Web Services

Theory and Practice

Anura Gurugé

ELSEVIER
DIGITAL
PRESS

AMSTERDAM • BOSTON • HEIDELBERG • LONDON
NEW YORK • OXFORD PARIS • SAN DIEGO
SAN FRANCISCO • SINGAPORE • SYDNEY • TOKYO
Digital Press is an imprint of Elsevier

Digital Press is an imprint of Elsevier
200 Wheeler Road, Burlington, MA 01803, USA
Linacre House, Jordan Hill, Oxford OX2 8DP, UK

 Recognizing the importance of preserving what has been written, Elsevier prints its books on acid-free paper whenever possible.

Library of Congress Cataloging-in-Publication Data
Gurugé, Anura
    Web services / Anura Gurugé.
       p. cm.
    ISBN 1-55558-282-6
       1. Web services.   I. Title.

    TK5105.88813.G87 2003
    005.7'2--dc22   2003062588

British Library Cataloguing-in-Publication Data
A catalogue record for this book is available from the British Library.

For information on all Digital Press publications
visit our website at www.digitalpress.com and www.bh.com/digitalpress

04 05 06 07 08 10 9 8 7 6 5 4 3 2 1

Printed in the United States of America

Web Services

To Deanna, with love.

Contents

Foreword

Web services are probably the most often written-about technology paradigm in today's trade press. Not a single day goes by, when I read at least one article daily touting the values of Web services. If you are new to Web services, you may be wondering why there is so much coverage about Web services. There are several reasons for the wide following of Web services, and this book provides a very good perspective of the business and technical benefits of Web services. Web services are positioned as the ideal solution to efficiently integrate the IT infrastructure. Let me explain the challenges of today's IT infrastructure in order to fully understand Web services.

Businesses are increasingly relying on IT to achieve their business goals. There is no question that businesses can increase their efficiencies by automating the business processes. There are scores of business applications available in the marketplace to automate your business processes. You can pick and choose the business application based on any number of criteria. For example, an enterprise might have purchased an accounting package 15 years ago that runs on IBM's AS/400, a home-grown inventory system that was built 5 years ago using Oracle Database running on HP UNIX, and a CRM system bought from a leading vendor last year. These applications typically work in a "Silo"; that is, the business process associated with the application starts and ends within that application and doesn't interact with other applications. Although each of the applications delivers the business service that it has been designed for, it does not truly address the need for today's business challenges.

Today's business processes are all about collaboration. Business processes have to leap over departmental, divisional, and enterprise boundaries. In other words, a business process may have to collaborate with specific services offered by the "Silo" applications. For example, in a supply chain management process, a buyer in the United States may have to interact with local and global suppliers. The supply chain process for the buyer may involve collaborating with the suppliers' inventory, shipping, and billing systems. Implementing such a process that spans multiple systems is quite a challenge. One has to know how to interact with the systems as each of the systems may have its own programming interface. This pushes up the complexity of integration and hence the cost.

The IT industry has been battling the problem of managing distributed processes for quite sometime. One way to solve the integration problem is to make all applications support a common integration standard. It is easier said than done as we have had several software vendors pursuing their own proprietary integration framework and selling their own middleware. Though such middleware is helpful in integrating applications, there are limitations. We have also seen the emergence, as of the 1990s, of distributed computing standards like CORBA and COM. Although they have been successful in their own domains, they have not provided a common integration framework for all the vendors to agree upon.

In the past few years, vendors have realized that the market is well served if handled collectively. The Web services initiative is a set of standards to facilitate easy integration of business artifacts. Web services have a wide following and are being actively supported by all the major software vendors including IBM, Microsoft, Sun, Oracle, SAP, and BEA. Because of the wide support from the industry, Web services are flourishing and are expected to stay around for a long time. In my view, the Web services paradigm is similar to reaching the "nirvana" in distributed computing.

The Web services paradigm is completely based on XML and consists of several standards including SOAP, UDDI, and WSDL. There are standards designed to address each component of integration. For example, SOAP is a transport-agnostic protocol that lets applications communicate with each other. This book explains important standards of Web services in detail. The Web services model segregates the implementation detail from the description. Because of this, any existing legacy IT asset can be described as a Web service. Once created as Web service, it can be consumed by any other application.

The biggest advantage of Web services is to build applications on the fly by leveraging existing assets. As Web services evolve, you will see most common services will be made available as Web services. This will facilitate the evolution of a service-oriented architecture in which software is available and consumed as service components.

Web services offer several benefits. It promotes reuse. A service component can be used by anyone, anywhere, from any platform. Hence, once created as Web service, it is guaranteed for reuse. Web services offer much-needed flexibility for enterprises as components can be outsourced. Web services lower the barriers to switching. As all Web services conform to common standards, buyers can switch poor suppliers with good ones by simply changing the Web service.

As Web services evolve, CTOs have to be knowledgeable in choosing the right vendors for Web services. Even though Web services vendors conform to common standards, there are differences in how they are implemented. This book provides guidance on how to choose the vendors and on the associated implementation issues.

My recommendation is that you take a serious look at Web services. It is widely supported by the industry and getting popular rapidly. Given the network effect, your business may be soon touched by Web services and you would be forced to think of Web services. If you have not thought about a Web services strategy, it is time to get to know more and this book will help you.

—Chandra Venkatapathy
Market Manager, IBM

Preface

Every act of dishonesty has at least two victims:
the one we think of as the victim, and the perpetrator as well.
Each little dishonesty makes another little rotten spot
somewhere in the perpetrator's psyche.

—Lesley Conger

Web services are going to be very big in time, despite their faltering, behind-schedule start. Of that there can be no doubt, given that Web services, very soon, will impinge on everything to do with applications—whether they have to do with development, ownership, usage, or commercialization. Web services set out to simplify application development. They will reduce application development costs and compress development schedules. They can be a brand-new source of software revenue. They can be used as a means to capture, reuse, and possibly even resell valuable business logic contained within "legacy" mission-critical applications. This book deals with all of these aspects and more.

This book will show you how to exploit the vast potential of Web services—whether you intend to be a Web service consumer, developer, provider, reseller, consultant, or commentator. If you are an executive, it will help you evaluate the issues that swirl around Web services and make sure you know what questions to ask from those you have tasked with making Web services real. This book will make sure that you will not be blindsided when it comes to Web services.

Web services are enigmatic. They can also be rather confusing and confounding. Much of this has to do with their actual name. Web services are not "services" in the conventional sense! Web services in reality are *application enablers*. They are software components. They typically are not meant to have a user interface. Instead, the input and output of Web services are meant to be in the form of XML documents. Web services as such are not meant for direct end-user consumption. They are meant to facilitate the creation of end-user applications. SOAP, WSDL, and UDDI, contrary to what you may have read in the trade media, are not Web services. Headlines such as "Intel to Support Web Services" are about as inane as a headline that says "Ford Motor Company to Support Spark Plugs." There are still a lot of misconceptions and mystery surrounding Web services. This book will demystify Web services. This is not just a promise; it's a *guarantee*.

Value proposition

This book is a comprehensive guide to all aspects of Web services. It was written when Web services appeared after a 2-year gestation. Consequently, it can address the real, practical issues as opposed to focusing on the initial, theoretical aspects of Web services. It tries to be provocative, exciting, and inspiring. It is certainly objective, nonpartisan, factual, and accurate. Though IBM, Microsoft, Sun, BEA, Oracle, and others are mentioned quite a bit, this book is definitely vendor-neutral.

This book provides an incisive executive view on how to exploit Web services—whether in terms of creating Web services, using Web services, identifying new Web services, marketing Web services, or supporting Web services. In all cases it presents a balanced viewpoint with the pros and cons clearly laid out. The book will also highlight potential issues pertaining to the topic in discussion and when appropriate identify germane solutions from multiple vendors that could be used to realize the requisite functionality.

The 10-item Q&A section at the end of each chapter is an easy way to reprise all the pertinent topics discussed in that chapter and make sure that you have not "misplaced" anything—especially if you were interrupted and distracted, as is likely to have been the case, multiple times during the course of reading a chapter. The numerous illustrations and tables will also help in this area. This book appreciates the time pressures on today's executives. It thus tries hard to convey the necessary information as easily as possible.

This book is not meant for an overtly technical readership looking for a "bits-and-bytes" guide to developing or using Web services. This is not a guide for writing Web services–related software. If you are already a C++, Java, or Visual BASIC programmer who knows exactly what an XML namespace is all about, then this book is really not for you, though you may want to skim through Chapter 1 and the illustrations in the other chapters and look at a few of the definitions to make sure that you will be on the right track when it comes to developing or using Web services. A quick story may help to clarify exactly what this book is striving to achieve.

I live on a relatively large lake in New Hampshire. One evening I was on the lake in a boat and I was waved down by a group of college-age kids driving around in what we refer to around here as "Dad's boat." They were a bit "disoriented" (to use a euphemism) and wanted to know how best to get to Jonathan's Landing in Moultonborough. I took out my map and started giving them precise directions using compass bearings, island names, and buoy numbers. A few seconds into this, one of the young men interrupted me and said, "I don't want to be rude, but don't get technical with us. Just point." Well, that is what I am doing with this book—trying to point you in the right direction, pointing out what you should be looking out for and what your final destination should be.

If nothing else, even if you just speed-read through this book, it will stop you from being blindsided at meetings where issues related to Web services are raised, discussed, or acted upon. As already mentioned, there is a lot of confusion, misinformation, and mystery surrounding Web services—part of this stemming from different people misconstruing what a Web service is supposed to be. For example, the concept of managing a Web service is really only germane if you are going to be a provider of a Web service. If, on the other hand, you are on the consumption side of Web services, you would want to manage the applications using Web services—and monitor the performance and availability of the Web services being used by your applications. This is because the Web services being used by your applications would typically be in the management domain of the Web service provider. It is the nuances like this that can trip you up when it comes to Web services. The express goal of this book is to ensure that you do not get misled by others when it comes to Web services.

From experience, from both sides of the table, I know that meeting scenarios at which technology gets debated is where management can best benefit most from the corporate equivalent of *Cliff Notes* that address the specific technology issues being discussed. When it comes to Web services, this book is that set of it-will-make-you-look-real-good crib notes. It will enable you to appreciate what the technical folks are talking about, the issues involved, and, most important, the right questions to ask and get answers to. This book is without bias and totally unsponsored by any vendor or organization. Thus, it freely cites, without any bias or prejudice, technology and products from as many germane vendors as possible. If there are any Web services–related vendors that I have not mentioned, and there are bound to be many given how quickly this market is expanding, it does not mean that I do not consider them to be viable. It just means that despite my best efforts they managed to remain below my radar screen.

If you are reading this book, the chances are that you are currently trying to evaluate what Web services are all about. In that case, this is indeed the right book for you—even if you discount my innate partisanship when it comes to this book. This book does set out to provide as comprehensive a view as possible, without getting overly technical, as to what is viable today when it comes to developing or using Web services.

Web services, as you will discover, change everything when it comes to applications. It really is, without in any way being trite, a new and exciting paradigm in the annals of software development. Web services elevate software component technology to a whole new plateau and then combine that with the reach and convenience of the Web. Web services also happen to be the killer applications for XML! Those of us who can remember life prior to the Web, often wonder and even openly ask others: How did we manage before the Web? Well, by 2010, there will be application developers who will ask, albeit rhetorically: How did we manage before Web services? It is as basic as that. This is where this book comes into its own. This book will make sure that you will be a player in the emerging world of Web services.

Web services are a highly dynamic arena. There is constant development in terms of new specifications, technologies, and offerings. A new Web site, www.xmlweb.org, has agreed to work with me to provide up-to-date, vendor-neutral information of interest to readers of this book. I will use this Web site to ensure that the information presented in this book continues to be alive and vibrant. Thus, it will serve you well to visit www.xmlweb.org while reading this book and then to bookmark it for regular visits to stay on top of this subject.

What is covered?

This book sets out to cover everything that an executive needs to know about Web services both in terms of theory as well as practice. It cites many practical scenarios for Web services and has many diagrams that clearly show how Web services will be invoked and used across the Web. It addresses the standards and technologies that make Web services possible, and the roles that Java and Microsoft's .NET can play when it comes to deploying and executing them. It discusses security from multiple perspectives. It also looks at reliability, performance, platform, and scalability issues. It discusses why Web services, despite their incontrovertible appeal, are considered to be behind schedule. In effect, no stone is left unturned. Over the eight chapters that make up this book, everything that has to do with Web services is identified and analyzed in a systematic and logical order.

Chapter 1 provides a thorough reconnaissance of the lay of the land when it comes to Web services. It is a mini-tutorial. At the end of this chapter you will already have a keen appreciation as to what Web services are all about. You will know the rationale for Web services and the growing family of standards that pertain to them. You will already know what roles SOAP, WSDL, and UDDI play and why there is such a buzz over the potential of Web services. Chapter 1 sets the groundwork for the rest of the book. Given that everything to do with Web services is contingent on XML, Chapter 2 provides a background on XML. It also includes an introduction to WSDL, the XML derivative used to define the functionality of a Web service.

Chapter 3 discusses, in considerable detail, the role of Microsoft and Microsoft .NET when it comes to Web services, and the issues, valid and otherwise, that some may have about invoking Web services running on Microsoft servers. Chapter 6 is the counterpoint to this chapter and looks at the role of Java. In between, Chapters 4 and 5 examine SOAP and UDDI, the two seminal standards associated with Web services, with the third being WSDL. Chapter 7 looks at deployment-related issues, including security and platforms, while Chapter 8 summarizes the themes, technologies, methodologies, and recommendations covered in the previous chapters.

There are a glossary and a list of acronyms at the end of this book, though I strive to describe (at least once) the terms, technologies, or buzzwords that are mentioned in the text—at or near the first time they are mentioned so as to make sure that you are not left in the dark. There are also an index and a detailed table of contents.

Headings and subheadings are used extensively after the introductory prose to identify and delineate the topics being addressed. The table of contents, which does list all of the headings and subheadings, can serve as a detailed navigational road map through this book. Given this structure, where each chapter starts off with an overview, many topics may appear multiple times within a chapter—typically with incremental levels of detail or refinement. Each chapter ends with a 10-item Q&A, which sets out to recap the important issues addressed in that chapter.

Navigating through this book

This book, of course, is structured to be read sequentially from chapter to chapter, page by page. If read in such a conventional manner, the issues, options, technologies, and solutions will be presented in a systematic, step-by-step manner, replete with detailed figures. It could, however, also be used in reference-guide mode, where the reader pursues a particular technology or theme—for example, the role of Web services vis-à-vis corporate portals. If you intend to use this book in this reference-guide mode, please use the index or the table of contents as the optimum means of locating the topics being sought. Starting with the Q&As at the end of each chapter is also a possibility, since they provide a quick snapshot of what is covered in that chapter.

Following the post-Y2K economic downturn, which was then exacerbated by the dot.com implosion and 9/11, these continue to be challenging times for the software industry. Web services will play a pivotal role in pulling this industry out of its slump. Web services can thus be thought of as a powerful empowering technology. Knowing what Web services are all about will in turn empower you.

—Anura Gurugé,
Lake Winnipesaukee, New Hampshire
October 2003

Acknowledgments

A book such as this, which strives to present a relatively high-level narrative of a somewhat complex and rapidly evolving sphere of technology, would ill serve its readers unless my views and interpretations were continually and consistently challenged by a motivated and knowledgeable devil's advocate. In this respect I was most fortunate in having the help of Chandra Venkatapathy. Chandra, who also very kindly agreed to write the Foreword to this book, is IBM's Market Manager for Web services–related integration solutions for small and medium businesses. Chandra is an out-and-out Web-services expert who has been actively involved with Web-services technology since early 2001. He was instrumental in developing IBM's Web Services Gateway—a proxy firewall for using Web services outside of an intranet/extranet.

Chandra, despite a heavy workload at IBM, reviewed and critiqued each chapter as soon as it was written. He pointed out various shortcomings, suggested alternate interpretations, and provided invaluable insights into the technology. He did his level best to keep me honest and accurate. If not for Chandra's efforts, I would have let you down in some areas. Thank you, Chandra. If you have not already read the Foreword, you really should do so in order to gain Chandra's uniquely privileged perspective on Web services, since he is one of IBM's evangelists in this arena. Despite Chandra's gallant efforts, any errors, omissions, and shortfalls you may still discover in this book are, alas, all due to my inadequacies, and I will, as ever, readily take all blame for them. Feel free to e-mail me at anu@wownh.com with any of your views and also to regularly check www.xmlweb.org for updates that may rectify omissions or errors.

Stuart McIrvine, IBM's Program Director for IBM's WebSphere Integration solutions, who was the devil's advocate for my previous book, introduced me to Chandra with the recommendation that Chandra would be the ideal person for my needs. As ever, Stuart was correct. Thank you, Stuart. You continue to be a hero. Tod Yampel, Mr. ResQNet, a friend of long standing from my days in Web-to-host and another technocrat of no mean repute (with multiple patents to his credit), did read Chapter 1 with care and assured me that I was on track. Thank you, Tod. I wish you had had the time to look through the rest of the book as well. But c'est la vie!

Thanks are also due to a few select individuals from the corporate world for their continued help and support over the years. These include my "bro" Carlson Colomb, once with Aviva but now a buccaneering Web entrepreneur in Canada; Mark Lillycrop of Arcati; Fiona Hewitt, the incomparable editor of *TCP/SNA Update* for Xephon; Tim Clark of eG Innovations; Jim O'Connor, still at Bus-Tech; Susan Verrecchia of the eponymous Verrecchia Group; Gregory Koss, Bill Koss, and Larry Samberg at Internet Photonics; Xavier Chaillot and Rana Aluraibi of Hummingbird; Adrienne Stevens, Richard Padova, Sandra Sanborn, Karen Muncaster, and Jane Torrey of Southern New Hampshire University; and David Wilson of Open Archive.

It would be remiss if I did not also mention a few special friends, since writing books can be a lonely, introspective task, and one needs the spark of others so as not to get lost. Susanne Weldon Francke (sometimes also my lawyer) and Dr. Gary Francke still keep an eye on me on a regular basis but not as much as they had to in the past now that I am married. Robert Rosenbaum is still related, though, alas, no longer via our goldens. Dony and Marcia Lamontagne have proved to be dear and durable friends, as has John Kimball. I should also add my new mother-in-law, Anna Gay Sellars, for brightening my day, without fail, with her daily stream of e-mails.

My father, Dr. Ananda Guruge, a considerably more prolific and gifted author than his son, has always been a driving influence in my life. As ever, I need to yet again acknowledge my debt to Dr. Tom Westerdale, of Birkbeck College, who labored hard to teach me how to write—though he should no longer be held responsible for all the bad habits I have succumbed to in the last two decades. Matthew Gordon and Danielle, now young adults, are busy with their lives and having seen their names in so many prior books had little interest in this book. But then there is Devanee, at three, who has made up for that with her verve and cheer. Along with Ulysses, my latest golden retriever, they make sure that there is still plenty of exercise in my life. Then there is Deanna, my wife, who I met shortly after I started working on this book and who has proceeded to enchant my life. Though our whirlwind romance did delay the completion of this book, Deanna's subsequent contributions to this effort were substantial. Thank you all. Without all of you I could not have gotten this done. Cheers!

Web Services: What, Why, and Where?

What's in a name? That which we call a rose
by any other name would smell as sweet.

—Shakespeare

Web services are modular, self-contained "applications" or application logic developed per a set of open standards. That much is immutable and indubitable. There is even concurrence of this application-centric viewpoint from the World Wide Web Consortium (W3C) (http://www.w3.org), the ultimate ratifiers of Web-related interoperability standards and in effect the godparents of Web services. W3C now has a definition, albeit in draft form, of Web services, within the emerging Web Services Architecture specification, which states categorically that a Web service is indeed a *software system*. This stake in the ground from W3C goes a long way toward helping rationalize prior conflicting views on exactly what constitutes a Web service, though it is only fair to note that this decisive description was formulated 2 years after the advent of Web services.

A Web service, however, is typically not meant to be a full-blown, feature-rich application in its own right—even though, there are no restrictions as to how long, big, or complex a Web service can or should be. First, a Web service does not necessarily have to possess a user interface. This alone runs counter to most people's concept of what constitutes an application. Consequently, a Web service, though it needs to be characterized as an application for technical integrity, is better thought of as a "mini-application," possibly even an application "segment," or better still as an *application enabler*.

Some other terms that may also be used to convey the true essence of a Web service are as follows:

- Subroutine

- Software building block

- Reusable object

- Software component

- Chunk of business logic

- Entry (or member) from a software library

- Remote procedure (or even possibly remote procedure call)

- Business process representation

The absence of terms pertaining to protocols, software services, or middleware in the previous list (such as a reference to SOAP or WSDL) is intentional, as opposed to being an omission or anomaly. A few examples of what Web services can be, at this juncture, should help clarify the choice of terminology that has been used so far. It will also permit the discussion of why a Web service is not necessarily a middleware service in the traditional sense to be deferred until a bit later. Here are some quintessential examples of the type of functions that can and should be provided by a Web service:

- Credit card authorization

- International currency converter (e.g., U.S. dollars to U.K. pounds)

- Purchase or VAT tax calculator

- Stock quote provider

- Package delivery status locator

- Shipping rate calculator

- Customized search capability

- Local weather "bug"

- Driving directions between two places

- Insurance rate quote provision (e.g., auto insurance)

- Personalized horoscope readings

- Local traffic report updates

- Airline flight schedules between designated cities

- Specialized user authentication techniques (e.g., two-factor authentication, as with RSA's SecurID system)

- Customer warranty status lookup

- A specialized purchase order processing mechanism between two companies

- Personnel (e.g., service technicians or equipment installers) dispatch scheduling per a workflow management scheme

A picture is worth a thousand words at this point. Figure 1.1 illustrates how a future Web application could make use of Web services. This hypothetical Web application is intended to provide a "wish you were there" vacation planning and vacation reservation function. To achieve this objective, this application is shown gainfully exploiting multiple Web services,

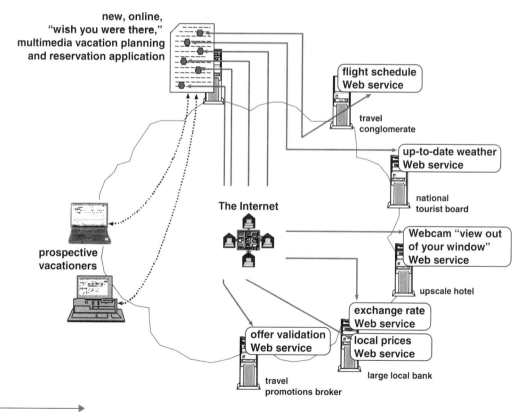

Figure 1.1 *A hypothetical, very persuasive, "wish you were there" multimedia vacation planning and vacation reservation application that relies heavily on software functionality obtained in the form of Web services from diverse sources.*

from disparate sources, to synthesize a highly compelling, very up-to-date, full-function, and seamless user experience. The rich and topical functionality, available in the form of Web services from third parties, ensures that this application can be flexible, extensible, easily modifiable, and, above all, highly effective.

Rather than trying to create and maintain all the software required by such an application, Web services enable the application developers to pick and choose, at will, proven, best-of-breed "utility" functions from around the Web—and easily plug them into their applications. This is the crux of what Web services are all about. Web services elegantly and systematically extend the potential sources for remotely invocable software components to now include the Web.

All the excitement about Web services revolves around this Web-centric value proposition. The reach and diversity of the Web is obviously incomparable when it comes to a 24/7 super-mall for software components. The Web is already awash in software of every conceivable type, and Web services provides a formal mechanism by which some, if not much, of this existing functionality can be repackaged, formally publicized, and then profitably reused. Moreover, the software talent pool available via the Web, both commercial and altruistic, is unprecedented and beguiling.

With Web services, the Web can become a mouthwatering, veritable software smorgasbord for application developers—hence, the basis of the name: Web services (i.e., software services for applications obtained over the Web). In exactly the same way that the Web has now become the undisputed, "must check first" source for merchandise and services, whether it be rare Alexandrite gems from Sri Lanka, first editions of John Irving, or ocean-view hotel rooms in Newport, Rhode Island, with Web services the Web becomes a primary source for modular software. Thanks to Web services, you can now develop new Web applications, relatively quickly, that consist of software components from multiple, diverse sources that have been dynamically assembled and loosely coupled together. Figure 1.2 sets out to present a generic view of what Web services are all about (i.e., the concept of Web applications that rely heavily on remotely invoked software functionality from third parties). It is, however, worth keeping in mind that Web services could also be gainfully used on an intranet basis (i.e., within a single enterprise) without recourse to the Web.

The "pick-and-choose" and "plug-and-play" of Web services are only possible because of standards—in particular, XML (i.e., the eXtensible Markup Language). XML is a platform, programming language and markup language independent scheme for sharing data in an unambiguous

Web Services
(i.e., software functionality [application "services"] invoked across the Web)

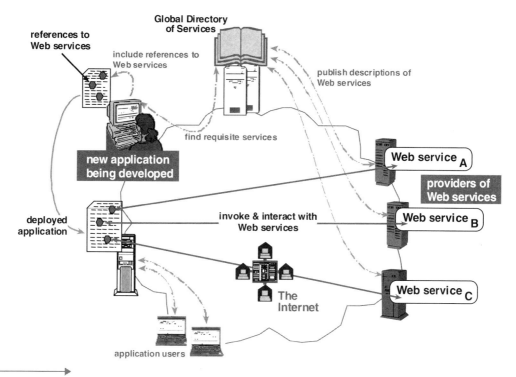

Figure 1.2   *Generic view of what Web services are all about—which is the concept of applications being able to readily invoke required software functionality across the Web.*

and consistent manner. It is, however, the underlying basis for Web services, so much so that within some technical circles today's Web services are referred to as *XML Web services*.

Web services operate by interchanging data that is in the form of XML. The reliance on XML-based data is the fundamental premise of Web services. To be even more precise, it should be noted that the data interchange is done using XML documents. Thus, the input parameters to a Web service are in the form of an XML document. The output of a Web service will also always be an XML document.

Though a Web service is a software component, XML per se is not a software component, a programming language, or even a scheme in any way associated with programming or software. Nor is it an enhancement or replacement for HyperText Markup Language (HTML), the format control standard for contemporary Web pages. Instead, XML is a meta-markup language for documents—in particular, documents containing structured information. Most documents have some level of structure in that the information they contain is invariably made up of content (e.g., text and graphics) and context (e.g., headings, tables, captions). XML's forte is its ability to clearly, cleanly, and consistently describe the context and meaning of the data vis-à-vis that document.

XML enables all types of information to be exchanged across disparate systems in an easier and better manner than was possible in the past. XML provides data from disparate applications and platforms with a standardized "interchange" format. This is the pivotal XML capability that is leveraged by Web services. With XML it does not matter whether the data were produced by a proprietary application and were originally structured in a manner that could only be interpreted by that application. XML thus becomes a standard way to describe structured data irrespective of whether these data belong to a spreadsheet, an electronic address book, a customer relationship management (CRM) application, an operating system configuration file, a financial transaction, or to a technical drawing. Web services would not be possible if not for the universal, "no strings," no caveats, any-application-to-any-other-application data interchange capability made possible by XML.

XML permits data to be shared. Web services extend this to permit software functionality, in particular existing business logic, to be shared and reused when it comes to application development. This software interoperability is realized through the exchange of XML documents. Let us take as an example a package tracking application as offered by the likes of FedEx, UPS, and the U.S. Postal Service, where Figure 1.3 shows the heavily used FedEx tracking system. The applicability and appeal of such a tracking function vis-à-vis e-commerce, supply chain management (SCM), or even some CRM applications are intuitive. Nonetheless, in the absence of Web services (or similar), embedding existing tracking functionality (e.g., the FedEx service) into other applications is not being practical. Instead, most e-commerce applications provide a tracking number and a "clickable" hot link to the tracking function of the shipper being used.

This approach works, and works well, but has various drawbacks—the primary one being that the e-commerce application is relinquishing the user to another site. This runs counter to the concept of keeping a customer captive and captivated. From an e-commerce standpoint it is the equivalent of a store clerk telling a customer who inquires about gift wrap options that he or she needs to go to another store to get that done. If package tracking functionality from the various vendors were available as Web services, then

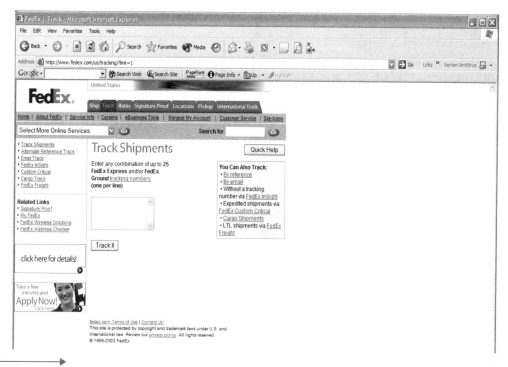

Figure 1.3   *The package tracking function on the FedEx portal, which debuted way back in 1994. A package tracking function such as this, or from another source, is an ideal candidate to be made into a Web service that can then be dynamically invoked by other applications—for example, e-commerce applications—so that users can continue to log on to that application to check the status of their shipments rather than having to link or be redirected to another site to gain access to the tracking functionality.*

the e-commerce, SCM, and CRM applications could have them neatly integrated within the applications and thereby obviate the need to redirect users to other Web sites. Web services enable applications to offer additional value-added functionality via the seamless integration of third-party software components.

The bottom line here is that Web services can simplify the application development process. This potential simplification can be exploited to realize, at a minimum:

1.   Marked compression of application development schedules—with a commensurate reduction in development costs.

2.   Specialized and customized "niche" applications, which would have been difficult to cost-justify in the past.

3.   Additional value-added functionality within applications without incurring the dreaded penalty of prolonged development schedules.

4.   Quick updates to application functionality to reflect changing circumstances (e.g., activation of new tax regulations), since the necessary changes will be made to the various affected Web services by their providers, obviating the need for the application support team to identify and implement all the changes. On this note it is worth reflecting that the Y2K application conversion extravaganza would have been considerably easier, less expensive, and more low-key if these legacy applications had been developed using dynamically invoked third-party software functionality via something similar to Web services, rather than being all-inclusive monoliths.

5.   Faster application testing and certification, since the functions being provided by the Web services will, at least in theory, have already been field-tested and proven.

6.   More reliable and resilient applications immediately, since the use of proven, best-of-breed third-party Web services for some of the functionality minimizes the amount of brand-new, in-house developed code content within an application

These factors can have a very positive influence on sacrosanct corporate criteria, such as competitiveness, productivity, profitability, and even the bottom line. Furthermore, the applicability of Web services is not restricted to companies or individuals developing software. Any company that owns its own suite of applications, irrespective of their type, nature, and vintage, can consider offering some of the software functionality embodied in these applications as Web services. Thus, Web services are a way that Fortune 5000 companies that have spent small fortunes developing their own mission-critical applications over the last 3 decades can now reap additional ROI from these highly proven pieces of software. Hence, large corporations with in-house application development teams could end up being both consumers and providers of Web services.

This is why there is so much fuss and excitement about Web services. Web services usher application development into a new, highly Web-centric era. Web services provide a formal and systematic framework whereby the reach of the Web can be leveraged to promote and foster software reuse.

1.1   **What are Web services?**

Web services represent a new breed of Web-specific software component methodology. They are a new type of object-oriented (OO) programming à la the Web. Web services are modular, self-contained, self-describing software components. These software components are available over the Web (i.e., they are "published" on the Web). They can be readily located and "checked out," online and dynamically, using a new directory and corresponding search mechanism known as Universal Description, Discovery, and Integration (UDDI). They are also invoked and "consumed" (i.e., used) across the Web—hence, the term *Web services*, reflecting the fact that these are software services for application developers that are totally Web-centric.

Web services are truly platform independent. This platform independence, furthermore, applies to both sides of a Web services "configuration" (i.e., the usage side as well as the provision side). Thus, applications that use Web services can run on any platform. Web services themselves, in turn, are also totally platform independent. There are also no restrictions as to what platforms they can be developed upon. Hence, there are no platform-related restrictions whatsoever as to which Web services can be used by which applications—or as to how and where the Web services, or for that matter the applications, were developed. Therefore, it is possible to have a Web application running on a Windows 2000 server that relies on three Web services: one running on a UNIX server from Sun, a second on a Unisys mainframe, and the third on an IBM iSeries machine. The Web service running on the iSeries machine may have been developed on a PC using IBM's WebSphere Studio Application Developer, whereas that running on the Sun UNIX server could have been developed using BEA's WebLogic Workshop running on a RedHat Linux system. Figure 1.4 highlights this no caveats, platform-independent, any-to-any capability of Web services, whereas Figure 1.5 shows how it would be possible to have applications running on different platforms acting as Web service users and providers to each other, at the same side.

The platform independence of Web services is, however, not in any way associated with or dependent on Java, despite appearing to promulgate the same message popularized since the mid-1990s by the Sun-led Java camp. Since it is now one of the leading programming schemes of the Web era, Java inevitably does have a major role vis-à-vis Web services, particularly since the Web services initiatives of industry super-heavyweights such as IBM, H-P/Compaq, Oracle, BEA, and Sun are all highly Java-centric.

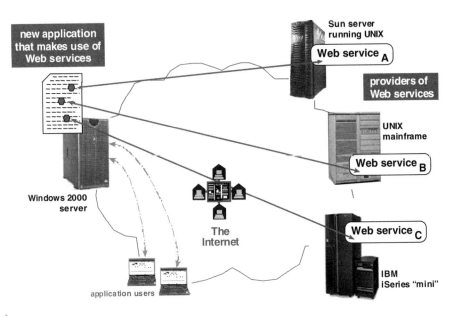

Figure 1.4   *Web services are totally platform independent, with no caveats, and as such it is possible for an application running on a Windows 2000 server, for example, to rely on functionality obtained from Web services running on vastly different platforms.*

Nonetheless, Web services, in addition to being platform independent, are also totally programming language agnostic. Thus, it would be eminently feasible for an application being written in Visual BASIC or C++ to readily use Web services functionality being provided by a legacy program written in COBOL, PL/I, or even BAL. Needless to say, Java presents no problems, either on the usage or on the supply side. Applications being developed in Java can use Web services being provided by software written in any language, including Java, while Web services emanating from software written in Java can be used by applications written in any language.

Just as with platform independence, the programming language neutrality of Web services has no boundaries. It is truly any-to-any when it comes to programming language interoperability. It also provides a bridge between the old and the new when it comes to software programming methodology. This is another key reason why so many enterprises, in addition to the computer vendor community, are so interested in Web services. Web services provide a structured and regulated means by which mission-critical software functionality developed decades ago, prior to the advent of the PC, let alone the Web, can be "brushed off" and profitably reused with brand-new Web-centric applications.

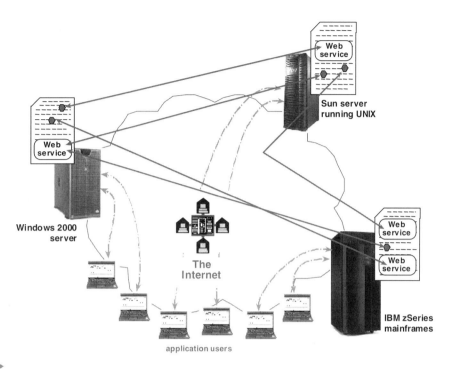

Figure 1.5   *Given the total platform independence of Web services, it is even possible for applications running on different platforms to act as Web service users and providers to each other, at the same time.*

Web services provide a means for "modernizing" legacy applications, particularly those developed to run on mainframes and mini-computers (e.g., IBM AS/400s and HP 3000s). With Web services you can squeeze yet more ROI from these tried and trusted software workhorses, despite them having already earned their keep, many times over, a long time ago. This legacy reusability aspect of Web services is an area of particular interest to IBM and other host access vendors (e.g., Jacada, SEAGULL Software), not to mention the Fortune 1000 companies that together have invested trillions of dollars in their application software portfolios.

1.1.1   Linking to remote functionality

Web services, to cut to the chase, are a remote procedure invocation mechanism. The data interchange (i.e., the I/O) with the remotely invoked procedure is, however, always realized using XML documents—hence, the platform and programming language independence. The software code that makes up a Web service is never embedded within an application that requires that functionality. Instead, the new application includes a programmatic call to the Web service using XML documents as the means to convey input parameters and receive the required output.

Web services are thus a remote procedure call (RPC) mechanism in the true sense of that phrase. This RPC mechanism operates via the exchange of XML-based documents. It can even be accurately categorized as an XML-centric messaging scheme. The use of the term RPC in this context, however, should not be confused or associated with the heavily used UNIX RPC scheme that popularized this acronym. Web services are not in any way tied to the UNIX RPC mechanism, though, to be fair, it should be noted that UNIX RPC is one of the many transport mechanisms that can be used to invoke and consume Web services. HTTP (i.e., the ubiquitous HyperText Transfer Protocol of the Web), though, is likely to be the most widely utilized of the transport options that are open to Web services. Some of the other transports that could also be used include native TCP (as in TCP/IP), the Simple Mail Transfer Protocol (SMTP) as used by Internet e-mail, message queuing schemes such as IBM's WebSphere MQ (née MQSeries) and Microsoft's MSMQ, the File Transfer Protocol (FTP), and nascent Internet-oriented protocols such as Blocks Extensible Exchange Protocol (BEEP).

The remote procedure call mechanism of Web services is realized using a protocol known as SOAP—which stands for Simple Object Access Protocol. SOAP is an XML-based messaging scheme that is platform and programming language agnostic. It is a simple, lightweight mechanism for exchanging structured and typed information peer to peer in decentralized and distributed environments à la the Web. In the context of Web services, it is SOAP that flows across the various possible transport options such as HTTP, RPC, TCP, SMTP, message queuing, FTP, and BEEP. Thus, the data transfers that take place between applications and Web services occur in the form of XML documents exchanged via SOAP—where SOAP in turn relies on a lower-level transport scheme such as HTTP or TCP for connectivity and networking across the Web.

Web services were originally meant to be programmatic, as opposed to visually interactive solutions. In other words, they were targeted for program-to-program consumption rather than for human-to-program interactions. In a sense Web services were going to provide new applications with ready access to a rich set of Web resident functionality comparable to what people had been enjoying on the Web since the mid-1990s (e.g., stock quotes, weather updates, traffic reports, news feeds, package tracking, currency conversions, insurance rates, and so forth). Web services would thus enable diverse software components to be integrated across the Web using open, standardized protocols (e.g., SOAP), which are decoupled and independent of any proprietary application programming interfaces (APIs). The goal of Web services is to facilitate simple, but pervasive, program-to-program programmatic interactions around the Web.

The initial (around 2000) program-to-program "charter" of Web services has, however, already started to evolve. In early 2002, IBM, a very influential and proactive force in the Web services arena, proposed a new standard, referred to as Web Services for Remote Portals (WSRP) via OASIS (i.e., Organization for the Advancement of Structured Information Standards). OASIS (http://www.oasis-open.org) is a not-for-profit, global consortium with more than 600 corporate and individual members in 100 countries around the world that drives the development, convergence, and adoption of e-business standards. WSRP advocates visual, user-facing Web services—that is, Web services that come replete with their own presentation services, ideally in the form of a contemporary graphical user interface (GUI).

WSRP's rationale, as implied by its name, is to make Web services that much easier to integrate into portals. (A portal, where Yahoo!, Excite, and www.schawb.com are classic examples of the genre, is an intuitive, transactional, focal point of access to a diverse range of content, services, resources, and applications.) Many functions desirable for inclusion within portals (e.g., stock quote retriever, stock price ticker, weather report "bug," search engine, and local traffic report "window") will in the future be available in the form of Web services.

What WSRP and a related specification known as Web Services for Interactive Applications (WSIA), which is now being amalgamated into WSRP, contend is that having a built-in GUI will simplify and expedite the deployment of such services within portals, rather than portal developers having to locate and rely on additional software to implement an appropriate user interface front end. To be fair, there are certain portal-specific, as opposed to Web services–specific, methodologies that can also be used with panache to tackle this user interface issue. Key among these are the so-called XSL portlets, which will automatically render XML-defined content (and remember that the output of a Web service is indeed an XML document) within specific portal "window panes," where a portlet, as illustrated in Figure 1.6, is a piece of software that handles and controls a specific, autonomous window pane within an overall portal view (or window, or even page). The importance of Web services vis-à-vis portals will be discussed further in Sections 1.2 and 1.3.

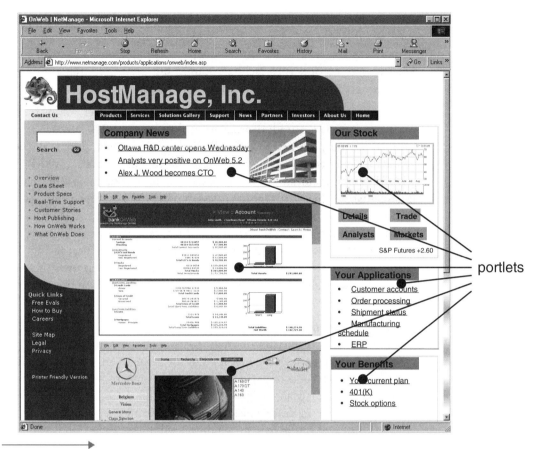

Figure 1.6   *Portlets, the individual window panes within an overall portal view.*

1.1.2   Self-promoting, as in blowing your own trumpet

Even more so than the platform and programming language independence, it is their self-advertising and self-describing aspects that make Web services truly special, revolutionary, and pragmatic. A Web service, by definition, has to always maintain an accurate self-portrait. Its operational model, interfaces, I/O parameters, and binding requirements have to be clearly and cleanly described—with these descriptions posted on the Web so that software developers can quickly determine what they can expect from a given Web service. Web services describe themselves using a new, XML-based dialect known as WSDL (i.e., Web Services Description Language).

Similar to how HTML describes the format of Web pages using tags, WSDL, typically pronounced *whiz dull*, provides a means for accurately describing contemporary Web-oriented communications protocols and messaging schemes. In the case of Web services, the messaging mechanism that will most often be described using WSDL is likely to be SOAP-based exchanges. The goal of WSDL is to ensure that automated processes (e.g., applications running on a PC) can automatically determine the exact networking capabilities of remote systems (e.g., mainframe or UNIX server) without human intervention or prior definitions. The WSDL-based definition of interfaces, parameters, and bindings ensures that a Web services "client" (i.e., a new application) can readily invoke a remote Web service programmatically, without regards to how or where the Web service is actually implemented.

While WSDL takes care of the self-describing part, the self-advertising aspect of Web services, along with the ability to locate these "blowing their own trumpet" Web services via a directory mechanism, is handled by UDDI. In much the same way that you could today use a search engine such as Google to find Italian olive oil producers or no-fee dating services, it is now possible, using UDDI, to search the Web for Web services that offer the exact software functionality required by an application (or portal) developer. By 2005, professional software developers tasked with delivering any new software functionality are likely to start by searching the Web, via UDDI, for pertinent Web services that may facilitate their tasks. It would be very akin to the current modus operandi of seasoned, "never-pay-the-full-rate" travelers or insurance buyers. These bargain hunters first scour the Web looking for deals before they ever think about talking to an actual travel or insurance agent. Similarly, application developers will also start looking for deals that will make their life that much easier—with these deals, however, being in the form of Web services.

Starting soon, the first, automatic knee-jerk reaction of application developers when confronted with the need to "reinvent the wheel" (so to speak) in terms of some software functionality will be to check if appropriate reusable software is available in the form of a Web service. They would do this using UDDI and a UDDI registry. It could be done manually by a person or programmatically by an application. The UDDI registry will contain WSDL-based descriptions of Web services. There is, however, no overt relationship between UDDI and WSDL. They are independent standards that can be used independently of each other. Thus, it is indeed possible to have services listed in a UDDI registry that are not described using WSDL. Such services, bereft of the WSDL self-describing prerequisite, will, however, not fall into the category of Web services. They would instead be non–Web services–related software ventures or nonsoftware-related services (e.g., consulting). It is also possible to have WSDL descriptions of Web services that are maintained outside a UDDI registry.

A UDDI Business Registry (UBR) to propagate use of Web services is already operational. This registry is sometimes also referred to as the UDDI Global Registry, since it is the cornerstone of the UDDI imitative. The UBR is operated as a Web-based, distributed service, which is made up of multiple, autonomously maintained registry nodes. At the start of 2003, registry nodes making up the UBR were being maintained by IBM, Microsoft, the Japanese NTT Communications Corporation (http://www.ntt.com), and SAP, the German-based world leader in Enterprise Resource Planning (ERP) software.

The UBR provides a central and formal directory where companies and individuals can register their businesses and the services that they offer. It is an online, category-based Yellow Pages for Web services (that can also be used as a white-page directory in that it supports name-based searches for companies and individuals). People who are looking for a service can now turn to this UBR to locate the businesses and individuals that provide such services.

Figure 1.7 shows the Microsoft UDDI registry node in action doing a search for services having to do with the weather, while Figure 1.8 shows the same search conducted on the IBM node to illustrate that the UDDI registry nodes will differ in their implementational details, though based on the same underlying UDDI standard. When searching for a Web service to source via UDDI, one does not have to limit the search to specific platforms, formats, APIs, or programming languages. Web services, through the use of XML-based documents and protocols, transcend all of these issues, which up until now were still pertinent concerns when talking about using external software functionality.

Now that the roles that XML, SOAP, WSDL, and UDDI play in making Web services possible have been broached, Figure 1.9 extends the Web services model introduced in Figure 1.2 to show where these enabling technologies come into play. The bottom line here is that thanks to XML, WSDL, and UDDI, Web services have propelled object-oriented technology to the next logical plateau.

1.1.3   The salient characteristics of Web services

At this juncture, with the general lay of the land when it comes to Web services mapped out, it is appropriate to look at the definition for Web

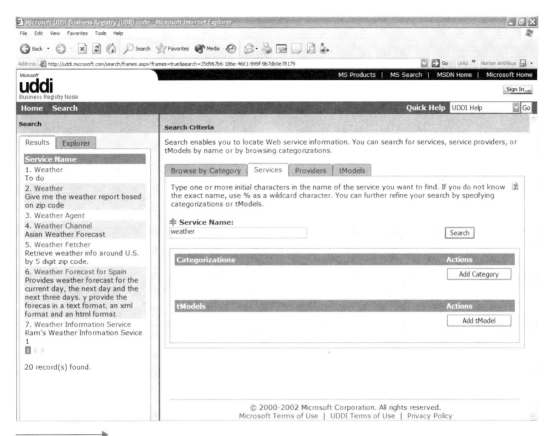

Figure 1.7   *Performing a search for weather services using Microsoft's UDDI registry, where the first 7 of the 20 services found are displayed on the left-hand "results" tab.*

services being proposed by the W3C as a part of the draft, November 14, 2002, Web Services Architecture specification. The authors of this specification, acutely aware of the confusion that has swirled around the issue of what actually constitutes a Web service, begin with this caveat: Although there are a number of varied and often seemingly inconsistent motivations for, and uses of, the term *Web service*, at its core the following definition captures what we believe to be the shared essence of the term.

With that out of the way, they set out to define a Web service in the following terms:

> *The W3C draft definition:* A Web service is a software system identified by a URI, whose public interfaces and bindings are defined and described using XML. Its definition can be discovered by other

software systems. These systems may then interact with the Web service in a manner prescribed by its definition, using XML-based messages conveyed by Internet protocols.

The term *URI* in this definition refers to a Uniform Resource Identifier—which is a short string that uniquely identifies resources on the Web, with Uniform Resource Locators (URLs) of the form "www.somename.com" being the best-known examples of a URI. "Software systems" in

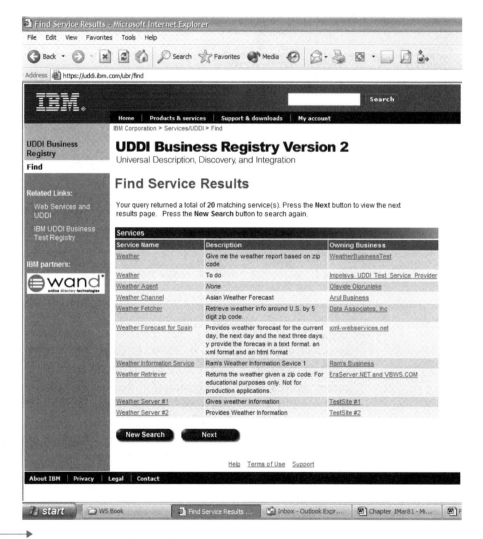

Figure 1.8   *Another search for weather services, this time using IBM's UDDI Business registry, which serves to illustrate that the UDDI register nodes will differ in their implementation details.*

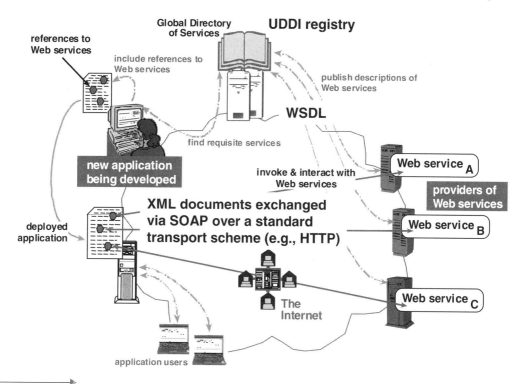

Web Services

(i.e., software functionality [application "services"] invoked across the Web)

Figure 1.9   *The generic Web services operational model introduced in Figure 1.2 is now extended to show where XML, SOAP, WSDL, and UDDI come into play.*

this context can be thought of as a broad umbrella term, which sets out to cover most things software related, including applications and possibly even small operating systems. This W3C definition, though striving to be as broad and open-ended as possible, is still consistent and very much in line with the Web services model presented at the very beginning of this book. The pivotal issue here is that Web services are "problem-solving" applications (or software systems), as opposed to being just networking protocols (e.g., SOAP) or a utility messaging functionality provided by some middleware suite.

The key, immutable, and defining characteristics of Web services, on top of the fact that they are applications, can now be summarized as follows:

1.   Modular

2.   Self-contained

3.   Self-describing

4.   Self-advertising

5.   Uniquely addressable

6.   XML-centric

7.   Standards based

8.   Platform independent

9.   Programming language agnostic

10.   Amalgamative in mix-and-match mode

Of these, the Web services feature that is most often and consistently cited by the cognoscenti is that of modularity. That makes sense, since it captures the "object" or "component" nature of a Web service. It also alludes to the fact that the overall Web services–oriented application development paradigm revolves around the concept of integrating diverse software modules to realize the requisite end results. It is a Lego block model, with application developers being able to mix and match and then snap together the various modules with a minimum of effort—confident that not only will it fit, but also that the whole will stick together with aplomb, without the need for glue.

The self-contained aspect of Web services builds on the idea of them being modular. It highlights that a given Web service has a clearly stated charter—in the form of operational characteristics and promised results. This charter is what is specified using WSDL. Furthermore, a Web service is supposed to deliver the entire functionality it promises without recourse to other external dependencies. This does not preclude a Web service from being able to call other Web services within its code to deliver the overall functionality it promises. What it means is that all such external calls and dependencies have to be handled entirely within the original Web service. All external dependencies have to be totally transparent to a subscriber of that Web service. A Web service thus has to be a well-behaved, uniquely identifiable black box with predefined inputs and outputs and no unexpected variations in behavior.

Of the 10 quintessential Web services characteristics listed earlier, at least six, and possibly seven, can be explicitly attributed to four key enabling technologies—namely, XML, SOAP, WSDL, and UDDI. The following chart takes the nine quintessential Web services characteristics and shows which of the four key enabling technologies are responsible, in the main, for that feature:

Web Service Characteristic	Made Possible By
Modular	—
Self-contained	—
Self-describing	WSDL
Self-advertising	UDDI
Uniquely addressable	Internet protocols (e.g., DNS)
XML-centric	XML
Standards based	XML, SOAP, WSDL, and UDDI
Platform independent	XML and SOAP
Programming language agnostic	XML and SOAP
Amalgamative in mix-and-match mode	XML, WSDL, and SOAP

Table 1.1 expands on this chart and shows all of the standards and specifications associated with Web services as of the spring of 2003. Note that the four key enabling technologies are now just the cornerstones in a rising pantheon of Web services–related methodologies. This list of methodologies will, of course, continue to expand and evolve for a long time to come. At present there is no formal body that promises to maintain an accurate and up-to-date list of these methodologies in an easy-to-reference, tabular basis—particularly in light of some of the intercompany (e.g., IBM versus BEA) or "interfaith" (i.e., Java versus .NET) politics that swirl around during the preliminary phases when such specifications are being formulated. The de facto standards bodies (e.g., W3C, OASIS, and so forth), understandably, do not want to get embroiled in the early wrangling and wish to stay aloof and impartial until there is some consensus.

For example, in early summer 2002, IBM, Microsoft, and a consortium made up of BEA, Sun, and SAP were each vociferously promoting its own specific scheme for business process orchestration, with IBM's Web Services Flow Language (WSFL) being the most cited in the media as the frontrunner for becoming the eventual standard. Nonetheless, in a few short weeks spanning July and August 2002, IBM and Microsoft decided, quite suddenly, to bury their hatchets vis-à-vis this issue, merge their competing schemes, and, moreover, collaborate, along with BEA, on creating the Business Process Execution Language for Web Services (BPEL4WS)—now one of the de facto standards in the still nascent business process orchestration sphere. Similar fluid and unpredictable dynamics are also afoot in the crucial and fast-growing Web services security arena. Hence, the difficulty in

Table 1.1   *Standards and Specifications Associated with Web Services as of Spring 2003*

Standard or Specification	Category	Purpose	Maintained By	Original Vintage	Original Sponsors
Core Backbone Standards					
XML	Description	Generalized data description scheme to facilitate data sharing	W3C	February 1998	Derived from SGML
SOAP	Messaging	Peer-to-peer exchange of messages using a remote procedure call mechanism	W3C	May 2000	IBM and Microsoft
WSDL	Description	XML derivative for describing Web-oriented communications protocols and messaging schemes	W3C	September 2000	IBM, Microsoft, and Ariba
UDDI	Advertising/Publishing	Web-based registry mechanism to publicize and locate services	OASIS	September 2000	IBM, Microsoft, and Ariba
Business Process Representation					
Business Process Execution Language for Web Services (BPEL4WS)	Business Process	Notation for describing business process behavior and interactions within the context of Web services	—	First draft July 2002	IBM, BEA, and Microsoft
Description					
Web Services Architecture	Description	Reference architecture that defines the key components and the relationships among them	W3C	First draft November 2002	Software AG, IBM, Iona, and BEA
Discovery					
Web Services Inspection Language (WS-Inspection)	Discovery	XML-based scheme that complements UDDI and WSDL, which allows a WS requester to drill down into the services offered by a provider	—	First draft November 2001	IBM and Microsoft

Table 1.1   *Standards and Specifications Associated with Web Services as of Spring 2003 (continued)*

Standard or Specification	Category	Purpose	Maintained By	Original Vintage	Original Sponsors
Messaging					
Reliable HTTP (HTTPR)	Messaging	Guarantees reliable delivery of HTTP packets (which could include SOAP messages) between a server and client	—	June 2001	IBM
Web Services Attachments	Messaging	Extension to SOAP to facilitate attachments (e.g., images) without explicit XML encoding	IETF—draft RFC	First draft June 2002	IBM and Microsoft
Direct Internet Message Encapsulation (DIME)	Messaging	Lightweight binary message format for encapsulating multiple payloads—and targeted to work with Web Services Attachments	IETF—draft RFC	First draft June 2002	IBM and Microsoft
Security					
XML Signature Syntax and Processing	Security	XML-based digital signatures	W3C	March 2001	Motorola, Citi-group, and W3C
XML Key Management Specification (XKMS)	Security	XML-oriented scheme to integrate Public Key Infrastructure (PKI) with the Internet	W3C	March 2001	VeriSign, Microsoft, and webMethods
Web Services Security (WS-Security)	Security	Enhancement to SOAP to provide message integrity, confidentiality, and authentication	—	April 2002	Microsoft, IBM, and VeriSign
WS-Security Addendum	Security	Clarifications to WS-Security, along with use of message timestamps, X.509 certificates, and password transmittal	—	August 2002	Microsoft, IBM, and VeriSign
WS-Security Profile for XML-Based Tokens	Security	Framework to permit XML-based security tokens (e.g., Security Assertion Markup Language [SAML] and Extensible Rights Markup Language [XrML]) to be used with WS-Security	—	August 2002	Microsoft, IBM, and VeriSign

Table 1.1 *Standards and Specifications Associated with Web Services as of Spring 2003 (continued)*

Standard or Specification	Category	Purpose	Maintained By	Original Vintage	Original Sponsors
Web Services Trust Language (WS-Trust)	Security	Builds on top of WS-Security messaging to cater to security token exchange and multidomain credential management	—	December 2002	IBM, Microsoft, VeriSign, and RSA
Web Services Policy Framework (WS-Policy)	Security/Policy	Framework to describe and communicate the policies of a WS, including service requirements, preferences, and capabilities	—	December 2002	IBM, Microsoft, BEA, and SAP
Web Services Policy Assertions Language (WS-PolicyAssertions)	Security/Policy	Details general messaging-related assertions for use with WS-Policy, such as character encoding and preferred language	—	December 2002	IBM, Microsoft, BEA, and SAP
Web Services Policy Attachments (WS-PolicyAttachments)	Security/Policy	Specifies three attachment mechanisms for using policy expressions with existing WSs	—	December 2002	IBM, Microsoft, BEA, and SAP
Web Services Security Policy Language (WS-SecurityPolicy)	Security/Policy	Model and syntax for describing and communicating security policy assertions within the context of WS-Policy	—	December 2002	IBM, Microsoft, VeriSign, and RSA
Web Services Secure Conversation Language (WS-SecureConversation)	Security/Policy	Builds on top of the WS-Security and WS-Policy models to provide secure communications between services	—	December 2002	IBM, Microsoft, VeriSign, and RSA
Web Services Secure Conversation Language (WS-SecureConversation)	Security/Policy	Builds on top of the WS-Security and WS-Policy models to provide secure communications between services	—	December 2002	IBM, Microsoft, VeriSign, and RSA

Table 1.1   *Standards and Specifications Associated with Web Services as of Spring 2003 (continued)*

Standard or Specification	Category	Purpose	Maintained By	Original Vintage	Original Sponsors
Transaction Processing					
Web Services Coordination (WS-Coordination)	Transaction	Extensible protocols for coordinating the actions of distributed applications, especially in the context of completing a specific business process	—	August 2002	IBM, Microsoft, and BEA
Web Services Transaction (WS-Transaction)	Transaction	Works with WS-Coordination to monitor the success or failure of short- or long-duration transactions	—	August 2002	IBM, Microsoft, and BEA
User Interface					
Web Services for Remote Portlets (WSRP) and Web Services for Interactive Applications (WSIA)	User interface	Standard set of user-facing interfaces for facilitating the plug-and-play integration of WSs with portals or interactive applications	OASIS	January 2002	IBM, Epicentric, and WebCollage
Web Services Experience Language (WSXL)	User interface	Component model for interactive WSs to facilitate commercial distribution via multiple channels and synthesis of new services	—	Late 2001	IBM

attempting to present an objective snapshot of the various standards in play without in some cases appearing to be backing the wrong horses.

All this said, IBM, a major proponent of Web services, has been maintaining a very useful list of pertinent Web services specifications in the Web services section of its *"developerWorks"* portal—which can be accessed by going to http://www.ibm.com and then selecting the "developers" link, which will typically appear in one of the navigation bars. If you need an up-to-date list of the Web services–related standards and specifications, this would be the best place to start, always assuming, of course, that IBM continues to maintain and post this list. In addition to this useful IBM list, it will also be worth consulting the Web Services Industry Portal at http://www.webservices.org, OASIS at http://www.oasis-open.org, the World Wide Web Consortium (W3C) at http://www.w3.org, and possibly even the new, vendor-oriented Web Services Interoperability Organization at http://www.ws-i.org to determine what these groups are portraying as the standards being adopted by the industry.

The ability to easily obtain incisive software functionality in the form of one or more Web services should positively influence all future decisions about new application development. It is important not to lose sight of this. Web services have the potential to dramatically compress schedules, enhance the functionality of applications, increase the competitive element of applications, and even reduce cost. This is not idle hyperbole. These are the things that Web services are really supposed to deliver.

1.1.4   Web services—not

Web services would be easier for people to accept if they were called by a slightly more descriptive term. The current name is ambiguous, misleading, and misused, so much so that "Web services" in time may even surpass the infamous Physical Unit (PU) in IBM's very influential Systems Network Architecture (SNA) as being the most misunderstood term in the computer industry. An SNA PU, despite what the name connotes, was not a piece of hardware. Instead, it was a piece of software that controlled a hardware device. In much the same way, a Web service, as we now know with conviction, is not a service in the sense that most people think of computer, network, or Internet services. "Services," in computer circles, mean many things to many people but invariably with a common underlying theme. The term is used, quite appropriately, to refer to any external entity that does work on your behalf, so people are used to print services, directory services, file services, security services, and so forth.

It has come to the point where, in the context of enterprise networking, there is an overall connotation that services are provided by middleware, such as Java 2 Enterprise Edition (J2EE), IBM's WebSphere Application Server, BEA WebLogic, IBM MQSeries, and Microsoft BizTalk Server. The problem is that Web services are not middleware in the conventional sense. They are "problem-solving" software components (e.g., specific segments of business logic) that deliver specific functionality (which would be described using WSDL) rather than utilities used to create or sustain software functionality. In other words, a Web service is the actual thing when it comes to application functionality rather than being supporting (or utility) functionality required to realize the application logic.

SOAP, WSDL, UDDI, and the nascent BPEL4WS are innovative and strategic technologies used to make Web services possible. Though they are indeed middleware services, they themselves are not Web services. They are enabling technologies for Web services, but there continues to be confusion about this distinction in the media, where it is yet possible to read three articles about Web services in trade journals where two are talking exclusively about the enabling technologies while the third is actually talking about Web services as modular applications. Also, it is not unusual to see headlines such as "Intel to Support Web Services," where the services in question are the enabling technologies as opposed to the high-level, application-oriented services. However, by now it should be abundantly clear what is what when it comes to Web services and the enabling technologies needed to sustain them.

1.2   Why there is a need for Web services

It is safe to say without any fear of contradiction, if one wants to cut to the chase, that Web services transform everything to do with applications. Furthermore, this bold assertion, bereft of any qualifiers, caveats, or verbs relative to the term *applications*, is not mere hyperbole. Web services really do positively impact everything associated with applications—both on the supply and demand side. Anybody and everybody who is exposed to software, in whatever role, whether as an application user, developer, financier, portal visitor, salesperson, or sustainer, will enjoy some tangible benefits made possible by Web services—hence, all the hoopla about Web services. Web services go beyond just changing the paradigm when it comes to applications. Web services are truly iconoclastic!

Though one can think of Web services as being an application development–specific methodology, this is far from being the whole picture. Web services also have a very productive role to play when it comes to existing applications. This is particularly the case when it comes to the so-called mission-critical applications that sustain the operations of medium- to large-scale commercial, academic, and research enterprises. Web services enable problem-solving logic from existing applications to be reused. Web services are thus a way to recycle software.

Web services are a standardized, universal, and sure-fire mechanism for isolating, capturing, and modularizing software functionality so that it can be easily reused—with alacrity. Thus, Web services, in effect, can make application owners into application software moguls! Therefore, one cannot just say that Web services only transform the application development process. Web services, instead, also transform application ownership—in a hitherto unprecedented manner. To emphasize this key bilateral feature of Web services, Figure 1.10 highlights the software recycling aspect of Web services, while Table 1.2 shows the primary advantages that can be accrued by software providers and software owners through the availability of Web services.

In addition to its "both sides can win" capability, the impact of Web services is also not restricted to any one particular type or class of application. Though at first blush it is easy to assume that large enterprise class applications (e.g., ERP, CRM, and so forth) are likely to be the main benefactors and thus consumers of Web services, this is not necessarily the case. Down the road, most new applications, whether they be for single-user desktop productivity or multiuser, pan-enterprise, transaction processing, are likely to rely on one or more Web services. This will certainly be the case with Web-related applications, in particular e-business suites and portal-related applications. Portals, as mentioned earlier in the context of the

Figure 1.10
Web services are a standardized, platform, and programming language–independent mechanism for recycling software functionality.

Application Developers

Web Services

Application Consumers Who Own Applications [e.g., Enterprises]

Table 1.2   *Advantages Made Possible by Web Services*

Supply Side		Demand Side
New Application Developers:	Owners of Previously Developed Applications:	Enterprise Class Application Consumers:
■ Obviate need to develop all necessary software.	■ Easily add new functionality to old applications through the use of third-party software modules.	■ Access to incisive, feature-rich applications.
■ Standardized, platform, and programming language–independent access to third-party software functionality.	■ Possibly remove platform dependencies of an old application by making the application a Web service which can then be invoked from a new platform-independent (e.g., Java) "widget" (i.e., a micro application).	■ Faster availability of new applications, new features, and software upgrades.
■ Compress development schedules by being able to utilize third-party software functionality.		■ More reliable and resilient software.
■ Reduce software testing needs through the use of proven third-party software functionality.		■ Possibly more variety, options, and competition vis-à-vis different types of applications—and thus better pricing and service?
■ Reduce application development costs by minimizing development and testing requirements and schedules.		■ Availability of hitherto economically infeasible specialized, niche applications.
■ Expedite time to market.		
■ Offer specialized, additional functionality sourced from third parties.		
■ Enhance product competitiveness by offering value-added and best-of-breed functionality.		
■ Minimize lost opportunity costs caused by product delays, lack of functionality, or product instability.		

■ Ability to promote and market specific software functionality from existing, pre-owned applications in the form of Web services.

WSRP specification, are likely to be major and pioneering consumers of Web services.

1.2.1   Why Web services complement portals

A portal is a Web-based, easy-to-use, transaction-oriented, focal point of access to a diverse range of content, services, resources, and applications. MSN, Yahoo!, Lycos, Excite, AOL, Netscape, and iVillage are all examples of portals—or, to be more precise, public Internet portals. FedEx.com,

Schwab.com, Citi.com, AA.com, and CNN.com, on the other hand, are examples of corporate portals, whereas PBS.org, Dartmouth.edu, and IRS.gov are examples of service-oriented noncorporate portals.

A corporate portal differs from a static, "home-page" Web site in two fundamental ways: personalization and transactional capability. A home-page Web site does not make any attempts to identify and distinguish its visitors. All visitors are treated equally and have access to the same set of content and services. A portal, on the other hand, even if it is a public Internet portal, tries to identify each and every visitor so that it can try to provide a personalized experience. Thus, the content, applications, and services available via a portal, especially corporate portals, will in most cases be tailored and personalized to meet the exact demands of specific users or user groups. Portals will identify users (i.e., visitors) either via an authentication process (i.e., a user-ID/password exchange) or via an automated "self-describing" scheme involving some kind of "cookie" (or applet) technology. Portals, and in particular corporate portals, also enable authorized users to conduct bidirectional, self-service transactions—for example, query account balances, make payments using credit cards or electronic checks, order goods or services, check the status of an order delivery, and so forth.

Portals, with their powerful personalization capabilities, have proved to be an extremely economical, efficacious, and efficient means for dealing with "clients." Corporations, irrespective of their size, have realized unequivocally that portals, at a minimum, can increase their reach, reduce operational costs, expedite customer service, bolster customer loyalty, and enhance competitiveness. Corporate portals can, at a stroke, simplify, streamline, and speed up all client-to-corporate interactions. A portal, in effect, is a fully automated, Web-based emulation of a highly proficient, well-motivated call-center operation devoid of on-hold delays, annoying voice response prompts, and incompetence. Consequently, the deployment and usage of portals are on the ascent, and the Web is now studded with heavily used portals.

Portals, given their transactional nature, thrive on functionality. Whereas compelling content is the key to a successful static, home-page Web site, the popularity of a portal, whether public or corporate, is largely contingent on the services it offers (i.e., its functionality). Portal users want features that enable them to get things done quickly (e.g., pay bills, sell options, check bank balances, book vacations, and so forth). They also want to be edified, gratified, and entertained—so much so, that one could easily extend that adage about never being able to be too rich or too thin to also say that a portal can never have enough functionality. Dedicated portal users will always be able to clearly articulate additional functionality that would enhance their visits to a portal. Consequently, portal providers, as well as the developers of portal software, are continually looking at ways to expedite and simplify the process of adding new functionality to portals. Given this pressing need, Web services have indeed been a hugely welcome panacea.

Web services, as a Web-centric, component-oriented software technology, are an obvious and easy way to add functionality to portals. Their platform and programming language independence further enhances their appeal in this respect, given that UNIX/Linux, Windows NT/2000, and iSeries machines are all popular platforms for portal deployment, with some large corporate portals even being hosted on IBM mainframes. The growing reliance on portlets (or similar mechanisms) within portal architectures and offerings further simplifies Web service integration, as discussed earlier. (Microsoft's "Web parts," Plumtree Software's "gadgets," and SAP's "iVews" are some of the other terms used to describe portlet-like constructs in the context of portals.)

In a portlet-based portal each application, service, and utility (e.g., search function) will be associated with a specific portlet. Consequently, each application, service, and utility can be developed, maintained, and updated independently. Within this framework it is easy to see how the functionality being provided by a portlet could be delivered using one or more Web services. Figure 1.11 highlights the potentially very powerful, synergistic, and symbiotic relationship between portlets (or equivalents) and Web services. This figure also helps to demonstrate that the Web services to portlet relationship may be one-to-one (i.e., a portlet relies on a single Web service) or many-to-one (i.e., a portlet synthesizes functionality obtained from multiple Web services). It is also worth noting that it would also be possible (and even normal) for a particular Web service (e.g., a currency or metric unit converter) to be used by multiple portlets within the same portal view.

Portlets provide modularization and function isolation. Web services, in turn, provide modular, self-contained, remotely invoked software functionality. Furthermore, the software functionality available in the form of Web services will be totally standards compliant and will work on any platform irrespective of the portal server software being used. In addition, the software functionality being provided by a Web service can easily be modified or upgraded on the fly without any changes whatsoever to the portal application, the portal server, or even the portlet per se. This is the beauty of

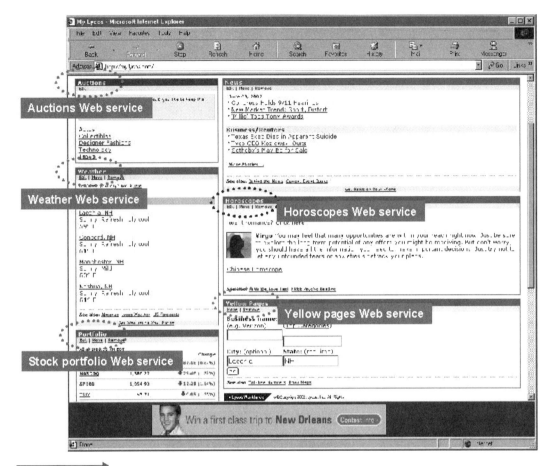

Figure 1.11　*The possibilities of using Web services to provide content and services for portals are immense and hard to ignore. Here we see just a few examples using a personalized Lycos public Internet portal. It highlights how individual portlets making up a portal view can be driven by one or more Web services working in the background.*

bringing together Web services and portlets. It provides a near-perfect, foolproof mechanism for conveniently obtaining portal functionality via a highly standardized outsourcing model.

Rather than trying to develop functionality in-house or obtain specific functionality by purchasing a software package, portal providers can now start thinking about a powerful, best-of-breed, mix-and-match, software component–oriented solution model based on Web services. Consequently, it should not come as a surprise that portal server providers in general are extremely supportive of Web services—with market leaders Oracle and IBM going out of their way to demonstrate how Web services can enhance

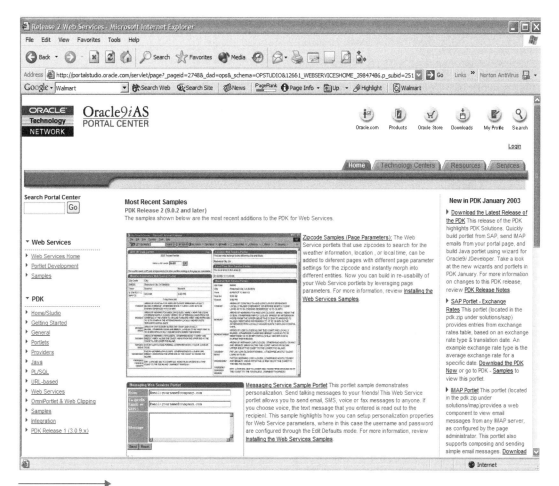

Figure 1.12   *A Web page from Oracle that sets out to demonstrate how Web services can be easily integrated with its market-leading portal server offering by showing various sample applications, with the first one shown being a zip code–driven local information retrieval scheme; the second example is a generalized, media-agnostic messaging service.*

portals. To this end, Figure 1.12 shows a Web page from Oracle showing sample applications of how Web services can be integrated into a portal, with the first example being of a zip code–driven Web service that delivers various local information feeds in real time, such as current weather and time.

The bottom line in this instance is that portals can be considered to be the "killer" application for Web services. This bodes well for the eventual success of Web services because portal deployment, as well as overall portal usage, is on the ascent. Most mid-size to large-size enterprises now realize that portals are an optimum, very low-cost, far-reaching way to interact with customers, prospects, employees, partners, and investors, whether it be to deliver information, provide transactional services, communicate with them, or collaborate with them in real time (e.g., Web-based "Webex"-type conferencing). Within this context it is also important to note that portals have also become the preferred vehicle through which enterprises want to deliver new e-business applications. Portals, in addition to offering unprecedented total global reach via the Internet, also offer proven security, user authentication, personalization, usage tracking, and change management. Portals thus make the whole process of new application rollout that much easier, efficient, and efficacious. Therefore, portals are also playing a key role in promoting the deployment of new e-business applications—another acknowledged growth area for Web services.

1.2.2   Why Web services are galvanizing legacy modernization

When it comes to Web services, legacy modernization is at the other end of the spectrum from where portals fit into the picture. Portals represent the consumption side of Web services. Legacy modernization, in the main, has to do with the supply side. Portals, in this context, are all about new applications (and portlets) obtaining requisite functionality by invoking Web services. Legacy modernization, on the other hand, is about using Web services to capture and expose existing business-critical functionality. This functionality would be located within proven mission-critical applications.

Web services thus enable existing and highly proven business logic to be gainfully reused within new applications. Interestingly, portal applications happen to be prime candidates for reusing functionality culled from existing mission-critical applications—given that portals are becoming the preferred corporate mechanism for "hosting" new applications. Modernization as such, in this context, refers to the creation of new applications based on functionality found in legacy applications.

It is now widely accepted within IT technical circles that much of the proven, highly valuable, business-critical functionality that is still embodied within decades-old legacy applications needs to be converted over the next few years into Web services. This is especially true when it comes to the $20 trillion worth of IBM mainframe and AS/400 applications that were known as SNA applications—where SNA, which stands for IBM's once-legendary Systems Network Architecture, represented the networking scheme used by these applications to serve large populations of online users. So, to paraphrase that adage about old soldiers, one can now say, without really any fear of contradiction, that old SNA applications, though now over 20 years in age, never die—they just fade away to become Web services.

Web services provide a standards-based mechanism whereby timeless legacy software functionality, which has been in daily production use since the 1980s, can be profitably reused when developing new applications in 2004 or beyond. This is what legacy modernization is all about. Legacy modernization is possible without Web services. However, Web services make it that much more structured and sanitized. Web services, in effect, legitimize the rationale and the expense of legacy modernization.

Legacy applications, as previously mentioned, are prime candidates to be *sources* of Web services—as opposed to *consumers* of Web services. An application that relies on software functionality provided by a Web service can be thought of as a Web service consumer. Though there is nothing technical that precludes existing legacy applications from becoming Web service consumers, this, however, is unlikely to be the case in practice. A legacy application will only need to become a Web service consumer if one is thinking of extending its current functionality to include capabilities best obtained in the form of Web services.

Web service consumption by legacy applications, in the end, boils down to the economics and practicality of modifying and extending applications that in many cases were developed even before the advent of the PC. Most of these applications were written in COBOL, BAL, PL/I, or possibly even FORTRAN. Rather than trying to modify the code of these applications (which is what many enterprises had to do to accommodate Y2K), a better way to extend their functionality would be in terms of what is known as *host integration*. Host integration, a technology that evolved from host access and Web-to-host, can be thought of as a precursor to legacy modernization.

Since at least 1999, host integration was always positioned as the final frontier of the Web-to-host repertoire of solutions, where Web-to-host dealt with how applications running on mainframes, IBM AS/400s, and other mini-computers (including UNIX servers) could be accessed using Web technology. Applet-based terminal emulation, as with IBM's Java-based Host On-Demand product, was one way to realize Web-to-host. Another approach was to rely on 3270/5250-to-HTML conversion (e.g., Hummingbird's e-Gateway), which enabled cost-effective Web browser–based access to existing SNA applications running on mainframes or AS/400s.

Host integration went to the next step and talked about how existing SNA applications can complement new Web applications. It was all about reusing the proven software functionality found within SNA applications. Web services provide the ideal mechanism for this software reuse scenario—hence, the now-close interplay between SNA applications, host integration, and Web services. Figures 1.13 and 1.14 illustrate different

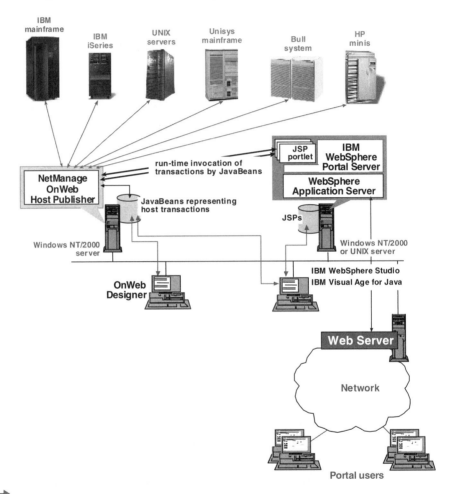

Figure 1.13   *A typical host integration scenario, in this instance for a portal application that is to be realized with JavaBeans and JSP portlets, using NetManage's OnWeb host integration product to create the JavaBeans and IBM's WebSphere Portal Server to run the Java-Beans bearing JSPs and invoke the necessary host transactions via OnWeb at run time. In the future the legacy application functionality could be provided in the form of Web services rather than JavaBeans using this same overall setup.*

host integration scenarios and show how Web services will come into play vis-à-vis host integration in the future. However, after all the monies that were expended on the Y2K conversion, most IT organizations are reluctant to make any more large-scale extensions to decades-old legacy applications. Consequently, legacy applications are unlikely to be major consumers of Web services.

On the other hand, legacy applications (and in particular SNA applications) are veritable smorgasbords when it comes to pertinent business logic that can be packaged for reuse as Web services. This also ties in with the very hot and strategic interest in business process integration and enterprise process management.

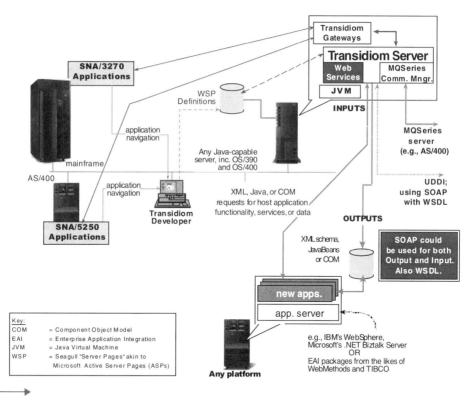

Figure 1.14   *Another host integration scenario, in this case showing Seagull Software's Transidiom offering, which happened to be the first product of this genre to support Web services vis-à-vis host integration. Transidiom allows legacy business logic that is captured in the form of its proprietary WSP definitions to be used by new applications in the form of Web services.*

1.2.3   Why Web services impinge on business processes

The lifeblood of any enterprise is its business processes. Processes are what make any business tick. It is these processes that shape and sustain a business. They are the internal nervous system of an enterprise that makes sure that things get done. It is processes that differentiate businesses that are engaged in the same line of business. The success of a business is shaped to a large extent by the efficacy and efficiency of the processes it employs. Processes even influence the vision of a corporation.

Let us use an insurance company as an easy-to-visualize example (Figure 1.15). In an insurance company there will be multiple processes that relate to the issuance, updating, and canceling of customer policies. Though there may be some processes, and especially subprocesses, that are manual, these days most insurance companies, in most countries, would rely on automated (i.e., computerized) processes for much of their mission-critical operations. Consequently, each automated business process will typically involve the invocation of multiple applications or the use of one integrated

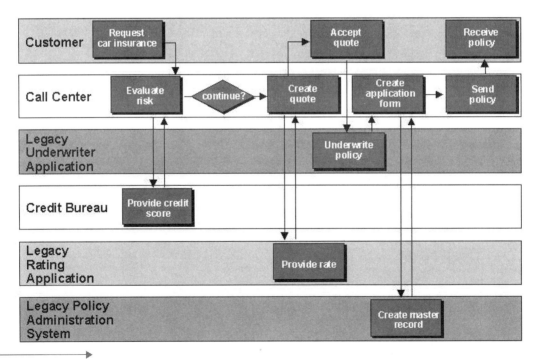

Figure 1.15   *A typical insurance company–related business process—characterized here by CRM heavyweight Siebel Systems. It depicts a generalized new policy issuance process. Note that it involves six applications, including the call-center application.*

application that performs multiple tasks. Figure 1.16 uses a new policy issuance process that is likely to be employed by a typical insurance company to show the overall subprocess-oriented composition of a business process and how these subprocesses are likely to be handled by different applications.

Automated business processes are thus made possible by applications. Business applications (and in particular mission-critical legacy applications) therefore embody umpteen proven and critical business processes. Trying to accurately reproduce these processes in new software can be a difficult, arduous, and risky endeavor, since even the slightest deviance from the original (e.g., even the way that numbers are rounded at the sixth decimal point) could significantly alter the desired end result. Thus, the existing software representation of these processes has intrinsic value. This is the software equivalent of knowledge. Web services provide an ideal mechanism for profitably reusing these process-related software assets. Figure 1.16 highlights this capability by taking the new policy issuance process shown in Figure 1.15 and showing how some of the subprocesses can be associated with Web services—either in terms of consumption or resale.

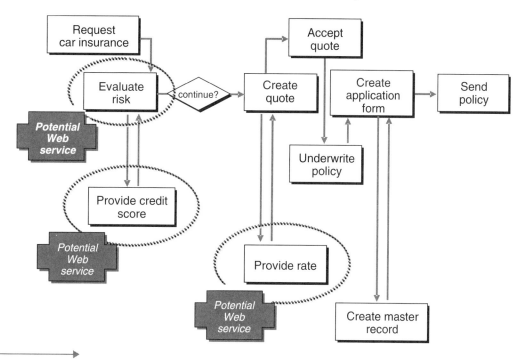

Figure 1.16   *Associating Web services with subprocesses that make up a process—in this case the new insurance policy issuance process, courtesy of Siebel Systems, shown in Figure 1.15.*

With Web services, business processes can be isolated, neatly packaged, and readily marketed for use by new in-house applications being developed (as in legacy modernization)—or even by other companies. On the flip side, Web services also now become the obvious way by which to source required process-related functionality when developing new applications. Web services, moreover, as previously discussed, are totally platform independent, so there are no real issues whatsoever about whether an application being developed to run on a particular set of platforms will be able to use Web services culled from legacy applications that are running on a different set of systems.

Web services provide those involved with business process software with an elegant, platform-independent, distributed computing mechanism based on remote invocation. With Web services, the process-related software functionality that is being reused, rather than being cut and pasted from the old application to the new, continues to run on a host platform and interacts with the new application in terms of dynamic (XML-based) I/O calls. Furthermore, thanks to Web services, the functionality of business process–related applications can be significantly enhanced without requiring any changes whatsoever to the source code of the original application. Rather than adding new code to the existing application, you can create new code based on Web services that run as separate software instances and interact with the original application at run time.

1.3   When to implement Web services

With Web services, given their unique and incontrovertible value proposition as a Web-based software component methodology and the near-universal industry backing, there was never any question about *if.* It was always about *when.* That "when," per all predictions as well as expectations, has come and gone, but among those actively involved in propagating Web services, the question of *when* (albeit sotto voce) still persists, even in late 2003.

A big part of the issue here, in terms of timing, is that Web services are an application development–related technology, which is most applicable to the development of large corporate applications. Thus, the supply and demand dynamics of Web services, to a very large extent, were going to be influenced from the start by the overall vigor of the software industry. The depressing economic downturn that followed in the wake of the dot.com implosion, which was then further exacerbated by 9/11, could not have come at a worse time in terms of Web services. In essence, the software industry has been treading water since Y2K. This is the backdrop against which the "when" question has to be rethought and reanswered.

XML Web services in their current form can no longer, by any stretch of the imagination, be considered nascent. They were postulated in early 2000 and were being vociferously promoted by the summer of 2000. In addition, the key prerequisite enabling methodologies, in the form of SOAP, WSDL, and UDDI, as shown in Table 1.1, were formalized and in place by October 2000. Consequently, given current technology adoption trends, Web services, in theory, have been ready for prime-time usage since at least the latter part of 2002. IBM, Microsoft, Oracle, and BEA (just to mention the super heavyweights) have also been actively promoting them and offering viable Web services development solutions, most of which appear to have the word "Studio" in their title, for even longer.

Thus, one could, if one wishes, begin Web services–based initiatives right away—without any further delay. Even a cursory search of the UDDI registries (e.g., IBM's or Microsoft's), as of the beginning of 2003, will show that there are plenty of Web services already available. Most of what is offered, however, is best characterized as yet being prototypical (of the "hello World" genre) as opposed to representing sophisticated business logic functionality. In essence, it is safe to say that Web services have arrived (around 2003), though, as is to be expected, they are still in the early stages of growth.

How and when one decides to "exploit" Web services is unfortunately not as straightforward as one would think, based on all that has been said about them in the media over the last few years. The biggest problem here is that Web services by themselves are not a product. They are not a "killer" application in their own right. Thus, you cannot buy, market, or sell Web services per se. Web services are a methodology. Hence, what you can buy, market, or sell (not counting the inevitable consulting services) are as follows:

1. Software components that have been developed per the Web services model

2. Tools that facilitate the creation, deployment, adoption (i.e., integration and invocation), testing, and popularization (e.g., automated UDDI registry) of Web services–based software components

3. Applications that have been developed using best-of-breed, third-party Web services–based software components

This list also immediately highlights another pivotal issue related to the vexing *when* question. The timing of your entrée onto the Web services stage will, and should, depend on what you intend to do with Web services—keeping in mind that it is best to put the horse in front of the cart, rather than the other way around. Consequently, if your interest is in providing tools to facilitate the creation and use of Web services, you ideally need to be ahead of those who want to develop Web services, use Web services within applications they are developing, or acquire new applications that are heavily Web services–oriented.

Those who want to create tools should be at it now! That sector of the market is already in high gear, and, thanks to IBM, Microsoft, and BEA, there is already a wide selection of compelling and effective tools. Therefore, one should assume that much of the Web services–related activity in the 2003–2006 time frame will and should revolve around the creation of business problem-solving Web services, but even this might get sidetracked to an extent while people await the solidification of some of the auxiliary standards associated with Web services, as listed in Table 1.1. From an enterprise standpoint, security- and management-related standards and practices will continue to be of particular issue, since mission-critical processes are likely to be the primary users of Web services.

Because of incessant virus and hacker threats, enterprises are understandably shy of any software technology that can in any way increase their potential vulnerability. Security concerns, essentially the same bugbear that has plagued the widespread adoption of so many other Web-related software ventures (e.g., e-business, Web-to-host, corporate portals), will again be a gating factor. Availability of solid security measures will dictate, more than anything else, as to when major enterprises will feel comfortable about adopting Web services. Thus, at this juncture it is worth looking at all of the various factors that have and will influence when the market will be ready to adopt and absorb Web services on a consistent and widespread basis.

1.3.1   The issues weighing down upon *when*

Though a few media columnists have been brave enough to express some doubts, Web services should not be summarily dismissed as mere marketing hype just because they have yet to live up to the enormous expectations that have surrounded them since their inception. There is no doubt that Web services have been slow in gaining real traction in real-life, enterprise-class production use despite the near-unprecedented push that they have received, without exception, from every quarter of the computer industry.

Although most saw 2002 as the year that Web services would begin to flourish, only a staggering amount of effort was expended by the supply side (i.e., vendor community) on defining and publicizing Web services–related standards, particularly in the security and business process "orchestration" fronts, rather than any real proliferation of mission-critical Web services. Despite these very public setbacks, Web services are, as stated earlier, very real, viable, and here to stay. Furthermore, they will be around for a very long time to come given the invaluable role they can play in application development, software reuse, and legacy modernization. The reason that one can make such unequivocal claims is that there are some valid and justifiable rationales that support why Web services have been slow in living up to their expectations.

The necessary technical infrastructure for Web services, in the form of XML, WSDL, SOAP, and UDDI, is in place and beyond reproach. The key issues, as such, have nothing to do with the underlying technology. Instead, all of the real impediments, in one way or another, relate to what it takes to make Web services mission critical and secure for enterprise usage. A good analogy here, which can, furthermore, be dramatically used to great effect in corporate meeting settings, is that of Russian-built commercial airliners such as those from Ilyushin or Tupolev (Figure 1.17). What makes North American and European travelers somewhat uneasy about these aircraft, which on the whole have a respectable track record in terms of airworthiness, is not their fundamental aerodynamic or propulsion capabilities, but the apparently haphazard nature of their passenger safety (e.g., oxygen masks) and passenger comfort–related equipment. Ditto for Web services. You cannot question their ability to fly. What is at issue is whether the cabin will remain pressurized during the flight.

With this Russian aircraft analogy in mind, the key auxiliary concerns that are currently slowing down the widespread adoption of Web services are as follows:

1.   Security and integrity

2.   Reliability (including guaranteed delivery of input/output)

3.   Performance and scalability

4.   Manageability

5.   Pricing model

6.   Ongoing support and updates

All of these issues, most of which are somewhat self-explanatory once they have been enumerated, will continue to be discussed in the remainder

Figure 1.17   *A Russian Ilyushin IL-96-300 jetliner is a great analogy to the factors slowing down the widespread adoption of Web services.*

of this book. Security, as already mentioned, is the big issue. As reusable pieces of business logic, sourced and invoked over the Web, Web services have the potential to be the ultimate in Trojan horse–type threats—even taking into account that the Web services code is executed, remotely, on a third-party server.

The first and biggest concern when it comes to security is making sure that the provider of a Web service is honorable and genuine and is really who he or she claims to be—especially if you intend to be dealing with sensitive data. Although it will not be disastrous if you send a zip code to a bogus organization masquerading as a provider of a weather forecast Web service, it would be a totally different matter if you were sending credit card information to a credit card authorization Web service that has been compromised or is being run by two teenagers out of an apartment in Azerbaijan.

Then there is the whole issue as to what happens to the information you have shared with a Web service. What rights, explicit and implicit, does a provider of a Web service have when it comes to storing, analyzing, and, above all, exploiting (e.g., selling) information that has been sent to the Web service? This opens up a whole Pandora's box of issues. Today we worry about the information that portals (e.g., Amazon) automatically and transparently extract from visitors via what is referred to, euphemistically, as "collaborative filtering." The scope for this type of intrusion in the case of Web services is equally high—and more insidious. Thus, there is an obvious need to determine that Web services are not unscrupulous, and the problem here is that scruples, in today's world, come in many shades of gray.

Securing the privacy of the information flowing to and from Web services, though a major concern, is not, fortunately, a real issue. Proven solutions such as SSL-based encryption will work and are more than adequate for the time being, but, alas, there are other problems. Think of the various buffer overflow–type vulnerabilities that have been exploited in Windows NT systems and some Web servers. Web services, at least in theory, can take such threats to a whole new dimension. Related to this is the possibility of denial-of-service attacks propagated through the Web services connections—especially because SOAP-based WS traffic typically is configured to flow through ports 80 and 443—that is, standard HTTP and SSL-encrypted traffic flows, respectively, for Web servers. All in all, it is not surprising that IT professionals are very anxious to ensure that all of the security-related issues pertaining to Web services are securely nailed down before they commit to this methodology.

The good news is that, as shown in Table 1.1, there is much activity taking place on the security front. There is even a forum—namely, XML Web Services Security (XWSS) (http://www.xwss.org)—to act as a central clearinghouse for all Web services–related security issues. It is definitely worth visiting this forum to get acclimatized to what is happening in this fast-evolving arena. Consequently, there is considerable belief that by mid-2004 there will be adequate security measures to enable enterprises to evaluate Web services from certified and credible sources with a significant level of confidence and trust.

As with any other type of new software methodology, IT professionals, understandably, have nagging concerns about the reliability, performance, scalability, and manageability of Web services. These concerns are exacerbated by the fact that many of those who intend to offer Web services are likely to be previously unknown entities. Also, there is the whole issue of platform independence, which in this context could be a negative, given that it enables Web service providers the option of using underpowered and possibly unreliable platforms. Obviously, there is nothing in the Web services standards per se that say that these software components have to be any different from other software in any of these crucial areas! To assume that Web services will somehow miraculously break the mold when it comes to all the standard RAS issues (i.e., reliability, availability, and serviceability) that have hounded software for the last 4 decades would be a case of taking optimism to unheard of heights. In terms of these RAS issues, a new Web service, at best, is not going to be that different from a new release of Netscape for the Mac. Diligence, testing, and vigilance are thus going to be essential when evaluating and integrating new Web services.

Pricing and the mechanism for ongoing support are other areas that have yet to be adequately addressed. The pricing model for Web services at present is in its embryonic stage. What is abundantly clear already is that there will be a very wide spectrum of pricing schemes, ranging from freeware to expensive, premium offerings. In addition, in the case of the non-freeware offerings, there will invariably be many permutations as to how the pricing will be structured. The pricing options available will definitely include one-time charge schemes, periodic licensing (e.g., monthly or yearly), and umpteen usage-based options. In addition, it is likely that there could be third-party Web service distributors—though the inherent dynamic discovery capability of Web services dilutes some of the potential value that can be offered by a distributor.

1.4   How to create and use Web services

As with most issues pertaining to Web services, the first thing to note when thinking about "implementing" Web services is that there are two very distinct and different scenarios that have to be taken into account—that is, Web services as a consumable versus Web services as a deliverable. Hence, implementation per se depends, and depends greatly, on whether your interest lies in using Web services to develop new applications or providing Web services to be used by others. Therefore, the first cut that has to be taken when looking at implementation-related issues is determining what side of the fence you intend to be on (i.e., the demand side as a consumer or the supply side as a provider). To make matters more interesting, each of these two camps can have very widely divergent players within them—each with different motives and needs.

Let us start with the demand side. It is easy to see how Web services will be of immense interest and value to in-house programmers employed by corporations to develop and enhance proprietary corporate applications. These in-house programmers are thus seen by many as the predominant target market for enterprise-level Web services. This will no doubt be the case when the previously discussed issues such as security and manageability have been adequately addressed, but these are not the only enterprise-class software developers who are likely to want to use Web services.

Developers employed by software vendors are also likely to want to avail themselves of best-of-breed functionality available in the form of Web services—provided, of course, they meet the reliability, integrity, and cost (i.e., pricing) expectations of the company as well as the particular software project. In many instances there is likely to also be political and support-related issues as to the desirability (and even wisdom) of including dynamically invoked third-party software components into a commercial application that is meant to be sold to other corporations. However, that, fortunately, is not the issue at hand at this point. The issue here is that even on the demand side there can be considerable variance as to how and when somebody would want to use Web services—and consequently also as to how he or she would want to go about realizing the implementation.

There are at least three distinct scenarios on the supply side, as originally highlighted in Table 1.2. These are as follows:

1.   Software vendors (or individual software developers) interested in delivering new functionality in the form of Web services

2.   Software vendors with existing commercial applications interested in making some of the functionality from these applications available in the form of Web services

3.   Enterprises, which are not software vendors, and which may now wish to use Web services as a mechanism to market and deliver proven, business process–related software functionality culled from existing, mission-critical legacy applications

Suffice to say that each of these camps will require somewhat different tools to realize their objectives. For a start, the enterprises that want to get into the legacy modernization game, as discussed earlier, will want to start off with business logic–capturing, host integration tools such as IBM's WebSphere Host Publisher. Host integration tools, in the main, rely on a highly visual (i.e., screen I/O oriented) paradigm that isolates and captures specific elements of business logic by stepping through an actual transaction associated with that business logic (Figure 1.18).

They do not require access to the application's source code or the expertise of programmers familiar with the inner working of the application. They can, in general, be used very successfully by software developers who have instructions as to how to invoke and navigate through the required transactions. Host integration tools may also be of use and value to the software vendors that want to market functionality from existing applications—though they typically have the advantage of having ready access to the source code of the applications in question. Consequently, they have

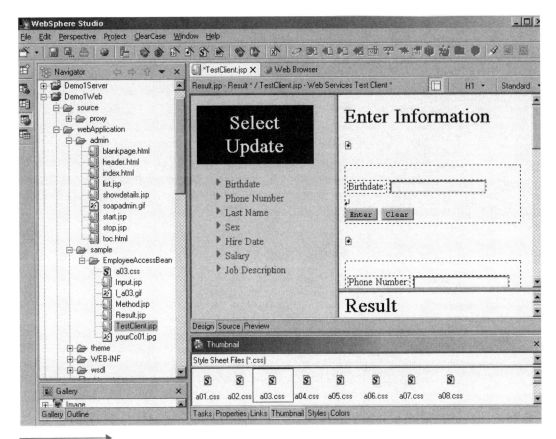

Figure 1.18   *A screen shot related to testing a newly created Web service from IBM's WebSphere Studio—one of the premier tools for developing, deploying, and using Web services.*

the option of culling and packaging the requisite functionality into Web services form—from scratch, so to speak. Similarly, software vendors interested in offering new functionality, in the form of Web services, will typically opt to do that using their preferred, in-house development methodology, given that competent programmers can, within reason, create bona fide Web services using any programming language and software development environment.

1.4.1   How to circumvent implementational pitfalls

There are three fundamental issues that any person involved with implementing Web services, whether on the supply or demand side, will invariably encounter at some stage—in one form or another. These three issues are as follows:

1.   Platform selection

2.   The role of Java versus Microsoft's .NET

3.   Advantages of utilizing Web services development tools such as those offered by Microsoft, IBM, BEA, and so forth

At this juncture, it has to be stressed that Web services are truly platform independent. This platform independence applies to both sides of a Web services configuration (i.e., the usage side as well as the provision side). This is indeed the case, because a Web service is a run time–invoked external subroutine, running on a different machine that functions by accepting input parameters in the form of an XML document and returning the required results also in the form of an XML document. Therefore, applications that use Web services can run on any platform. Web services are also totally platform independent. They can run on any platform, whether a mainframe or a PC. Web services also may be developed on any platform without any implication whatsoever as to where or how they are going to be deployed. Hence, there are no platform-related restrictions of any sort when it comes to any aspect of Web services. This all-around platform independence should never be forgotten or underestimated. Consequently, there are no limitations as to which Web services can be used by which applications or where they can be developed or dcployed.

The platform independence of Web services, as previously discussed, is also in no way related to Java. Though many of the super heavyweights that promote Web services have Java-centric offerings, Java is just another programming scheme as far as Web services are concerned—keeping in mind that Web services, in addition to being platform independent, are also totally programming language agnostic. Thus, Web services can be developed in any language. Web services may also be used by applications written in any programming language—irrespective of the vintage of that language.

Therefore, applications being written in Visual BASIC or C++ can readily invoke Web services functionality being provided by legacy programs written in COBOL, PL/I, or even BAL. In the same way, Java may be used to create Web services or to develop applications that use Web services. Applications being developed in Java can use Web services being provided by software written in any language, including Java, whereas Web services emanating from software written in Java can be used by applications written in any language. Just as with platform independence, the programming language neutrality of Web services has no boundaries. It is truly any-to-any when it comes to programming language interoperability. It thus also provides a bridge between the old and the new when it comes to software programming methodology.

Despite the platform and language impartiality, Web services, in their role as the new programming paradigm for the next iteration of Web evolution have, nonetheless, become the latest battlefield in the now decades-old IBM versus Microsoft vendetta. This is, however, somewhat ironic, since many of the pivotal Web services–related standards (e.g., SOAP, WSDL, UDDI, BPEL4WS, WS-Security, and so forth), as shown in Table 1.1, are the result of open and close collaboration between IBM and Microsoft. What is clear, though, is that the standards were created by technocrats, whereas the vendetta is being fought by the combatant and aggressive marketers. Microsoft's Web services push revolves around .NET, whereas that of IBM now revolves around the Java-based WebSphere Application Server and WebSphere Studio. Chapters 3 and 6 are devoted to addressing this issue from all angles.

The one major downside to the .NET initiative is its lack of platform independence. Although Web services developed by or running on a .NET server can be used with impunity by applications running on other platforms, including IBM mainframes and iSeries, the .NET-based applications, Web services, and tools can only run on the Windows system—with the Windows servers, in turn, only running on PCs. Many, especially those who have become hooked on Java, find this platform restriction galling.

The Java-based Web services solutions, whether Web services or tools, in marked contrast, can and will run on multiple platforms—including Windows 2000/2003 servers. This is the rub. However, as stated unequivocally earlier, you have to be very careful when trying to draw a fine line here about platform independence. In some cases, possibly even most, it may not really matter where a Web service is running—provided that it meets the requisite reliability, resilience, security, and performance expectations. Thus, it makes sense not to get too religious about this issue. There will be more on this later in the book. With the major Microsoft and Java tools for developing Web services being discussed in Chapters 3, 6, and 8, it is sufficient to close this chapter by noting that proven tools for developing, deploying, and testing Web services are available, at a minimum, from IBM, Microsoft, BEA, Sun, SAP, webMethods, and so forth.

1.5   Q&A: A time to recap and reflect

Q: What are Web services?

A: Web services are a new genre of Web-specific software component methodology that deal with modular, self-contained, self-describing software components whose public interfaces are described using XML. Hence, one can build applications by reusing or assembling existing components from within and outside of an enterprise. Thanks to Web services, these applications will be able to cross systems, programming language, and platform boundaries. New applications being developed can obtain software functionality in the form of Web services. All data transfers that occur between applications and the Web services they invoke are in the form of XML documents that are exchanged using a messaging mechanism—with SOAP being the preferred and recommended messaging scheme.

Q: Are SOAP, WSDL, and UDDI Web services?

A: No. These are enabling technologies that are used by Web services. Web services are software components that solve problems or perform some business logic. They are not just networking protocols provided by middleware.

Q: What is the role of XML in relation to Web services?

A: XML is the underlying basis for today's Web services (with Web services, in this context, being used, per common usage, to describe reusable, remotely invoked software components), so much so that they are referred to within some technical circles as "XML Web services." Web services are defined and described using XML. Web services operate by exchanging XML documents. Thus, the input parameters to a Web service are always in the form of an XML document, whereas the output of a Web service will also always be an XML document.

Q: Why is there a need for Web services?

A: Web services dramatically and positively alter everything related to applications, both on the supply and demand side. Web services expedite, simplify, and reduce the cost of new application development by providing application developers with systematic access to standards-compliant third-party software functionality that is invoked across the Web. It also allows valuable software functionality embedded within existing applications to be isolated and reused. Since they are totally Web-centric, developers looking for sources for best-of-breed software functionality now have ready access to the entire worldwide software community without the hindrance of geographic, political, or trade boundaries.

Q: Are Web services platform independent?

A: Web services are truly platform independent. The platform independence, furthermore, applies to both sides of a Web services "configuration" (i.e., the usage side as well as the provision side). This is because a Web service is a run time–invoked external subroutine, which runs on a machine different from that of the application invoking it. Therefore, applications that use Web services can run on any platform. Web services themselves, in turn, are also totally platform independent and can run on any platform. There is never a need for any commonality. It is a true any-to-any scheme. Web services also may be developed on any platform without any implication whatsoever as to where or how they are going to be deployed.

Q: Is Java a prerequisite for Web services?

A: No. The platform independence of Web services is not in any way related to Java. In addition to being platform independent, Web services are also programming language neutral. Web services may be written in any programming language (including Java). In turn, Web services may also be used by any application, written in any programming language.

Q: Is there a rational explanation as to why the widespread adoption of Web services has been much slower than expected?

A: Yes. Web services are an application development–related methodology. The economic downturn that started in 2001 has impacted and slowed down the whole software industry. This has delayed the promulgation of Web services. It is also true that all of the pertinent standards to cover the security, manageability, and reliability aspects of Web services were yet to be formalized in the spring of 2003. These factors, understandably, have slowed down the widespread adoption of Web services, though it should be noted that the UDDI registries testify to the availability of a relatively large number of bona fide Web services. Note, however, that UDDI only comes into play when you are looking for Web services from hitherto unknown external sources (i.e., a bit like looking for a florist in some distant city in a foreign country in an online Yellow Pages directory). Enterprises, however, can also source and use Web services from within the enterprise or from trusted partners—without obviously having to resort to UDDI.

Q: Has a "killer" application for Web services been identified as yet?

A: To an extent, yes. Portals, or, to be more specific, portal applications, whether they are for public or corporate portals, are likely, at present, to be the leading candidates for Web services consumption. Portal applications thrive on functionality. Providing value-added, best-of-breed functionality is the primary raison d'être for Web services. Thus, Web services are ideally poised to provide portal application developers with the value-added functionality that they constantly crave.

Q: What are UDDI, SOAP, and WSDL?

A: UDDI is a directory and corresponding search mechanism that enables Web services to be readily located and checked out on the Web—online and dynamically. WSDL is an XML dialect used to describe the external interfaces of Web services. These WSDL descriptions will typically be maintained in a UDDI registry. SOAP is the remote procedure call mechanism preferred by Web services. It is a platform and programming language messaging scheme that is XML based.

Q: What are the salient characteristics of Web services?

A: Web services are modular, self-contained, self-describing, self-advertising, uniquely addressable over the Web, XML-centric, standards based, platform independent, programming language agnostic, and amalgamative in mix-and-match mode.

2

XML—The Backbone of Web Services

Tell me, tell me if anything got finished.

—Leonardo da Vinci

Extensible Markup Language (XML) is what makes Web services possible. Everything to do with today's Web services are based, one way or another, on XML. The link between XML and Web services is inextricable and incontrovertible. All data transfer to or from a Web service always has to be in the form of an XML document. That is a given. The input parameters to a Web service are thus structured and defined using XML, as is the output generated by a Web service. In addition, the input/output operations of a Web service, which are implemented in the form of a remote procedure call mechanism, are realized using an XML-based messaging scheme—namely, SOAP.

The workings of a Web service are also described using XML, in this case WSDL, which is an XML derivative. The W3C's proposed definition of what a Web service is supposed to be states categorically, in the very first sentence, no less, that the public interfaces and bindings of a Web service are defined and described using XML. Many of the auxiliary standards associated with Web services (as shown in Table 1.1), such as those related to security and discovery (e.g., WS-Inspection), also happen to be XML-centric. Even the proposed GUI standard for Web services (i.e., WSRP), though not XML-specific, given that information presentation per se is not exactly XML's "cup of tea," still makes sure that it includes support for presentation-oriented dialects of XML, such as VoiceXML. Table 2.1 highlights the deep-rooted relationship between XML and Web services—Web services now assume the role of the "killer" application for XML. Figure 2.1 builds upon the Web services model introduced in Figures 1.2 and 1.9 to show the role of XML vis-à-vis the workings of a Web service.

Table 2.1   *XML and Web Services Relationship*

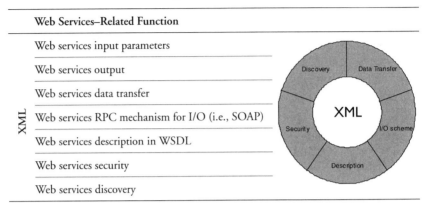

Web Services–Related Function
Web services input parameters
Web services output
Web services data transfer
Web services RPC mechanism for I/O (i.e., SOAP)
Web services description in WSDL
Web services security
Web services discovery

It is also the total dependence on XML that ensures that Web services are indeed platform neutral and programming language independent. Hence, it is XML that truly differentiates and distinguishes today's Web services from all previous software component methodologies. Web services, in their current form, would not be here if not for XML. This is why

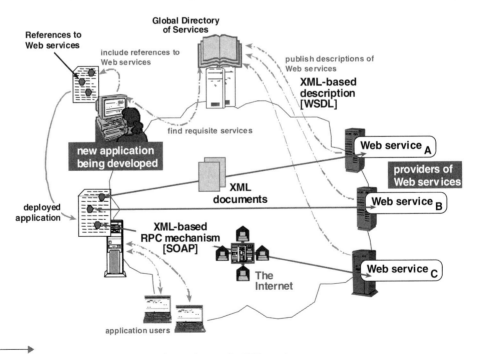

Figure 2.1   *Role of XML vis-à-vis the workings of a Web service.*

they are often referred to as *XML Web services* by technocrats in order to unequivocally convey the inescapable link between XML and Web services.

Web services have become the "killer" application for XML. XML was formulated in the 1996–1997 time frame to facilitate data interchange between incompatible systems. It is a standardized, platform- and programming-language–independent mechanism for sharing data in a consistent, unambiguous, and meaningful manner. It provides a framework for describing data. XML, in effect, makes data self-describing. Figure 2.2 illustrates the overall concept of data description à la XML by showing how the composition of a well-known poem could be defined using XML.

It is the any-to-any data interchange capability made possible by the self-describing data that makes XML so indispensable to Web services. Thanks to the availability of XML, which was ratified as an industry standard by the W3C in February 1998, Web services did not have to come up with their own scheme for data exchange. Instead, Web services were able to piggyback on the ground swell building up around XML. One could even say that it was the presence of XML that provided the impetus for the creation of Web services. It is also safe to say that the credibility and acceptance that Web services enjoyed, from the get-go, from within the technical community can be largely attributed to the fact that they were based

```
<?xml version="1.0"?>
<POEM>
    <TITLE>Lines Written in Early Spring</TITLE>
    <AUTHOR>
        <FIRSTNAME>William</FIRSTNAME>
        <LASTNAME>Wordsworth</LASTNAME>
    </AUTHOR>
    <STANZA>
        <LINE N="1">I heard a thousand blended notes,</LINE>
        <LINE N="2">While in grove I sate reclined,</LINE>
        <LINE N="3">In that sweet mood when pleasant thoughts</LINE>
        <LINE N="4">Bring sad thoughts to the mind.</LINE>
    </STANZA>

    <STANZA>
        <LINE N="5">To her fair works did nature link</LINE>
        <LINE N="6">The human soul that through me ran;</LINE>
        <LINE N="7">And much it griev'd me my heart to think</LINE>
        <LINE N="8">What man has made of man.</LINE>
    </STANZA>
</POEM>
```

Figure 2.2   *A poem by William Wordsworth described using XML. Courtesy of Rutgers, State University of New Jersey (www.ceth.rutgers.edu).*

squarely on the XML standard and did not try to espouse any new mechanisms for data interchange.

2.1   **XML from 33,000 feet**

IT "technicians," particularly those with a programming background, rarely, if ever, have a problem appreciating the need or rationale for XML. They can see the possibilities afforded by XML, even if it is just at a philosophical level. This is because they have typically experienced first hand the issues involved with trying to import data from one application into another—even if it was that of trying to get "comma-separated" contact information from one type of electronic address book into a different address book used by another e-mail client.

Those who work for corporations that utilize multiple, disparate IT platforms have, in addition, invariably encountered the challenge of trying to make data used by an application suite on one platform be available, in a meaningful and thus useful manner, to another unrelated application suite running on another platform. Sometimes it does not even matter if the application suites are on the same platform. Any-to-any data interchange could never be taken for granted. For example, a corporation might have tried to take data that was being used by its in-house ERP application suite and make it available to a new CRM application. Realizing such a data exchange, which, though obvious and justifiable, may have been far from straightforward.

The Web accentuated the need for a generic but global mechanism for describing data so that it would not be misunderstood or misconstrued. Search engines (e.g., Google) looking through HTML-based Web pages would locate and index keywords, oblivious to their context. A "chip" would be a "chip," irrespective of whether it was being used in the context of a micro-chip, a chocolate-chip cookie, "Chip" as in a first name, or even a wood chip. Not having a standard means to associate meaning and context to data made business-to-business (b2b) e-business propositions that much more taxing, since each and every data interchange permutation required between corporations and applications had to be dealt with on an individual basis.

Thus, it was no wonder that XML, from its inception, was hailed as the great unifying technology for the Web. It was meant to be the lingua franca for e-business. It was the next big thing (until Web services came along a few years later). It was, even independent of Web services, going to revolutionize the Web, applications, and b2b transactions. That is still in the cards—albeit now with an increased dependence on Web services. XML, in cahoots with Web services, still dominates much of the thinking, planning, and positioning (not to mention posturing) when it comes to new corporate applications (including desktop applications), e-business, corporate portals, and the future makeup of the Web.

XML is powerful in that it has no inherent functional limitations. XML imposes no caveats or restrictions as to what types of data or the nature of the data that can be defined and described using its syntax. It is flexible and, per its name, extensible. It is also, nonetheless, disarmingly simple and straightforward. It eschews arcane codes and conventions. Furthermore, it is totally textual and is meant to be readily comprehensible to humans. With XML, data are always described in terms of an XML document. An XML document consists of the original data delimited and annotated by XML tags. XML, particularly in comparison to HTML, has strict and rigid rules but is painfully consistent.

XML, like Web services, has been slow to live up to its lofty expectations. As with Web services, there are, fortunately, some rational explanations as to why this has been the case. The innate simplicity and flexibility of XML do mean that XML can be verbose and cumbersome. Though data defined using XML are said to be self-describing, deciphering what the data mean does require intelligence. People typically have no problems understanding XML-defined data—provided, of course, that they have, at a minimum, average common sense. However, computers and applications do not have any inherent smarts. Intelligence has to be supplied in the form of programming. XML cannot get around that.

For applications to understand XML data, they need "guidance"—that is, a level of mutual intelligence shared by the creator and the consumer. In essence you need common, application-specific vocabularies (e.g., a vocabulary for CRM applications, another vocabulary for funds transfer applications, and so forth). It has taken a while for these vocabularies, particularly those needed for the pertinent e-business scenarios (e.g., supply-chain management), to be formulated. The good news, however, is that by the beginning of 2003 there was adequate progress and consensus on this front so as to preclude it from being an impediment for much longer.

By the beginning of 2003, most popular commercial software offerings supported XML in some form or another. The types of software supporting XML include commercial applications (e.g., Siebel's Siebel 7 Customer Relationship Management suite, SAP's Supply Chain Management, and IBM's WebSphere Business Integrator); database management systems (e.g., Oracle 9i and IBM's DB2 Ver. 7); software development tools (e.g., IBM's

WebSphere Studio Application Developer, IBM's latest COBOL compiler, and Microsoft's Visual Studio .NET 2003); corporate portal solutions (e.g., BEA WebLogic Portal); application servers (e.g., IBM's WebSphere Application Server V4); message queuing middleware (e.g., WebSphere MQ); and even desktop applications.

Microsoft's Excel 2002, in Office XP, has an XML Spreadsheet file format that allows users to import, export, and analyze XML data. Figure 2.3(a, b) illustrates Excel's XML support by showing a small, sample Excel spreadsheet and the initial part of the XML representation of that spreadsheet. (The full XML document for this simple and small spreadsheet is still too long to be included in total—testifying to the previously mentioned verbosity of XML.) Microsoft also supports XML in its SQL Server 2000, Access 2002, and BizTalk Server 2000 offerings. Microsoft's Word 2003, which will be a part of the new Microsoft Office 2003, will enable documents to be saved in XML form, as well as the integration of XML-defined data within Word documents. The bottom line here is that the repertoire of widely used commercial applications supporting XML is now reaching critical mass, thus making XML more accessible and tangible than ever before. Plus, there is the growing impetus around Web services—the "killer" application for XML.

Figure 2.3(a)
A small and simple Excel spreadsheet.

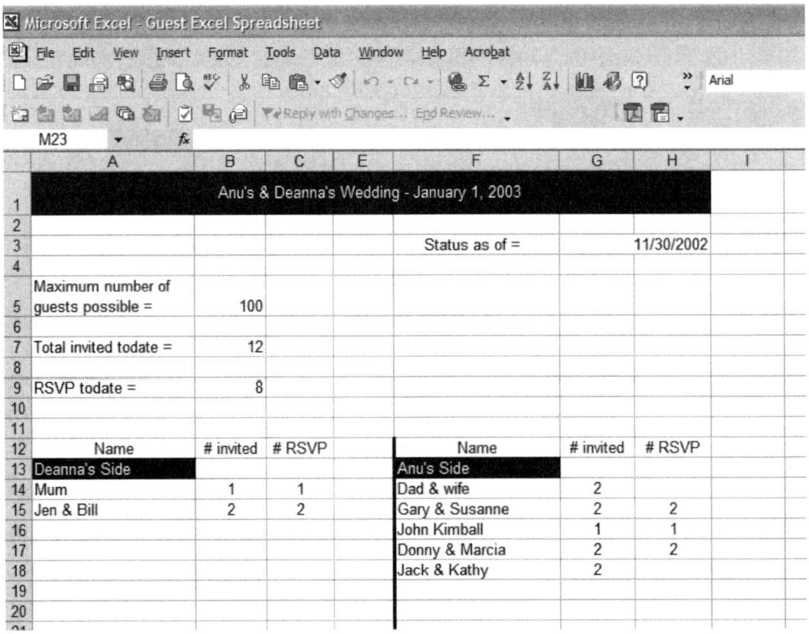

```
<?xml version="1.0"?>
<Workbook xmlns="urn:schemas-microsoft-com:office:spreadsheet"
 xmlns:o="urn:schemas-microsoft-com:office:office"
 xmlns:x="urn:schemas-microsoft-com:office:excel"
 xmlns:ss="urn:schemas-microsoft-com:office:spreadsheet"
 xmlns:html="http://www.w3.org/TR/REC-html40">
 <DocumentProperties xmlns="urn:schemas-microsoft-com:office:office">
  <Author>Anu Guruge</Author>
  <LastAuthor>Anu Guruge</LastAuthor>
  <Created>2003-05-18T01:13:19Z</Created>
  <LastSaved>2003-05-18T01:33:46Z</LastSaved>
  <Version>10.4219</Version>
 </DocumentProperties>
 <OfficeDocumentSettings xmlns="urn:schemas-microsoft-com:office:office">
  <DownloadComponents/>
  <LocationOfComponents HRef="file:///\\"/>
 </OfficeDocumentSettings>
 <ExcelWorkbook xmlns="urn:schemas-microsoft-com:office:excel">
  <WindowHeight>10230</WindowHeight>
  <WindowWidth>16155</WindowWidth>
  <WindowTopX>480</WindowTopX>
  <WindowTopY>30</WindowTopY>
  <ProtectStructure>False</ProtectStructure>
  <ProtectWindows>False</ProtectWindows>
 </ExcelWorkbook>
 <Styles>
  <Style ss:ID="Default" ss:Name="Normal">
   <Alignment ss:Vertical="Bottom"/>
   <Borders/>
   <Font/>
   <Interior/>
   <NumberFormat/>
   <Protection/>
  </Style>
  <Style ss:ID="s27">
   <Alignment ss:Horizontal="Center" ss:Vertical="Center"/>
   <Font ss:Color="#FFFFFF"/>
   <Interior ss:Color="#000000" ss:Pattern="Solid"/>
  </Style>
  <Style ss:ID="s31">
   <Alignment ss:Horizontal="Left" ss:Vertical="Bottom"/>
  </Style>
  <Style ss:ID="s34">
   <Font ss:Color="#FFFFFF"/>
   <Interior ss:Color="#000000" ss:Pattern="Solid"/>
  </Style>
  <Style ss:ID="s37">
   <Font ss:Color="#FFFFFF"/>
   <Interior/>
```

Figure 2.3(b)   *The initial part of the XML document created by Excel to describe the spreadsheet shown in Figure 2.3(a).*

```
 </Style>
 <Style ss:ID="s38">
  <Alignment ss:Horizontal="Center" ss:Vertical="Bottom"/>
 </Style>
 <Style ss:ID="s39">
  <Alignment ss:Vertical="Bottom" ss:WrapText="1"/>
 </Style>
 <Style ss:ID="s44">
  <Alignment ss:Vertical="Bottom"/>
  <Font/>
  <NumberFormat ss:Format="Short Date"/>
 </Style>
 <Style ss:ID="s46">
  <Borders>
   <Border ss:Position="Right" ss:LineStyle="Continuous" ss:Weight="3"/>
  </Borders>
 </Style>
</Styles>
<Worksheet ss:Name="Sheet1">
 <Table ss:ExpandedColumnCount="8" ss:ExpandedRowCount="34" x:FullColumns="1"
  x:FullRows="1">
  <Column ss:AutoFitWidth="0" ss:Width="106.5"/>
  <Column ss:AutoFitWidth="0" ss:Width="46.5"/>
  <Column ss:AutoFitWidth="0" ss:Width="43.5"/>
  <Column ss:Hidden="1" ss:AutoFitWidth="0"/>
  <Column ss:AutoFitWidth="0" ss:Width="39"/>
  <Column ss:AutoFitWidth="0" ss:Width="106.5"/>
  <Column ss:Index="8" ss:AutoFitWidth="0" ss:Width="49.5"/>
  <Row ss:AutoFitHeight="0" ss:Height="27">
   <Cell ss:MergeAcross="7" ss:StyleID="s27"><Data ss:Type="String">Anu's &amp;
Deanna's Wedding - January 1, 2003</Data></Cell>
  </Row>
  <Row ss:Index="3">
   <Cell ss:Index="6" ss:StyleID="s31"><Data ss:Type="String">    Status as of = </
Data></Cell>
   <Cell ss:MergeAcross="1" ss:StyleID="s44" ss:Formula="=DATE(2002,11,30)"><Data
     ss:Type="DateTime">2002-11-30T00:00:00.000</Data></Cell>
  </Row>
  <Row ss:Index="5" ss:Height="25.5">
   <Cell ss:StyleID="s39"><Data ss:Type="String">Maximum number of guests possible
=</Data></Cell>
   <Cell><Data ss:Type="Number">100</Data></Cell>
  </Row>
  <Row ss:Index="7">
   <Cell><Data ss:Type="String">Total invited todate = </Data></Cell>
   <Cell ss:Formula="=R[23]C+R[23]C[5]"><Data ss:Type="Number">25</Data></Cell>
  </Row>
  <Row ss:Index="9">
   <Cell><Data ss:Type="String">RSVP todate =</Data></Cell>
   <Cell ss:Formula="=R[21]C[1]+R[21]C[6]"><Data ss:Type="Number">10</Data></Cell>
```

Figure 2.3(b)   *(continued)*

```
 </Row>
<Row ss:Index="12">
 <Cell ss:StyleID="s38"><Data ss:Type="String">Name</Data></Cell>

 <Cell ss:StyleID="s38"><Data ss:Type="String"># invited</Data></Cell>
 <Cell ss:StyleID="s38"><Data ss:Type="String"># RSVP</Data></Cell>
 <Cell ss:Index="5" ss:StyleID="s46"/>
 <Cell ss:StyleID="s38"><Data ss:Type="String">Name</Data></Cell>
 <Cell ss:StyleID="s38"><Data ss:Type="String"># invited</Data></Cell>
 <Cell ss:StyleID="s38"><Data ss:Type="String"># RSVP</Data></Cell>
</Row>
<Row>
 <Cell ss:StyleID="s34"><Data ss:Type="String">Deanna's Side</Data></Cell>
 <Cell ss:StyleID="s37"/>
 <Cell ss:Index="5" ss:StyleID="s46"/>
 <Cell ss:StyleID="s34"><Data ss:Type="String">Anu's Side</Data></Cell>
</Row>
<Row>
 <Cell><Data ss:Type="String">Mum</Data></Cell>
 <Cell ss:StyleID="s38"><Data ss:Type="Number">1</Data></Cell>
 <Cell ss:StyleID="s38"><Data ss:Type="Number">1</Data></Cell>
 <Cell ss:Index="5" ss:StyleID="s46"/>
 <Cell ss:StyleID="s31"><Data ss:Type="String">Dad &amp; wife</Data></Cell>
 <Cell ss:StyleID="s38"><Data ss:Type="Number">2</Data></Cell>
 <Cell ss:StyleID="s38"/>
</Row>
<Row>
 <Cell><Data ss:Type="String">Jen &amp; Eric</Data></Cell>
 <Cell ss:StyleID="s38"><Data ss:Type="Number">2</Data></Cell>
 <Cell ss:StyleID="s38"><Data ss:Type="Number">2</Data></Cell>
 <Cell ss:Index="5" ss:StyleID="s46"/>
 <Cell><Data ss:Type="String">Gary &amp; Susanne</Data></Cell>
 <Cell ss:StyleID="s38"><Data ss:Type="Number">2</Data></Cell>
 <Cell ss:StyleID="s38"><Data ss:Type="Number">2</Data></Cell>
</Row>
<Row>
 <Cell><Data ss:Type="String">Lisa, Stephen &amp; kids</Data></Cell>
 <Cell ss:StyleID="s38"><Data ss:Type="Number">4</Data></Cell>
 <Cell ss:StyleID="s38"/>
 <Cell ss:Index="5" ss:StyleID="s46"/>
 <Cell><Data ss:Type="String">John Kimball</Data></Cell>
 <Cell ss:StyleID="s38"><Data ss:Type="Number">1</Data></Cell>
 <Cell ss:StyleID="s38"><Data ss:Type="Number">1</Data></Cell>
</Row>
<Row>
 <Cell><Data ss:Type="String">Melody &amp; friend</Data></Cell>
 <Cell ss:StyleID="s38"><Data ss:Type="Number">2</Data></Cell>
 <Cell ss:StyleID="s38"/>
 <Cell ss:Index="5" ss:StyleID="s46"/>
 <Cell><Data ss:Type="String">Donny &amp; Marcia</Data></Cell>
```

Figure 2.3(b)   *(continued)*

```
<Cell ss:StyleID="s38"><Data ss:Type="Number">2</Data></Cell>
<Cell ss:StyleID="s38"><Data ss:Type="Number">2</Data></Cell>
</Row>
<Row>
<Cell><Data ss:Type="String">Mike &amp; Penny</Data></Cell>
<Cell ss:StyleID="s38"><Data ss:Type="Number">2</Data></Cell>
<Cell ss:StyleID="s38"><Data ss:Type="Number">2</Data></Cell>
<Cell ss:Index="5" ss:StyleID="s46"/>
```

Figure 2.3(b)   *(continued)*

2.2   **What XML is all about**

XML is a mechanism for describing data. It can be used with any type of data, irrespective of the nature of the data. XML describes data using markup language conventions. The term *markup*, in this context, has its roots in preelectronic document publishing (i.e., prior to the mid-1980s). Previously, authors, editors, and proofreaders used a standardized set of marks (typically written in red) to make all necessary corrections to a manuscript, as well as to convey formatting instructions to the typesetter. Figure 2.4 shows some of the editing and proofreading marks that used to be widely used, and Figure 2.5 shows an actual facsimile of a book manuscript containing edit markups.

Markup was a way to add descriptive and instructional annotation around the content of a document without overtly interfering with the original content. This is the motivation and philosophy around today's electronic markup languages—that is, the ability to annotate a document (e.g., a Web page) for a particular purpose (e.g., formatting or collaborative review) without impacting the content of that document. Most of today's electronic markup languages have evolved from the Standard Generalized Markup Language (SGML) that was developed by IBM in the early 1980s.

HyperText Markup Language (HTML) is by far the most widely known and the most widely used of contemporary, electronic markup languages. HTML is a classic markup language in the true sense of the term. It comes with its particular set of markups (e.g., <B> for bold text, <H1> for level 1 heading, <P> for paragraph, and so forth). Though it could have been used to do more, HTML from the start gravitated toward being a formatting-specific markup language. It is an electronic version of the markup notation previously used to instruct typesetters on how to lay out and present the contents of a manuscript. HTML, as such, has remained true to the roots of markup languages and has propagated their legacy.

Instruction	Editing Marks (in the line only)	Proofreading Marks (in the line and in the margin)	
delete	Boulders campus events	Boulders campus events	
delete and close up	Boullder campus events	Boullder campus events	
replace	Boulder campus events (Denver)	Boulder campus events	Denver
insert	Boulder events (campus)	Boulder events	campus
insert and close up	Boulde campus events	Boulde campus events	
transpose	Boulder events campus	Boulder events campus	
insert space	Boulder campus events	Boulder campus events	#
insert hair space	"Boulder campus 'events'?"	"Boulder campus 'events'?"	
close up extra space	Boulder campus events or Boulder campus events	Boulder campus events or Boulder campus events	extra # extra #
insert line space	Boulder campus events Denver campus events	Boulder campus events Denver campus events	ℓ #
delete line space	Boulder campus events Denver campus events	Boulder campus events Denver campus events	ℓ #
equalize spacing	Boulder today	Boulder today	ℓq #
run on/no new paragraph	She runs. He jogs.	She runs. He jogs.	run in
new paragraph	She runs. He jogs.	She runs. He jogs.	¶

Figure 2.4 *A sample of some of the editing and proofreading marks (i.e., markup symbols) that were employed when a manuscript was being prepared for publishing in the pre-electronic era. Source: inkwelleditorial.com.*

XML, on the other hand, is not a true markup language in the conventional sense. First, it does not come with its own set of markups, as does HTML. Instead, XML is a meta-markup language. It allows one to create markup languages to address any particular need. There are no restrictions as to what can be marked up (i.e., annotated) with XML. In essence, it allows you to create application-specific markups. This is what the "extensible" part of its name alludes to. It affirms that with XML there are no preset bounds as to what you can deal with. It is flexible and pliable. Thus, you could use XML, à la HTML, to describe the layout and presentation of data. There is even an emerging XML-based W3C sanctioned standard known as Extensible Stylesheet Language (XSL), discussed later in this chapter, that does exactly this—that is, provide an XML vocabulary for specifying data (or document) formatting semantics.

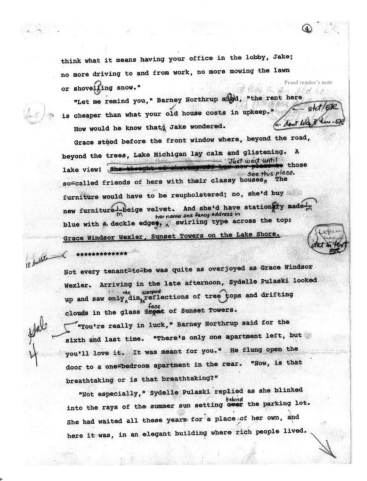

Figure 2.5   *Actual example of a marked-up manuscript, in this case a book by Ellen Raskin, as shown on the University of Wisconsin–Madison Web site.*

XML is thus a generalized, no-holds-barred meta-markup language for describing data. Though it can be used with any type of data, it is most effective in describing data that have some type of structure associated with them. Much of the data used by people and computers have some level of innate structure—particularly if they are thought of in terms of a document. A poem, as shown in Figure 2.2, has a structure made of stanzas and lines. A book, at a minimum, is made of chapters, chapter headings, and paragraphs. A spreadsheet, as illustrated in Figure 2.3, is made up of cells.

Consequently, one can think of any document as consisting of data that are structured in some manner. The information contained in a document is invariably made up of content (e.g., text, graphics) and context (e.g., headings, tables, captions). XML excels in describing this type of structured data. XML describes the context of the data relative to a document—where "document" in this context is just an arbitrary and generic file (or even just a placeholder) containing the data in question. The bottom line here is that XML deals with the context of data. HTML, by marked contrast, rather than dealing with the context of data, instead deals purely with how data should be formatted and presented for visual consumption. This fundamental difference between XML and HTML will be demonstrated further in Sections 2.3 and 2.4. For the time it suffices to note that XML was never intended to be just an enhanced version of HTML.

XML, though a meta-markup language as opposed to a specific markup language in its own right, is nonetheless derived from SGML. SGML became an ISO standard (i.e., ISO 8879) around 1985. SGML has become the de facto standard for defining the structure of different types of electronic documents. It has been widely used by the U.S. military, the U.S. government, and the aerospace industry over the last decade. HTML is also a derivative of SGML. SGML, by design, is very detailed, powerful, and complex. It was too unwieldy to be easily adopted for the Web and e-business.

XML is in essence SGML "lite." XML retains enough of the SGML functionality to make it useful and powerful but removes much of the optional and redundant features that can make SGML somewhat convoluted and unwieldy.

Before moving on, it is salutary to list some of the things that XML is not and that XML cannot do—just to dispel any possible lingering misconceptions. XML is not a programming language, a database scheme, or a networking protocol. XML documents can and are transported across networks using standard, widely used protocols, such as FTP, HTTP(S), SOAP, and SMTP. Since they are standard text documents, there are really no limitations or caveats as to how they can be transported, installed, or viewed. Databases (e.g., DB2 V7) will support XML data and even permit its data to be described in XML form, but the database will not be in the form of a large XML document.

The bottom line is that XML really does address what has been the Holy Grail of networking, right from the very early days—that of universal data interchange that transcends platforms, networking protocols, and programming languages. Now, with the Web providing global connectivity, XML does what previous networking schemes (e.g., IBM's SNA and OSI) always wanted to provide—a consistent, universal data interchange capability, without barriers.

2.3   The very basics of XML

XML always deals with data within the context of documents. Data (i.e., content) are included in an XML document as strings of text. The data are bracketed by XML text markup, which sets out to describe these data (i.e., give them context). The basic building blocks of an XML document are called "elements"—where an element is a specific unit of data along with the XML markup describing these data. An XML element is made up of a name and some content.

The XML markup, in much the same way as HTML, is in the form of tags. A tag thus appears within angled-brackets (e.g., `<tag>`, `<name>`, `<price>`, `<wife>`, and so forth). The big difference between XML and HTML when it comes to tags is that unlike HTML, XML does not come with its own set of tags. Instead, in XML you make up custom tags unique to the data that is to be described.

Though there are no predefined tags per se, XML does, however, have the concept of optional "processing instructions," which can be used, in the vein of comment statements, to convey information about an XML document. Key among these is the XML declaration that, though optional, is nonetheless often inserted at the top of an XML document. This XML declaration, which is in the form `<?xml version="1.0"?>` if one is dealing with the initial and most widely used version of XML, is used to specify the version of XML that is being used to describe the contents of that XML document. Process instructions appear within tags that have "?" at the start and end (i.e., `<? …?>`). These processing instructions are the closest thing that XML has in terms of predefined constructs.

An XML element is delimited by two tags: a start tag and an end tag—where an end tag corresponds to a start tag but has a forward slash (i.e., "/") before the name (e.g., `</tag>`, `</name>`, `</price>`, `</wife>`, and so forth). The element will typically consist of these two tags with text (i.e., data) in the middle (e.g., `<name>Nelson Mandela</name>`, `<price>$120.00</price>`, `<wife>yes</wife>`).

2.3.1   XML elements and element names

The start tag is what gives the element its name. In the example, `<e-mail>anu@wownh.com</e-mail>`, the element name is "e-mail" and the content of this element is "anu@wownh.com." XML, in its quest to be extensible, does not specify the tags and hence element names you can use within an XML document. XML gives users carte blanche when it comes to defining elements. There are, however, strict rules as to the composition of the XML names that can be given to an XML element.

First, XML names must begin with either an alphabetic letter (i.e., A to Z) or the underscore character (i.e., "_"). It is important to remember that XML names cannot start with numeric digits. XML names can be of any arbitrary length. Following the first character, the remainder of the name can be made up of the following:

- Alphabetic letters

- Numeric digits

- Underscore character

- Dot character (i.e., ".")

- Hyphen character (i.e., "-")

- Colon character (i.e., ":")—however, this is a special, reserved character associated with XML namespaces, which are described later

Note that spaces are not valid within XML names. The only other restriction is that names cannot start with the words "xml"—which is reserved for use by the XML specification per se. The string "xml" may, however, occur within a name.

In marked contrast to HTML, XML tags (and hence XML names) are case sensitive. Hence, `<name>`, `<NAME>`, and `<Name>` represent three very different tags. Thus, `<Name>Deanna Gurugé</name>` would not be a valid element in XML. `<Zipcode>` and `<ZipCode>` would also be treated as different names. Given this case sensitivity, there are two popular conventions, as opposed to rules, when it comes to XML names. The first is that where possible people stick to using just lowercase when it comes to XML names. If the name consists of multiple words and it helps to separate them, then hyphens are used between the words (e.g., `<product-item-number>`). Others prefer what is referred to as the "Camel Case" convention. They capitalize the first letter of each word (e.g., `<ProductItemNumber>`). But these, one should not forget, are conventions and not rules.

In some cases there can be more XML markups between the original start and end tags, for example:

```
<name>
<given-name>Nelson</given-name>
<surname>Mandela</surname>
</name>
```

However, nested elements cannot overlap each other. In other words, the tags making up a nested element cannot be overlapped. Thus, in the previous example, the given-name element must be terminated prior to the start of the surname element—that is, the `</given-name>` tag must appear before the `<surname>` tag. In the same way, the surname element must be completed before the name element is terminated.

It is possible to have attributes associated with XML elements, as was shown in Figure 2.2, where the N = *"value"* in each `<LINE N = "n">` tag is an attribute. Attributes provide a mechanism whereby small amounts of data can be quickly and easily associated with an element. Thus, in the case of the XML used to describe the Wordsworth poem in Figure 2.2, the attribute N = *"value"* is used to quickly associate a line number with each line in the poem. If the N = *"value"* attribute was not used in this instance, then one would have to use a separate line number element to realize the same effect, which, as can be seen here, would be slightly more cumbersome:

```
<STANZA>
    <LINE-NUMBER>1</LINE-NUMBER>
    <LINE>I head a thousand blended notes,</LINE>
    <LINE-NUMBER>2</LINE-NUMBER>
    <LINE>while in grove I sate reclined,</LINE>
```

The ability to have attributes results in one of the very few syntactical oddities in XML—these being the so-called empty elements made up using "empty tags." An empty element does not contain any content. You could create one using an opening and closing tag with no content between them. Usually this would be somewhat redundant if not for the fact that you can still include information within this element using attributes. The concept of empty tags makes this useful XML "construct" that much simpler to use. With an empty tag you do not need a corresponding closing tag. Instead, just one tag serves as both the start and end tag. An empty tag is enclosed in angle brackets (`<>`) per the norm but contains a forward slash right in front of the closing angle bracket (`/>`), for example:

```
<wife name="Deanna Guruge" birthday="June 27" phone="555-
2293"/>
```

With the exception of empty tags, all other XML tags have to appear in matching start and end pairs. This is another big difference between XML and HTML, given that HTML does permit certain tags to be used without corresponding end tags, with `<br>`, `<p>`, `<hr>`, `<col>`, and `<img>` HTML tags being classic examples.

2.3.2 Special characters in XML and XML "entities"

By carefully restricting the special characters that may appear within names, XML deftly gets around the issue of restricted characters (e.g., the angle brackets) that may appear within XML names. However, XML cannot, and does not want to, control the characters that may appear within the content (or data portion) of an XML element. Given XML's tag-oriented syntax, the appearance of restricted characters, such as the angled brackets, within the content of an element would wreak havoc with the XML-related structure of that document. Consequently, there are five special symbols in XML that have to be entered differently. In essence, there are "escape sequences" assigned to these five special symbols so that their presence does not disrupt the syntax of XML. XML handles this escape sequence to special symbol mapping via a generalized reference insertion mechanism built into XML known as "entities."

In XML, an entity is a symbol that represents—or identifies—a predefined resource, where this resource may be a file or a text character. Entities are included within a document via entity references. An entity reference is defined using an ampersand (&) at the beginning and a semicolon (;) at the end (e.g., &copyright; &UK; &NH; or &wstp;). An XML parser will automatically replace the entity reference via the value assigned to that entity. Values are assigned to entity references via an entity declaration, which has the form:

```
<!ENTITY entityname entitydefinition>
```

Thus, some of the entities mentioned previously could be defined as:

```
<!ENTITY UK "United Kingdom">
<!ENTITY NH "New Hampshire">
<!ENTITY WSTP "IBM WebSphere Transcoding Publisher">
<!ENTITY copyright "&#169;">
```

Unlike the others, the copyright entity is nonintuitive in that it in turn illustrates another XML feature. This feature is the ability to directly enter character references in the form of Unicode character references—in this example the "169" represents the character code for the copyright symbol ©. If you are using Windows, use the "Character Map" utility, found under "Programs" and then "Accessories" off the Windows "Start" button, to find these character codes. Character code references are prefaced by &#. Hence the "&#169." The character code for an "e with an accent acute" (i.e., "é") is 233. So you could define an XML entity reference for it that reads:

```
<!ENTITY eacute "&#233;">
```

These entity references could be used in an XML document as follows:

```
<article-body>

What you always wanted to know about XML

&copyright; Anura Gurug&eacute;
</article-body>
```

Once the workings of entity references are understood, the way that XML handles the five special characters becomes obvious. XML predefines five entities to represent these special characters, as follows:

- Left angle bracket or less than symbol (<) as `&lt;`

- Right angle bracket or greater than symbol (>) as `&gt;`

- Ampersand symbol (&) as `&amp;`

- Double quote symbol (") as `&quot;`

- Apostrophe symbol (') as `&apos;`

Thus, in XML, the company name Johnson & Johnson will have to appear as:

```
<CompanyName>Johnson &amp; Johnson</CompanyName>
```

There are two other related concepts that should be dealt with within this concept of names and entities, and they have to do with language specification and how to denote space characters that are "meaningful." There is a special attribute, `xml:lang`, that is provided within XML that enables one to specify the language in which the content that follows it is written. In essence, you can have an `xml:lang` attribute per element that specifies the language in which the content of that element is written. Thus, you could distinguish between U.K. English and U.S. English as follows:

```
<articlebody xml:lang="en-GB">The foreground color is
green.</articlebody>
<articlebody xml:lang="en-US">The foreground color is
green.</articlebody>
```

The codes that can be used to specify the "root" language, in this case English (i.e., "en") but it could equally well have been French (i.e., "fr") or Hindi (i.e., "hi"), are defined by ISO 639. Visit http://lcweb.loc.gov/standards/iso639-2/englangn.html for more information. In the case of languages with "dialects," a subcode, in our example "GB" and "US," can be used to get very specific. In the case of French, Canadian French can be specified as `xml:lang="fr-CA"`. The subcodes for this purpose are defined by ISO 3166. Visit http://www-old.ics.uci.edu/pub/ietf/http/related/iso3166.txt for more details.

The other special attribute that can be used within an element is `xml:space`. It can have one of two values: preserve or default (with default, obviously, being the default if this attribute is not included within an element). Stating `xml:space="preserve"` instructs XML applications that the spaces appearing within the content of this element are meaningful and should be preserved.

2.3.3 The need for mutual understanding

XML thus takes a flat stream of text, which represents data of some sort, and transforms it into a set of self-describing objects. This is what XML is all about. It provides a flexible, open-ended mechanism for describing any type of data. The goal of XML is to ensure that a recipient of an XML document is able to easily, unambiguously, and consistently determine the nature and structure of the data contained within that document. This then enables the recipient to correctly manipulate and process the data without mistaking what the data are supposed to represent (albeit subject to a caveat discussed in a second). Thus, if XML were used to describe Web pages, search engines would be able to better identify the context and meaning of keywords, since they would now contain XML-based descriptive tags. Since XML documents are always in text form, they can invariably be read and deciphered by people, but people have innate intelligence. Computer applications do not, and that is a significant issue when it comes to XML.

In order for an application to be able to successfully process an XML document, it needs to know what the various elements represent. In other words, the recipient application needs to know what the tags mean. Since the meaning of a tag can differ significantly between different organizations, countries, and industry sectors, an application really needs to know what each tag means within a specific "application domain." This is the problem when it comes to XML. Just because you have a well-formed XML document does not guarantee that it can and will be correctly interpreted by any and all applications.

An analogy widely used in the mid-1980s to explain the need for networking protocols and architectures can now be conveniently reused to highlight XML's reliance on shared understanding at both ends of a transaction. This analogy relates to making a direct-dial phone call between

London and Moscow. Though you will, with luck, get a connection, there is no guarantee that you will be able to hold a meaningful conversation unless both of you happen to know a common language, whether it be Russian, Esperanto, English, or French. The same is true with XML.

To successfully process XML, you need a mutual understanding at both ends of the transaction. XML provides mechanisms to facilitate this mutual understanding. The two main schemes for this are called Document Type Definitions (DTDs) and XML schema. In some special cases it is possible to have DTD-less XML documents, provided the elements are structured in some type of self-explanatory manner. DTDs and XML schema are described in Section 2.5.

2.3.4   XML namespaces

Extensibility is the beauty and the bane of XML. Enabling users to define tags and, as such, element names at will, though desirable, can lead to ambiguity and misunderstandings—especially if the same names appear to mean different things in different XML documents. DTDs and XML schema are not the answer here, since they tend to be document specific. One option would be to implement a global naming registry, as IBM tried to do to ensure unique network identifiers (i.e., NETIDs) for SNA and APPN networks in the mid-1980s, or the Domain Name System (DNS) now used for Web addresses (i.e., URLs). This would be unwieldy and impractical and compromise the underlying principles and flexibility of XML.

Let us assume that you create an XML document listing your favorite PC games and post this on a Web site as a public domain document. One of your friends could take this list and decide to rate the various games. To do this your friend might add a new "rating" element. Another one of your friends might decide to rate the games by their suitability for various age groups using the General (G), Parental Guidance (PG), PG-13, and so forth rating system used in North America for movies, TV shows, and even some PC and video games. Given that this is also a rating system, they too may decide to add this new classification using a "rating" element. However, these two "rating" elements, though they apply to the same base document, mean very different things.

One way to overcome such a conflict problem is to qualify (or prefix) the various element names (e.g., "fun rating" and "age rating"). This works but can be limiting, since qualifying the element names is contingent on one anticipating potential conflicts. XML's strategic solution for preventing this type of conflict is the use of namespaces. Namespaces are an elegant and nonintrusive mechanism to enable unique identification of XML elements—without in any way restricting the flexibility or extensibility of XML. Namespaces are implemented by attaching a prefix, identified by a colon (":"), with each element and possibly even with each attribute. Thus, with namespaces, the rating elements would be defined as fun:rating and age:rating, where the prefixes now refer to namespaces. These prefixes are mapped to what is called a Unified Resource Identifier (URI). These URI mappings typically appear near the start of the XML document and have the following form:

```
<pc-games xmlns:fun=http://www.wownh.com/funrating
          xmlns:age= http://www.wownh.com/agerating
```

where xmlns identifies this as an XML namespace (ns) declaration. Note that this URI scheme is similar to how you define an external DTD.

The exact use of URIs in XML is somewhat complex and confusing, especially since there is no requirement that a URI is valid! In other words, a URI does not have to point to anything. In the context of namespaces, URIs are only used as identifiers. Since URIs do not need to be valid, they are essentially treated as case-sensitive text strings. After stating these caveats, it is fair to say that for practical purposes most XML "developers" use valid URLs as their URIs. These URLs will then point to a file that contains the exact definition of the element being qualified. The Internet Engineering Task Force (IETF) is working on another alternative to URIs known as Uniform Resource Names (URNs). Whereas URLs usually start with a protocol designation such as "http" or "ftp," URNs start with a "urn:" prefix. URNs are supposed to define a unique, location-independent name for a resource that then typically maps to one or more URLs. The XML namespace recommendation can be found at http://www.w3.org/TR/REC-xml-names/.

2.4   Contrasting XML against HTML

The fundamental distinction between HTML and XML is that HTML defines data presentation (or data rendering), whereas XML defines the meaning of the data. This is best illustrated with an example. Let us start with some sample HTML codes that could be found within a document containing contact information for an individual:

```
<p><b>Mr. Anura Guruge</b>
<br>
Principal
```

```
<br>
i-net guru
<br>
4 Varney Point Road, Left
<br>
Gilford, NH 03249
<br>
USA
<br>
anu@wownh.com</p>
```

In this HTML example the `<p>` tag represents the start of a new paragraph, the `<b>` tag calls for bold text, and the `<br>` tag specifies a line break. Note that, as mentioned earlier, HTML does not require or define a `</br>` tag. This type of asymmetrical tag usage would not be permissible in XML—with the exception of empty tags, which, in reality, include a closing "/" at the end of the tag. In all other instances XML expects all open tags to be explicitly closed. This HTML code, when rendered by a Web browser, would show "`Mr. Anura Guruge`" in bold with the rest of the information underneath it—in separate lines per the breaks dictated by the `<br>` tags, as illustrated in Figure 2.6.

The problem with this HTML example is that it only describes the layout for the data contained in the document. There is no description as to what the data mean. A person could interpret what the data mean, but it would be difficult for an application to determine what all these fields meant unless it was explicitly programmed to look for contact information in this type of format. A good example of the potential for ambiguity with

Figure 2.6   *Example HTML code rendered by a Web browser.*

HTML documents can be seen by doing a search for a keyword such as "bill" using any of the popular Web search engines, such as Google.com. Such a search will return thousands of entries covering people's names (e.g., Bill Gates), laws (e.g., Bill of Rights), theater playlists, and monetary notes.

With XML, the contact information will be organized between tags that set out to describe the data. Thus, one possible XML representation for some of these data might look like:

```
<contact_info>
 <name>
  <salutation>Mr.</salutation>
  <first-name>Anura</first-name>
  <last-name>Guruge</last-name>
 </name>
 <title>Principal</title>
 <company>i-net guru</company>
 <address>
  <street>4 Varney Point Road, Left</street>
  <city>Gilford</city>
  <state>NH</state>
  <zip>03249</zip>
 </address>
 <e-mail>anu@wownh.com</e-mail>
</contact_info>
```

The first thing to note here is that the XML representation shown here is totally arbitrary and just reflects my preferences and foibles. You could describe these data in other ways using tags with different names—true to the extensible nature of XML. In marked contrast to HTML, XML does not come with its own set of fixed tags and elements that has to be used by everybody to cover all applications. That would obviously be much too restrictive and impractical.

XML lets you define the elements you want as you go along to best fit what you are trying to achieve. Thus, with XML you can design your own customized markup languages for limitless different types of documents. You can have elements specific to organizations and industries. Consequently, there are already numerous discipline- and industry-specific variants of XML, such as Chemical Markup Language (CML) for representing molecular information; Mathematical Modeling Language (MathML) for describing mathematical notation; and Human Markup Language (HumanML) to enable consistent description of human emotions, intentions, gestures, and so forth. The key thing to remember is that you will need a DTD or XML schema that describes what is expected and acceptable within a specific XML document—especially if you want that XML document to be processed by applications written by others. This is unfortunately the downside of not having a specific, predetermined set of markup tags à la HTML.

A quick example with MathML will help reinforce the need for a mechanism (such as a DTD), outside and independent of the original XML document per se, to describe what the tags are supposed to represent within that document and how they are intended to be structured. Let us look at a possible MathML depiction of the structure of a relatively simple mathematical expression: $(a + b)^2$. Given that it is the actual structure of the expression that is being articulated, it will be described as a "base" $(a + b)$ with a superscript of "2." This can be realized with the following lines of MathML:

```
<msup>
 <mfenced>
  <mrow>
   <mi>a</mi>
   <mo>+</mo>
   <mi>b</mi>
  </mrow>
 </mfenced>
 <mn>2</mn>
</msup>
```

In this MathML example, the <msup> element indicates that a base and superscript notation is being expressed and the <mfenced> element denotes the use of parentheses (or brackets), whereas the <mrow> element signifies a horizontal row of characters. The <mi> and <mo> elements refer to identifiers and operands, respectively, whereas the <mn> element indicates a specific number—in this instance 2. Although the overall flow of MathML may be intuitive enough for some to determine what is being expressed, it should be clear by now that a total, unambiguous interpretation of MathML, like other dialects of XML, is only possible if the recipient is aware of what the elements are supposed to represent.

The application "specificity" of XML can be further highlighted by noting that the previous MathML representation is not the only way in which the $(a + b)^2$ expression could have been described using MathML. The MathML lines shown focused on the structure of the mathematical expression—that is, its presentation (or what it looks like). MathML also enables one to describe mathematical expressions in terms of their content rather than their structure. The content representation would look like this, where `<apply>` refers to an operation—which is typically represented by empty elements such as `<power/>` and `<plus/>`.

```
<apply>
   <power/>
   <apply>
    <plus/>
    <ci>a</ci>
    <ci>b</ci>
   </apply>
   <cn>2</cn>
   </apply>
```

Although this representation may be somewhat more easier to follow than the previous scheme, it is still fair to note that unequivocal interpretation would only be possible with an explanation of what the elements are supposed to represent (e.g., that `<ci>` must in this instance represent identifiers).

In marked contrast, all it would take with HTML to convey $(a + b)^2$ would be:

```
(a + b)<sup>2</sup>
<br>
```

where the `<br>`, in this instance at least, is optional. Note that the HTML representation is primarily visual—that is, the base `(a + b)` appearing as just a string of text with no indication as to what it represents mathematically. This visual representation would make programmatic interpretation somewhat more difficult—and in effect would require the recipient application to include the type of logic found within a compiler (or interpreter) to parse and then evaluate the mathematical expression. In the end, it still boils down to the fact that HTML does not attempt to convey meaning, whereas XML's very raison d'être is to impart context and meaning to data.

The lack of predefined markup in XML means that it is possible to invariably come up with different hierarchies and schemes to describe the same set of data. The availability of attributes adds another level of flexibility and extensibility. Consequently, the contact information example shown earlier could be represented in quite a few different XML "hierarchies"— with all of them within reason being equally germane and valid. Thus, another possible XML schema to describe contact information could be:

```
<contact_info>
   <entry name="Anura Gurugé">
     <address>
```

```
      <street>4 Varney Point Road, Left</street>
        <city>Gilford</city>
          <state>NH</state>
            <zip>03249</zip>
        </address>
      </entry>
  </contact_info>
```

At this juncture, note that an XML attribute is made up of a name-value pair that is attached to an element's start tag. The name and value making up a particular name-value pair will be separated from each other by an equals sign and optional whitespace. The value of a name-value pair is enclosed in either single or double quotation marks. It is possible to have multiple attributes per element, with each attribute consisting of a valid name-value pair separated by whitespace as in the previously shown example:

```
<wife name="Deanna Gurugé" birthday="June 27"
phone="555-2293"/>
```

When contrasting and comparing HTML with XML, another key factor that becomes immediately obvious is that XML does not provide any predefined formatting guidelines as to how data should be presented. The data presentation issue per se is not an issue if the recipient of an XML document is an application. In such an application-to-application programmatic scenario, all that would be required is that the data in the XML document, which would be in the form of a string of text, are structured correctly and are valid. However, as can be seen with even the simple XML examples used so far in this chapter, it certainly helps people if they can view an XML document with some amount of formatting to highlight the structure of the elements.

It should also be apparent by now that a standard browser would be able to interpret the XML structure and display the data portion of an XML document. This is indeed the case. Microsoft Internet Explorer 5 (and greater) and Netscape 4.x (and greater) can both display XML documents—albeit bereft of any significant esthetic formatting. The XML in Figure 2.3(b), which shows an Excel spreadsheet as an XML document, is, as can be seen, rendered using Internet Explorer (where the "–" symbols that appear at the very start of certain lines enable one to expand or contract the display of that "element" by clicking on it). Stylized and customized presentation of XML documents is not possible with this basic browser-based display mode. In order to display XML documents in visually pleasing formatted mode, one has to use either Cascading Stylesheets (CSS) or eXtensible Stylesheet Language (XSL)—as discussed in Section 2.6. XHTML is not an option in this context, given that it is an XML-compliant version of HTML (i.e., HTML that adheres to XML's rules), as opposed to a formatting mechanism for XML.

2.5   DTDs and XML schema

XML borrows the concept of Document Type Definitions (DTDs) from SGML. A DTD is a formal description of a particular class of XML documents. It defines what the XML document is supposed to mean. It is what specifies the particular XML markup that is being used within that class of XML documents. The XML markup specific to a given class of XML documents that is being defined with a DTD is specified using an XML declaration syntax. A DTD specifies what structures are permissible within an XML document. A DTD thus spells out what names are to be used for the different types of element, where they may occur, the attributes that can be assigned to elements, and how they all fit together.

Every element that can appear within an XML document needs to be declared within that document's DTD with an element declaration statement. The basic structure of an element declaration statement looks like:

```
<!ELEMENT element_name (content_description) ['?' | '*' |
'+']>
```

where the "?," "*," and "+" are "wild-card" references, with "?" indicating that the preceding name (or associated content description) can occur zero or one time, "*" denoting zero or more times, and "+" denoting one or more times.

Thus, a simple DTD for an XML document containing contact information, as in the example used in the previous sections, may look like:

```
<!ELEMENT person (name, company*)>
<!ELEMENT name (salutation?, first_name, middle_name*,
last_name)>
<!ELEMENT salutation (#PCDATA)>
<!ELEMENT first_name (#PCDATA)>
<!ELEMENT middle_name (#PCDATA)>
<!ELEMENT last_name (#PCDATA)>
<!ELEMENT company (#PCDATA)>
```

The term "#PCDATA" that is often seen in DTDs refers to "Parsed Character Data" (i.e., essentially a string of text). If an element is defined as being of type #PCDATA, then it cannot have subelements (or child elements). So, for example, if you define an element "phone_number" as being `<!ELEMENT phone_number (#PCDATA)>`, you will, within the corresponding

XML document, have to just define the phone number as a string of text. You could not, in this instance, subdivide it further into separate elements corresponding to "country_code," "area_code," "extension," and so forth. If XML attributes are permitted, they will be defined, relative to the appropriate element name, via an `<!ATTLIST>` declaration.

A DTD would typically be stored as a file (with a ".dtd" suffix), separate from the XML documents it describes. It could also be included within the XML document it describes. The location of the DTD that describes a given XML document is specified within that document via a Document Type Declaration. A typical Document Type Declaration would look like:

```
<!DOCTYPE contact_info SYSTEM "http://www.wownh.com/
dtds/contactinfo.dtd">
```

The `<!DOCTYPE>` declaration usually follows the `<?xml version= …?>` statement that kicks off an XML document. If the DTD is to be included within the XML document, then it is embedded as a part of the Document Type Declaration statement, as follows:

```
<?xml version="1.0" encoding="UTF-8"?>
<!DOCTYPE person [
  <!ELEMENT person (name, company*)>
  <!ELEMENT name (salutation?, first_name, middle_name*,
last_name)>
  ….
]>
<person>
 <name>
  <salutation>Mr.</salutation>
  <first_name>Anura</first_name>
…..
…..
</person>
```

The DTD for the XML document describing a Wordsworth poem, as shown in Figure 2.2, provided by Rutgers State University of New Jersey, would look like:

```
<!ELEMENT POEM      (TITLE, AUTHOR, STANZA*)>
<!ELEMENT TITLE     (#PCDATA)>
<!ELEMENT AUTHOR    (FIRSTNAME, LASTNAME)>
<!ELEMENT FIRSTNAME (#PCDATA)>
<!ELEMENT LASTNAME  (#PCDATA)>
<!ELEMENT STANZA    (LINE*)>
<!ELEMENT LINE      (#PCDATA)>
<!ATTLIST LINE N CDATA #REQUIRED>
```

As repeatedly mentioned in this chapter, the success of XML is totally contingent on a common understanding of what an XML document represents at both ends of a "transaction." Without that mutual understanding, XML is but an unnecessary overhead. DTDs are one of the ways to achieve this common understanding. XML schema is the other. Given the imperativeness of the mutual understanding if XML is to be applicable, there is now a relatively rich body of public DTDs for various industry sectors and applications (e.g., loan processing within the financial sector, property description within the context of real estate, engineering change [EC] management as it applies to supply chain management, and so forth). A collection of public DTDs for various industry sectors can be found at http://www.xml.org/xmlorg_registry. This site is maintained by the Organization for the Advancement of Structured Information Standards (OASIS), which is now endorsed and supported by the United Nations (UN). Public DTDs can also be found at http://www.schema.net and Microsoft's BizTalk site at http://www.biztalk.org. Figure 2.7 shows a proposed DTD available at xml.org submitted by the HR-XML Consortium,

```
<!-- Copyright 2000 The HR-XML Consortium (TM) -->
<!-- version 1.0  October 17 2000 -->
<!-- 11/05/2000
Changed all elements to UpperCamelCase
 -->
<!ELEMENT PersonName  (FormattedName* , GivenName* , PreferredGivenName? , MiddleName? , FamilyName* , Affix* )>

<!ELEMENT FormattedName  (#PCDATA )>
<!ATTLIST FormattedName  type  (presentation | legal | sortOrder )  'presentation' >
<!ELEMENT GivenName  (#PCDATA )>

<!ELEMENT PreferredGivenName  (#PCDATA )>

<!ELEMENT MiddleName  (#PCDATA )>

<!ELEMENT FamilyName  (#PCDATA )>
<!ATTLIST FamilyName primary  (true | false | undefined )  'undefined' >
<!ELEMENT Affix  (#PCDATA )>
<!ATTLIST Affix  type  (academicGrade |
                        aristocraticPrefix |
                        aristocraticTitle |
                        familyNamePrefix |
                        familyNameSuffix |
                        formOfAddress |
                        generation )  #REQUIRED >
```

Figure 2.7   *A proposed DTD from the HR-XML Consortium for describing a person's name in XML form for HR applications, where the term "#PCDATA" refers to "parsed character data," which is a fancy way of saying that this is a string of text. This and other DTDs and schema can be found at xml.org.*

Inc., for describing a person's name in the context of XML-based HR applications.

Since the roots of DTDs go back to SGML, their forte is that of describing conventional text documents. Consequently, DTDs just specify the structure of an XML document—in terms of the elements that make up that document. DTDs, however, do not have a mechanism for expressing the content of elements in terms of specific data types. A DTD cannot be employed to specify numeric ranges for an element, to define limitations of what can occur, or to check on the text content. Furthermore, the syntax of DTDs is relatively complex and cumbersome, as you can see if you look at some of the public DTDs available at their Web sites. In addition, and ironically, DTDs are written in their own special syntax rather than in XML. The bottom line here is that DTDs are now being usurped by XML schema per a W3C recommendation, which can be found at: http://www.w3.org/TR/xmlschema-0/.

XML schema are written in standard XML. The XML dialect used to create a schema is referred to as the XML Schema Definition (XSD) Language. An XML schema can provide a far more comprehensive and rigorous description of the contents of an XML document in a modular, typed, and object-oriented manner. Since they permit data types to be rigorously specified, developing a good XML schema will require more thought and work than was required to create a DTD—especially so if the XML document being described contains complex data types.

As with DTDs, industry- and application-specific XML schema are already available and many new ones are in the process of being defined. There are vendor-independent initiatives sponsored by the likes of OASIS, such as ebXML (for "electronic business XML" for e-business) and tpaML (for Trading Partner Agreement Markup Language). Industry-specific XML "dialects" are also being promoted by the likes of RosettaNet.org—a self-funding, nonprofit consortium of major IT, electronic components, and semiconductor manufacturing companies.

2.6   XSL and XSLT: Making XML presentable

Once you have an XML document, people invariably want to be able to display it on various devices—with Web browsers and intelligent cell phones being in the lead in this respect. However, it does not end here. There is a lot of work currently taking place on VoiceXML for voice-based applications such as the voice response systems used by call centers. XML documents are typically displayed on a browser or cell phone by associating a stylesheet with the XML document. In some cases this can be achieved by using standard Cascading Stylesheets (CSS).

Stylesheets, or CSS, per se are not new concepts. They were introduced to enhance HTML in the early 1990s, with CSS Level 1 becoming a W3C recommendation in December 1996 (well before the advent of XML). CSS is a simple but powerful mechanism for adding style (i.e., different fonts, colors, spacing, borders, and backgrounds) to Web documents. Though it took some time before CSS was adequately supported by browsers, this is no longer an issue and full CSS support is available in contemporary versions of the popular browsers. Given that many Web page developers are now familiar with CSS, it provides a quick and easy way to add visual embellishments to an XML document.

XSL, however, is the more strategic approach for presenting XML documents, given that CSS uses a non-XML syntax. (There is a parallel here with DTDs and XML schema, where DTD's lack of XML compliance is one of the key reasons why XML schema is deemed to be more strategic than DTDs.) XSL defines the format for an XML document. XSL is divided into two parts: XSL Formatting Objects (XSL-FO) and XSL Transformations (XSLT). XSL-FO is deemed to be an XML application that can be used to precisely describe the layout of a page in terms of blocks of text, graphics, and horizontal lines. Most people, however, do not create XSL-FOs. Instead, they write an XSLT Stylesheet, which transforms the XML in your document into the corresponding XSL-FOs.

XSLT is also called an XML application. It specifies how one XML document can be transformed into another. XSLT works through the use of XSLT stylesheets, which are sometimes referred to as XSLT documents. XSLT stylesheets contain templates and are XML documents in their own right. XSLT works by comparing the elements in an input XML document being converted with the templates appearing in the stylesheet. When it finds a match, it creates a corresponding output per what is specified in the template. You can have multiple stylesheets for the same XML document: one for displaying the document in HTML form within a browser and another for displaying it in some type of WML form on an intelligent phone.

Internet Explorer 5.5 (and greater) has a built-in XSLT processor that enables it to accept XML documents and corresponding stylesheets and process the necessary XSLT transformations on the fly. If the browser does not support XSLT, a separate XSLT processor will have to be used—for example, the "open-source" Apache Software Foundation's Xalan (in Java or C++) from http://www.apache.org.

XHTML per se, despite any connotations evoked by its name, is not a formatting-related adjunct to XML. Instead, it is an XML-based variant of HTML 4.0—and is an official W3C recommendation. It reformulates HTML 4.0 to ensure that it lives up to XML's syntax requirements. There are three DTDs available that describe HTML 4.0 in terms of XML. The big thing with XHTML is that it imposes strict discipline on HTML. First, unmatched tags are not allowed, so all start tags have to have matching end tags. All attribute values now have to appear within quotes. Whereas HTML is not case sensitive, XHTML, consistent with XML being case sensitive, enforces case sensitivity in the case of tags—deeming <p> to be valid and <P> to be invalid. Most of today's browsers, irrespective of their vintage, can adequately render most XHTML documents.

2.7   XML editors and XML APIs

Given the strategic importance associated with XML since its inception, there is no shortage of tools to help developers create and validate XML documents. These tools fall into three categories:

1.   XML authoring tools for creating XML documents from scratch

2.   Automated XML converters that will take an existing document and convert it into a valid XML document—for example, Excel 2002 (as discussed earlier), which will now save a standard Excel spreadsheet in the form of an XML document, as depicted in Figure 2.3(a, b)

3.   XML validators

Given that an XML document, by definition, is a flat text file, one could, as with HTML, create and edit XML documents using a simple text editor such as Windows Notepad, which is included as a standard, no-cost accessory with all flavors of today's Windows operating systems. However, as with HTML, many will find using a pure text editor to create XML to be tedious and frustrating. They would prefer an XML-cognizant editor, which would simplify some of the mundane but crucial tasks (e.g., keeping track of open tags). The good news is that there are plenty of such XML-specific editing tools.

A free graphical XML editor, which would allow you to display and manipulate XML documents per their XML structure, was available from Microsoft. It was called XML Notepad. Though no longer available directly from Microsoft, this still-popular editor can be downloaded for a fee from:

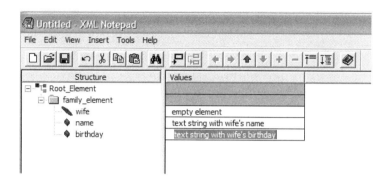

Figure 2.8   *Microsoft's XML Notepad showing its two-pane structure, where the left-hand pane maps out the XML structure, whereas the right-hand pane shows the values associated with the various XML elements.*

http://www.devhood.com/. XML Notepad is a standard Windows application, which allows you to create and edit XML documents quickly and easily. It displays the structure of an XML document as an easy-to-follow tree structure. The interface, as shown in Figure 2.8, presents two panes: one for the XML structure and the other for the values. You can add elements, attributes, comments, and text to an XML document by creating the tree structure in the left pane and then entering the required values in the corresponding text boxes shown in the right pane.

Other, but not free, XML editors are available from the likes of XML Spy at http://www.xmlspy.com and Corel/SoftQuad at http://www.xmetal.com. These editors come in two forms. XML Spy, like Microsoft's XML Notepad, deals directly with XML code and expects you to know XML. On the other hand, XMetaL hides the XML from you. You concentrate on the structure of the document using Word processor–like techniques. The editor, behind the scenes, generates the XML on your behalf. These types of automatic XML "generators" are similar to MS FrontPage or MacroMedia DreamWeaver in the context of HTML. These user-friendly HTML tools allow you to compose Web pages using visual, drag-and-drop, graphical techniques. The HTML is generated automatically by the editor without the user having to know anything about it.

If you plan to use XML extensively, you might want to get one of each of the two different editor types. Use the automatic generation editor to get you started. Then use the XML-centric editor to refine, optimize, and customize the automatically generated XML. Then there are the XML converters, which will take a document, typically a document in a word processing format, and then represent it as an XML document. XML validators, on the other hand, take an existing XML document and parse it to make sure that it is valid in that it meets all of the XML requirements.

At present there are two popular XML APIs: Document Object Model (DOM) and Simple API for XML (SAX). These APIs allow applications to read XML documents independent of the XML syntax. These APIs are geared toward different applications. DOM is geared for display type applications involving XML-oriented browsers and editors. SAX, on the other hand, is targeted for interprogram interactions.

2.8   **WSDL in a nutshell**

Web Services Description Language (WSDL), one of the three seminal standards behind Web services, is an XML dialect that relies heavily on XML namespaces and XML schema. It is used to define the high-level functionality of a Web service in terms of its external interface and to describe how that Web service can be accessed over the Web. It is, in effect, an abstract model per an XML-based format for describing Web services.

Potential users of a Web service would typically locate the Web service using its textual description as published in a UDDI repository. Initially this Web service description per se will usually not be in WSDL form. However, when a potential user wants more details as to how a Web service actually functions, particularly in terms of what it accepts as input and what it will return as its output, the user will request it in WSDL form. The link to the WSDL definition of a Web service will be maintained in the UDDI Registry as a part of the overall description of the Web service. The WSDL description will also specify where the service can be found (i.e., its location within the Web) and how it should be invoked. WSDL enables one to separate the description of the abstract functionality offered by a service (i.e., its interface) from specific details of a service description, such as "how" and "where" that functionality is offered.

The mechanics of WSDL are such that in reality WSDL is a scheme for generically describing network services as a set of endpoints that function via exchanging messages containing either document-oriented or procedure-oriented information. These message exchange operations and messages are described abstractly in an implementation-neutral manner.

A WSDL-based description of a Web service starts with the messages (i.e., the inputs and outputs) that will be exchanged between the service provider and service requester. These messages are described abstractly in terms of their name and type (e.g., character string, date/time, and so forth). Each message is then bound to a concrete network protocol (e.g., SOAP, HTTP, and so forth) and message format. Thus, a message consists of a collection of typed data items. An exchange of messages between the service provider and requester, as in a transaction, is then described as an operation. A WSDL operation thus consists of a set of previously defined messages. A set of operations is, in turn, called a port type.

Within this context, a (Web) service per se is thought of as being made up of a set of *ports*, where each port is an implementation of a port type. With WSDL, operations and messages are described abstractly and then bound to a concrete network protocol (e.g., SOAP) and message format to define an endpoint. WSDL can be used with SOAP, HTTP, and MIME (i.e., Multipurpose Internet Mail Extensions, the popular and official Internet standard that specifies how messages must be formatted so that they can be exchanged between different e-mail systems). If we take SOAP as an example, then a WSDL definition describes a set of SOAP messages and how those messages are to be exchanged.

Figure 2.9 illustrates an example of a WSDL definition, as found in the W3C specification for WSDL Version 1.2. This example is for a flight reservation–related Web service, which can be used both to query flights available on a particular date and time between a specific origin city and a destination as well as to make a reservation for a specific flight identified in terms of its flight number, origin/destination city names, and the departure data and time.

The goal of WSDL is to ensure that automated processes (e.g., e-business applications running on client PCs) can automatically determine the exact networking capabilities of remote systems (e.g., mainframe) without human intervention or prior definitions. The key WSDL constructs, per the current WSDL specification available at w3.org, are as follows:

1. WSDL Types—a container for data-type definitions using some type of system

2. Message—an abstract, typed definition of the data being communicated

3. Operation—an abstract description of an action supported by the service

4. Port type—an abstract set of operations supported by one or more endpoints

5.   Binding—a concrete protocol and data format specification for a particular port type

6.   Port—a single endpoint defined as a combination of a binding and a network address

7.   Service—a collection of related endpoints (or port types)

```xml
<?xml version="1.0" encoding="UTF-8"?>
<definitions name="TicketAgent"
    targetNamespace="http://airline.wsdl/ticketagent/"
    xmlns="http://schemas.xmlsoap.org/wsdl/"
    xmlns:tns="http://airline.wsdl/ticketagent/"
    xmlns:xsd="http://www.w3.org/2001/XMLSchema" xmlns:xsd1="http://airline/">
    <import location="TicketAgent.xsd" namespace="http://airline/"/>
    <message name="listFlightsRequest">
        <part name="depart" type="xsd:dateTime"/>
        <part name="origin" type="xsd:string"/>
        <part name="destination" type="xsd:string"/>
    </message>
    <message name="listFlightsResponse">
        <part name="result" type="xsd1:ArrayOfString"/>
    </message>
    <message name="reserveFlightRequest">
        <part name="depart" type="xsd:dateTime"/>
        <part name="origin" type="xsd:string"/>
        <part name="destination" type="xsd:string"/>
        <part name="flight" type="xsd:string"/>
    </message>
    <message name="reserveFlightResponse">
        <part name="result" type="xsd:string"/>
    </message>
    <portType name="TicketAgent">
        <operation name="listFlights" parameterOrder="depart origin destination">
            <input message="tns:listFlightsRequest" name="listFlightsRequest"/>
            <output message="tns:listFlightsResponse" name="listFlightsResponse"/>
        </operation>
        <operation name="reserveFlight" parameterOrder="depart origin destination
flight">
            <input message="tns:reserveFlightRequest" name="reserveFlightRequest"/>
            <output message="tns:reserveFlightResponse" name="reserveFlightResponse"/>
        </operation>
    </portType>
</definitions>
```

Figure 2.9   *An example of a WSDL definition of a Web service, in this case a Web service for airline reservation applications, as shown in the W3C specification for WSDL Version 1.2.*

2.9   Q&A: A time to recap and reflect

Q: Why is XML important in the context of Web services?

A: Web services are totally and unabashedly XML-centric. All data transfers to and from a Web service are always in the form of XML documents. The input parameters to a Web service are thus structured and defined using XML, as is the output generated by a Web service. In addition, the I/O operations of a Web service, which are implemented in the form of a remote procedure call mechanism, are realized using SOAP, which happens to be an XML-based messaging scheme. The workings of a Web service are also described using XML, in this case WSDL, which is an XML derivative.

Q: Is XML the newfangled replacement for HTML?

A: No, XML is definitely not a replacement for HTML. Though they share a common ancestry (namely, SGML), XML and HTML serve different purposes. HTML deals with the presentation of data for visual consumption. It does not address what the data means or attempt to categorize the data. This, on the other hand, is what XML is all about. Thus, XML per se, in marked contrast to HTML, does not concern itself about how data should be formatted. If you want the data contained within an XML document to be presented in formatted mode, then you need to use Cascading Stylesheets or XSL, so XML is certainly not a replacement for HTML. At a stretch you could contend, if you want to be generous, that they complement each other, but that is about as close as you can get. HTML is chalk and XML is cheese. That is how different they are.

Q: What is the purpose of XML?

A: XML is a flexible, no-holds-barred mechanism for describing data in a systematic manner. It can be used with any type of data, without exception, and is, moreover, platform, programming language, and application independent. Consequently, it is a powerful, standardized means for facilitating data interchange between incompatible systems—provided, of course, that the data description is suitably described using a DTD or XML schema.

Q: Is XML a programming language?

A: XML is certainly not a programming language, nor is it associated with any programming language. XML is very much a technology that is programming language and computer platform independent. It is a standard for creating application-specific markup languages.

Q: If XML is a markup language of sorts does it come with its own set of tags, as does HTML?

A: Unlike HTML, XML does not come with its own set of markup tags, though it has a few, strictly optional, processing instructions, which appear within tags that are delimited with "?" marks (e.g., `<?xml version=1"?>`). With XML, users define and create custom, application-specific tags that optimally describe the data that are being described. There are really no overly restrictive rules or caveats as to which tags can be created, what they can be called, how they can be structured, or how many different tags you can have—other than some minor naming conventions (e.g., names cannot start with numeric digits) and a need to ensure that tags are correctly nested without "hanging" overlaps.

Q: How does XML work?

A: XML deals with data within the context of documents. Data are included in an XML document as strings of text. The data are bracketed by XML text markup, which sets out to describe these data. The basic building blocks of an XML document are called "elements"—where an element is a specific unit of data along with the XML markup describing these data. An XML element is made up of a name and some content. The XML markup is in the form of tags. An XML element is delimited by two tags: a start tag and an end tag. The start tag is what gives the element its name.

Q: How does a recipient of an XML document know how to interpret the data contained within that document?

A: To successfully process XML, you need a mutual understanding at both ends of the transaction. XML provides mechanisms to facilitate this mutual understanding. The two main schemes for this are called Document Type Definitions (DTDs) and XML schema. In some special cases it is possible to have DTD-less XML documents, provided the elements are structured in some type of self-explanatory manner.

Q: If XML itself is not a data formatting scheme à la HTML, are there any mechanisms available to present XML documents in a visually compelling manner?

A: Yes, there are at least two key means by which to present the data contained within an XML document in a visually compelling manner; these are Cascading Stylesheets (CSS) and eXtensible Style Language (XSL).

Q: What kinds of tools are available to facilitate the use of XML?

A: At a minimum there are XML authoring, XML conversion, and XML validation tools. XML authoring tools help one create valid XML documents from scratch, whereas XML converters will take an existing structured document (e.g., spreadsheet or word processing file) and automatically generate a corresponding XML document. XML validators carefully parse XML documents and determine if they are valid per XML conventions and check that they meet all the XML requirements.

Q: What is the role of WSDL vis-à-vis Web services?

A: WSDL is used to define the high-level functionality of a Web service, in terms of its external interface, and to describe how that Web service can be accessed over the Web. WSDL will specify how a Web service actually functions, particularly in terms of what it accepts as input and what it will return as its output. The WSDL description of a Web service will specify where the service can be found and how it should be invoked.

3

Microsoft's Web Services

A battle is only great or small according to its results.

—Mark Twain

Microsoft's Web services initiative, as embodied within its .NET program, is incisive, pervasive, and aggressive. This is to be expected. It is also remarkably realistic and pragmatic, which may come as a surprise to some, but let's face it—Microsoft, as the idiom goes, "put skin in the game." Actually, Microsoft, the world's most successful software company has a lot of skin in this game. Microsoft, one of the founding fathers of Web services, along with IBM, knows exactly what is at stake here. Ironically, this very alliance with IBM accentuates to Microsoft's senior management on a daily basis the dangers of what can happen if you do not pay adequate attention to a potentially important software technology.

Twenty years ago, IBM and Microsoft also collaborated, not as the peers that they are today but very much on a David and Goliath basis, on desktop software for the then-nascent PCs, in particular the OS/2 operating system. IBM, sated by continuing success in the mainframe and mid-range sectors, was somewhat lackadaisical in rallying its considerable resources to decisively exploit this emerging market in a timely manner. IBM took its eyes off the ball. Microsoft stalked it like a hawk. The rest is history.

IBM is still paying the price for this miscalculation and hoping that the new Web services–oriented software model, coupled with the growing acceptance of Linux, might give it a chance to redress the balance when it comes to PC software. Microsoft, innately more street-smart than most, and certainly more so than IBM, knows that. It does not intend to slip up and give IBM, or anybody else for that matter, an unexpected opening.

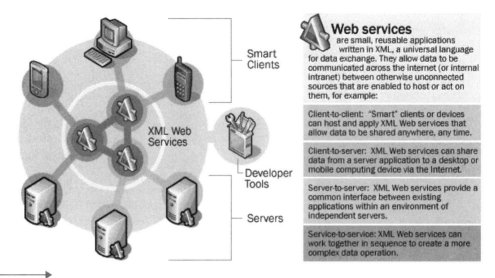

Web services are small, reusable applications written in XML, a universal language for data exchange. They allow data to be communicated across the Internet (or internal intranet) between otherwise unconnected sources that are enabled to host or act on them, for example:

Client-to-client: "Smart" clients or devices can host and apply XML Web services that allow data to be shared anywhere, any time.

Client-to-server: XML Web services can share data from a server application to a desktop or mobile computing device via the Internet.

Server-to-server: XML Web services provide a common interface between existing applications within an environment of independent servers.

Service-to-service: XML Web services can work together in sequence to create a more complex data operation.

Figure 3.1 *One of Microsoft's perspicacious depictions of Web services (see Web services model introduced in Figure 1.2).*

Rather than let Web services weaken its desktop franchise in any way, Microsoft is committed to making sure that Web services fall within its franchise.

Microsoft coauthored the SOAP, WSDL, and UDDI specifications in 2000 (as shown in Table 1.1). By April 2001 it had one of the first widely used implementations of SOAP—namely, the Microsoft SOAP Toolkit 2.0. It is now one of the four companies responsible for maintaining the global UDDI Business Registry, as discussed in Section 1.1.2; the other three companies are IBM, NTT Communication Corporation, and SAP. It is still extremely active, one could even say proactive, in the Web services standards front (as shown in Table 1.1), and has had a hand in creating many of the key auxiliary standards, including business process representation (BPEL4WS), Web services discovery (i.e., WS-Inspection), messaging, XML key management (XKMS), security (e.g., WS-Security, WS-Trust, and so forth), and transaction processing (WS-Coordination). The bottom line here is that it is fair and safe to say that Microsoft really does know what Web services are all about and furthermore is making sure that rather than just having a finger on the pulse, it has a stethoscope on the heart.

Given this level of familiarity and involvement from day one, it is not surprising that Microsoft's characterization of Web services is perspicacious and snappy (Figure 3.1). Two of the high-level definitions favored by Microsoft are as follows:

- Web services protocols enable computers to work together by exchanging messages. Web services are based on the standard protocols of XML, SOAP, and WSDL, which allow them to interoperate across platforms and programming languages.

- Web services are small, reusable applications written in XML, a universal language for data exchange. They allow data to be communicated across the Internet (or internal intranet) between otherwise unconnected sources that are enabled to host or act on them.

Despite what its many distracters may ardently hope, there is no question that Microsoft is destined, even preordained, to play a pivotal role when it comes to Web services. This is a given. To look at this in another way, one can even say, without any fear of contradiction, that Web services cannot really take off without the help of Microsoft offerings, whether it be Windows, Microsoft's ubiquitous Internet Information Services (IIS) Web server, Microsoft BizTalk Server 2000, or any of Microsoft's Visual application development suites (e.g., Visual BASIC, Visual C++, or Visual Studio).

The reality here is that given Microsoft's current control of basic corporate IT infrastructure, especially at the desktop and the Web interface, it is inconceivable to see how Web services can truly flourish without in some way impinging upon Microsoft technology. Furthermore, Microsoft's development tools are widely used and highly popular within the application development community. Consequently, many Web services will be developed using Microsoft tools and deployed on Windows NT, Windows 2000, or Windows 2003. That is ineluctable.

Web services, particularly in the case of Microsoft and IBM (and to a smaller degree in the case of IBM and BEA), have added a whole new twist to the "co-opetition" (i.e., cooperating with your competition) concept favored by Novell's founder, Ray Noorda. When it comes to Web services–related standards and the task of maintaining the global UDDI Business Registry, Microsoft and IBM appear to work hand in glove and advocate the same values. There has been more productive collaboration between these two companies on the Web services front than between any other two companies. Together they account for at least 60% of the standards-related work done to facilitate Web services.

However, the cooperation and chumminess end abruptly when it comes to marketing Web services–related solutions. IBM is all Java and Microsoft is all decaf. The gulf could not be any wider or more fundamental. Rather than getting better over time, this dispute continues to escalate and get more acrimonious. Microsoft's decision not to include an industry standard–compliant Java Virtual Machine (JVM) that was acceptable to Java's creator Sun Microsystems within the Windows XP operating system precipitated the latest showdown—which yet again included lawsuits and injunctions.

A JVM is also not installed as part of a typical Internet Explorer 6.0 (or greater) installation, though one is automatically downloaded and installed on the fly when a user encounters a Web page that relies on Java Applets. The upshot of all of this is that Microsoft, as of February 2003, is claiming that it will not include any sort of JVM in any Microsoft products as of January 2004—and moreover will stop distributing its Java-oriented Visual J++ product as well. Those who want a JVM with Microsoft products, including the newer Windows platforms, will have to get JVM from a third party. In reality this is not a big deal, since free and highly automated downloads for all major releases of Windows are available from the http://www.java.com Web site.

At this juncture, to avoid any future confusion or misunderstandings, it is important to point out that Microsoft does have a relatively widely used Java-based software development suite known as Visual J++ (Figures 3.2 and 3.3) and that the latest version of this software development package, known as Visual J#, is integrated into Microsoft's Visual Studio .NET. The pivotal issue here, however, is that Microsoft's Java is not platform independent!

Software developed using Microsoft's Visual J++ or J#, as is also the case with most other Microsoft software development tools, will only run on the Windows platform. That is the rub. This issue is so germane to the discussion here that it is worth repeating what Microsoft has to say about this: "Visual J# .NET 2003 is not a tool for developing applications intended to run on a Java virtual machine. Applications and services built with Visual J# .NET 2003 will run only in the .NET Framework; they will not run on any

Figure 3.2   *The product packaging of Microsoft's Visual J++ Release 6.0 offering.*

Java virtual machine. Visual J# .NET 2003 has been developed independently by Microsoft. It is neither endorsed nor approved by Sun Microsystems, Inc." This terse set of statements tells it all and confirms that there is indeed a basic difference of opinion and sentiment between Microsoft and the Java camp. As of 2004, this split could reach the point of being irreconcilable.

IBM likes to claim that its WebSphere family is the best route by far for implementing Web services–related solutions. Microsoft disagrees vehemently. As far as Microsoft is concerned, its .NET initiative is a much more practical and cost-effective approach than anything IBM can offer. Both camps have ardent, dyed-in-the-wool supporters, in roughly equal quantities. Many of these are active, knowledgeable practitioners who make a good living developing software. They can cogently argue as to why they opted to use one scheme rather than the other. They cite practice as opposed to theory.

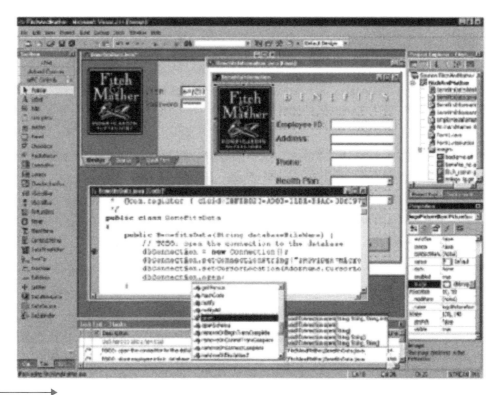

Figure 3.3   *An example from Microsoft of the highly visual, integrated development environment available with the Java-based Visual J++ software development tool.*

Both sides, given their ample war chests, also have mercenaries in the form of consultants and analysts. These, though typically more articulate and prolific with the written word than the software practitioners, tend to disseminate what is essentially party propaganda. Media journalists for their part, though hoping to elucidate, tend to vacillate between the camps depending on who they last spoke to at length. Acrimony, on the whole, is such that both camps even go to the trouble of writing white papers or commissioning others to write white papers that are no more than just rebuttals of each other's methodologies vis-à-vis Web service development and deployment. In these documents, each side agrees, albeit grudgingly, that the other's technology works. What they bicker about incessantly is what approach is easier to use, the significance of platform independence, and the overall cost of one approach over the other.

In reality, much of this "my approach is faster than yours" or "my approach will save you money" carping is not that useful in relation to the big picture, even when these claims are categorized by empirical data such as "12 steps rather than 9" or "an average programmer can complete the task 3 hours quicker, thus saving $360 in development costs." Preference when it comes to programming methodology, as anybody who has programmed for a living will know, is a very subjective personal thing akin to whether one prefers briefs or boxers. Experience and familiarity with one approach will invariably outweigh the apparent superiority of alternate schemes—hence, the futility of these claims and counterclaims.

A programmer or a team of programmers, who have spent the last 5 years (or more) working with Microsoft Visual InterDev tools, are unlikely to want to, or need to, switch to using a totally Java-based approach, because the Microsoft scheme involved a few more steps when it came to developing Web services. The learning curve will invariably be too steep, and the retraining costs too high. On top of this there is all the very real but hard to quantify "lost opportunity costs," such as higher programming error rates, longer debugging cycles, and a propensity for more testing. Obviously, the converse case—that is, seasoned Java programmers with no prior exposure to Microsoft development methodology being expected to decamp—is equally unrealistic. Retraining programmers is a slow and costly undertaking—particularly so if they were perfectly content with the methods they were using before. Major switchovers invariably only happen over a protracted period of time, because of major changes in overall corporate IT policy, such as those brought about by a merger or acquisition, change in company mission, or the hiring of a new CTO. Section 3.1 highlights the real issues in methodology and points out those factors that are but mere noise.

The bottom line here is that both camps have their pros and cons, and both sides have important roles to play within the emerging Web services market relative to their constituent bases. The die is already cast. Microsoft and IBM, whether they like it or not, have no choice whatsoever other than to share the stage. That is not going to change. Nonetheless, it is safe to assume that, at least for the foreseeable future, IBM will continue to be petulant that Microsoft has the audacity to want to play an active role in the Web services market.

It seems hard for IBM to reconcile that Microsoft really is a bona fide, credible, and influential player when it comes to enterprise-class, server-side application software. However, the reality is that Microsoft now has a huge and ardent following in the programming community, with many casual and part-time practioners only being conversant with Microsoft tools. At this juncture it is also obligatory to point out that this is not just a two-horse race between Microsoft and IBM, or even Microsoft and Java. There are also the very viable and compelling software development options provided by the open source software initiatives, such as Perl and PHP from the Apache Software Foundation (http://www.apache.org) or the increasingly popular Python (http://www.python.org), which appears to be the new no-charge BASIC for the masses. There will be more on this in subsequent chapters.

3.1   The real and not-so-real issues

The key issues that really need to be considered in the Microsoft versus non-Microsoft debate vis-à-vis Web services can be categorized as follows:

- Nature of the software being developed, given that a Web service is like a cake in that your feelings about it will vary significantly on whether your role is limited to making it or eating it

- The applicability of platform independence, since Microsoft solutions tend to be Windows specific

- Security—especially since Microsoft muddied the waters at the outset by trying to juxtapose its Passport initiative with Web services

- Scalability, which, if crucial, is one of the legitimate factors that can influence the choice of platform decision

- Resilience, given that programmers appreciate that any time or steps saved during the development phase can be totally overshadowed by the time that can be expended trying to debug, rectify, and regression test unstable software

- Freedom of choice if one does not want to be locked into the solution set of one particular vendor, whether Microsoft, IBM, or Sun

When talking about Web services–related software development, it is sometimes easy to lose sight of the fact that there are two very distinct and different sides to this. Web services–related software development, as highlighted in Figure 3.4, embraces both:

1. The creation of reusable Web services

2. The consumption of previously created Web services

From a software development perspective, these are very different endeavors—as diverse as chalk and cheese. Web services, as stated in Microsoft's own definition and shown in Figure 3.1, are small, reusable "applications" that are XML based. Web services, in essence, are software "widgets." They are components. On the other hand, applications that are

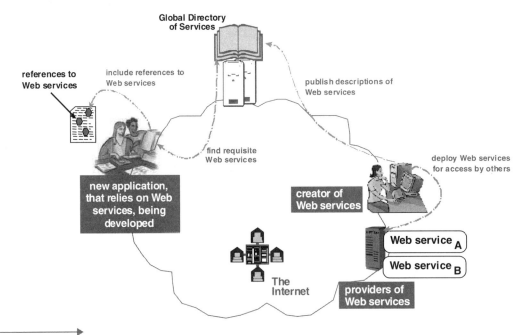

Figure 3.4   *Web services–related software development is always a two-prong operation, with the creation of the Web services being a very separate exercise from that of developing the applications that use them.*

built using one or more Web services are, by implication alone, expected to be larger and more complex than a typical Web service. The whole point of having Web services is to simplify and expedite the development of sophisticated, feature-rich, problem-solving applications.

It is indeed possible to have "nested" Web services, where one Web service invokes other Web services from other external parties to obtain functionality that it requires. This, however, is unlikely to be widely adopted for relatively obvious performance, security, and commercial considerations, given that with Web services you are dealing with dynamic, run-time invocation of functionality, as opposed to an embedded software–oriented software component model. Unless there is a watertight means for total disclosure upfront, and WSDL in its current form alone may not be adequate for this, a person who elects to call a Web service to obtain a certain function may not be comfortable to find out that that Web service in turn is going out to other Web services behind the scene.

Suffice to say that such nested calls, if they involve multiple undisclosed entities, could be a potential can of worms. For the discussions at hand, it is adequate to categorize such nested services based just on the number of nested calls involved. If a Web service only has one or two calls to other external Web services, for the sake of the issues here, it could still be treated as a "large" Web service. If, however, a Web service has many calls to other external Web services, it starts to cross over the boundary and should be thought of more as an application—rather than a single Web service.

There is meant to be a definite subset-superset, component-system relationship between a Web service and the application that uses it. The Web service is a subset (or component), whereas the end application is the larger, total picture. The end application, as the system in this case, is a superset of the Web services invoked by it. Consequently, it is fairly easy to appreciate that the needs of programmers developing Web services are likely to be different from those developing the applications that will be using Web services.

Thus, one cannot look at Web services–related software development as a single, homogeneous continuum that spans both the creation and consumption aspects. Instead, what we have are two disjointed, decoupled endeavors—each with its own unique set of goals and requirements. This distinction is vital when trying to objectively evaluate the Java versus decaf debate, given that one could be better for creating Web services, whereas the other is more suited for developing the larger applications that will be using Web services. Immediately it is possible to envisage win-win scenarios involving both methodologies, which could even prove to be synergistic.

Table 3.1   *How Web Services Differ from the Applications That Use Them*

	Web Service	Application Using Web Services
Purpose:	Reusable, commodity component	Address an overall business or entertainment need
Typical size in terms of code length:	Small	Medium/large
Functionality:	One specific function	Multifunction
Typically developed by:	Individual or 2–4 people	Team of programmers
Complexity (in general):	Relatively simple	Relatively complex
Development time frame:	Days	Months

At this juncture, however, it would be useful to characterize some of the key differences between Web services and the applications that use them, as well as to categorize the motives that will spur the development of Web services. Table 3.1 address the former, whereas Table 3.2 tackles the latter relative to corporations and individuals.

The bottom line here is that it is a fallacy to assume that Web services and the applications that intend to use them are or will be birds of the same feather. Instead, they are likely to be (one could even say that they really should be) very different entities—developed by different types of people, with very different motivations and software development requirements. This plays to Microsoft's advantage. Given this distinct dichotomy, one could develop Web services using Microsoft tools—in particular, the new .NET solution set—without immediately confronting the challenge that Microsoft-based solutions are not appropriate for use in large data center–related scenarios. The reason is that a given Web service could have many different takers—all of them not necessarily wanting to use that Web service in a large-scale, mission-critical application being developed for a Fortune 500 corporation. However, the contention that a Web service deployed on a Windows server may not be rugged enough for use by enterprise-class applications may still have some justification in certain situations, as will be discussed shortly.

3.1.1 No real glory in making it complicated

By now, especially after the characterizations depicted in Tables 3.1 and 3.2, it has to be clear that Web services, in general, are supposed to be compact,

Table 3.2 *Motivations for Developing Web Services*

Corporations	Individuals
1. Gain revenue by marketing them as a software products	1. Gain some revenue by marketing them as a software products—possibly as "shareware"
2. For internal use to facilitate developing in-house applications	2. Gain kudos, repute, and satisfaction within the software development community by providing useful, value-added software functionality in the form of open-source software (i.e., freeware)
3. For use in applications being developed for resale	
4. For use by partners, suppliers, and affiliates when developing e-business-related "extranet" applications (e.g., a Web service to process a specific type of invoice)	3. For subsequent use as reusable components when writing new applications
	4. To help out friends who are developing applications
5. Gain competitive advantage by offering a promotional "no-charge" Web service, for use by applications being developed by other companies (e.g., specialized search capability, currency converter, and so forth)	5. To try out new programming techniques and methodology
6. Gain publicity, kudos, and repute within the software development community by providing useful, value-added software functionality in the form of open-source software	
7. Capture and preserve valuable functionality hitherto buried inside legacy mission-critical applications for future use	
8. Serve as a real-world proving ground for trainee programmers who want to write some production software on their own	
9. Enable specific departments (or lines of businesses) to develop specialized software routines that reflect the work they perform	

self-contained pieces of software. It is tempting to also add the word "slick" to this description, though this, alas, is not a mandatory prerequisite, though one would like to think that this indeed is likely to be the case much of the time. "Agility" is the other word—one could even say theme—that should come to mind, especially as one gets more and more exposure to Web services. Everything about a Web service is supposed to be quick, nimble, and, above all, easy. These agility-related attributes thus apply not just to the use of a Web service, but equally so to the development of a Web service.

Somebody planning to, or tasked with, developing a Web service should not typically view this as being a major, long-drawn-out project. Developing a

Web service is meant to be a relatively quick and easy endeavor. A couple of metaphors at this juncture should help reinforce this key point. A Web service, to use an analogy, is not meant to be a novel. It is not even supposed to be a 50-page short story. Instead, it is meant to be a set of paragraphs. In this analogy, the novel will be one of the new applications that makes use of the Web service. This analogy should provide a fairly accurate handle as to the level of effort and time commitment one should associate with the development of a Web service. If it takes more than a couple of weeks to create, then it could likely be more than a Web service. The metric for measuring the time required to develop an average Web service really has to be days rather than anything larger. It may also help to think of Web services as the TV dinners of the software industry—with ease of preparation, quick results, and fast gratification being the keywords here.

Developing typical Web services is thus meant to be a small project. It is not meant to take a long time, and it is expected to be relatively easy to complete. This is good for Microsoft and .NET. The flip side of the Microsoft in the data center argument now comes into play—more or less by default. If Microsoft solutions are not industrial strength for enterprise-level deployment, then they must at least be easy to create and deploy. The rationale for this is that one has to believe that Microsoft software must have some redeeming attributes, given that Microsoft as a company serves more software users, by far, than any other company.

In essence, the "not industrial strength" gibes, by implication, tend to convey the perception that Microsoft solutions have to be less complex, less cumbersome, and, in general, "lighter." It makes Microsoft's approach feel more user friendly, more approachable, and less intimidating—exactly the type of approach you would want if you were looking for a way to develop a small piece of software without expending too much time, effort, and money—so this leads to a definite schism. The non-Microsoft camp, in particular IBM, comes across as being heavy duty, somewhat involved, and complicated. Microsoft, on the other hand, can now revel in being "light and easy," and, to Microsoft's delight, there are tens of thousands of programmers, if not more, who will heartily concur with this sentiment.

To be fair to all sides, the popularity and effectiveness of Microsoft's software development solutions are not just a perception issue, or, for that matter, one that is even subjective. Microsoft's visual family of programming tools, now exemplified by Visual Studio .NET 2003, has a huge, faithful, and avid following. Visual BASIC (Figure 3.5), introduced in 1991 after Microsoft obtained the underlying technology from Alan Cooper in 1988, struck a chord, especially with noncorporate programmers. BASIC,

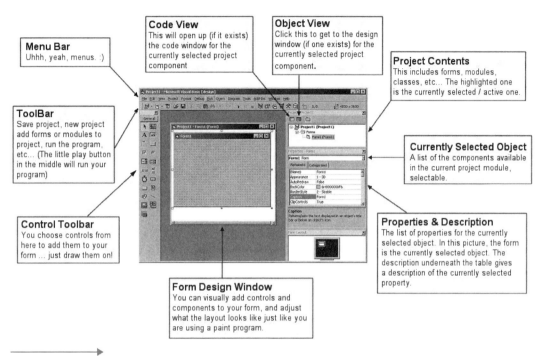

Figure 3.5   *The visual programming paradigm of Microsoft's Visual BASIC software development environment with annotations by Professor Saul Greenberg, University of Calgary, Canada.*

ever since its inception at Dartmouth College in the mid-1960s, had enjoyed an unblemished reputation for ease of use, convenience, and user friendliness. BASIC, even when available in compilable as opposed to interpretive mode, was, however, never considered as a serious contender to the likes of COBOL, FORTRAN, PL/I, and C when it came to developing large, mission-critical applications. BASIC was more for the casual and entertainment (e.g., DOS games for the initial PCs) market.

With Visual BASIC (VB) Microsoft changed some of the ground rules as to the applicability of BASIC. VB was integrated with the then emerging Windows. VB enabled programmers to quickly and easily create Windows-compatible, event-driven (e.g., clicking a button) graphical user interfaces (GUIs). VB was thus a quick and obvious way to develop true Windows applications as opposed to clunky DOS applications. VB was compelling to programmers trying to capitalize on the fast-breaking Windows wave, particularly if they were working with modest budgets and aggressive schedules. The ensuing rapid embracement of VB by a large segment of the programming community, further bolstered by a whole new legion of

VB-inspired freelance programmers, gave VB credibility and respectability. The "mainly for kids" stigma factor associated with BASIC was dissipated by the sheer weight of numbers, both in terms of VB-qualified programmers as well as VB-based applications on the market.

VB, however, was only the beginning. Since then, there has been Visual C, which has since evolved into Visual C++ and Visual C#. There has also been Microsoft's popular COM- and Active X–based object-oriented methodology, as well as the heavily used Active Server Pages (ASP) scripting scheme for developing server-side software for dynamic Web applications. The hard and cold facts are irrefutable. VB, Visual C++, COM/ActiveX, and ASP are not just popular; they border on being ubiquitous. Whether one likes it or not, much of what makes up today's Web, whether Web content, Web applications, Web servers, or Web browsers, have some Microsoft connection.

Given this presence and popularity, Microsoft's influence and role when it comes to the development of future Web services is already assured. That is beyond debate. It has already happened. Microsoft's Visual Studio .NET, with its integrated support for VB and Visual C#, has from day one been explicitly targeted as a premier tool for developing XML Web services. Programmers who have been relying on Microsoft tools in the past are apt to look at Visual Studio .NET before evaluating other development schemes. However, it should be noted that Visual Studio .NET per se is not a prerequisite for developing XML Web services. You could develop them using older Visual C++ or VB products.

All of today's highly visual software development "studio" suites, whether from Microsoft, IBM, BEA, Sun, Oracle, or the open-source eclipse.org Consortium, go out of their way to facilitate the development of Web services. However, the reality here is that the compact, small project nature of developing a typical Web service nonetheless still plays to all of Microsoft's advantages vis-à-vis software development. The key ones here are, however, worth enumerating, given that it is sometimes easy to forget exactly what they are since they can be so obvious as to be transparent. Some of the key issues that will favor Microsoft, when programmers have to consider options for developing new Web services include the following:

■ Despite what one may feel about Microsoft, particularly in regard to software resilience (e.g., "blue screen of death" with most versions of Windows, including NT) and cost (e.g., new version of Office), Microsoft, thanks to its inescapable presence on desktops, still falls into the category of the "known devil."

- Again, thanks to Windows, Internet Explorer, and Office, Microsoft and its offerings come across as being approachable—particularly in terms of downloading the necessary tools from Microsoft and trying them out on a Windows machine.

- Software developed with Microsoft tools can be quickly, easily, and inexpensively debugged and tested on "commodity" Windows platforms.

- VB and Visual C++ have a reputation for delivering fast results.

- It is difficult to feel isolated or be stranded high and dry during the development, debug, or deployment process, since no-charge, near instantaneous tips, help, and encouragement are available online, 24/7, from a large and committed fraternity of knowledgeable and experienced like-minded practitioners from around the world who frequent a number of very active bulletin boards.

- There is a vast network of practical online resources, including sample code, much of it on a no-charge basis, available from Microsoft, other companies, and individuals to help one get started on a development project.

- Given that many well-known software packages only work on Windows-based server platforms, or are initially released just for Windows with UNIX support only available much later, one cannot be easily ostracized for developing a Windows-specific solution—especially since Web services, by definition, are platform agnostic.

Thus, the bottom line here is that Microsoft tools, in particular the .NET repertoire, will continue to play a major role when it comes to the development and deployment of Web services. That really is incontrovertible. The one big downside, however, of using Microsoft development tools, including Visual Studio .NET 2003, is the lack of platform latitude. Software developed using most Microsoft development tools can typically only be deployed on Microsoft Windows platforms. Figure 3.6, which is a screen shot of Microsoft's System Requirements for Visual Studio .NET 2003 Web page, shows that the only operating systems supported by Microsoft for the deployment of applications created by Visual Studio .NET 2003 just happen to be various flavors of Windows.

3.1.2   Mounting the platform—gingerly

The platform independence of Web services, as repeatedly stressed at the beginning of this book, is truly bona fide, universal, and without exception

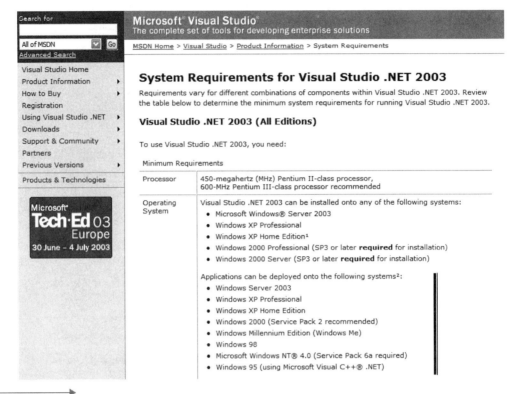

Figure 3.6   *Part of the system requirements for Visual Studio .NET 2003 Web page from Microsoft's Web site showing that applications developed using this tool set can only be deployed on Windows platforms. Highlighting, in the form of the vertical bar, was added by the author.*

or caveats. This is so because Web services operate by exchanging XML documents on a run-time basis. XML, as should be now clear, is a simple methodology based entirely on the use of documents consisting of plain text. Platform independence and programming language independence are two of XML's primary precepts. Consequently, the platform independence of Web services is not just restricted to one side of the requester-provider model.

Web services can be deployed on any platform, as can the applications that rely on the functionality provided by Web services. It is always any-to-any. There are no interoperability limitations or unacceptable permutations. There are also no mandated optimum permutations, though there will be those who claim that UNIX/Linux to UNIX/Linux, mainframe to UNIX/Linux, mainframe to iSeries, iSeries to iSeries, or iSeries to UNIX/Linux pairings are unlikely to give any cause for concern when it comes to

performance, security, reliability, or scalability. The XML-oriented operation model employed by Web services also dictates that there are no requirements or restrictions as to how Web services or the applications that use
them are developed. Since all data exchange takes place in the form of XML
documents, there are no programming language–, database-, or file format–
related interoperability issues.

Given this background, one has to be very careful and have plausible
justification prior to claiming that some platforms may not be as good as
others when it comes to hosting (i.e., running) Web services. Note that the
keyword is that of hosting Web services (i.e., the platform on which a Web
service is to be deployed). The platform issues for the applications that will
use Web services are invariably very different and are dictated by a separate
set of criteria. However, in order to establish a baseline for the ensuing discussion, Table 3.3 sets out some of the key platform-related factors as they
apply to Web services and the applications that use them.

In general, the platform preference and selection for the application side
will occur independent of any consideration being given to the intended
use of Web services. That is perfectly legitimate and acceptable—as it
should be. The application is the driving force in this instance. It is the
goal. Web services are but enablers. The tail should not wag the dog—and
in this instance, the application is very much the dog. Consequently, any
Web services–related platform issues per se should not influence the platform or platforms targeted for a Web service invoking application. Thus, it
is really business as usual on the application side when it comes to platform-
related issues.

Typically the platform(s) for an application is preordained by a number
of "set-in-concrete" factors. If the application is being developed for use by
just one company (e.g., a large Fortune 1000 company), then the platform
preferences of that company, both existing and those targeted for the future,
will be the deciding factor. If it is a large company that has relied on mainframes for much of its IT needs for the last 3 decades, and the new application is to replace a 25-year-old mission-critical application running on
those mainframes, then the chances are that the new application will be targeted, at least initially, to be mainframe-compliant. This is where Java is
such a boon. Developing the application in Java is likely to cover all bases—
current as well as future.

A Java application can be easily hosted on a mainframe, UNIX/Linux,
iSeries, or even a Windows platform. It will even adroitly accommodate any
plans to migrate some of the mainframe workload to Linux server images
running on a mainframe. Thus, for this type of corporate application, Java

would appear to be the optimum choice, with C++ being the second choice if performance is paramount—given that a C++ application could also be ported to any of these applications, albeit with the need for it to be first recompiled on that platform.

Then there are the applications that are developed, by enterprises or individuals, so that they can be sold, leased, or given to others—where the recip-

Table 3.3 *Factors That Can Influence Platform Preference for Web Services and the Applications That Use Them*

	Web Service	Application Using Web Services
Likely to be a replacement for an existing (legacy) piece of software:	No	Yes
Relative size (i.e., code length or memory requirements):	Likely to be small	Likely to be large
Reliance on "backbone" services (e.g., database, directory, messaging):	Limited, if any	Significant
Potential consumption of computing resources (i.e., processor cycles, memory, I/O):	Likely to be low (per instance)	Likely to be high
Likely to be mission-critical:	No	Yes
Size of potential target audience known in advance:	No	In general, yes—even when targeted for public access over the Web
Need for scalability:	Unknown	Likely to be a concern
Developed with specific response time expectations:	No	Yes
Culled from a legacy, mission-critical application:	Possible	No
Importance of platform resilience:	Of some concern	Likely to be very high
Importance of security:	High	High
Ability to dictate need for a new, more powerful server platform:	Limited	High
Ability to justify higher server costs because of mission criticality or number of users for the server:	Limited, if any	High
Importance of potential portability between diverse platforms:	Unlikely to be a major concern in general	Likely to be a concern

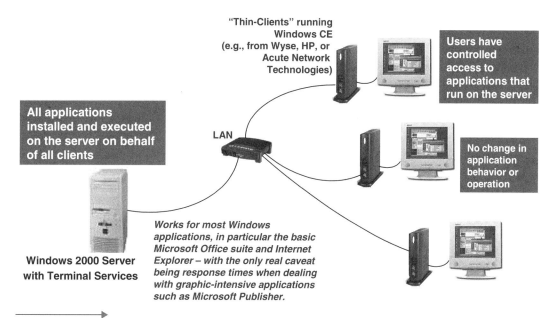

Figure 3.7   *The overall architecture of the compelling "thin-client" solution available with Windows 2000 Terminal Services, which obviates the expense and effort of having to install and maintain Windows applications on individual desktops.*

ients could be commercial corporations, noncommercial organizations, or individuals. This is the trillion-dollar application software market. The platform issues in this instance are obviously more convoluted and complicated. First, there is the pivotal issue as to whether the application is for the client side or the server side. The ongoing popularity of mobile clients (e.g., intelligent cell phones, PDAs, Pocket PCs, and tablets) and "thin clients" (e.g., Windows 2000 Terminal Services, Citrix solutions, or Web browser–based access), however, starts to blur this client-side versus server-side demarcation, as does the whole concept of Web server–resident Web applications.

Figure 3.7 illustrates the overall "thin-client" model postulated by Windows 2000 Terminal Services, whereas Figure 3.8 shows the contemporary application delivery architecture advocated by Citrix Systems. With "thin-client" solutions, in essence what you end up with are client-side applications that nonetheless execute on a server, as opposed to the actual client.

The traditional desktop client market, irrespective of whether it is enterprise or home related, is dominated by Windows. Linux could start changing this down the road—and it is salutary to note that it is possible to easily port UNIX/Linux applications to run on the Mac OS X (and later) platform. The issue here is relatively simple. Applications being developed for the traditional

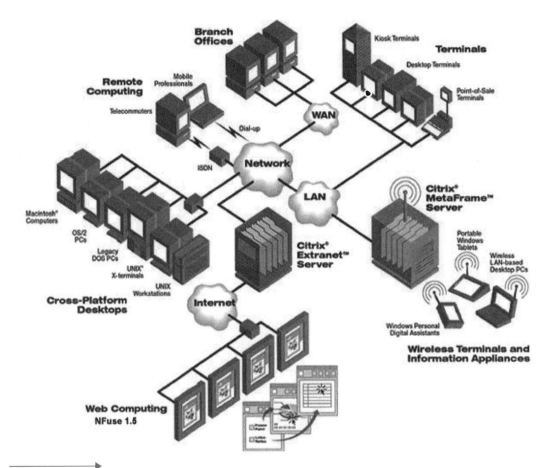

Figure 3.8   *The latest "thin-client" application delivery architecture postulated by Citrix Systems showing how "client" applications running on a Citrix server can be conveniently accessed by a wide range of legacy, desktop, terminal, kiosk, Web, and wireless clients.*

desktop client market are invariably going to favor Windows, at least for the foreseeable future, given that this is the predominant market. The availability of Windows subsets for mobile devices (e.g., Windows CE), in particular, a feature-rich version of Windows XP for PC tablet platforms, is likely to make a Windows-oriented decision even more compelling.

Things, however, are more complicated on the server side—given that there are at least four major and widely used server platforms—namely, UNIX, Linux, Windows, and iSeries (née AS/400). Fortunately, there is a distinct market stratification that helps provide a first cut as to which platforms will be of relevance to which types of applications. Though enterprises of all sizes and shapes use Windows server platforms, the larger enterprises invariably also rely on other server platforms (e.g., UNIX) for some or all of their crucial IT functions—with the Windows server being used in the main for file/print server and departmental applications.

On the other hand, smaller businesses and organizations (e.g., restaurants, convenience stores, small professional firms, and health-care practices) tend to rely entirely on Windows platforms, so much so that Microsoft even runs print ads for its Windows 2003 server that state: "You need UNIX-level performance and reliability. You don't have a UNIX-level budget." Thus, in essence, the primary target market for a given server-side application more or less steers the platform decision one way or another.

Windows will continue to be the preferred platform for applications designed for small businesses and organizations. Though applications written in Java could be made to work on Windows platforms, many software developers will see this as an unnecessary (and costly) exercise if the application is meant to be just for Windows. They will further argue that developing these applications in Java will make them less efficient—possibly even sluggish. In marked contrast, platform flexibility becomes a big issue when an application is being developed for use by mid- to large-size enterprises—hence, the preference for Java or C++ for this class of application.

The bottom line here is that the platform selection issue for applications that will be using Web services will invariably be made independent of any concern as to (or possibly even any thought given to) where the requisite Web services will actually be located. To be fair, in most cases developers might not even know exactly what Web services they want to use until they are much further into the actual software development process. Remember that finding and sourcing necessary Web services, using a combination of UDDI and WSDL at a minimum, is meant to be easy, dynamic, and flexible. Furthermore, developers are likely to ditch certain Web services and look for alternatives if they are not satisfied with the functionality or integrity of a particular Web service.

However, the issue here is that the platform being used by a Web service could, in some circumstances, have an impact on the calling application. In effect, the platform selection for an application could get undermined, unintentionally, by the platforms being used by the Web services being invoked by that application.

3.1.3   Ease of development, however, is not everything

To cut to the chase, the underlying concern here has to do with Web services that are to be deployed on Windows platforms. The preceding discussions should have demonstrated, irrefutably, that Microsoft development tools, in particular the Visual Studio .NET, VB, Visual C++, and Visual J++ offerings, will play a major role in the foreseeable future when it comes to the creation of Web services. Individuals, as well as small to medium-size enterprises, are likely to opt for a Microsoft scheme as their weapon of choice when thinking about developing a new Web service. These Web services will end up being deployed on Windows server platforms. This is because software, including Web services, created using Microsoft's development tools tends to be Window-specific. Furthermore, other developers may opt, justifiably, to have their Web services deployed on a Windows platform, even if they are not using a Microsoft development scheme, given that Windows platforms are ubiquitous, inexpensive, and are always within easy reach.

Consequently, Windows, incontrovertibly, will be a dominant platform on which Web services are hosted. There is even a possibility that in the 2004–2007 time frame roughly half of the Web services (if not more) made available via the global UDDI Registry are running on Windows platforms. This predilection vis-à-vis Windows could have potential ramifications— and that is the real nub of this issue.

The concern here relates to Windows-resident Web services being invoked by applications running on a non-Windows platform. This is not an interoperability issue. The genuine platform-independent, any-to-any principle of Web services mandates that applications running on non-Windows platforms should be able to profitably make use of Web services running on Windows platforms. Moreover, an application should not even have to care about which platform a Web service it is invoking is executing on. It should be transparent and immaterial. However, the reality is that there could be a potential expectation mismatch if an application explicitly developed to run on a non-Windows platform ends up relying on one or more Web services running on a Windows server (e.g., a mainframe application invoking a Web service running on a Windows NT server).

The potential mismatch here pertains to four extremely key factors, namely:

1.   Security vis-à-vis platform vulnerability

2.   Reliability and resilience of the platform

3.   Performance attributes of the platform as it relates to being able to quickly service a large number of requests within acceptable response time criteria

4.   Scalability of the platform when it comes to adroitly accommo-
        dating increasing workloads

The problem here is that Windows servers, particularly Windows NT
and the earlier versions of Windows 2000, are invariably at a disadvantage
relative to these four factors when matched up against UNIX, mainframe,
and even iSeries platforms. Thus, the question becomes whether a Web
service running on a Windows platform could compromise the integrity
and performance of a mission-critical application running on an "enterprise-class" server. To put it more graphically, could using a Web service
running on a $2,500 Windows server potentially damage the credibility of
a million-dollar application running on a $1,800,000 top-end UNIX server
with 24 processors and 64 GB of memory?

The answer, alas, has to be: Yes, it could.

This is where the "Windows is still not ready for the enterprise-class data
center" argument comes in. Windows 2003, available as of June 2003 and
explicitly developed to cogently address the exacting data center needs of
large enterprises, may start to change this—but this has yet to be demonstrated. In the meantime, it is only fair to say that Windows platforms are
invariably not in the same class when it comes to security vulnerability,
high-end performance, high availability, and scalability as the more expensive UNIX and mainframe solutions. That is the rub. Figure 3.9 depicts the
four, somewhat intertwined, factors of any server platform running Web
services, but in this case, Windows platforms in particular, that could prove
to be a source of concern if their operational characteristics are significantly

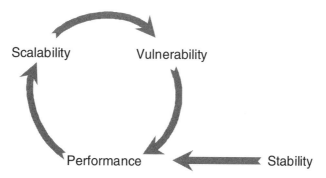

Figure 3.9   *These four key factors of a server platform dictate the desirability of that platform as a
host for Web services, since exposure in any one of these areas can undermine the value of
the Web service vis-à-vis applications running on other platforms with significantly better operational characteristics.*

inferior to those of the platforms hosting the applications invoking the Web services.

Over the last few years the security vulnerability of Windows platforms, particularly those exposed to the Internet and running Microsoft's IIS Web server or e-mail server, has been a major concern to enterprises around the world. The ubiquity of these servers, coupled with the fact that it is easy and inexpensive to obtain one for experimentation, has meant that most hackers invariably opt for Windows as their favorite, and in most cases *only,* platform to seek and attack.

Think about it. It is not that easy or practical to fire up a mainframe in your one-bedroom apartment so that you can poke around looking for soft-ware vulnerabilities (e.g., buffer overflow processing or profile "flipping") that could be exploited for nefarious purposes, and savvy hackers usually do not like the risk of snooping around and trying blatantly suspicious pro-gramming activities on data center computers—which, moreover, are harder to gain unauthorized access to in the first place. Thus, it is much more convenient and safer to pore over a Windows server, which can be installed on any halfway-decent PC, and determine ways to attack other similar Windows platforms.

On the whole, Windows platforms to date have been a fertile field for hackers and the creators of viruses. They have found and exploited numer-ous—in many cases profound—security "holes." The resulting security breaches have been far-reaching, disturbing, and costly. They have repeat-edly disrupted e-commerce and e-business activities and caused millions to lose sleep over the potential loss of their credit card information. It reached a point when influential IT analyst firms started issuing high-priority alerts to their large corporate customers, advising them to migrate away from Windows server platforms—especially in the case of servers being used for Internet-related endeavors.

Consequently, most IT professionals at medium to large enterprises now tend to be somewhat leery of Windows NT and Windows 2000 servers—particularly if they are conversant with other server platforms. With Win-dows 2003 Microsoft promises to provide significantly tighter security, but it will take quite some time, with zero violations during that time, before people will feel that they are not at some risk if they start using an Internet-connected Windows platform. The bottom line here is that IT professionals used to dealing with UNIX, mainframe, or iSeries platforms will, justifi-ably, be anxious about having to rely on Web services running on a Win-dows platform.

A "rogue," unscrupulous Web service could do untold damage. It could put viruses to shame when it comes to stealth, cunningness, and potency. A rogue Web service masquerading as a bona fide service can in effect commit hard-to-detect, white-collar crime in the context of IT processing. It can be the ultimate Trojan horse. The Web services of concern here are not those offering innocuous functions such as weather reports, zip code location, shipping charge calculation, or flight availability look-up. Given that any and all data sent back from a Web service have to be in the form of an XML document (i.e., a text file), a Web service cannot infiltrate the calling system by sending back a virus or worm. To put it another way, a Web service cannot send back an executable piece of code that can damage or compromise the calling system. The danger has to do with sensitive information being sent to a rogue or compromised Web service.

The most obvious example here would be credit card information. Let us assume that a Web service that has to do with some form of credit card processing is not what it claims to be—or is being run on a Windows server that has been infiltrated and compromised by a hacker. Now you have a situation where sensitive information is being sent out, unbeknownst, to an "unsafe" destination. The nature and threat of this danger are easy to see and really do not need much further elaboration.

Microsoft unintentionally further muddied the whole security landscape vis-à-vis Web services running on Windows platforms by trying to associate its single sign-on authentication system, Passport, with Web services. Passport is essentially a digital wallet system to obviate the need for the same user to be repeatedly authenticated by different service providers—particularly in the context of e-commerce, private portals, or subscription-based Web pages. It predates the advent of Web services and really is totally independent and orthogonal to Web services. Nonetheless, in early 2001, when Microsoft was trying to promote the then-fledgling concept of Web services to the public at large, it bandied about Passport as an enabler for Web services prior to the subsequent efforts of one of the potential authentication schemes for Web services.

Just as with the Windows servers, as well as the other Microsoft Web-related servers, hackers (and security experts) have probed and tested Passport and found it to be more porous than it really should have been—particularly given that toward the end of 2001 more than 200 million Web users had signed on to avail themselves of Passport's single sign-on convenience. Disquieting security flaws continue to be unearthed, with a major flaw discovered in the spring of 2003 that would enable a hacker to change the password of a Passport account and gain access to that account! The digital wallet aspect of Passport (i.e., a supposedly secure repository for maintaining credit card information needed for e-commerce) meant that the credit card information stored in their Passport "wallets" by unsuspecting Passport users could have been stolen. The security vulnerabilities found in Passport, which was meant to be a security-enhancing service, were another major, highly visible, and embarrassing black eye to Microsoft.

Although slow response times and unreliability are not as catastrophic as security flaws, one should now be able to easily extrapolate how a Web service running on a sluggish, crash-prone platform could undermine the delivery goals of a mission-critical application running on a high-power, high-availability system. This whole issue can be summed up by saying that there is not much point in implementing a high-volume, 10,000 concurrent user, mission-critical application on a "zero downtime" mainframe claimed to deliver a 99.999% uptime if this application relies on making constant calls to a Web service running on a Windows server that needs to be rebooted three times a week.

3.1.4   Circumventing the Windows server issue

If you are in any way concerned about Web services that are deployed on Windows platforms, the first thing that you have to do is determine whether applications that are being developed within your purview need access to such Web services. This is something that will have to be done on a case-by-case basis—each time your developers identify a function that is best addressed using an externally sourced Web service (unless, of course, you obtain all of the required Web services from just a few previously qualified and selected vendors and you know beforehand that they do not deploy any of their Web services on Windows platforms).

Typically an application developer will have to contact the Web service provider to ascertain the platform on which a particular Web service will be offered. As in the case with those offering Web site hosting, there could be scenarios where a Web service provider may offer the same service on different platforms—possibly with a price differential between them—but the bottom line here is that explicit contact with the service provider is invariably going to be the best way to establish on which platform a particular Web service is deployed—and what options there may be in terms of having that service offered on another platform.

When dealing with Web services for mission-critical applications, it would not be amiss to start thinking about service-level agreements (SLAs)—similar to what large corporations would have with their telecommunications provider and ISP to ensure that they receive a guaranteed minimum level of service. The use of Web services has not yet reached a point where this concept of SLAs is being widely bandied about, even though IBM has already done some pioneering work on this front relative to its Web Services Management Middleware project. One can, however, definitely see an emerging call for such SLA-based guarantees when it comes to mission-critical scenarios.

Sluggish or unreliable Web services could definitely result in lost opportunity costs (e.g., loss of business) in the context of mission-critical applications. Consequently, it makes sense to ensure that a Web service provider is willing to guarantee some level of performance and uptime—albeit at a cost. This would thus be the ideal mechanism and framework through which to ascertain the platform on which a Web service is being offered. It can also serve as a good litmus test to determine the service provider's level of confidence and commitment vis-à-vis that Web service.

The ideal workaround, if having a key Web service running on a Windows server is a concern, whether for security, performance, reliability, or scalability, would be to have the option of porting that Web service to a different platform. This, however, is the problem. Web services developed using Microsoft's popular software development tools, particularly the now heavily promoted Visual Studio .NET, tend to be Windows-specific. Some of these Web services, especially if developed using Microsoft's Java (i.e., Visual J++), C#, or C++, could conceivably be ported to other platforms by extracting the basic source code and "recompiling" it using a non-Microsoft compiler—provided that the Web service is not too heavily dependent on Windows-specific software technology such as Microsoft's COM components. However, such porting will by nature necessitate some level of rework of the original software. If the Web service is heavily reliant on Windows-specific content, rework may not be feasible or practical.

Another option that could be considered at this juncture is the overall ROI of rewriting the necessary Web service in-house, such that it can be deployed on a non-Windows platform. Though this would appear to go against the grain of gainfully reusing functionality developed by others, it has two hard-to-ignore virtues. The first, of course, is that it eliminates the concern about using a Windows-based Web service. The second is that the new software component developed in-house, being a Web service, could be marketed for profit to other enterprises that may also feel queasy about using a Windows-based service. If there are insufficient resources in-house to develop the necessary Web services, a variation on this theme is to find a contract software house, a consultant, or an application development company that would undertake the development as a revenue-generating proposition.

If porting to another platform or rewriting the Web service is not possible or justifiable, another alternative would be to acquire the rights to the Web service from its provider and deploy it in-house (i.e., behind the corporate firewall, so to speak) on a secure Windows 2003 server. At least this will enable you to have some level of control over performance, scalability, and hopefully also reliability.

The bottom line here is that those involved with mission-critical applications are justified in wanting to make sure that a Web service running on a Windows platform will not compromise the operational characteristics of their offering. However, the issues involved are not black and white. There are many shades of gray. Much depends on the exact circumstances of the calling application relative to that of the Web service. This section has addressed as many of these as possible and tried to put them all into perspective. There will be a lot of Web services that are only available on Windows servers. Do not dismiss all of them out-of-hand. Evaluate those that are of interest to you, on a case-by-case basis, and consider whether a service-level agreement might provide you with the assurances you need.

3.2   The .NET initiative

.NET, if Microsoft has its wish, is meant to be a dynasty. What Ming was to porcelain is what Microsoft wants .NET to be when it comes to Web services–inspired Web applications.

.NET is meant to encompass all of Microsoft's initiatives that pertain to XML, Web services, and post-Y2K e-business. With .NET, Microsoft is borrowing a concept that for so long was quintessentially IBM's. This is the concept of a "blueprint" or "marketecture" à la IBM's Systems Application Architecture (SAA) in 1987, the Networking Blueprint in 1992, or the more recent WebSphere "framework." .NET is in effect Microsoft's Web services–oriented SAA for the first decade of the twenty-first century—where, ironically, the one big difference is that IBM, a decade ahead of Java, was trying to promote the concept of applications that could run on disparate platforms, whereas with .NET Microsoft is assiduously promoting a platform-specific solution.

Figure 3.10   *Microsoft's depiction of .NET Framework as a "sausage machine" for churning out XML Web services.*

.NET is not a single product. It is an umbrella term, which, like IBM's WebSphere, spans a plethora of products—in this case Microsoft software offerings for clients (both desktop and mobile), servers, application suites (e.g., Microsoft Office XP), services, and software developer systems. .NET Framework is the program execution layer of .NET.

The .NET Framework, Microsoft claims, is the first software environment built from the ground up to provide native support for XML Web services, in addition to other more traditional types of applications, so much so that Microsoft has a graphic, as shown in Figure 3.10, which depicts the .NET Framework as a "sausage machine" for delivering Web services.

To realize the intended native support for Web services, .NET Framework is tightly and fully integrated into the latest Windows operating systems—namely, Windows 2003 Server family, Windows 2000 (with Service Pack 3 or 4), or Windows XP. It is thus a Windows component. The .NET Framework (which was at Version 1.1 as of June 2003) includes everything you need to run applications built using the .NET Framework, including the Common Language Runtime (CLR) and the necessary class libraries.

Having .NET Framework integrated into Windows thus obviates the need for a separate "application server" to run .NET-compliant applications and Web services. This is one of Microsoft's main value propositions for .NET—that is, the supposed elimination of costly middleware (e.g., IBM's WebSphere Application Server) to run Web services or applications making use of Web services. The problem here, however, is that .NET only supports applications and Web services developed using .NET-compliant products. It does not support Java applications. To run Java applications, especially J2EE-based Java applications, one would typically need to install a Java application server.

If an older Windows 2000 or Windows XP system does not have the .NET Framework installed, Microsoft provides a free and easy download of the .NET Framework 1.1 as a part of the now-standard "Windows Update" process. You can check whether the .NET Framework is installed on a Windows system by using the standard "Add or Remove Programs" control panel—as illustrated in Figure 3.11.

There is also a free, downloadable Software Development Kit (SDK) Version 1.1, which includes everything one needs to write, build, test, and deploy .NET Framework applications. This SDK 1.1 consists of documentation, application samples, command-line tools, and compilers. Since the

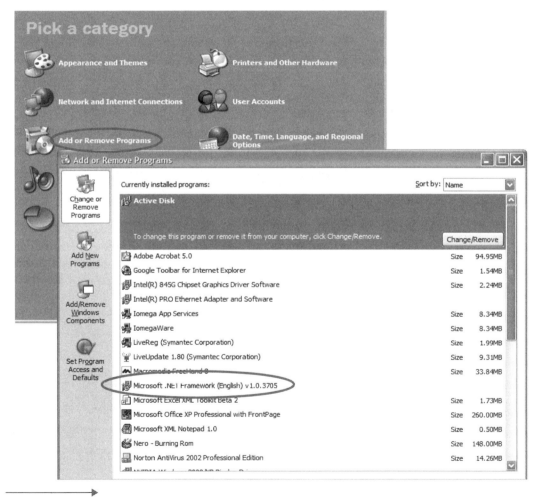

Figure 3.11 *Checking to see if the .NET Framework is installed on a Windows system using the standard Windows "Add or Remove Programs" control panel.*

.NET Framework 1.1 (or greater) is required to run any application, including Web services developed by others using a .NET Framework 1.1 (or greater) offering, it is best to have .NET Framework installed.

Microsoft describes the .NET initiative as being software that connects information, people, systems, and devices. Within that overall context, the .NET Framework becomes the programming model of the .NET environment for building, deploying, and running Web-based applications, smart client applications, and XML Web services. .NET, per Microsoft, will take care of much of the "software plumbing" (i.e., interfacing and necessary service location), thus enabling software developers to focus on the problem-solving aspects of their programs.

3.2.1   The composition of .NET

.NET, which spans clients, servers, application suites, and development tools, is made up of (at a minimum):

1.   The .NET Framework

2.   Developer tools

3.   A set of servers

4.   A repertoire of clients

5.   Application suites

6.   A group of services

The .NET Framework is .NET's universal application execution environment. .NET-centric XML Web services, as well as other applications, are tested, deployed, and run on the .NET Framework of a Windows system—whether that Windows system is installed on a server or client. On the server side, .NET is supported on Windows 2000 (with SP3, SP4, or later), and Windows 2003. However, support for .NET is also included in other related server products, particularly Microsoft's BizTalk Server and Microsoft SQL Server. In all cases, .NET functionality as it relates to executing, operating, and managing XML Web services and other Web-centric applications is integrated with the Microsoft server code in the form of the .NET Framework.

On the client side, .NET is embraced by Windows XP, Windows CE .NET 4.2 (for non-PC devices, such as cash registers, automated teller machines, and medical recording systems that require an embedded OS), and Windows Mobile 2003 for Pocket PCs. Note the absence of Windows ME and the still widely used Windows 98, but this makes sense. Windows

XP, based on the Windows NT code set, is indubitably the most stable and resilient release of Windows to date.

Until now, I was never a big proponent of upgrading Windows on client systems just because a newer version was available. However, Windows XP is so palpably superior that I am willing to concede that upgrading to XP, where possible, is worth the trouble and cost—and should typically result in a positive ROI within a year just from the minimization of "lost opportunity costs" (i.e., downtime), without even factoring in the inevitable increase in user satisfaction.

On the development tool front, the flagship Microsoft offering when it comes to .NET is the Visual Studio .NET—which in its latest incarnation is known as Visual Studio .NET 2003. Visual Studio, like all the other "point-and-click," "drag-and-drop" software development studios on the market, is a GUI-based integrated development environment (IDE). It has obviously been optimized to ensure developer productivity when developing Web services or other applications to be deployed to run on the .NET Framework. Visual Studio .NET is discussed in more detail next.

Microsoft, predictably, classes Microsoft Office XP as a .NET-compliant application. This is a bit of a stretch, but, to be fair, Microsoft, as earlier pointed out, has imbued significant XML capabilities into the pertinent applications—in particular, Excel and Word. Based on these criteria, one would have thought that Microsoft would have mentioned the XML Notepad as another .NET application, but Microsoft appears to have abandoned this freeware product, as mentioned in Section 2.7. One assumes that Microsoft and its partners will label other germane applications as being .NET-compliant down the road.

As of the summer of 2003, there were at least four Microsoft services that fell, albeit loosely, within the category of .NET-related services. These were as follows:

- .NET Alerts

- .NET Passport

- MSN Messenger Connect

- Microsoft MapPoint Web Service

Microsoft .NET Alerts has evolved from a real-time, e-mail-based change in flight status notification system (i.e., flight delayed or flight canceled) that Microsoft postulated in early 2001 as a part of its HailStorm initiative (discussed later). Since then, Microsoft has expanded this concept of real-time notification to encompass any type of high-priority, critical information (e.g., dramatic swing in the price of a stock, news on a merger or acquisition). Microsoft's .NET Alerts, as such, are time-sensitive notification messages that service providers can send to customers, in real time, at the customer's request—in the event that something of interest and value to that customer transpires. Not surprisingly, changes in flight status, including notification of possible upgrades, continue to be a major application for this service—with United Airlines, for one, supporting .NET Alerts. Users can receive .NET Alerts on their desktop computers through Windows Messenger (i.e., an "instant messenger" [IM] scheme), in e-mail, or on a mobile device, such as a phone or PDA.

.NET Passport, which is described in more detail in Section 3.4, is Microsoft's now star-crossed user authentication scheme to facilitate a common single sign-on to multiple Web sites, portals, and services. The goal of Passport, as with any single sign-on scheme, is to eliminate the need for users to maintain (and remember) multiple user IDs and passwords for different sites, applications, and services. Most other single sign-on schemes (e.g., IBM's Express Logon feature on its host integration products) focus on providing single sign-on at an enterprise or data center basis (i.e., on an intranet or extranet basis).

Passport, on the other hand, set out from the get-go to offer single sign-on across organizations, Web sites, and even countries. It was to be the strategic single sign-on scheme for the Web. According to Microsoft, at the beginning of 2003, there were more than 200 million Passport accounts (i.e., users) around the world—and more than 3.5 billion Passport-based authentications were being made each month. Nonetheless, Passport, always an obvious target for security attacks, has of late (i.e., 2002 onward) been beset by major, high-profile security exposures. Though Microsoft has scrambled to fix each of these incidents, it suffices to say that Passport's credibility continues to be undermined.

The Liberty Alliance Project was initiated in September 2001 by such super heavyweights as AOL, Sun, H-P, Novell, VeriSign, Sony, General Motors, American Express, Nokia, and Fidelity Express to provide an open, standards–based alternative to Passport. The problem here is that whereas Passport, for all its flaws, is a tangible, operational offering, the Liberty Alliance, at least as of the time of this writing, only deals in specifications and draft standards. Consequently, there is really no viable alternative to Passport. A single sign-on, despite its usefulness, may as yet be too premature for the Web. Though inconvenient, maintaining separate user IDs and passwords for different Web sites and services may still be the best, if not the only, option for those who value their privacy and are concerned about the security of their personal information.

Microsoft Network (MSN) Messenger Connect for Enterprises is in essence a variation of the .NET Alert services. It enables companies to interact with their customers in a "secure" and audit trail–maintained manner using MSN Messenger instant messaging (IM). Companies can gainfully use it to share time-sensitive information with their customers and process transactions in real time. All messages are authenticated so that recipients can be assured of their bona fide nature. All messages are also logged so that they could be audited in the future if there is ever a need to check a particular set of communications. Ironically, this might not be as attractive as it may first appear. Following all of the recent lawsuits involving corporations, including the antitrust case against Microsoft, where archived e-mail correspondence was unearthed to be used as evidence, many corporate executives have resorted to using IM as a "no paper trail" mechanism to communicate sensitive or provocative information.

Microsoft's nascent MapPoint Web Service is a good example of Web service technology in practice. It is a programmatic XML Web service for integrating maps, driving directions, distance calculations, proximity searches, and other geographic location–related intelligence into new applications. All of you are probably very familiar with the hot links to MapQuest (or equivalent) available on many Web pages when referring to a street address (e.g., a restaurant or hotel) or geographic location so that you can click on it to get a map of the area in question. MapPoint now offers this capability as a Web service, as opposed to a hot link, so that mapping services can be seamlessly integrated into new applications. This, as discussed in Chapter 1, is what Web services are all about.

3.2.2   The .NET Framework

The .NET Framework is now an important and strategic new integrated component within the Windows family of operating systems—whether for servers, PC clients, mobile clients, or non-PC "terminal clients" running an embedded Windows OS (i.e., Windows CE 4.2 or greater). Though it is the native execution environment for XML Web services and other Web applications, it is meant to be unobtrusive, to the point of transparency, as far as end users are concerned. End users will just be running a relatively new version of Windows (e.g., Windows XP or Windows Mobile 2003 Software for Pocket PCs). Most will not be aware that they also have .NET Framework running on their Pocket PCs or smart phones.

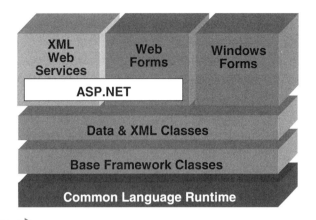

Figure 3.12   *The high-level architecture of the .NET Framework, per Microsoft, which is made up of the Common Language Runtime (CLR) and a .NET Framework Class Library.*

The .NET Framework, as illustrated in Figure 3.12, consists of two key subcomponents, namely:

1.   The Common Language Runtime (CLR)

2.   A unified set of class libraries referred to as the .NET Framework Class Library

CLR is a Windows-specific execution environment. You could even think of it as a virtual machine, à la a Java Virtual Machine (JVM) or Java container, but in this instance for .NET applications—including Web services. As with a VM or Java container, it provides all the common services required by .NET applications. Some of the key services provided by the CLR include language integration, security, memory allocation, process control, thread management, and unified error handling. It also provides development time services to applications being developed within the .NET Framework—particularly to facilitate cross-language integration.

Microsoft claims that it and its vast network of partners provide .NET Framework–compliant compliers for over 20 programming languages. These languages include C, C++, C#, COBOL, Microsoft Visual BASIC, FORTRAN, RPG, Pascal, Perl, APL, Python, and Microsoft Jscript. Microsoft also claims that over 350 tools are already available from third-party vendors to aid in .NET Framework–centric software development, including nearly 250 add-ons for the Visual Studio .NET.

The .NET Framework Class Library includes prepackaged software components that application developers can use to expedite and simplify their software development process and cycle. Software functionality available as base class components include those for input/output handling, string manipulation, security enforcement, networking, thread management, text processing, and GUI design.

The .NET Framework Class Library is made up of the following three key subcomponents:

1.   ASP.NET, Active Server Pages (ASP) software functionality to facilitate the development of server-based Web applications and Web services

2.   ADO.NET to provide XML-based database interaction, including search and translation functionality, through OLE DB, ODBC, Oracle, and Microsoft SQL Server interfaces

3.   Windows Forms software classes, which are made available to help developers create GUIs for smart clients

3.3   The pivotal .NET offerings

From a Web services perspective, the two pivotal .NET offerings will be:

1.   Windows Server 2003 family

2.   Visual Studio .NET 2003

The Microsoft BizTalk Server, scheduled for 2004, will also be important, particularly for e-business integration—but not to the same extent as Windows Server 2003 and Visual Studio .NET 2003. BizTalk Server can best be thought of as an e-business-specific .NET server whose forte is that of software component integration (via adapters), enabling multivendor interoperability and software modularization to promote Web services such as component-based application development.

BizTalk Server promotes e-business application development and application integration, in the main, via the provision of BizTalk adapters and BizTalk vertical (market) accelerators. Third-party integration and interoperability are realized using these adapters. There are BizTalk adapters from Microsoft for interfacing with IBM's MQseries, as well as popular application suites from the likes of SAP, PeopleSoft, and J. D. Edwards. There is even a Web services adapter that enables applications to interact with others using XML-specific Web services methodology. There are also a slew of non-Microsoft adapters for interfacing with other application suites and technologies, such as those from Siebel, Oracle, Ariba, and i2.

The BizTalk Server vertical (market) accelerators are targeted at specific industry sectors or industry applications. At present, the emphasis is on health care and manufacturing (as in SCM). These accelerators are meant to significantly reduce the time, cost, and effort associated with integrating applications within a specific sector (e.g., health care). There is also a generic accelerator for b2b applications.

The Windows Server 2003 family, which consists of the Standard Edition, Enterprise Edition, Datacenter Edition, Web Edition, and Small Business Server Edition, will, however, still be the primary platform on which .NET-based Web services will be deployed. This is only likely to change down the road, when Windows Server 200x, where x is most likely to be greater than 5, hits the market.

Windows 2003, referred to as WIN2003, is the latest incarnation of the Windows NT family of server OSs. Windows NT, where the NT stands for "new technology," was introduced nearly a decade ago. It was a big step for Microsoft. At that time Novell, with NetWare, dominated the LAN-centric PC server market. NT was good but never stellar. IT professionals at enterprises always agonized about its scalability and reliability. When these servers, as highly popular platforms for Web servers and e-mail servers, became exposed to the Web, security became the other overriding concern.

Though NT was never big when it came to data center–type IT applications, it was effective for small business and departmental-level server applications. This segment accounts for a large chunk of the overall server market. Suffice to say, Windows NT, last seen as NT 4.0 with Service Pack 6a, has been a phenomenal success, despite its known shortcomings—with the legendary "blue screen of death," so well known that it even gets mentioned by late-night TV comedians. Its biggest claim to fame was that it managed to successfully and conclusively usurp NetWare.

With Windows 2000, Microsoft tried to address some of the reliability, security, and scalability issues that still lingered with NT 4.0. Windows 2000, if nothing else, was significantly more reliable and resilient. As of June 2003, there was WIN2003. According to Microsoft, Windows 2003 takes the best of Windows 2000 and makes it better—specifically in the areas of scalability, security, performance, and ease of use. Microsoft's performance claims when it comes to WIN2003 indeed appear to be true. Third-party tests appear to indicate that file server functionality, on average, is roughly 20% quicker, whereas the new IIS 6.0-based Web serving, in general, appears to be at least 10% faster.

This improvement in performance is indeed good news vis-à-vis Web services, given that overall performance is one of the main issues at hand when considering a server platform for Web services that will be used by high-volume, mission-critical applications. In addition to software rewrites to improve the performance of core functions, WIN2003 addresses performance and scalability in two other ways:

1. Increased symmetrical multiprocessing (SMP) capability

2. Enhanced clustering support

The Windows Server 2003, Datacenter Edition, is capable of supporting 64-way processor partitions, each with up to 512 GB of RAM with the 64-bit version. The 32-bit version will support up to 32 processors and a maximum RAM size of 64 GB. This level of SMP capability, which is now similar to what is available on UNIX server platforms, provides horizontal scalability. Clustering, on the other hand, delivers vertical scalability, as well as failover protection. The Datacenter Edition will support up to 8-node clustering replete with dynamic load balancing and failover protection. Thus, it is fair to state that WIN2003 has also made a concerted effort to address the hitherto perennial scalability concerns. This is also encouraging in the context of Windows-based Web services for mission-critical applications.

Given the spate of widely publicized and credibility sapping security attacks on Windows platforms in the 2000–2002 time frame, it is not surprising that Microsoft devoted considerable efforts trying to make WIN2003 above reproach in this area. The jury, however, is still out on this, since WIN2003 is still very new and as yet to be deployed in volume. Nonetheless, WIN2003 is supposed to be the first Microsoft server that attempts to conform to Microsoft's avowed Trustworthy Computing initiative. It is said to meet the three sacrosanct "Ds" of the Trustworthy Computing initiative, namely:

1. Secure by design

2. Secure by default

3. Secure when being deployed

In terms of expanded security capabilities, WIN2003 includes a built-in firewall, integrated public-key infrastructure (PKI) management for digital certificates, Network Address Translation (NAT) support for even more secure Virtual Private Network (VPN) operation, and enhanced encryption support. However, the most noticeable security "overlay" with WIN2003 comes in the form of disabled and "locked-down" services. Many of the attacks on Windows servers over the Internet were realized by hackers exploiting services on the server that IT professionals did not even know were active—let alone vulnerable.

To prevent this, more than 20 services (e.g., Telnet, WebClient, license logging, NetMeeting remote desktop sharing, and so forth) are turned off, by default, when WIN2003 is first installed. Neither is IIS 6.0, the latest version of the popular Web server, automatically installed each time a WIN2003 is deployed. Instead, IIS 6.0 has to be explicitly installed and activated. Even then, it starts up in a locked-down mode with many "value-added" capabilities—for example, the ability to run scripts embedded in Web pages—turned off. The bottom line is that compared with its predecessors, WIN2003 at least sets out to be security conscious from the get-go. This is obviously good news, but IT professionals are unlikely to drop their guard until WIN2003, in large numbers, has been successfully running around the world for at least 2 years.

Whereas WIN2003 is the .NET-specific back end when it comes to Web services, Visual Studio .NET 2003, incontrovertibly, is the front end—as clearly demonstrated by Microsoft in Figure 3.10. Microsoft claims that by the spring of 2003, there were more than a million developers using Visual Studio .NET! That is plausible. As unequivocally stated at the beginning of this chapter, Microsoft's visual development technology, now epitomized by Visual Studio .NET 2003, is the choice of the masses when it comes to "cottage industry" application development—hence why it is ludicrous to think that Microsoft platforms will not play a pivotal role when it comes to the future of Web services. When you have a user base this large, it really is somewhat immaterial to harp on the idea that a Java IDE might allow you to build a comparable Web service with three fewer steps. That is really akin to telling the CTO of an enterprise with 5,000 Windows clients, all of them using Office and Outlook on a daily basis, that Linux is a more resilient OS.

In general, based on current PC technology, the system requirements for Visual Studio .NET 2003, as shown in Figure 3.13, are not overtly onerous. One could even say that they are somewhat reasonable, given the multilanguage support inherent with this product. It should also be noted that Visual Studio .NET 2003 includes built-in support for developing applications for mobile devices. The bottom line here is that for the foreseeable future, Visual Studio .NET 2003 and its successors will be the premier software development tool, within the Microsoft world, when it comes to XML Web services and new Web applications.

Minimum Requirements

Processor	450-megahertz (MHz) Pentium II-class processor, 600-MHz Pentium III-class processor recommended
Operating System	Visual Studio .NET 2003 can be installed onto any of the following systems: • Microsoft Windows® Server 2003 • Windows XP Professional • Windows XP Home Edition[1] • Windows 2000 Professional (SP3 or later **required** for installation) • Windows 2000 Server (SP3 or later **required** for installation) Applications can be deployed onto the following systems[2]: • Windows Server 2003 • Windows XP Professional • Windows XP Home Edition • Windows 2000 (Service Pack 2 recommended) • Windows Millennium Edition (Windows Me) • Windows 98 • Microsoft Windows NT® 4.0 (Service Pack 6a required) • Windows 95 (using Microsoft Visual C++® .NET)
Memory	• Windows Server 2003: 160 megabytes (MB) of RAM • Windows XP Professional: 160 MB of RAM • Windows XP Home Edition: 96 MB of RAM • Windows 2000 Professional: 96 MB of RAM • Windows 2000 Server: 192 MB of RAM
Hard Disk	• 900 MB of available space required on system drive, 3.3 gigabytes (GB) of available space required on installation drive • Additional 1.9 GB of available space required for optional MSDN Library documentation

Figure 3.13   *Minimum system requirements for all editions of Visual Studio .NET 2003, per Microsoft's Web site.*

3.4   **Microsoft's .NET passport**

As of this writing, it is safe and fair to say that Passport is under siege—and that its reputation as a secure, widely accepted single sign-on scheme is severely tarnished. As a single sign-on mechanism, Passport literally holds the keys to Web security. If the Passport service, which is run by Microsoft, is infiltrated and compromised, a hacker, in effect, gets an "open sesame" pass to roam the Web at will masquerading as another—to see what information, services, and even goods can be hijacked using preapproved validations activated by the single sign-on scheme.

Microsoft's .NET Passport home page is shown in Figure 3.14, which highlights the fact that it is a free service with Microsoft's proud claim that one can "Use one name and password to sign in to all .NET Passport-participating sites and services."

Passport violations can obviously result in e-commerce disruption, as well as identity theft. Credit card information could be at risk—though Microsoft now no longer offers the Passport Wallet service that maintained credit card and user information as a part of the overall Passport initiative. The Passport Wallet, with all those ready-to-use credit card numbers and expiration dates, was always an irresistible temptation to hackers. Thus, it was not surprising that a major flaw in Passport Wallet was exposed in late 2001. This flaw was so significant that Microsoft had no choice but to temporarily suspend the Wallet functionality. The Wallet capability is now no more. Rather than risk further exposures, and possible financial liability, Microsoft has totally withdrawn it. Today what remains of Passport is just the single sign-on capability, with the option to store some personal information so that one can receive personalized service at those sites that recognize and accept the information passed on by Passport.

Even without Wallet, Passport, when compromised, provides unscrupulous individuals with enormous amounts of unauthorized logon and service activation capability—especially with portals that will react and activate personalized services based on the personal information (i.e., cookies) passed on by Passport—enough to disrupt, if not severely damage, global trade. It could destabilize all aspects of e-business and e-commerce. Consequently, the U.S. Federal Trade Commission (FTC) felt obliged, quite rightly so, to intervene and check out Passport's security claims at the beginning of 2002, alleging that Microsoft made false security and privacy promises vis-à-vis the integrity of Passport!

On August 8, 2002, Microsoft entered into settlement with the FTC. The first paragraph of the FTC Press Release, which was entitled "Microsoft Settles FTC Charges Alleging False Security and Privacy Promises," reads as follows: "Microsoft Corporation has agreed to settle Federal Trade Commission charges regarding the privacy and security of personal information collected from consumers through its Passport Web services. As part of the settlement, Microsoft will implement a comprehensive information security program for Passport and similar services."

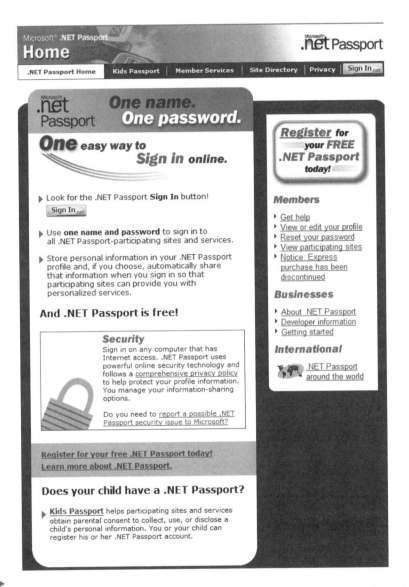

Figure 3.14 *Microsoft's .NET Passport home page at www.passport.net, which talks about the free, single sign-on service, as well as the powerful security features that are there to protect one's profile information.*

This press release then went on to categorize the areas where it felt that Microsoft had misrepresented what Passport did or did not do. This part of the press release, which can be found in its entirety at http://www.ftc.gov, reads as follows and is scathing to say the least:

According to the Commission's complaint, Microsoft falsely represented that:

- It employs reasonable and appropriate measures under the circumstances to maintain and protect the privacy and confidentiality of consumers' personal information collected through its Passport and Passport Wallet services, including credit card numbers and billing information stored in Passport Wallet.

- Purchases made with Passport Wallet are generally safer or more secure than purchases made at the same site without Passport Wallet, when, in fact, most consumers received identical security at those sites regardless of whether they used Passport Wallet to complete their transactions.

- Passport did not collect any personally identifiable information other than that described in its privacy policy, when, in fact, Passport collected and held, for a limited time, a personally identifiable sign-in history for each user.

- The Kids Passport program provided parents control over what information participating Web sites could collect from their children.

Microsoft's settlement with the FTC hinged on its pledge to do a better job protecting the information contained in Passport, as well as the submission of audits pertaining to the safety of Passport every 2 years for the next 2 decades. Microsoft faced $11,000 per violation fines, where each Passport account put at risk could be counted as a violation—and to this end it is worth remembering that Microsoft claims that there are more than 200 million active Passport accounts.

Since this landmark settlement, Microsoft has been forced to admit to two more serious vulnerabilities in Passport. The die has been cast. At the time of this writing, the FTC has yet to respond to these breaches. There is a possibility that the FTC could bring pressure upon Microsoft to close down Passport.

This, alas, is the somber background against which Passport needs to be discussed and evaluated. Microsoft launched Passport on October 11, 1999, as a means of streamlining commerce and communications on the Web. As such, Passport predates Web services per se by nearly a year when one takes into account that Microsoft, IBM, and Ariba did not get around to formalizing WSDL and UDDI until September 2000. To be fair, there was, and still is, a need for single sign-on and even digital wallets. E-commerce is not possible without explicit user identification and payment information (e.g., credit card number). Most portals, even public portals (e.g., Excite and MSN), now prefer users to log on (albeit even by using a cookie) so that they can enjoy a personalized service. This means that an active Web user is forced to maintain umpteen user IDs and corresponding passwords. This was the problem that Passport was going to solve.

Single sign-on has always been a double-edged sword. If you do not provide a single sign-on (or equivalent), users are forced to compromise security by either writing down all of their user IDs/passwords (where this list could be found by others) or to using "simple" (i.e., easy to guess) permutations. Single sign-on attempts to obviate this by enforcing stricter and tighter authentication—but only by doing this once. The problem here is that if the single sign-on is compromised, a hacker gets access not just to one application or service—but to a whole bunch of them. This is why many IT professionals have agonized over the years about the desirability of offering single sign-on.

Passport, with its security vulnerabilities, unfortunately shows single sign-on in its worst possible light. This said, it is important to remember that there is nothing that ties Passport with Web services—even Web services provided by Microsoft. Passport is but an optional user authentication scheme. Yes, Microsoft, at least in the early days, tried to continually intertwine Web services and Passport. This was marketing. There are, as discussed in Chapter 1, Web services–specific security standards now being formulated. There is also the multivendor Liberty Alliance project. Down the road, one has to believe that Passport is unlikely to be an industry-standard security scheme that is in any way endorsed as a preferred way to authenticate Web services users, whether consumers or providers.

3.5   HailStorm

HailStorm was unveiled by Microsoft on March 19, 2001, 6 months after it had been instrumental in launching WSDL and UDDI, and 9 months since its joint efforts with IBM to formalize SOAP. HailStorm was very much a trial balloon, one could even say a shot in the dark, to initiate a dialog with the marketplace on the possibilities of XML Web services. It also gave Microsoft an opportunity to expound on its then-nascent .NET strategy. It was a political manifesto on Microsoft's vision when it came to Web services and .NET.

HailStorm was an amorphous set of services, all of them in the form of Web services, meant to help developers create other Web services. They were as such best viewed as enabling Web services. Microsoft even talked about a

HailStorm architecture that would ensure that these enabling Web services could be seamlessly and consistently exploited by other Web services.

At the time of HailStorm's relatively high-profile rollout, Microsoft stated that several big names, including American Express, ClickCommerce, eBay, Expedia, and Groove, already had conceptual demos that made use of the HailStorm services and as such were showing an interest in this new .NET technology. However, much of these initial machinations involving HailStorm revolved around the then still somewhat new Passport and Passport Wallet. This was how the perception came to be that Passport was somehow intrinsically intertwined with all of Microsoft's Web services initiatives.

The quintessential HailStorm application touted by Microsoft involved the online purchase of an airline ticket—after one had profitably perused the Web for the desired schedules and ticket pricing. This is where Passport and Passport Wallet kicked in. Passport, with its single sign-on, would enable you to easily flit from site to site, accessing premium members-only services without the inconvenience of having to repeatedly log on.

The personal information maintained, and possibly even automatically accumulated, by Passport Wallet would then simplify service selection by remembering your preferences and habits. Finally, when you were ready to actually purchase a ticket, Passport Wallet would provide all of the necessary credit card and ticket delivery (e.g., street address) information—as well as seating and dietary preferences. This was pretty close to a utopian Web experience, but it did not end here.

When you made a reservation through HailStorm/Passport, HailStorm would actively monitor the "status" of that reservation on behalf of the user. If the flight was delayed or canceled, HailStorm, in theory, would notify you, in real time—à la today's .NET Alerts service. One could even take this scenario further. In the event of a flight cancellation, HailStorm, while in the process of notifying you of this annoying event, could also be diligently looking for alternate flights and preparing a list that you could conveniently look through. All of these are well within the realms of today's software technology.

The problem, vis-à-vis HailStorm, is that Passport Wallet, so key to the automated e-commerce applications envisaged for HailStorm, is no more. Furthermore, Passport itself is under threat. Consequently, the overall, grandiose manifesto of HailStorm has to be diluted. Rather than the interconnected, long-duration transactions originally envisaged, as in the flight reservation scenarios, what we are likely to see are more self-contained services such as .NET Alert and MSN Messenger Connect. The bottom line here is that HailStorm, though now no longer a mainstream, strategic initiative, did show the world some of the possibilities inherent with Web services technology.

3.6   Q&A: A time to recap and reflect

Q: Will Microsoft be a major player vis-à-vis Web services?

A: Yes, incontrovertibly. Microsoft already is one of the key players when it comes to Web services, and this role is unlikely to diminish in the coming years. Microsoft has had a hand in the development of most of the pivotal Web services standards (e.g., SOAP, WSDL, UDDI, BPEL4WS, WS-Security, WS-Coordination, and so forth). Furthermore, Microsoft is one of the four companies around the world providing a UDDI Business Registry (UBR) to facilitate Web service location and identification using UDDI. Microsoft's strategic .NET initiative is highly Web-centric, and Microsoft is already offering at least one bona fide programmatic Web service—namely, MapPoint Web Service. If all of this alone is not enough, Microsoft claims that more than a million developers use its Visual Studio software development methodology. One has to assume that some of these are already hard at work developing Web services using Visual Studio .NET—which Microsoft touts as a premier means for Web service creation. The bottom line here is that Microsoft, whether one likes it or not, will continue to be a powerful and pivotal mover and shaker when it comes to Web services.

Q: What is the relationship between Microsoft and IBM when it comes to Web services?

A: There is a beguiling love-hate, "co-opetition" relationship between Microsoft and IBM when it comes to Web services. As shown in Table 1.1, Microsoft and IBM have collaborated extensively when it comes to the development of the pivotal Web services–related standards. No other two companies have done as much as Microsoft and IBM when it comes to promoting and propagating the Web services vision and technology. However, this camaraderie ends markedly and abruptly when it comes to marketing Web services–related products. They are at loggerheads with each other. IBM is all Java and Microsoft is all decaf. Microsoft claims .NET is the best way to develop and deploy Web services, and IBM disagrees, vehemently.

Q: What is Microsoft's attitude toward Java?

A: Microsoft was never a big fan of Java. The hallmark platform independence of Java is of no real interest to Microsoft. It only supports and endorses one platform—that being Windows. Unlike IBM, Sun, and H-P, it is not a purveyor of computer hardware systems. Consequently, Microsoft always appeared to see Java, rightly so, as a threat to its platform-specific strategy. Lawsuits by Sun to get Microsoft to become more Java conscious have, in effect, backfired. Rather than agreeing to try to be Java compliant, Microsoft, at least for the time being, has decided to sever all ties with Java. In February 2003, Microsoft claimed that it will stop including a Java Virtual Machine (JVM) in all Microsoft products as of January 2004. It is also withdrawing its Java-oriented, but Windows-specific, Visual J++ product. The noninclusion of JVMs by Microsoft will not, however, mean that Java support will not be available on all popular Microsoft products. Various organizations, led by Java.com, are already providing proven and free JVM downloads for Microsoft products such as Windows XP.

Q: Are Web services developed with Microsoft's Visual Studio .NET 2003 platform independent?

A: No, they are not platform independent in terms of where they can be deployed and executed. Web services, as well as other applications developed with Visual Studio .NET 2003, will only run on Windows systems. This, however, does not preclude them from being used by applications running on other platforms. Consequently, the sacrosanct platform independence of Web services is not violated in that the Windows specificity of Web services developed with Visual Studio .NET are still freely interoperable with applications running on all other platforms.

Q: Are there any valid reasons to be concerned about Web services deployed on Windows servers?

A: This could be a potential concern if a Web service running on a Windows server is going to be repeatedly invoked by a high-volume, mission-critical application, serving tens of thousands of concurrent users, and running on a mainframe or large UNIX server. The performance, reliability, and scalability of the Windows server may not be adequate to match the 99.999% availability and response-time criteria demanded by the mission-critical application. Security vulnerability of the Windows server could also be a concern if sensitive information, such as credit card numbers, is to be sent to the Web service from the mission-critical application.

Q: Is it possible to port a Web service developed to be deployed on a Windows server to another platform (e.g., Linux or UNIX)?

A: This, to a large extent, is contingent on how much Windows-specific technology—for example, Microsoft COM objects or the ASP scripting scheme—is used by the Web service. In general, given enough time, money, and patience, any piece of software, especially if written in a popular high-level language such as C or C++, can be ported from one platform to another. In some cases, however, such a port might end up being akin to a total rewrite. The pivotal issue here is cost—and the cost will be greater as the amount of Windows-specific functionality increases.

Q: What is Microsoft's .NET?

A: .NET is meant to encompass all of Microsoft's initiatives that pertain to XML, Web services, and post-Y2K e-business. .NET is not a single product. It is an umbrella term, which spans a plethora of products—in this case Microsoft software offerings for clients (both desktop and mobile), servers, application suites (e.g., Microsoft Office XP), services (e.g., .NET Alerts), and software developer systems.

Q: What then is .NET Framework?

A: .NET Framework is the program execution layer of .NET. It is the programming model within the .NET initiative for building, deploying, and running Web-based applications, smart client applications, and XML Web services. The .NET Framework, Microsoft claims, is the first software environment built from the ground up to provide native support for XML Web services in addition to other more traditional types of applications.

Q: What are the major advantages of Windows Server 2003 over previous Windows servers?

A: Windows Server 2003 is faster than prior versions when it comes to file server and Web server transactions. It is also significantly more scalable in that it can support 64-way SMP configurations with up to 512 GB of memory. It also supports 8-node clustering with dynamic load balancing and failover protection. It is also meant to be more secure, by design and default, than prior versions, including Windows 2000.

Q: What exactly is .NET Passport?

A: .NET Passport is Microsoft's now-beleaguered single sign-on service for the Web. Passport obviates the need for repeated logons to various Web sites, applications, and services using different user IDs and passwords. With Passport a user is authenticated once per Web "session." Once authenticated, that user can automatically log on to Web sites and services that support Passport without needing to identify himself or herself again. Passport as such is a valuable and compelling service. There was an adjunct to Passport, known as Passport Wallet, which could be used as a secure, digital repository for credit card information. Passport-authenticated users could then use the credit card information contained in their digital Wallet for e-commerce transactions. Following security exposures, Microsoft has now withdrawn the Wallet service. The true security of Passport also continues be questioned, with people still managing to uncover disturbing holes in this supposedly highly secure service. Consequently, Passport's credibility is tarnished and its future is under a dark cloud.

4

Universal Description, Discovery, and Integration

UDDI is in effect the publicity arm for Web services. It satisfies the self-advertising mandate of Web services. It is a standardized process to publish and discover information about Web services (as well as other services) programmatically or via a graphical user interface, which would typically be Web based. OASIS, which took over the stewardship for this technology as of July 2002, has a subheading in the "UDDI.org" section of its Web site that states: "Universal Description, Discovery, and Integration of Web Services." Appending the two crucial words "Web services" to UDDI makes the goal of UDDI that much easier to perceive and appreciate.

A banner on that same OASIS Web page succinctly and elegantly highlights what UDDI is all about by saying: "UDDI is a key building block enabling enterprises to quickly and dynamically discover and invoke Web Services both internally and externally." UDDI as such is a universal, totally open, platform-independent mechanism for describing, discovering, and integrating (i.e., consuming) Web services, though it can also be used to describe and advertise non-Web services–related services (e.g., the 1-800 toll-free, mail-order telephone number for a traditional brick-and-mortar business).

The mission of UDDI is to provide a standard, uniform service, readily accessible by applications via a programmatic interface or by people via a GUI, for describing and locating the following:

- Business and organizations that offer various services—Web services being one such service

- Meaningful description of the services being made available by the businesses and organizations listed as service providers

- Technical information as to how to locate, access, and utilize a particular service

As with all things related to or inspired by Web services, UDDI is highly XML-centric. The core information model used by UDDI, irrespective of the kind of service being described, is based on an XML schema. This UDDI XML schema deals with the following four types of key information as it relates to service providers and the services they offer, whether Web services or otherwise:

1. Business information pertaining to a business or organization providing one or more services—which, in the context of the UDDI model, is referred to as the "businessEntity"

2. Sets of related services (e.g., a set of Web services concerning purchase order processing and another set concerning online inventory checking) being offered by a previously described business or organization—which are referred to as "businessService" elements

3. The binding information necessary to invoke and make use of a particular, previously described, service (whether a Web service or otherwise)—referred to as a "bindingTemplate" element

4. More technical information (or even a technical blueprint) about a service, over and above the binding information necessary to connect to it, such as pointers to detailed specifications, protocols used by the service (e.g., SOAP, HTTP, or SMTP in the case of a Web service), and possible type classification for that service—which is known as a "technical model" (tModel)

There is a prescribed hierarchy among these four data structures. This hierarchy is shown in Figure 4.1. These four core data structures have been a part of UDDI from the start. They form the nucleus of what UDDI is all about. Two other data structures have been added since, one in UDDI Version 2 and the other in Version 3. These two data structures deal with:

1. Relationships between business or organization entities (e.g., certification, alliances, membership, trading partnerships, and so forth), asserted to by one or both of those entities. This data structure, referred to as "publisher Assertion," was introduced with UDDI Version 2.

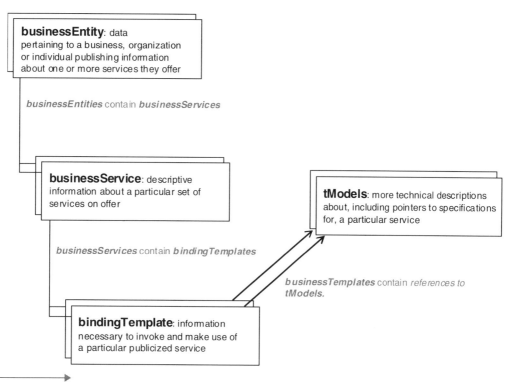

Figure 4.1   *The four key UDDI data structures, based on the model shown in various UDDI documents.*

2. Standing orders subscribed to by companies, organizations, or individuals requesting automatic notification in the event of a change to specific entities within the UDDI registry. This data structure, used for such automated change notification, which was introduced with UDDI Version 3, is referred to as "operationalInfo." It is used, at present, to provide a change-order subscription mechanism. Consequently, this data structure is also sometimes referred to as "subscription."

Figure 4.2 extends the data structure hierarchy shown in Figure 4.1 to show how these two additional structures come into play.

The UDDI specification per se describes the XML schema for this information model, SOAP messages to transport the XML-based information, and a set of APIs to manipulate and manage the UDDI data. There are two key APIs: the UDDI inquiry API, which can be used to search or browse through the information contained in a UDDI Registry, and the UDDI publication API, which enables programmers to create or delete the information

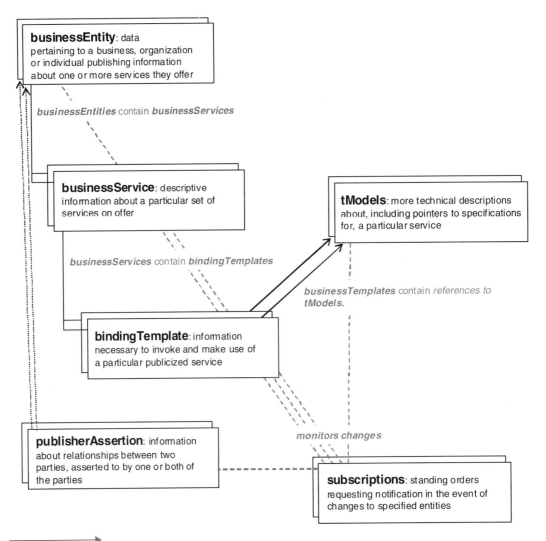

Figure 4.2   *The four core and original UDDI data structures shown in Figure 4.1 extended to show the two additional structures that were introduced in the later versions of the UDDI specification.*

structures within a UDDI Registry. Invoking a UDDI API results in one or more SOAP messages being generated. There are about 40 inquiry and publishing functions–related SOAP messages that can be generated against a UDDI-compliant registry by the UDDI inquiry and publishing APIs.

UDDI, however, is not just a sterile specification. The UDDI instigators—namely, Ariba, IBM, and Microsoft—made sure that there would also be publicly accessible sets of implementations of the UDDI specification. They also made sure that other companies would actively buy into the UDDI initiative. They were successful in that endeavor, too.

In September 2000, when UDDI was initially unveiled, it was endorsed by about 30 blue-chip companies, including Sun, Compaq, Dell, American Express, Merrill Lynch, and Nortel Networks. Today this number is in excess of 200. UDDI is also a standards-based interoperable service available for free on the Web—with both a user-friendly graphical interface and a programmatic interface that conform to the UDDI APIs.

The two pivotal standards exploited by UDDI are XML and SOAP. Note that WSDL is not one of the prerequisite standards used by UDDI. In reality there is no formal relationship between UDDI and WSDL. They do, however, complement each other. Given that WSDL can be used to describe the interface of a Web service, there is obviously a role that WSDL can play vis-à-vis UDDI. The tModel for a Web service could thus point to a WSDL description, as could the bindingTemplate.

UDDI enables enterprises, individuals, and software applications to quickly, easily, incisively, and dynamically locate and obtain Web services, as well as other services. Though originally intended as a global public service available via the Web, the UDDI specification does not preclude private and semiprivate implementations. The global public UDDI service, referred to as the Universal Business Registry or as the UDDI Business Registry (UBR), has been in operation since late 2000. The information maintained in the UBR can be accessed programmatically using a UDDI API, or via the Web-based user interface. Figure 4.3 shows SAP's Web-based user interface to the UBR. The equivalent Microsoft and IBM interfaces to the UBR are shown in Figures 1.7 and 1.8.

The UBR was originally run by the three companies that collaborated to develop the initial UDDI specification, which was published in September 2000 as Version 1.0. Today, the URB is being run by IBM, Microsoft, NTT Communications, and SAP—with Ariba, sadly, no longer involved. H-P, which was supposed to take Ariba's place when Ariba opted out, is also not a UBR player right now—partly due to the distraction of its merger with Compaq and partly to preclude the concept that the UBR was a wholly U.S. operation. In addition to the public Web-centric UBR, there is now also the concept of intranet UDDI implementations that serve just one enterprise, as well as extranet UDDI implementations that serve a group of enterprises collaborating with each other as partners.

Microsoft's new Windows Server 2003 includes a full-blown enterprise UDDI capability for realizing intranet or extranet implementations. IBM

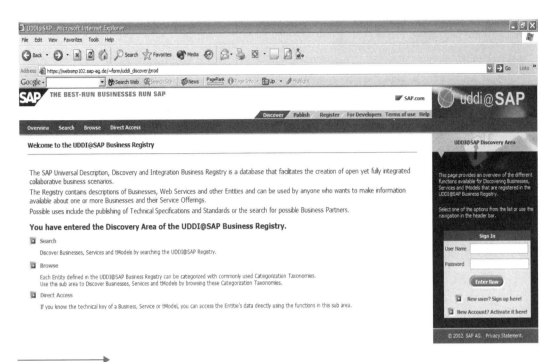

Figure 4.3   *The Web-based user interface to SAP's UBR node.*

also offers a similar capability in its new WebSphere Application Server Network Deployment (WAS ND) V5—which has subsumed the previously available WebSphere UDDI Registry offering. In addition, UDDI-related development tools, some of which include private UDDI registries, are available from a wide variety of other vendors, including BEA, Sun, Novell, Fujitsu, IONA, and Cape Clear Software.

With the ready availability of these products and tools, there will now be a surge in intranet and extranet UDDI implementations as businesses and organizations gingerly start to evaluate the potential and power of Web services by using them in-house and in conjunction with trusted partners for pilot projects. Enterprise UDDI registries will enable these "not-ready-for-prime-time-as-yet" Web services to still be properly categorized and represented, using standard UDDI mechanisms, within the privacy of intranets and extranets. Recognizing the appeal and applicability of enterprise UDDI registries, the latest UDDI specification, namely, Version 3, sets out to specify the concept of UDDI registry interaction (i.e., how private UDDI registries can coexist and interoperate with the public UBR).

UDDI, given what it sets out to do, is a directory. It is a directory of businesses and organizations that provide various services. Thus, it is not surprising that UDDI is invariably thought of as a kind of electronic telephone directory—particularly an electronic yellow pages of sorts. In reality, UDDI is more, much more, than just a yellow pages directory that is organized purely by service type. UDDI also is a white pages directory in that it lists service providers by name. Consequently, the information contained in UDDI is best thought of as being divided into three distinct categories, referred per telephone directory parlance as the following:

1. White pages

2. Yellow pages

3. Green pages

The white pages contain descriptive information about businesses and organizations providing various services. The business or organization name and a textual description of what they are will be included, where appropriate, in multiple languages. Contact information for that entity will also be included in terms of contact names, phone numbers, fax numbers, e-mails, and URLs. It will also list any known "industrial" identifiers, such as a Dun & Bradstreet (D&B) D-U-N-S nine-digit identification sequence, which uniquely identifies a particular business. The Thomas Registry identification scheme is another option.

The yellow pages, on the other hand, categorize businesses and organizations per industry-standard taxonomies. At a minimum, businesses and organizations will be categorized in terms of their industry, the products and services they offer, and their geographic location. The North American Industry Classification System (NAICS), which has superseded the U.S. Standard Industrial Classification (SIC) system, is one of the taxonomies that can be used to specify industry classification. Similarly, the United Nations Standard Products and Services Code System (UNSPSC) can be used to specify product/service classifications. UDDI is also innately extensible. Thus, it permits the use of new taxonomies provided that all users of the UDDI Registry have a means of interpreting the classification scheme used.

The green pages are where the technical information needed in order to use an available service is catalogued. The green pages, in effect, contain the information contained in the bindingTemplate and tModel data structures for a given service—as listed in a businessService entry (as shown in Figures 4.1 and 4.2). To wrap up this phone book analogy, note that the white pages contain the information found in the businessEntity data structures of a UDDI Registry, whereas the yellow pages categorize, per accepted taxonomies, the information maintained in the businessService data struc-

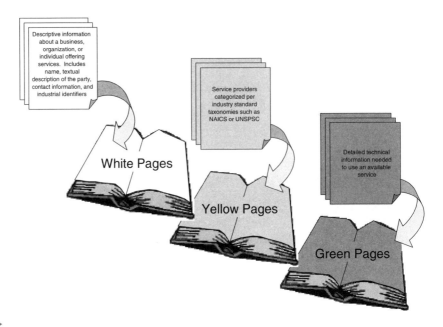

Descriptive information about a business, organization, or individual offering services. Includes name, textual description of the party, contact information, and industrial identifiers

Service providers categorized per industry standard taxonomies such as NAICS or UNSPSC

Detailed technical information needed to use an available service

White Pages

Yellow Pages

Green Pages

Figure 4.4   *The UDDI information content per the telephone directory model.*

tures. The green pages, then, augment the entries in the yellow pages by including the information found in the bindingTemplate and tModel structures for that particular service. Figure 4.4 depicts the UDDI information content in terms of the phone book model, whereas Figure 4.5 correlates the phone book model to the UDDI information hierarchy shown in Figure 4.1.

The bottom line here, for the time being, is that UDDI in general, and the public UBR in particular, are cornerstones of the overall Web services initiative. Given that it provides the search mechanism for locating applicable Web services, the eventual success and popularity of Web services are obviously going to be contingent, to a large degree, on the efficacy of UDDI. Given that the deployment and adoption of Web services have yet to live up to expectations, it is not surprising that the UBR, at present, is not brimming with germane entries.

Nonetheless the volume, the categories, and the amount of information per entry has been slowly but palpably growing since the summer of 2002. The availability of full UDDI functionality, as a standard, no-charge feature within Microsoft Windows Server 2003, will further increase UDDI awareness and promote enterprise-level implementations. Based on these trends, one has to assume that by 2010, professionals in the business community

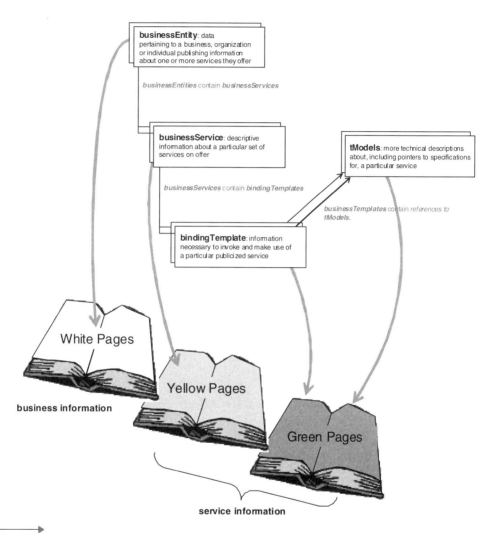

Figure 4.5   *Correlating the UDDI telephone directory model with UDDI's four core data structures.*

will often stop to ponder how they used to locate businesses and services prior to the advent of UDDI—in much the same way that percipient people today often wonder: How did we manage to do *that* before the Internet?

4.1   **The rationale and motivation for UDDI**

UDDI was conceived at the time that the dot.com frenzy was building to its crescendo. E-business seemed unstoppable as the long-sought-after panacea for expediting and streamlining commerce. Against this backdrop,

UDDI was initially envisaged as a standards-based, vendor-neutral mechanism for globalizing and simplifying Web-based, electronic b2b interactions. UDDI would automate many of the discovery and integration aspects of an eventual e-business transaction—particularly those having to do with locating the appropriate partners (e.g., suppliers in the case of an SCM scenario) and the mechanisms by which these potential partners conduct business.

UDDI would eliminate the guesswork and chance that was then an inherent part of e-business, given the lack of globally accepted directories for listing e-business participants. The main issues that UDDI intended to address included the following:

- How an enterprise, whether a business or organization, identifies other enterprises around the world that may be able to provide it with necessary services (or goods)

- How enterprises could describe themselves and the services they offered in a structured, systematic manner so as to attract prospects interested in such services

- How an enterprise could sift through and narrow down its list of prospective service providers to those that best fit its needs, based on specific criteria, given that unbounded searches on the Web could produce very large and unwieldy lists of results, considering the millions of enterprises that maintain a high-profile presence on the Web

- How one could obtain an accurate, detailed description of the services being offered by a selected enterprise

- How one could determine the mechanisms available for conducting e-business transactions with a selected enterprise

- How one could realize all of the above using programmatic interfaces—rather than having to do all of this manually using a user interface

UDDI strived to be as generic, inclusive, and flexible as possible when it came to the services it would accommodate. Though it wanted to promote Web services, it went to great lengths to ensure that its scope would not be restricted just to Web services. It wanted to facilitate all possible means of b2b, with Web services being just one, albeit a very strategic one, of the available mechanisms. The UDDI-based search and discovery process can thus be gainfully used, in theory, to realize the means for achieving any and all types of e-business transactions—hence, the reason why UDDI and the UBR are not limited purely to Web services.

Consequently, there is nothing to preclude a business that offers no Web services whatsoever from still publicizing the services it does offer (e.g., mail order service, consulting services, shipping services, import/export expertise, or financial services) on the UBR. This unalienable fact that UDDI is not restricted to just Web services is something that one should always keep in the back of one's mind when dealing with Web services– or UDDI-related issues.

The obvious question at this juncture is why the UDDI instigators, in particular IBM and Microsoft, did not pursue the option of extending the then-rampant Internet search engines (e.g., Yahoo!, Alta Vista) to include the envisaged UDDI functionality. Another option would have been to try to enhance one of the then-nascent e-business service registries, such as the ones being promulgated by WebMethods or CommerceOne, to fulfill the UDDI goals. The cynical and first blush answer to this would be that both these superpowers in the IT world, much to their chagrin, had "no skin" in search engine technology or in e-business registries. However, to be fair, search engine technology, then as it still is now, was unregulated, proprietary, and not based on any accepted standards other than HTML and URLs. The e-business registries were also proprietary and too closely associated with specific vendors.

The UDDI instigators wanted UDDI to be as standards based as Web services. Standards compliancy and, through that, vendor neutrality and platform independence were the main planks of the Web services platform. To sustain this value proposition, UDDI, as an enabling technology for Web services, also needed to be entirely standards compliant. In addition to the absence of relevant standards that governed their operation, some of the other key factors that made search engines unsuitable for the purposes of UDDI included:

- Search engines devoted all their efforts to locating and indexing just the URLs of the Web pages that contained keywords of interest. Search engines did not make any effort to identify other identification or contact information such as e-mail addresses, FTP sites, or even phone numbers. Search engines, even today, are very HTML-centric and URL specific. UDDI was seeking a more generalized search-and-discover mechanism.

- Search engines specialize in doing free text searches against unstructured data, whereas UDDI wished to promulgate structured data models.

- Search engines, in general, do not offer a no-charge, self-service, publishing mechanism whereby enterprises or individuals can enter specific information that they wish to publicize.

- Search engines, even today, do not typically offer programmatic access to the services they offer.

- Search engines have yet to become XML savvy.

Given all the previous limitations of search engines, it is understandable that the UDDI instigators wanted to create something that was considerably more compatible and consistent with the methodologies that they were in the process of introducing for Web services—in particular, SOAP and XML. At this juncture SOAP had just been introduced, so there were no SOAP-related standards per se that might have been of relevance for realizing UDDI. Therefore, there really was no other viable option than to create UDDI from scratch around SOAP and XML schema—and then put it forward as a proposed standard. That is exactly what happened.

At this point, those who are familiar with other directory schemes may be wondering, quite legitimately, why the OSI directory standard X.500 or the Lightweight Directory Access Protocol (LDAP), its equivalent in the TCP/IP world, could not have been used to achieve the goals of UDDI. The reality here, however, is that UDDI is meant to be at a higher level, a more logical level, than these two directory setup and directory access–oriented standards.

The parallel here is that of SOAP being developed as a transport-agnostic messaging scheme that can be used on top of HTTP, RPC, TCP, SMTP, FTP, message queuing, and so forth. Similarly, UDDI set out to define XML schema-based data models and APIs that generate SOAP messages, which, in theory, could be implemented on top of a standard directory scheme. Thus, it is indeed possible to build a fully conformant UDDI Registry on top of LDAP or X.500—and there are indeed specifications on the Web as to how such implementations can be realized. BEA even offers an enterprise implementation solution built on top of LDAP. That said, it is common knowledge that the UBR nodes, at present, are implemented using popular relational database systems (e.g., DB2 in the case of IBM).

Given this background, the advantages that UDDI bestows upon the global business community at large can be summarized as follows:

1.   Provide businesses, organizations, and even individuals with an unprecedented, no-charge, totally egalitarian mechanism to showcase all of their services in a systematic way to the entire

world—thus enhancing their market reach, competitiveness, marketing efficacy, and overall business prospects

2. Provide a very structured and consistent mechanism for locating and obtaining necessary details about pertinent services available on the global market

3. Facilitate businesses in identifying prospective b2b partners

4. Enable service providers and services to be registered, as well as located and invoked, using standardized, programmatic interfaces, thus bolstering the electronic infrastructure for the next generation of e-business

5. Simplify and streamline e-business-related software integration by ensuring that access to all of the pertinent technical information is available over the Web via a standard mechanism

4.2 The UDDI model

The "UDDI Version 3 Feature List" document, which was published by UDDI.org in mid-2002, starts off with this pithy (but uncharacteristically Web services–centric) description: "UDDI Version 3 builds on the vision of UDDI: a 'meta-service' for locating Web services by enabling robust queries against rich meta-data." Note that the term *meta* gets used not once but twice in this somewhat short description, with the first mention, intentionally or otherwise, having two very appropriate and germane connotations in the context of UDDI.

Technical "Webizens," whose lives revolve around the Web, will immediately interpret "meta-data," in this context, as referring to it being machine readable—in other words, data that are programmatically accessible, or in this case data that are programmatically searchable. This is consistent with the W3C's definition of meta-data, which happens to be: "Meta-data is machine-understandable information for the Web."

It also ties in with HTML's <META> tag, which enables one (among other things) to specify Web site identification and keyword information to help search engine Web crawlers to more easily categorize and index that Web page. Again, the concept here is that of automatic, programmatic searches. This programmatic aspect, as indicated by this meta-data reference, as should now be clear, is a fundamental plank of UDDI.

The prefix "meta," however, has a more traditional, pre-Web connotation. It is used to denote a description that is one level higher than the word being prefixed. Thus, if "x" is some entity, then meta-x is a description of "x." Therefore, a metasyntax is a syntax for describing other syntaxes. Similarly, a meta-language is a language that can be used to describe the makeup of other languages.

Hence, this is why XML is referred to as a meta-markup language. It allows one to describe the composition of other markup languages or, more commonly, to describe data that would otherwise be annotated with another, lower-level markup language. This now brings us to UDDI being a "meta-service." Given that UDDI is modeled around APIs that generate

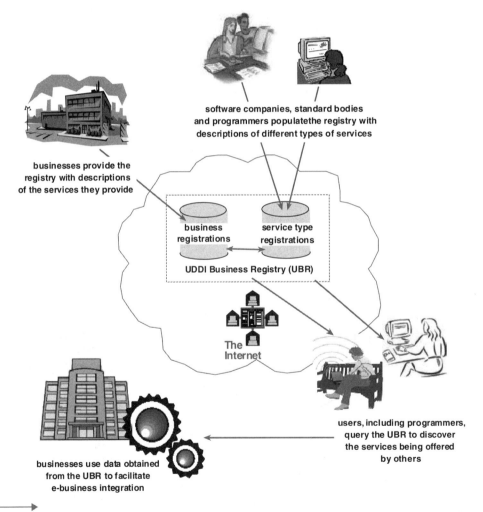

Figure 4.6   *A simplified and rationalized version of the original "How UDDI V1 Works" model postulated by UDDI.org in September 2000.*

SOAP messages, UDDI definitely falls into the category of machine-understandable service—if one were to extrapolate the W3C meta-data definition to cover meta-service.

However, UDDI, being a meta-service, also alludes to it being a service for locating other services—particularly Web services. Thus, this new mission statement, included with a UDDI Version 3 must-read overview document, hits the nail on the head quite squarely by highlighting the "service about other services" and programmatic aspects of UDDI. Relative to this backdrop, the initial UDDI model postulated with UDDI V1, in September 2000, is shown in Figure 4.6, whereas Figure 4.7 shows the multiregistry structure that is likely to be common in the future. This basic model still holds true for the UBR. The one big difference that has taken place since, particularly with UDDI V3, is the concept of the UBR being augmented by private and semiprivate UDDI registries. However, the non-UBRs also still conform to the overall precepts of the original model, albeit

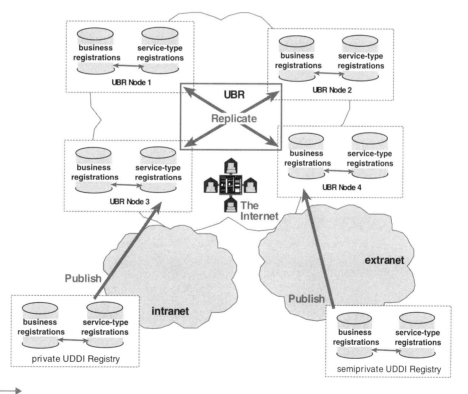

Figure 4.7   *Post-2003 UDDI scenarios, where the UBR will be complemented by affiliated private and semiprivate UDDI Registries.*

with less external entities participating in populating, categorizing, and interrogating a given private or semiprivate registry.

4.2.1   UDDI data structures

The UDDI information model is composed of instances of persistent data structures. A persistent data structure is one that automatically preserves its old versions. With a persistent data structure, one can make changes to the structure without destroying the old version. Thus, all versions of the structure persist. This enables previous versions of the structure to be queried, in addition to the latest version. The use of persistent data structures by UDDI means that one could have access to different versions of a service rather than just to the most recent.

UDDI's persistent data structures are referred to as "entities." An "entity" in XML is a special unit of storage. Entities are the basic building blocks of an XML document. Though UDDI does not make explicit reference to this connection, it is implied and will be appreciated by those familiar with XML. The UDDI information model is said to be composed of instances of six core entity types. These entity types, which are shown in Figure 4.2, are as follows:

1.   businessEntity

2.   businessService entity

3.   bindingTemplate entity

4.   tModel entity

5.   publisherAssertion entity

6.   subscription entity

All these entities are represented in XML, with each structure corresponding to predefined XML elements and XML attributes. They are stored, in a persistent manner, in one or more UDDI nodes. Each entity acquires the type of its outermost XML element.

There is a very definite and immutable hierarchy between these six UDDI data structures, as depicted in Figure 4.2, though if one wants to be ultra-pedantic, one would claim that this hierarchy relates to just the four original UDDI V1 structures, with publisherAssertion and subscription being more in the nature of "flags" or references that apply to the other structures. Each business or organization described in a UDDI Registry exists as a separate instance of a businessEntity data structure. Similarly, each service offered by a business or organization is maintained as a separate instance of data.

The fixed hierarchy between the UDDI data structures also results in an automatic, corresponding containment relationship between these structures. Thus, the businessEntity structure contains one or more unique businessService structures, whereas each businessService structure, in turn, contains specific instances of bindingTemplate data. The bindingTemplate structures will contain information that includes pointers (or references) to specific instances of tModel structures.

Within the UDDI hierarchy, no single instance of one of the core structure types is ever contained by more than one parent structure. Thus, as clearly depicted in Figure 4.2, only one specific businessEntity structure will ever contain information about a specific instance of a businessService structure. At this juncture it is best to look at a specific data structure in detail so as to reinforce what has been discussed so far—as well as to provide a basis for discussing a set of new UDDI concepts and constructs. Figure 4.8 shows the detail composition of the businessEntity structure. Figure 4.9 shows how an instance of data for a particular service provider (in this case IBM), as maintained per this structure, would be presented to a user of a UBR node.

Most of the elements in the businessEntity structure, such as "name," "contacts," "discoveryURLs," "businessServices," and so forth, are self-explanatory. Some, in particular "identifierBag" and "categoryBag," can,

```
<element name="businessEntity" type="uddi:businessEntity" />
<complexType name="businessEntity">
  <sequence>
    <element ref="uddi:discoveryURLs" minOccurs="0" />
    <element ref="uddi:name" maxOccurs="unbounded" />
    <element ref="uddi:description" minOccurs="0" maxOccurs="unbounded" />
    <element ref="uddi:contacts" minOccurs="0" />
    <element ref="uddi:businessServices" minOccurs="0" />
    <element ref="uddi:identifierBag" minOccurs="0" />
    <element ref="uddi:categoryBag" minOccurs="0" />
  </sequence>
  <attribute name="businessKey" type="uddi:businessKey" use="required" />
  <attribute name="operator" type="string" use="optional" />
  <attribute name="authorizedName" type="string" use="optional" />
</complexType>
```

Figure 4.8   *The businessEntity structure, as defined in the "UDDI V2.03 Data Structures Specification," in relatively easy-to-follow XML schema notation, showing which elements or attributes are required (i.e., use="required"), those that can be repeated (i.e., maxOccurs="unbounded"), and those that are optional (i.e., minOccurs="0").*

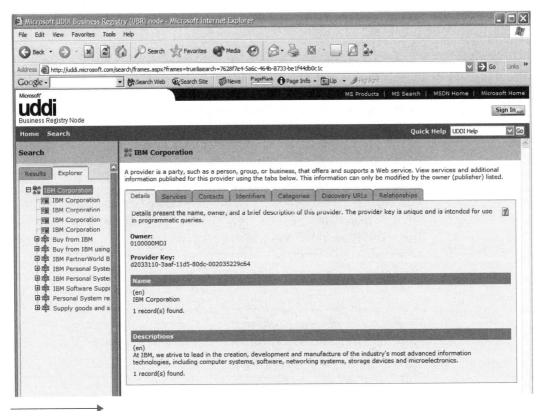

Figure 4.9   *The business provider information for IBM, as it appears in Microsoft's UBR node, illustrating how data maintained in a businessEntity structure, as shown in Figure 4.8, get utilized. The long, hexadecimal Provider Key, which appears near the middle of the Web page, corresponds to the unique business key identifier for this entry. Also note the tabs for services, contacts, identifiers, categories, and discovery URLs, which correspond directly to elements within the businessEntity structure. The Name entry, which appears after the first blocked-out horizontal bar, in this instance, only has one entry— and that is in English, as denoted by the (en). It would have been possible to have multiple entries here.*

however, be somewhat obscure or misleading. The postfix "Bag," in this case, was probably not the best word to use in this context. The term "bag" in this context strives to convey that it is possible to have a mixed list (i.e., a mixed bag) of identifiers or categories—albeit with both of these lists being optional. What is listed in the identifierBag are accepted industrial identification "numbers" as D-U-N-S, nine-digit identification codes. Figure 4.10 shows the D-U-N-S identifier for IBM as it appears in Microsoft's UBR node.

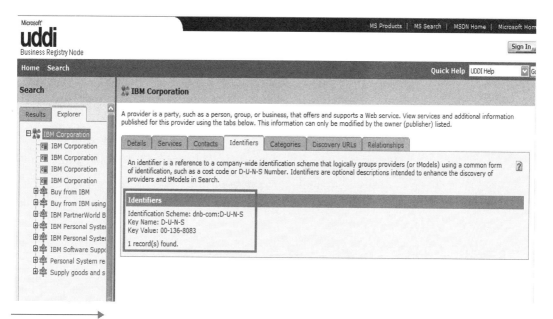

Figure 4.10   *The D-U-N-S, nine-digit identification for IBM shown in the Identifiers tab as it appears within IBM's entry at Microsoft's UBR node.*

Business or organization categories as they relate to a yellow-page taxonomy are listed in the categoryBag. Figure 4.11 shows the start of the list of 170 categorizations that IBM lists for itself using a combination of NAICS and UNSPSC codes. IBM's comprehensive list of categorizations of what it does ranges from "optical jukebox server software" to "sales financing." It also includes the UNSPSC codes for "spreadsheet software," "word processing software," and "presentation software."

All of these categorizations are germane, and one has to applaud IBM for its diligence in coming up with all of these codes. However, if you look at Microsoft's listing of categories, you will be surprised just to find one! That is the NAICS code for a software publisher. IBM happens to list that one, too. This highlights one of the unintended, but inevitable, shortfalls of UDDI. UDDI is unregulated, self-policing, and essentially unaudited.

The completeness and accuracy of the entries are left entirely to the discretion, professionalism, and motivation of the business or organization entering the data about itself. Until Microsoft gets around to updating its list of categorizations, there will be the irony that somebody doing a UDDI query for providers of word processing software will find IBM as a search result, but not that of the undisputed market leader Microsoft!

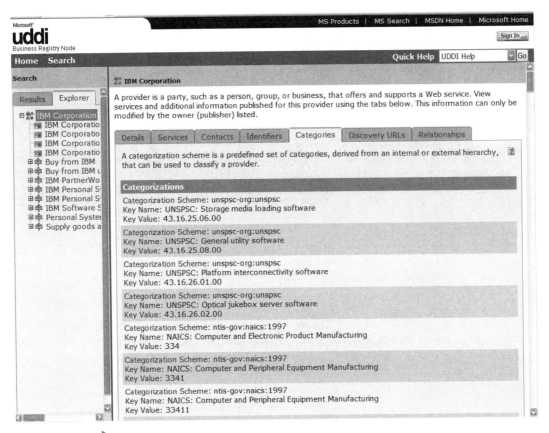

Figure 4.11   *The start of the 170 categorizations IBM lists for the services and products it offers using a combination of NAICS and UNSPSC codes. On the other hand, Microsoft, uncharacteristically self-effacing, only lists one category—that being the NAICS "51121" code for a "software publisher."*

4.2.2   UDDI keys

Each entity in a UDDI Registry, whether a business, a service, a service binding information, or a tModel, is assigned a specific UDDI identifier or UDDI key. An example of a UDDI key, which is actually my consulting services–related entry in the UBR, would be:

```
uddi:E05BE6A0-C043-11D7-9B41-000629DC0A53
```

Figure 4.12 is a screen shot from IBM's UBR node showing the businessEntity entry for "Anura Guruge," with the above key prominently displayed as the first item of information—albeit not showing the mandatory "UDDI" key. Compare this businessEntity presentation à la IBM with that shown in Figure 4.9, which depicts how such information is presented by Microsoft. This is something that you have to get used to when dealing with UDDI implementations—including the global UBR.

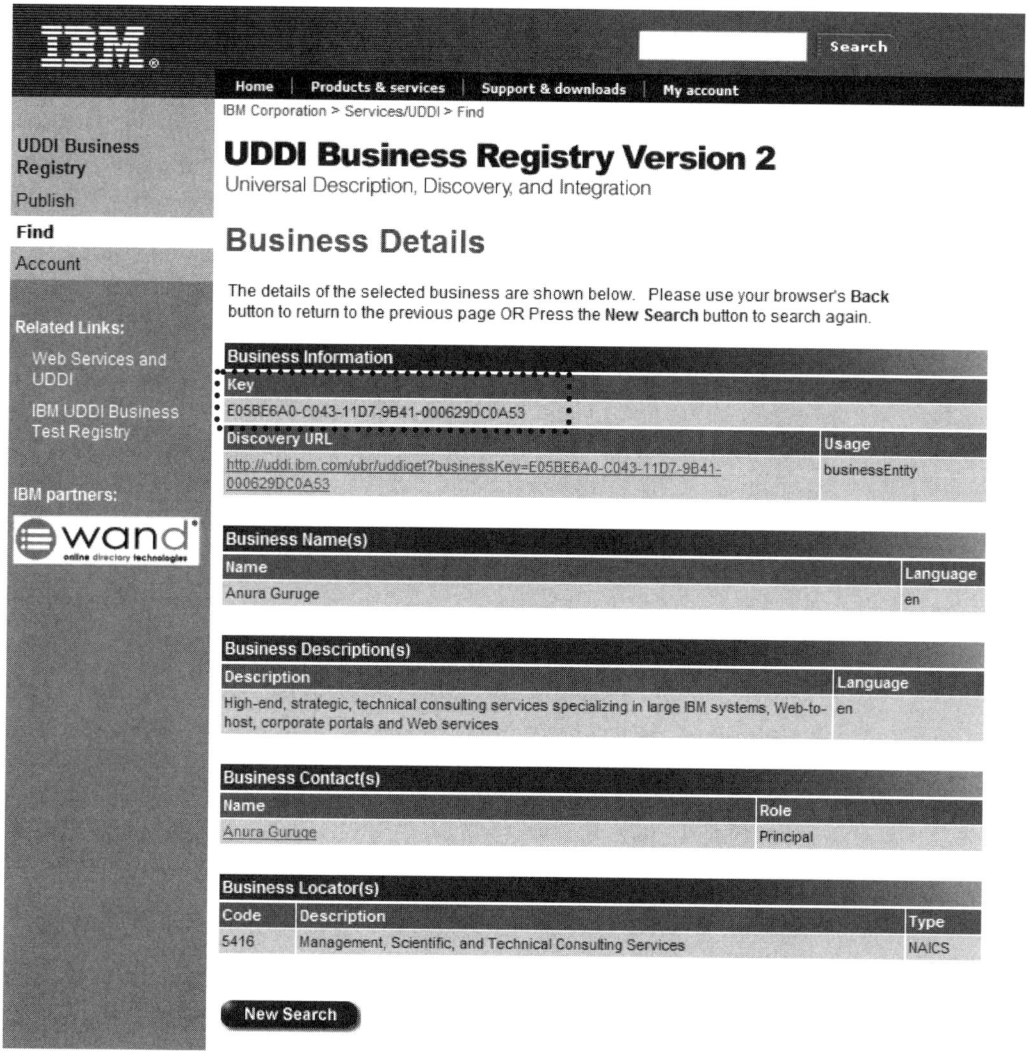

Figure 4.12   *A businessEntity presentation for another service provider, in this case for Anura Guruge, as displayed on IBM's UBR node, showing the 32-digit hexadecimal key for this entry. Compare this presentation with how Microsoft displays businessEntity information, shown in Figure 4.9, and note that although IBM just refers to the UDDI key as the "key," Microsoft calls it the "Provider Key" and uses lowercase to display the hexadecimal code, whereas IBM opts for the more traditional uppercase.*

The UDDI specification only deals with the information models, the APIs, the XML schema, and the SOAP messages. It does not talk about implementation details, so each UDDI implementation, including the various nodes that make up the global UBR, can have a different look and feel. However, all nodes of the UBR, given that they are working with the same set of information, uniquely identified by the UDDI keys, will always present the same information content—as well as information instances.

The UDDI key uniquely identifies that entity, for the duration of its existence, within the UDDI Registry. The persistence of UDDI data is related to the use of these unique keys. In the case of the UBR, all the nodes that make up the UBR will use and reflect the same UDDI key for a specific instance of information, given that all the nodes that make up the UBR work in concert when it comes to the information maintained by the UBR.

The "Provider Key" in Figure 4.9 is also an example of a UDDI key—in this case the key to this particular instance of IBM's businessEntity information. Figure 4.13 shows IBM's entry, as displayed on IBM's UBR node as opposed to Microsoft, to confirm that the provider key is still the same irrespective of the UBR node being used—though it looks different because Microsoft displays the hexadecimal digits in lowercase per the wont of XML and the Internet, whereas IBM, the godfather of hexadecimal notation since the early 1960s, opts for the more common uppercase-only representation. This is another example of how implementation details will vary from node to node, thus giving some users pause for thought if they skip from one implementation to another. UDDI keys, as with all XML-related entities, are, nonetheless, case sensitive, though this case sensitiveness does not apply to whether hexadecimal digits appear in lowercase or uppercase, given that these are in reality numeric digits, though shown using letters.

A UDDI Registry assigns one of these unique identification keys when a new registry entry is first published (i.e., saved). Once assigned, a UDDI key can be used at any later time to incisively access that specific instance of data—on demand. Prior to UDDI V3, all UDDI keys had to be generated by the "publishing" UDDI node to ensure the uniqueness of each key. UDDI nodes generated these unique keys in the form of Universally Unique Identifiers (UUID). A UUID, also called a Globally Unique Identifier (GUID), is a scheme that permits resources to be uniquely named over time and space.

UUIDs were originally created for use with remote procedure call (RPC) mechanisms in the context of the Network Computing System (NCS) initiative of the 1980s. This RPC mechanism was later adopted by the Open Group's Distributed Computing Environment (DCE) and further

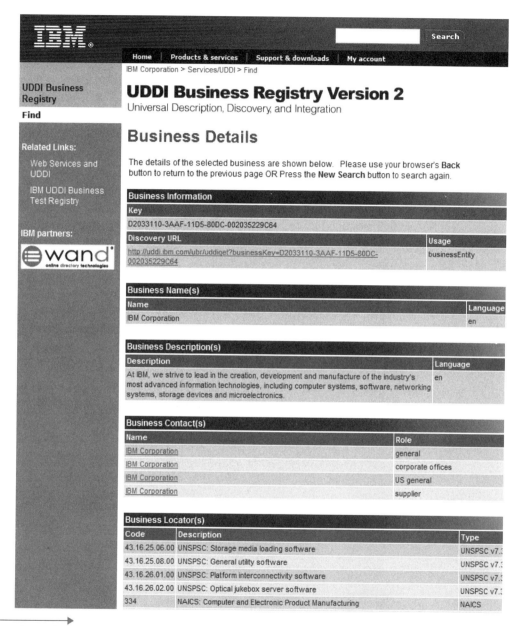

Figure 4.13   *BusinessEntity display for IBM, at IBM's UBR node, confirming that the UUID key for this entry is exactly the same as that shown in Microsoft's UBR node, per Figure 4.9, with IBM, however, displaying the hexadecimal digits in uppercase versus the lowercase depiction preferred by Microsoft. Also note that IBM's presentation includes the business description, as well as the categorizations (i.e., Business Locator[s]), and that these categorizations are listed in the same order shown in Figure 4.11.*

formalized by ISO within the framework of the once-rampant Open Systems Interconnection (OSI) model as ISO standard: ISO/IEC 11578:1996.

A UUID is 128 bits long. It can thus be represented by 32 hexadecimal digits, given that each hexadecimal digit corresponds to 4 bits. The UUIDs used as UDDI keys are depicted as 32-digit hexadecimal sequences by the current UBR implementations, as illustrated in Figures 4.9, 4.12, and 4.13. A UUID is guaranteed to be different from all other UUIDs generated until 3400 A.D., or, worst case, still likely to be extremely different from any other even if the UUID generation algorithm is not optimally implemented.

The algorithm used to generate UUIDs relies on a combination of hardware addresses (derived from IEEE 802 MAC addresses uniquely assigned to each and every LAN adapter), timestamps, and random seeds. It is the use of timestamps that results in the caveat that the uniqueness of UUIDs is only guaranteed up until 3400 A.D.! The 32-hexadecimal digit UUIDs, the only type of keys available with UDDI V1 and V2, are not well suited for use by people. They are arbitrary, unwieldy, and impossible to remember. With UDDI V3, it is possible to have keys that are considerably better suited for use by people. The creator (i.e., publisher) of a UDDI entity can even request a particular key or a type of key. These so-called "publisher-assigned keys" are one of the major new features of UDDI V3.

With V3 it is now possible to have so-called "domainKeys" in addition to the prior "uuidKeys." Domain keys are based on the now-commonplace Internet domain names. Since domain names have to be unique, keys based on domain names can also maintain UDDI's requisite individualism. A domain name–based UDDI key would look like this:

```
uudi:acmecompany.com:businessRegistration
```

Thus, a domain name–based UDDI key for my businessEntity could be:

```
uddi:inet-guru:AnuraGurugeBusinessName
```

Domain name–based UDDI keys are obviously much more flexible and meaningful than uuidKeys. However, the UDDI specification leaves as an implementation option whether a given UDDI Registry has to support domainKeys. In addition to these two orthogonally different key types, it is now also possible to have what are referred to as "derived keys." A derived key has either a uuidKey or a domainKey as its base (i.e., its start), but has in addition an alphanumeric ASCII character string, or arbitrary length, appended to it. This, especially in the case where a uuidKey is the base, provides further flexibility when it comes to UDDI key assignment.

The growing trend toward having enterprise UDDI registries, whether private or semiprivate, augmenting the UBR, does complicate the management of UDDI keys—especially if domainKeys are in use. The issue has to do with UDDI publishers that wish to copy the entire contents of a UDDI entity entry from one UDDI registry (e.g., private) to another while preserving the key assigned to the original entity. UDDI V3 includes a capability known as "entity promotion" to cater to such scenarios. With entity promotion, a UDDI publisher is permitted to propose the existing key for an entity as the preferred key for that entry. It is, however, left to the implementation and the exact policies of a given registry as to whether the new registry has to acquiesce to this request.

To facilitate publisher-assigned keys, in particular entity promotion scenarios, V3 introduces the concept of root and affiliate UDDI registries. The use of a root UDDI registry by multiple affiliate registries ensures that the affiliate registries can readily share data among themselves, relative to that root, and still make sure that they maintain unique UDDI keys, since this would be arbitrated by the root. It is suggested that the UBR should be considered, whenever possible, as the root registry in such distributed registry scenarios. In this case the UBR, through the use of either uuidKeys or domainKeys, will ensure the uniqueness of the necessary UDDI keys.

4.2.3   UDDI APIs

The UDDI inquiry and publication APIs, as mentioned earlier, are key to any UDDI implementation. They control the core functions related to publishing and locating entities in a UDDI Registry. Though presented so far as single APIs for simplicity, the UDDI specification treats all APIs as consisting of sets. It then further splits these sets into node versus client API sets. The API sets specified in V3 are thus as follows:

UDDI Node API Sets	*UDDI Client API Sets*
1. UDDI Inquiry	1. UDDI Subscription Listener
2. UDDI Publication	2. UDDI Value Set
3. UDDI Security	
4. UDDI Custody Transfer	
5. UDDI Subscription	
6. UDDI Replication	

The functionality made possible by these UDDI API sets can be characterized as follows:

- UDDI Inquiry: This API set is what a programmer would use to locate and obtain details on specific entries stored in a UDDI Registry. This API set supports three distinct patterns of inquiry to address all germane inquiry modes for this type of data. The three types of inquiry patterns supported are referred to as browse pattern inquiry, drill-down pattern inquiry, and invocation pattern inquiry. A browse pattern inquiry, as the name alludes, permits one to conduct an inquiry starting with a broad categorization and then refining the inquiry to more specific criteria as each set of search results is displayed. A drill-down inquiry involves using a UDDI key, obtained via a browse pattern inquiry or by other means (e.g., using a domain-Key), to access a specific entity. An invocation pattern inquiry is typically used in the context of bindingTemplate entries for Web services. As suggested by the name, it is used when the application invoking this search is happy to have the Web service located by the search to be dynamically invoked at the end of the search, so this becomes a search-and-activate operation.

- UDDI Publication: This API set is used to publish, update, and delete information contained in a UDDI Registry. It is left to the implementation policies of a particular registry to decide which node of a particular UDDI registry is used by a publisher to publish a given set of data. UDDI per se does provide an automated mechanism to check and reconcile information that may be published on different nodes of the same registry at different times. This again is an implementation issue.

- UDDI Security: This API set is currently used to obtain and manage authentication information.

- UDDI Custody (and Ownership) Transfer: The publisher who initially creates an entry has ownership of that entity. A custodial UDDI node (typically the one at which the entry was published) has to maintain a rigid relationship between an entity and its owner to ensure the integrity of the information in a UDDI Registry. In the case of a multinode registry (e.g., UBR), every node must guarantee the integrity of an entity's ownership and custody. Consequently, a node cannot permit changes to an entity unless it is the custodial node for that entity. The Custody (and Ownership) Transfer API set enables one node to transfer custody of certain entities to another node or to transfer ownership of an entity from the current owner to a new one—in an authorized and cooperative manner.

- UDDI Subscription: This is the API set that facilitates the subscription scheme introduced with UDDI V3. This API set enables clients, referred to in UDDI argot as subscribers, to register their interest in being notified if and when changes are made to specific entries in a registry.

- UDDI Replication: Used to replicate entries within a UDDI Registry.

- UDDI Value Set: This API set permits authorized third parties to validate certain information being published in a UDDI Registry based on registered "value sets."

4.2.4 UDDI nodes and UDDI registries

A software system that supports at least one of the UDDI node API sets described earlier is considered to be a UDDI node. The UDDI V3 specification tries to put some "self-serving" spin into this definition by stating: "A set of Web services supporting at least one of the node API sets is referred to as a UDDI node." What is noteworthy here is the introduction of the concept of Web services supporting the UDDI API sets. That is the self-serving part, since one can justifiably argue that it is not necessary to include Web services in this definition. On the other hand, some technocrats will argue that this is indeed a valid and necessary distinction, based on the fact that UDDI relies on SOAP.

The UDDI APIs, by definition, operate by generating SOAP interactions. Thus, any software system that supports a UDDI API set, by default, has to be able to accommodate SOAP. SOAP is considered by most, including the nascent W3C Web Services Architecture, to be a fundamental (if not a prerequisite) building block of Web services. When one subscribes to this SOAP-centric view of Web services, one could then go the next step and describe any SOAP-based piece of software as being a Web service.

At a minimum, one could claim that any piece of software that communicates using SOAP is Web services ready. At this juncture, all that is important to note is that the UDDI definition for a UDDI node calls for the node to support at least one of the node API sets. Whether the software that makes this possible is a set of Web services or not is not that critical, provided there is an appreciation of what is being alluded to here.

In addition to supporting at least one node API set, the three other criteria to which a UDDI node has to conform are as follows:

1.   It interacts with UDDI data via the appropriate UDDI API sets.

2.   A UDDI node can only be a member of exactly one UDDI Registry.

3.   A UDDI node, at least conceptually, has full access to and can manipulate data structures of a complete logical copy of the total data managed by the registry of which they are a part. All interactions made via that node's query or publish API sets must always apply to these data—and no other (i.e., the UDDI APIs should only be used to access and manipulate the data associated with the UDDI Registry).

A UDDI Registry is made up of one or more UDDI nodes. When a registry is comprised of multiple nodes, all the nodes have to work in a collaborative manner to ensure that all nodes have access to the same logical set of data. The nodes making up a registry are collectively responsible for managing the UDDI data associated with that registry. The nodes will typically achieve this goal by using UDDI replication between the nodes using the UDDI Replication API set.

As previously stressed, the UDDI specification does not specify any implementation criteria for realizing a UDDI node or a UDDI Registry.

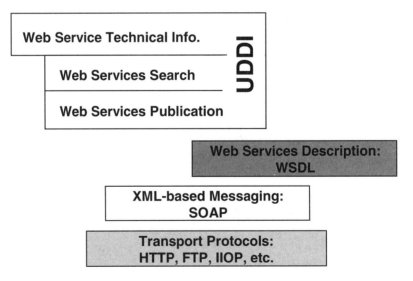

Figure 4.14   *The Web services stack showing the basic relationship between the various Web services enabling technologies and UDDI.*

Thus, the UBR was implemented, from day one, as a multinode registry. However, most private (if not semiprivate) registries are likely, at least to begin with, to just consist of one node. How a given registry implements policy decisions (e.g., authentication, integrity, support of digital certificates, and so forth) is also left as an implementation option. However, the necessary policy decisions have to be implemented in a consistent manner at each and every applicable point within the registry. A registry, however, has the option of delegating certain policy decisions to individual nodes—which is true in the case of the UBR.

Figure 4.14 brings this architecture-related section to a close by showing, in a "stack"-oriented depiction, how and where UDDI fits in relative to the other Web services–related methodologies.

4.3   How UDDI has evolved

Even by today's Internet-fueled pace, the evolution of UDDI has been relatively rapid and pronounced. There were only 22 months between UDDI V1 and V3. The overriding motivation to make UDDI a bona fide industry standard as soon as justifiably possible explains some of the haste to push out new specifications way ahead of the actual technology adoption curve. There is nothing wrong in this, and the key UDDI instigators—namely, IBM, Microsoft, and Ariba—need to be applauded for their commitment and drive.

When the UDDI Consortium was created in the summer of 2000 to bring forth UDDI V1, its charter was to oversee UDDI through V3. At that juncture UDDI was to be handed over to an accepted standards body. This indeed was exactly what happened, with the Consortium handing over the reins to OASIS in the summer of 2002, following the release of V3. OASIS (Organization for the Advancement of Structured Information Standards) is an accepted Web- and XML-related standards body. It started its life in 1993 under the name "SGML Open." This was a consortium of vendors and users committed to developing guidelines for interoperability among products that support the Standard Generalized Markup Language (SGML)—the granddaddy of XML. OASIS (http://www.oasis-open.org) adopted its current name in 1998 to reflect its expanded scope of interest, especially in the technical aspects of XML and e-business.

OASIS now bills itself as a not-for-profit, global consortium, which drives the development, convergence, and adoption of e-business standards—UDDI now being one of these. OASIS has more than 2,000 participants representing over 600 organizations and individual members in 100 countries. It also has close ties with the United Nations (UN), and together they jointly sponsor ebXML (Electronic Business using XML)—one of the first, and as yet one of the most credible, initiatives, alongside Web services, to promulgate the use of XML by enterprise applications.

OASIS sets out to produce respected and popular worldwide standards for security, Web services, XML conformance, business transactions, electronic publishing, topic maps, and interoperability within and between marketplaces. It achieves this goal by enabling its wide and well-represented membership to set the OASIS technical agenda. Cognizant of how heavy bureaucracy has successfully scuttled many standards efforts (and OSI comes to mind as a good example), OASIS favors a dynamic, lightweight, open process expressly designed to promote industry consensus and unite disparate efforts. Given these credentials, one cannot reasonably argue that

Table 4.1   *Evolutionary History of UDDI*

	UDDI Specification		
	Version 1	**Version 2**	**Version 3**
Published:	September 2000	June 2001	July 2002
Primary themes:	Create a framework for a UBR	Support complex organization models that include business units and subdivisions "Internationalization" in the form of permitting business-Entity description in multiple languages Support for more taxonomies	Private and semiprivate registries User-friendly UDDI keys "Operation information" (i.e., subscription service for change notification) Support for digital signatures
Data structures:	1. businessEntity 2. businessService 3. bindingTemplate 4. tModel	1. businessEntity 2. businessService 3. bindingTemplate 4. tModel 5. publisherAssertion	1. businessEntity 2. businessService 3. bindingTemplate 4. tModel 5. publisherAssertion 6. Subscription
Registry keys supported:	uuidKeys		uuidKeys, domainKeys, and derived keys

OASIS does not have the legitimacy to make UDDI a true, industry standard for the Web and e-business.

When UDDI was first conceived, realizing a UBR was the Holy Grail. UDDI V1, as characterized in Figure 4.6, focused on the needs for implementing a UBR. The initial UDDI.org Consortium, which consisted of around 30 well-known names, in addition to those of IBM and Microsoft, was indeed extremely successful in making sure that a three-node UBR was active and ready to roll when the initial V1 specification was unveiled to the world. Since then, the most profound change that has happened has been the growth in interest in private and semiprivate UDDI registries. Version 3's main thrust has to do with multiregistry-distributed UDDI environments with root and affiliate registries.

Table 4.1 sets out to highlight the evolutionary history of UDDI.

The bottom line here is that the UDDI standard is now well ahead of UDDI implementations, including the UBR—not to mention overall UDDI adoption. In reality, OASIS has time on its hands in terms of having to do much more on the standard—though, as is today's wont when it comes to Web services–related specifications, it is unlikely to be too long before we see UDDI V4. However, what is important right now is to ensure that UDDI and Web services become valuable business assets, rather than being technologically impressive paper tigers.

4.4   UDDI implementations—UBR and otherwise

UDDI found itself at an interesting and important crossroad in the summer of 2003—exactly a year after its custody was transferred over to OASIS. The UBR, now consisting of the four nodes after NTT joined IBM, Microsoft, and SAP as a node operator in October 2002, continues to be real and freely available. Figure 4.15 shows the front page of NTT's Japanese-centric UBR node to complete the set of UBR node screen shots included in Chapter 1 and this chapter.

Despite the no-cost, no-holds-barred, worldwide availability, the UBR's popularity, repute, and applicability are, however, still open to question. As with all things Web services–related, UDDI has not yet even come close to living up to its once-lofty expectations. On the other hand, the inclusion of a full-function, V2-compliant UDDI service as a standard feature within Microsoft's now flagship Windows Server 2003, which started shipping in June 2003, coupled with Visual Studio .NET's direct support for UDDI search-and-publish functions, gives UDDI a whole new breadth of exposure.

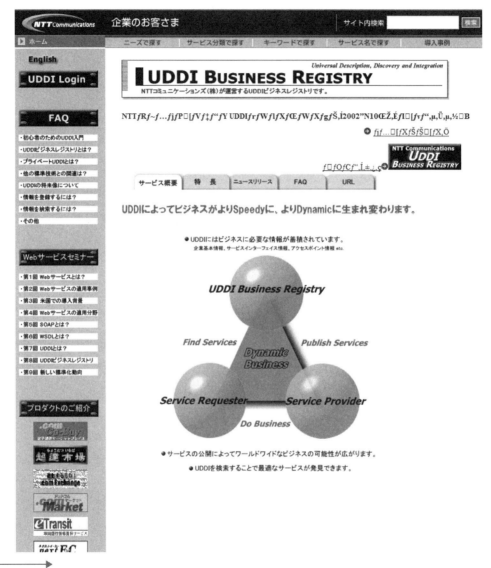

Figure 4.15   *NTT Communication's Japanese-centric UBR node.*

In addition, the availability of Java-based, multiplatform enterprise UDDI servers from the likes of IBM and BEA, as adjuncts to their highly popular application server offerings, gives UDDI even further credibility with application developers. The Java versions, moreover, enable UDDI implementations on UNIX and even iSeries platforms. The Java- and Windows-based enterprise versions of UDDI will certainly help make UDDI more real, tangible, and accessible vis-à-vis the IT community—

hence, why it is safe to claim that UDDI really is at a crossroad at the time of this writing.

Up until V3, the focus of UDDI implementations revolved around the UBR initiative. However, V3's explicit endorsement and support for multi-registry environments changes that in a profound manner. Over the next couple of years, the emphasis is going to shift toward enterprise UDDI registries, both private and semiprivate, and their interaction with the UBR. Consequently, before venturing any further, it is best to characterize the features of the key UDDI implementation types, in tabular form, so as to serve as a framework for the remainder of this section. This is done in Table 4.2.

4.4.1   The UDDI Business Register

The UBR is the public face of UDDI. In reality it was to be the be-all and end-all of what UDDI was all about. Though a UBR, per the original expectations, has now been in continuous operation for nearly 3 years, on a no-charge, open-to-all basis, it is fair to say that the UBR is still a little-used novelty—only appreciated by a select, Web services–centric cognoscenti. It is still far from being the oracle for e-business-related services that it was supposed to be.

In its defense, it is only fair to note that following the dot.com debacle, the spread of e-business slowed down dramatically in mid-2001—just as UDDI and UBR were trying to gain momentum. Then there were 9/11 and the resultant economic downturn, particularly severe in the high-tech sectors—as well as a huge, overall increase in cautiousness related to all security- and privacy-related issues. The ongoing epidemic of viruses, Internet attacks, relentless spam, and security exposures on Windows platforms justifiably fuels this "under-siege" mind-set.

Against this background, the UBR was and still is an unknown. Businesses are leery about disclosing too much information about themselves to strangers. They especially do not want to publicize too many electronic links into their organization. The original "free-world" climate within which the UBR was conceived has changed—irrevocably!

This security-inspired, technological "xenophobia," however, is not the only reason why the UBR has not flourished. The UBR is bereft of leadership. OASIS, true to its charter as a standards body, wishes to stay aloof from UDDI implementations—even if it is the egalitarian, "not-for-gain" UBR. There is no explicit reference to UBR on OASIS's UDDI-related front page. Instead, there is a misleading and obscure reference on the top navigation bar that says "Register"—with an exclamation mark in front of

Table 4.2   *Features of Key UDDI Implementation Types*

	Public UDDI Registries		Enterprise UDDI Registries	
	UBR Business Registry	**UBR Test Registries**	**Private Registry**	**Semiprivate, Shared Registry**
Purpose:	Global, unrestricted visibility to services available from businesses, organizations, and individuals from around the world	A test-bed version of the UBR provided at some UBR nodes mainly to provide software developers with a means to accurately try out the working of the UDDI APIs	1. Internal catalog, for use by in-house software developers of available (and approved) Web services that may be used in new applications 2. Test bed for use by in-house programmers developing programmatic access to the UBR 3. In the case of large multinational, multidivisional enterprises as a standardized, in-house directory, categorized by taxonomies, of all available services—Web or otherwise	1. List of Web services approved for use in b2b e-business applications being developed by or for use by members of this group of "partners" 2. Standardized list of all services, categorized by taxonomies, being offered by the various members that make up this "partnership"
Accessed via:	Internet		Intranet	Extranet
Behind firewalls:	No		Yes	
Cost:	No charge at present		UDDI server functionality typically included with a "larger" server product	
Administration:	UBR node operators		Private, in-house	Collaborative
Likely to be multinode:	Yes	No	No	Yes

it, as shown in Figure 4.16. Clicking on that then takes you to a page that is headed "Register." If you are just looking to sample and evaluate the UBR, this process is confusing and intimidating to say the least.

Typing in http://www.uddi.org in the hope that doing that would get you to the UBR does not work either. This intuitive URL takes you to the OASIS UDDI front page discussed previously. Also, http://www.ubr.org is currently for sale! That about sums it up! Doing a search for "UBR" with, say, Google, does produce results—but nothing that immediately says: "This is the global, no-charge, open-to-all, standards-based UBR." Instead, you get references to particular UBR nodes—typically starting with Microsoft's UBR node, at uddi.microsoft.com, given that most search engines use a weighting mechanism for ranking search results based on the

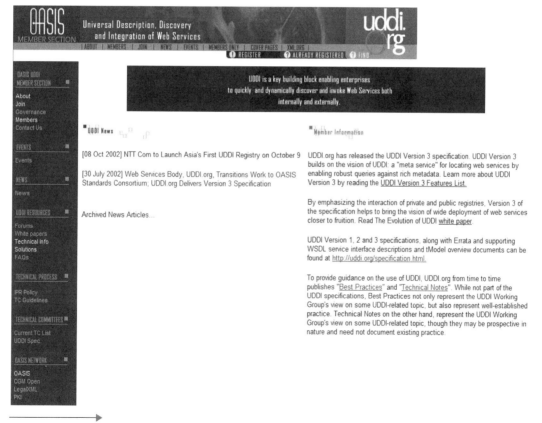

Figure 4.16   *The Register tab on the OASIS UDDI front page, which will take you to a page that shows how to access one of the UBR nodes.*

"how many links to this site have we seen" criterion, and Microsoft, in general, happens to be a heavily visited site.

The URLs for the various UBR nodes (e.g., uddi.microsoft.com, uddi.ibm.com, and uddi.sap.com) are another problem. The ".com" suffix detracts from the service-oriented theme that the UBR should project. Though one of the express goals of the UBR is to promote e-business, the ".com" connotations—especially when juxtapositioned against names such as Microsoft, IBM, and SAP—can understandably create some level of paranoia about how information maintained in the UBR may get exploited in the future. Then, as if to add insult to injury, typing in uddi.ntt.com results in a "page not found" error. Instead, to get the NTT node, you have to enter http://www.ntt.com/uddi.

The NTT node, as shown in Figure 4.15, is predominantly in Japanese and moreover appears to have "button" ads for other services and vendors. Overall, one can excuse an average business person from being suspicious of the UBR. The UBR, today, comes across as a "Big Brother is watching you"–type directory maintained by market superheavyweights. The UBR would be so much easier to swallow if it were indeed run by OASIS or an equivalent consortium as a uddi.org entity.

Ironically, however, another factor impacting the UBR is the lack of UDDI-related commercialization. To date, nobody, including IBM, Microsoft, or SAP, has made much money on Web services, UDDI, and, by implication, the UBR. UDDI- and UBR-related ROI have to be in the negative territory. This explains why the UBR, at present, is not as slick as one would expect—particularly in comparison to large search engines such as Google. First, a year after V3 was released, all of the UBR nodes were still at V2 levels. Given that it is V3 that permits cooperative coexistence of multi-registry environments, the lack of V3 support also has a dampening effect on enterprise-level implementations.

The bottom line is that the UBR has yet to show its true promise and potential. The UBR, overall, does set out to fill a noticeable void in today's global trading community—not just for Web services, but as a global repository of all available services. One hopes that as the UDDI message becomes better known within enterprises, thanks to the enterprise UDI implementations, the popularity of the UBR will increase—even if it is, to begin with, just to enumerate traditional services not associated with Web services. In the interim, the primary pros and cons of the UBR are summarized in Table 4.3.

Table 4.3 *Pros and Cons of the UBR*

Pros	Cons
1. Standards based, open service	1. Still lacks visibility, not to mention credibility
2. No charge (at present) and available to all without discrimination	2. No checks on the validity, accuracy, or completeness of the entries
3. Global, Web browser accessible service	3. Lacks consistency across the nodes
4. Published API-based programmatic access	4. Predominantly English oriented, with the NTT node being Japanese
5. Powerful, extensible architecture that permits complex queries	5. No perceived driving force
6. Multinode implementation fosters redundancy	6. Unintentionally succeeds in projecting a highly commercialized "sinister" image, though it is essentially a not-for-profit service
	7. Has yet to cogently quell security and integrity issues that businesses may have

4.4.2 UDDI enterprise registries

The growing interest in private and semiprivate UDDI registries echoes a fundamental ground shift that has occurred in the Web services world. When originally conceived, Web services, as testified by the all-important word "Web" in the name, were going to be all about standards-based software functionality available over the Web. Web services were the software methodology sector of the Web-based, "the whole world is the market," free-trade zone that transcended geographic, political, currency, cultural, and economic boundaries. Well, this utopian dream of application developers around the world, gainfully collaborating with each other over the Web, is not going to happen as quickly and as easily as originally envisaged.

There is too much mistrust and foreboding in the post-9/11 business world. In addition, the constant state of high alert in which businesses now have to operate when it comes to IT-related attacks, thanks to the never-ending news about various security flaws in heavily used software, further exacerbates all concerns regarding the security, privacy, and protection of all corporate assets. Consequently, more and more enterprises are looking at Web services as a technology they want to use either strictly in-house or just with trusted partners. Rather than "Web" services, it is now becoming "intranet" services or "extranet" services.

This situation is responsible for the increased interest in enterprise registry. Enterprise registry enables enterprises to faithfully recreate the entire Web services operational model—albeit now purely on an intranet or extranet basis. The in-house corporate phone book analogy immediately and obviously comes to mind. With private registries, enterprises can maintain their own listings of services, per the UDDI model—whether for Web services or otherwise. They will have total control of the access, administration, and security aspects of these in-house registries. They can be maintained on a strictly need-to-know basis.

Only those who are actively involved with particular projects need to even know that an enterprise has an in-house UDDI Registry. Just as with information listed in a corporate phone book, most enterprises will not want the contents of their private UDDI registries known to outsiders. As with other sensitive corporate information, there will be rules, policies, and procedures as to how information contained in a private UDDI Registry is treated.

Private and semiprivate UDDI registries can be a major boon for in-house software developers—particularly as they transition toward a Web services–centric software development model. These registries provide them with a standard mechanism for cataloging the new Web services they develop. No longer will they have to rely on e-mails, departmental meetings, and word of mouth to disseminate, plus acquire, information about the in-house Web services now offered. They can gainfully use the in-house registry—in exactly the same way that UBR was originally intended to be used as the self-advertising mechanism for Web services.

Private and semiprivate registries can also be the staging posts for automated, programmatic, Publish API set–based entries into the UBR, once the UBR nodes, as well as the enterprise implementations, are all at V3. As previously mentioned, IBM, Microsoft, and SAP offer test registries alongside their business registries for programmers who wish to test their software against a real, live UDDI implementation. However, using one of these test registries still means going outside the firewall, so the enterprise implementations, especially those that can be realized to be extremely economical using the bundled-in UDDI server inside Windows 2003, will satisfy an important need. Programmers like to try out their software. Now they have a real emulation that they can beat on, behind the privacy afforded by firewalls, to their hearts' content, before they have to trot their efforts out into the glare of the Web.

Private and semiprivate registries also allow programmers to have the option of developing truly dynamic, "don't bind until run time" applications based on Web services. Remember that the whole Web services model is contingent on invoking and binding with the necessary Web services modules at run time. Web services are an RPC mechanism. UDDI, through the bindingTemplate entities, can maintain all necessary invocation parameters for a Web service. Given this framework and the invocation pattern inquiry scheme supported by the UDDI Inquiry API set, it is possible to write new applications that only invoke Web services via their UDDI entry. This means that the actual Web service invoked could change as new Web services are added to a UDDI Registry. With enterprise registries, developers, when applicable, could exploit this highly dynamic Web service invocation model.

The bottom line here is that enterprise UDDI registries, as with employees-only intranet or partners-only extranet portals, are here to stay. In today's security-obsessed corporate culture, they fulfill an important need for providing full UBR compliance within the privacy and security afforded by a firewall. The sponsors of UDDI recognize this need—hence, the support for multiregistry environments in V3. All that is required now is for the UBR as well as enterprise implementations to be based on V3 so that the interoperability envisaged by V3 can be a reality.

4.5   Security and integrity in relation to UDDI implementations

As with all things Web-related, post-9/11 security, as already discussed in the preceding sections, has hampered the spread of UDDI and the UBR. However, when it comes to UDDI and the UBR, one has to be very careful and judicious as to what one means by security—and the scope of potential security exposures in this context. The first distinction that has to be made is between enterprise implementations and the UBR. Enterprise implementations, whether private or semiprivate, are meant to be closed user group affairs, which should only be accessible to authenticated and authorized users. The corporate phone book analogy has already been used.

In the case of private registries, system administrators should implement all appropriate access control mechanisms to ensure that only those with a need to know have the necessary rights to search, populate, or update the registry. This goes without saying. A private registry becomes just another sensitive corporate IT asset, and the type of corporation that would need a private registry will already have mature security policies about such IT assets. Obviously the one thing that you do not want is unauthorized users being able to snoop around or modify the contents of a private registry.

With semiprivate extranet registries, the issue of security becomes more difficult—but not insurmountable. First, having an extranet registry that is shared among trusted partners does not preclude you from also maintaining an intranet-only private registry. Thus, you can have multiple levels of security and access controls. Within this structure, you would only publish select and carefully vetted information in the semiprivate registry.

Companies looking at semiprivate UDDI implementations are most likely to already have some level of experience when it comes to b2b e-business. There is a high possibility that they already operate a partners-specific extranet portal. As a result, such companies will already know how to share and at the same time restrict information between partners using authentication, personalization, and access controls. All of these will come into play when implementing a successful and secure extranet UDDI registry.

The security issues surrounding the UBR are, however, totally different. One can even plausibly argue that when it comes to the UBR, what is at stake is not so much security—but integrity. What is important to remember here is that the UBR, by definition and intent, is meant to be a public repository. Hence, to read that the UBR node operators go to great lengths to encrypt the information maintained by a UBR node is incongruous. That is akin, if you think about it, to a public library having all of its books behind lock and key. The information published to the UBR is meant to be in the public domain.

What is key, however, is to maintain the integrity of the information in the UBR, and this is a challenge. Remember the bad old days when people poached domain names that should by rights belong to others? Well, a similar problem is still there with the UBR. As yet, there is no controlling authority that truly validates users who wish to publish new entries in the UBR. Consequently, an unscrupulous but resourceful "joker" could hijack the UBR entries for genuine businesses if those businesses have not already registered with the UBR. Thus, frivolous and inaccurate information is one of the big dangers facing the UBR and its users. To this end, recall that IBM lists 170 categories of services versus the one stated by Microsoft. Is one or both of these entries a joke? That is the problem. It is hard to tell.

Yes, the UBR nodes insist that you register with them before you can publish an entry. In the case of IBM, this involves selecting a previously unused user ID and an appropriate password and providing a set of contact information, with a valid e-mail address being sacrosanct. Your registration is only activated when you invoke a link to send to the e-mail address provided. This e-mail-based validation approach is not new and has been widely used in the last 5 years or so as a minimally acceptable, baseline method.

The rationale here is that the service provider (i.e., the UBR node operator) has at least an e-mail address that once worked and that points to the user trying to register. Suffice to say that this e-mail-based validation is really not worth the electrons used to execute it! A wily hacker will not have any problems opening numerous hard-to-track e-mail accounts. Microsoft insists that registration to use its UBR node has to be made via its now severely tarnished and undermined Passport service. This alone, as discussed in Chapter 3, may be enough to convince cynics that the integrity of the UBR is already compromised!

This is where digital certificates and digital signatures come in. UDDI V3 supports these mechanisms, but the exact use of these is left as policy decisions to the individual node operators. It now seems inevitable that down the road, all the UBR node operators will insist upon third-party certification, à la digital certificates, in order for one to register as a bona fide UBR publisher. Until this happens, there will always be concerns about the integrity of the information available in the UBR.

Once an entry is published, only the user who published that entry can modify or delete it. This is good and reassuring, assuming that the original user who did the publishing was legitimate and was who he or she actually claimed to be. The original publisher, through the custody transfer API set, also has the ability to assign ownership to another registered user—the key here, though, being that the original publisher has all the initial rights. This is why it is so imperative to ensure, via digital certificates, that the original publisher is not a charlatan. Once there is a validated publisher, a UBR node's policies could further dictate that it will only accept digitally signed entries from that user. With such policies one can put stock in the integrity of the information maintained in the UBR. During the transition to a digitally verified UBR structure, it will be possible, albeit with V3 implementations, for users to request that the searches they conduct on the UBR be restricted to those entries that have been digitally verified as to their authenticity.

4.6   Q&A: A time to recap and reflect

Q: What is UDDI?

A: Universal Description, Discovery, and Integration is a scheme for Web-based electronic directories that contain detailed information about businesses, the services they provide, and the means for utilizing these services. A UDDI directory, referred to as a registry, is meant to be platform independent and can be readily accessible via a Web browser–based GUI or by applications via published APIs. Its goal is to ensure that enterprises and individuals can quickly, easily, and dynamically locate and make use of services, in particular Web services, that are of interest to them.

Q: Is UDDI a standard?

A: Yes, it is a de facto industry standard under the auspices of OASIS (http://www.oasis-open.org). OASIS, which was formed as a consortium in 1993 to promote SGML, is now an accepted standards body for XML and e-business–related initiatives. Thus, it makes sense for UDDI to be under the stewardship of OASIS—which is a not-for-profit agency with more than 2,000 participants representing over 600 organizations and individual members in 100 countries. In addition, UDDI is based entirely on XML and SOAP, which in turn are acknowledged industry standards.

Q: Is it possible to use Web services without UDDI?

A: Yes. Unlike XML or SOAP, UDDI is not a prerequisite "protocol" that has to be used by a Web service in order for it to be deemed a Web service. UDDI is essentially an optional adjunct to publicize the availability, characteristics, and activation requirements of Web services. It is possible to write applications (and Web services) that can dynamically locate and invoke Web services by programmatically interrogating a UDDI Registry. However, this is by no means mandatory; it is an option. Most applications developers are unlikely to opt for such a dynamic approach, given the variables and uncertainty of this type of on-the-fly run-time binding. Though not a prerequisite per se, UDDI is the accepted means for realizing the self-advertising mandate for Web services—and as such should be considered as an integral part of a Web services landscape.

Q: How does UDDI relate to WSDL?

A: Despite what would appear to be a common goal when it comes to describing the characteristics of Web services, there is no prespecified relationship between UDDI and WSDL. In contrast to SOAP, WSDL is not one of the prerequisite standards used by UDDI. They do, however, complement each other. One of UDDI's express missions is to publicize the technical requirements and invocation criteria for Web services. WSDL happens to be the preferred and accepted way to describe the interface of a Web service. Thus, there is an obvious and natural role that WSDL can play vis-à-vis UDDI. The tModel information for a Web service within a

UDDI Registry could thus point to a WSDL description of that Web service, as can the bindingTemplate.

Q: What is a UDDI Registry?

A: A UDDI Registry is an instance of one complete set of UDDI-related data about businesses, the services they provide, and technical details of these services. A UDDI Registry is made up of one or more UDI nodes, where a UDDI node is a software system that supports at least one of the UDDI API sets. A given UDDI node can, at any one time, only be a member of just one UDDI Registry. In the case of a multinode registry, all the nodes are expected to work collaboratively with each other, representing one unified view of the data managed by that registry.

Q: Is UDDI based on LDAP?

A: No. UDDI is not built upon any of the popular directory schemes. UDDI is meant to be a high-level, "logical" overlay architecture that deals with data structures, in the form of XML schema, and SOAP-based messages, invoked from APIs, to manage and manipulate these data structures. The UDDI specification, now in its third version, does not specify or even suggest how one should go about realizing these data structures or the SOAP messaging. Those are left as individual implementation decisions. Thus, there is no formal relationship for the Lightweight Directory Access Protocol (LDAP) or even X.500. There are, however, specifications available on the Web as to how a UDDI node could be implemented on top of LDAP or X.500. At present, however, many of the UDDI implementations are realized using popular relational database systems such as IBM's DB2, though BEA, for one, offers an LDAP-based UDDI implementation.

Q: What is the UBR?

A: The Universal Business Registry, also referred to as the UDDI Business Registry, is a global, public UDDI service available on the Web that is open to all—currently on a no-charge basis. It has been in operation since late 2000. The UBR was initially operated by Ariba, IBM, and Microsoft. Today, the UBR consists of four UBR nodes, working collaboratively, with these nodes being run by IBM, Microsoft, NTT Communications, and SAP. You can locate the UBR by going to http://www.uddi.org and clicking on the "Register" tab at the top of the page.

Q: Is there a charge for using the UBR?

A: At present there is no charge for using the UBR—whether to publish information or to search for information. The UBR nodes, however, require those who wish to publish information in the UBR to be registered with them beforehand so that they can be authenticated. Anybody can freely search the UBR without being registered. Down the road it is highly likely that the UBR nodes will require potential publishers to be digitally authenticated and certified before they can apply for registration. There is likely to be a charge for this digital certification.

Q: Is it possible to have a private UBR?

A: Yes. Version 3 of the UDDI specification, which was published in July 2002, endorses the concept of multiregistry environments consisting of a root registry (typically the UBR) and multiple affiliate registries. Today, IBM, Microsoft, BEA, Sun, and others offer products for implementing so-called enterprise UDDI registries. An enterprise UDDI Registry could be private (i.e., restricted for use by one company) or semiprivate (i.e., shared between trusted partners). Microsoft's flagship Windows Server 2003, which started shipping in June 2003, includes a full-function UDDI Registry capability as a built-in feature.

Q: Are Web services the only type of service that can be included in the UBR?

A: No. Though UDDI and the UBR were conceived to promote e-business, and in particular Web services, neither the UDDI specification nor the UBR insists that the only services that can be included in a UDDI Registry are Web services. In reality the UBR is extremely generic and flexible. One can register any type of business, organization, or even an individual, as well as any arbitrary type of service.

5

SOAP

> *Pictures are for entertainment;*
> *messages should be delivered by Western Union.*
>
> —Samuel Goldwyn

SOAP is currently a fundamental, prerequisite building block for XML Web services. SOAP is used to send input to and receive output from conventional XML Web services. Thus, it is the underlying communications mechanism for today's Web services. Since a Web service requires input parameters in order to be activated, SOAP is also considered to be what invokes a Web service—because it delivers the input parameters.

The role and scope of SOAP, however, are not limited to Web services. SOAP is the latest in a long line of distributed computing initiatives, which in this context include CORBA and Microsoft's COM/DCOM, though it is not meant to totally displace either of these powerful, object-oriented methodologies. SOAP sets out to be a simpler alternative that does not provide all the high-end bells and whistles (e.g., automatic garbage collection).

SOAP is totally XML-centric. SOAP is a messaging scheme that works by exchanging XML documents. It is formally characterized as a lightweight communications protocol for exchanging XML-based information between applications in a decentralized, distributed environment like the Web. In the interests of putting a stake in the ground, think of SOAP, to begin with, as an XML datagram.

XML, as should now be abundantly clear, is a mechanism for describing the meaning and context of data—albeit based on both sides (i.e., creator and subsequent reader or consumer) being privy to some common "intelligence" (e.g., XML schema or DTD). XML's initial focus, understandably,

was all about being flexible and extensible and having the necessary indus-
try- and application-specific vocabularies (or dialects) to facilitate b2b e-
business, but the real scope of XML is limited to that of XML documents
(i.e., plain text files containing data annotated with XML notation). XML
does not deal with how XML documents can be exchanged between interested parties, which is where SOAP comes in.

Let's take a look at an obvious supply chain management (SCM) scenario, that of a supplier wishing to notify some of its customer base programmatically, with new pricing data, to appreciate the rationale for SOAP
in the context of XML. With today's expertise in XML and the ready availability of the appropriate industry-specific vocabularies, it would not be difficult to create the necessary price update XML document. The challenge
now becomes that of conveying this document to all the intended recipients—in an automated, program-to-program manner.

Obviously, sending the XML document over HTTP as an e-mail attachment or sending it via FTP to each of the recipients is not adequate. This
does not address the fundamental, program-to-program criteria—nor does
it offer XML-oriented, application-level "transaction" coordination, payload security, or guaranteed delivery. SOAP sets out to address all of these
distributed computing-related message delivery requirements. SOAP can
sustain any type of XML messaging application need, including those for
one-way messaging, multicasting (or broadcasting), request-response interactions, and coordinated, sequential workflow progressions. It also includes
the option for a simple but powerful RPC-type mechanism.

With SOAP one can conduct XML-based, program-to-program,
request/response-oriented, RPC-like transactions that can be visualized in
the form:

- placeOrder()

- getCreditRating()

- findCurrentWeather()

- getStockPrice()

- updatePurchaseOrder()

- obtainShipDate()

One can now see the relationship between XML documents, SOAP,
and Web services because each of the procedure calls shown above could be
to a Web service that performs that function. Though SOAP is invariably

associated with this type of RPC mode operation, it is important to note that this is only one of the messaging modes that can be used with SOAP. In reality, RPC mode representation is an optional SOAP capability.

What SOAP really does when it comes to RPCs is provide a generalized mechanism for representing and encapsulating them within SOAP messages. The SOAP approach is programming language and protocol agnostic. In theory, any of the schemes used by today's programming languages to define and invoke procedures or object-oriented "methods" can be mapped and represented by a SOAP message—which would typically be delivered to the remote "server" via an HTTP POST command.

Let's take, for example, the "findCurrentWeather" Web service, which when given a zip code returns an XML document that contains the current temperature, anticipated temperature range, current disposition (e.g., cloudy), and so forth. A SOAP-based call to this service, which is hypothetically assumed to be available as a method at "www.your-weather.com," would look like:

```
<w:findCurrentWeather xmlns:w="http://www.your-
weather.com/">
   <w:sZipCode xsi:type="xsd:string">03249</w:sZipCode>
</w: findCurrentWeather>
```

The response to this call will be returned in another SOAP message. At this juncture it is best to actually look at the overall structure of a representative but relatively simple, SOAP-based transaction. To this end let's consider a hypothetical online book ordering scenario between a book retailer and a publisher realized via an "eOrder" SOAP request.

The SOAP request sent from the book retailer to the publisher will contain retailer identification, PO details, and information about the book. To achieve this, the customer sends the following "orderItem" SOAP request to the supplier, which includes pertinent information such as the customer identification (i.e., RetailID), the item number, item name, item description, quantity ordered, wholesale price, and so forth—in this case using HTTP as the transport mechanism:

```
POST /Orders HTTP/1.1
Host: www.megapublisher.com
Content-Type: application/soap+xml; charset="utf-8"
Content-Length: nnnn

<?xml version='1.0' ?>
<soap:Envelope xmlns:soap="http://www.w3.org/2003/05/
```

```
soap-envelope">
 <soap:Header>
  <o:eOrder
      xmlns:o=http://www.megapublisher.com/orders
      soap:encodingStyle=http://megapublisher.com/
encoding
      soap:mustUnderstand="true">
  </o:eOrder>
 </soap:Header>
 <soap:Body>
 <m:onlineOrder>
   soap:encodingStyle=http://www.w3.org/2003/05/soap-
encoding
     xmlns:m="http:// www.megapublisher.com/orders/">
  <m:eOrder xmlns:m="http:// www.megapublisher.com/
orders">
  <m:retailerCode>UK0216987</m:code>
  <m:retailerName>TechBooks</m:retailerName>
  <m:invoiceNumber>MgTec533</m:invoiceNumber>
  <m:isbnNumber>1-55558-280-X</m:isbnNumber>
  <m:author>Guruge</m:author>
  <m:title>Corporate Portals</m:title>
  <m:quantity>100</m:quantity>
  <m:shipping>standard</m:shipping>
 </m:onlineOrder>
 </soap:Body>
</soap:Envelope>
```

This SOAP request, delivered to the book publisher (i.e., MegaPublisher.com) via HTTP, will result in the "eOrder" method to be invoked at www.megapublisher.com/orders/. SOAP itself does not specify or care how this method was implemented. It also does not get involved in how this request is processed. Its express goal is to deliver the request, in the form of an invocation, to the intended remote method—along with the enclosed input data. The receiver, in this case the HTTP server at "MegaPublisher.com," could use a standard CGI script, invoke a Java servlet or .NET process to process this order, and return an appropriate acknowledgment (e.g., order confirmation number and an estimated delivery date).

Even a cursory examination of this SOAP example will indicate that it consists of four distinct parts. The first four lines, starting with "POST," talk about HTTP, identify the (remote) host, and specify a content type for this message. These four SOAP transport-related lines are known as the SOAP "binding"—in this instance, the SOAP-HTTP binding, given that the transport is HTTP. Within this, the first two lines, which are HTTP specific, are understandably known as the HTTP request. Straight after the XML declaration, which comes next, you can find the start of a SOAP envelope. This envelope, which in essence subsumes the entire SOAP message, is in turn made up of two parts: the SOAP header and the SOAP body. All SOAP messages will conform to this overall structure, as will be discussed later in this chapter.

In addition, the abundance of colons in the previous example, since each element name is prefixed, as well as the four occurrences of the keyword "xmlns," should indicate that XML namespaces are an integral concept within SOAP. XML namespaces, as discussed in Section 2.3.4, are the standard XML mechanism to ensure that the meaning and intent of XML elements relative to a given XML document are not mistaken or misinterpreted. The prefixed element names, relative to a specific XML namespace, ensure the uniqueness of XML elements within a particular context.

This explains the significance of XML namespaces vis-à-vis SOAP. Since SOAP is a messaging scheme, the underlying implication is that the XML document transported by using SOAP will be read and interpreted at a site different from where the original XML document was originally conceived. Also, a recipient could receive XML documents from different sources that contain the same elements—but each with a slightly different nuance. The use of XML namespaces eliminates such ambiguity and makes sure that a recipient of an XML document has the means to unequivocally validate the intent of the elements contained in that document.

This preamble as to what SOAP is about can be concluded with the following summary of the salient SOAP attributes.

- SOAP is an XML-based messaging scheme.

- SOAP works between applications.

- SOAP can be readily used between disparate platforms.

- SOAP supports the encapsulation and remote delivery of RPCs.

- SOAP is programming language agnostic.

- SOAP enables XML to be communicated over HTTP.

- SOAP, however, is not restricted to HTTP.

- SOAP relies heavily on XML namespaces.

- SOAP is used by Web services for their I/O operations.

- SOAP is also considered to be what remotely invokes Web services.

5.1   **SOAP: The genesis and evolution**

SOAP, based on its XML pedigree, is meant to be platform and operating system independent. It is also supposed to be totally programming language agnostic—despite its prowess in serving as an RPC mechanism. It is thus ideally suited to be freely and gainfully used as a message-based communications scheme between disparate systems. This intersystem communications capability is the fundamental relationship between SOAP and Web services. SOAP serves as the means for realizing Web services I/O operations and consequently also for Web invocation. Despite the overt I/O-related role that it plays in Web services, SOAP nonethelessis not a transport mechanism.

SOAP is meant to be used on top of standard transport protocols. The layering of SOAP on top of the transport layer is clearly shown in the Web services stack diagram in Figure 4.14. SOAP can be used across HTTP, TCP, SMTP, FTP, message queuing (e.g., IBM's WebSphere MQ), BEEP, or other RPC mechanisms. However, HTTP is the preferred and most widely used transport scheme for SOAP—in the context of Web services as well as other scenarios.

HTML over HTTP is what the Web is all about, but with SOAP, you can have XML over HTTP. The SOAP specifications acknowledge this made-in-heaven relationship aspect of SOAP and HTTP. Though it is stated that SOAP is not limited to use with HTTP, the only transport "bindings" shown in the original SOAP specification (known as the 1.1 specification) were those for HTTP.

Given that SOAP is a messaging scheme that has structures known as "envelopes" and "payloads," it has become de rigueur to use a postal analogy to describe SOAP, though the analogy is somewhat limited. Nonetheless it would be remiss not to mention it in passing, given its widespread usage within the industry. SOAP is all about the item that is to be mailed. It describes how the item to be mailed (i.e., the payload) is to be packaged, in a modular manner. That is where the SOAP envelope comes in.

However, SOAP does not dictate how this envelope containing the payload (i.e., the message) is delivered to the intended recipient. When dealing with paper-oriented mail, you have multiple delivery options (e.g., normal mail, express mail service, courier [e.g., FedEx], and so forth). Those are transport options—same message, but very different delivery characteristics.

It is the same with SOAP and the various transports over which it can be used.

When used on top of HTTP, SOAP messages can typically traverse corporate firewalls and evade standard packet-filtering policies, since HTTP, as the basis for interacting with Web servers, is given carte blanche access. Ironically, one of the motivations for developing SOAP was the fact that when used with HTTP it could indeed be a powerful remote procedure call mechanism that would not be blocked by a corporate firewall. CORBA and the DCOM-based distributed computing approaches needed specific ports to be opened in the firewall for them to get through. Since network administrators are invariably hesitant to open up new ports on firewalls, this was yet another problem that beset the CORBA and DCOM approaches. Suffice to say SOAP's ability to get through firewalls by using HTTP is now a source of some concern and one of the security-related issues that has to be cogently dealt with in the context of Web services.

However, this firewall traversal capability is not an overt security exposure, the reason being that getting one or more SOAP messages through a firewall by itself is unlikely to pose any kind of threat or cause any damage. SOAP, as shown in Figure 5.1, always works in application-to-application, sender-to-receiver mode. Thus a SOAP message that traverses a firewall is but a harmless "lost transmission" unless it is received by and acted upon by an application (or Web service) running behind the firewall. The secret for enforcing SOAP-level security is to ensure that any SOAP-capable application (or Web service) deployed behind a firewall is authorized, trusted, and regularly monitored.

SOAP predates the advent of Web services. The origins of SOAP can be traced back to XML-RPC. XML-RPC was developed in early 1998 by a few inspired visionaries working for Userland Software, DevelopMentor, and Microsoft—with the names of Dave Winer of Userland Software and Don Box of DevelopMentor inextricably associated with the development of XML-RPC and its influence on the creation of SOAP. XMP-RPC, true to its name, is a simple RPC mechanism realized by using XML over HTTP. XML-RPC demonstrated that XML's scope did not have to be limited to that of representing the exact meaning of a structured document. XML, with XML-RPC, could also serve as the basis for a powerful, standards-based distributed transaction processing scheme. XML-RPC is still in use today, though SOAP has in many ways supplanted it as its more strategic and widely known descendant.

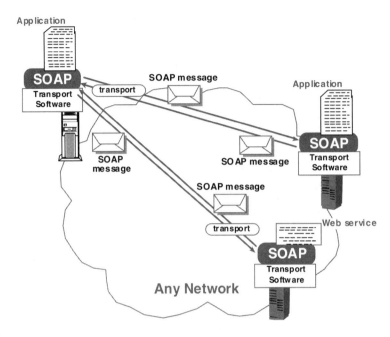

Figure 5.1   *SOAP's modus operandi. It is transport and network independent and always works application to application, application to Web service, Web service to Web service in sender-receiver mode, where a SOAP node can act as both a sender and a receiver since most SOAP interactions work via some form of request-response exchange.*

Following XML-RPC, Microsoft and DevelopMentor went on to investigate transport-independent, XML-based messaging schemes that could be used for distributed computing. They were striving for a mechanism that was simpler to deploy and use than either DCOM or CORBA—which were considered at that time the long-term solutions for component-based distributed computing, with the former being Microsoft specific while the later was "open" and vendor independent. The resulting specification, SOAP 1.0, was ready in September 1999. To garner sufficient market backing for this specification, Microsoft sought other partners. The result was the SOAP 1.1 specification, which was authored by representatives from Microsoft, DevelopMentor, IBM/Lotus, and UserLand Software.

The 1.1 specification was submitted to W3C on May 8, 2000. Collaborating on SOAP provided IBM and Microsoft with the inspiration and impetus to flesh out the concept of XML Web services that would use this new XML-based messaging scheme as their I/O mechanism. IBM, Microsoft, and Ariba thus went on to create the specifications for WSDL and UDDI, which were made public 6 months after the unveiling of SOAP.

In addition to the four companies that "authored" it (keeping in mind that Lotus is a division of IBM), the submission of the SOAP 1.1 specification to W3C was further endorsed by other then-big names in the industry, including Ariba, Compaq, H-P, SAP, IONA Technologies, and Commerce-One. Given this wide and influential industry backing, W3C did not subject this specification to the rigorous ratification process that is typically the norm. Bowing to the momentum that SOAP had already picked up by that juncture, and the fact that SOAP implementations were already in progress, particularly from Microsoft (i.e., Microsoft's SOAP Toolkit 1.0, which was available in summer 2000) and the Java camp, led by IBM and Apache, W3C accepted SOAP 1.1 as a de facto industry standard. By 2002, there were more than 70 separate SOAP implementations.

5.1.1   The SOAP 1.2 initiative

SOAP 1.1 was not as precise as some would have wished, and there were some interoperability issues between different implementations of the 1.1 specification. This led to the W3C's XML Protocol Working Group initiating work on a SOAP 1.2 specification that attempted to address the nearly 400 technical and editorial issues cited against the original specification. This working group was formally chartered with creating an XML-based standard—namely, SOAP 1.2—that would satisfy, at a minimum, the following criteria:

- Develop an "envelope-oriented" encapsulation scheme for XML data so that it could be transferred in an interoperable manner between disparate systems, allowing for future extensibility and evolution in terms of distributed systems—particularly in terms of possible intermediary nodes that may occur between the transmitter and the receiver where these intermediaries could be in the form of gateways, caches, or application-level "proxies."

- Ensure, with the cooperation of the IETF, an operating system (and programming language)–independent means for representing the contents of the SOAP envelope when SOAP is used for RCP-related operations.

- Define a mechanism based on XML schema data types (e.g., xsd:string, xsd:integer, xsd:decimal, and xsd:Boolean) to represent necessary data (where such a process for representing data so that it can be correctly interpreted at the remote end is referred to as "data serialization").

- To define, yet again with the cooperation of the IETF, a nonexclusive transport mechanism that could be layered on top of HTTP.

The SOAP 1.2 specification, sanctioned as an official W3C recommendation, was made available on June 24, 2003. This W3C recommendation status makes SOAP 1.2 a bona fide standard. The 1.2 specification consists of two parts:

1. *SOAP Version 1.2 Part 1: Messaging Framework*

2. *SOAP Version 1.2 Part 2: Adjuncts*

These two parts, which constitute the technical body of the specification, were edited by representatives from Canon, IBM, Microsoft, and Sun. This technical portion of the specification is augmented by an introductory primer, *SOAP Version 1.2 Part 0: Primer*. This document was edited by a representative of Ericsson. The complete 1.2 document set, however, is considered to consist of one other document—the *SOAP Version 1.2 Specification Assertions and Test Collection*. This document, which is essentially a test plan for 1.2, was created by representatives of Active Data Exchange, AT&T, IONA Technologies, Oracle, Unisys, and W3C.

The goal of the *Assertions and Test Collection* is to foster interoperability between diverse 1.2 implementations. Given that interoperability was an issue with 1.1, it is easy to appreciate the motivation for this specification-validating suite of tests. This document captures assertions found in the *SOAP Version 1.2 Part 1* and *Part 2* specifications and provides a set of tests that indicate whether the assertions are properly implemented in a given SOAP implementation.

These tests are meant to help SOAP implementors ensure that their creations comply with the actual specification. A SOAP 1.2 implementation that passes all of the tests specified in this document may claim to conform to the June 24, 2002, SOAP 1.2 Test Suite—this being the date that the document was accepted as a W3C recommendation. In theory, all implementations that successfully pass the entire suite of tests contained in this document should be able to cleanly interoperate with each other without encountering unexpected exceptions.

However, the successful completion of this test suite does not necessarily guarantee total SOAP 1.2 compliance, since this test suite admits up front that it does not test all aspects—particularly those facets of an implementation that are considered to reflect the core mandatory SOAP 1.2 requirements spelled out in the specification. The bottom line here, however, is that having a test suite that sets out to validate a relatively large part of the overall specification is definitely a worthwhile and sound basis for trying to enforce interoperability.

In a somewhat related vein, the 1.2 specification also strives to be as unambiguous as possible, especially when describing the structure of the XML-based documents, yet also strives to minimize the potential implementation variations that could result in interoperability issues. To this end, Part 1 of the specification, which deals with the composition of SOAP messages, resorts to the use of "XML Information Set" (XML InfoSet) conventions. XML InfoSet is a relatively new W3C standard that was formally ratified in October 2001.

The goal of XML InfoSet is to provide a consistent set of definitions for use in other specifications that need to refer to the information in a well-formed XML document. The XML InfoSet is an abstract data set for XML documents. It is, in effect, a guide for writing more-rigorous XML. It emphasizes the use of XML namespaces to eliminate ambiguity. Given this mission to promote better-structured XML documents, one can understand its appeal to those crafting the SOAP 1.2 specification. With the use of InfoSet, SOAP 1.2 also shifts the data serialization (i.e., "remote" data representation) issue to correspond with the transport that is to be used. Thus it is left to the specification for a transport binding to dictate the serialization scheme that will be used with that transport.

Other than the use of InfoSet, with its emphasis on namespaces, much of the other changes between 1.1 and 1.2 tend to be in the realm of technical refinement—and are somewhat esoteric. For example, with 1.1 it was possible to have other elements, known as "trailers," after the payload-carrying body element of a SOAP message. In other words, there could be elements between `</s:Body>` and `</s:Envelope>`. SOAP 1.2 does not permit such trailers.

SOAP, to be as flexible and extensible as possible, advocates a message transfer model in which there can be a chain of SOAP-cognizant nodes between the originator and receiver of a message. Each node in such a chain may process a part of the overall SOAP message. Nodes that perform some level of processing on a SOAP message are known as SOAP "endpoints." The processing performed by intermediary endpoints typically relates to header items within the SOAP message. Figure 5.2 illustrates some of the endpoint configurations possible with SOAP, highlighting that SOAP supports multicast/broadcast as well as chained workflow-type configurations.

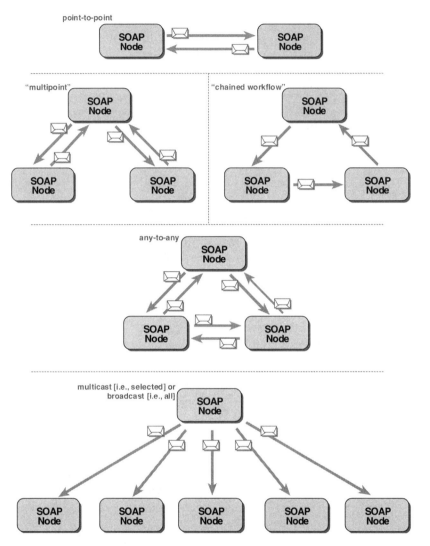

Figure 5.2   *Some of the possible SOAP node/endpoint configurations. The terms endpoint and node are essentially interchangeable when it comes to SOAP. The former was popular in the early days of SOAP, though SOAP 1.2 tends to emphasize the latter.*

In SOAP 1.1, header elements could contain an "actor=" attribute, which specifies which types of endpoints (which are defined via a URI) should process that particular header element.

SOAP 1.2 renames the "actor=" attribute to a more meaningful "role=" attribute while keeping its purpose and meaning the same as that for "actor="—discussed further in Section 5.2.1. The other changes in 1.2 are similarly arcane and are targeted at technocrats heavily involved in implementing rather than using SOAP. Consequently, these are beyond the scope and mission of this book, which is meant to be a "nontechnical" executive's guide to managers and decision makers.

However, there is one subtle but significant change regarding SOAP 1.2 that deserves exposition. As of 1.2, SOAP will no longer be considered an acronym for "Simple Object Access Protocol." Instead, SOAP will just stand for SOAP! The phrase "Simple Object Access Protocol" is misleading, and one has to suspect that it was contrived just to obtain the catchy acronym.

SOAP is a message transfer protocol rather than an object access mechanism. There is nothing that relates to object orientation when it comes to SOAP. SOAP does not even assume that any "objects" exist at the sending or receiving ends, so the "object" part is inappropriate. Furthermore, exactly how "simple" SOAP is, particularly as it evolves with 1.2, is also open to debate. In the early days of SOAP, people would claim that a SOAP implementation could be realized in a weekend, given that it was such bare-bones protocol. However, the consensus today is that it really would take a rather long weekend to successfully realize a SOAP implementation that conformed to the 1.2 test suite. So it is best to forget the "simple" and "object" references and just think of SOAP as what greases the skids when it comes to Web services I/O.

5.2   SOAP: The overall model

As is the case with XML, the power of SOAP emanates from the fact that it is based on a simple, modular, and highly flexible model that eschews restrictions. The core SOAP philosophy revolves around three fundamental precepts, as follows:

1.   SOAP messages consist of XML documents.

2.   SOAP messages, as illustrated in Figure 5.1, flow on an application-to-application basis, from a sender to a recipient, in a stateless, one-way message exchange scheme.

3.   There can also be a chain of recipients (i.e., endpoints or nodes) that process a given message—with each recipient in the chain being responsible for processing some part of the message.

Everything to do with SOAP, and its use in the context of Web services, is derived from these three basic precepts. The new SOAP documentation captures this with an opening that categorically but simply states: "SOAP Version 1.2 provides the definition of the XML-based information, which can be used for exchanging structured and typed information between peers in a decentralized, distributed environment." Subsequent sections in the introduction stress that SOAP is a lightweight protocol and that SOAP messages can be exchanged over a variety of underlying protocols. It also notes that the SOAP framework has been designed to be independent of any particular programming model and other implementation-specific semantics. Figure 5.3 shows several representations of SOAP "stacks" to show how SOAP can be layered on top of diverse transports.

Simplicity and extensibility are two major design goals for SOAP, which strives to realize these goals by trying to stay aloof from many of the networking-related issues normally addressed by other distributed computing paradigms. Some of these networking-related features that are not addressed by SOAP include reliability, security (including firewall traversal), message

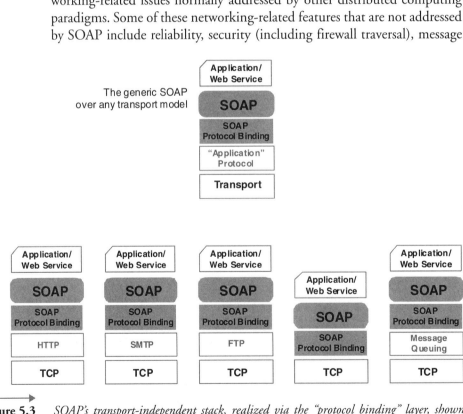

Figure 5.3   *SOAP's transport-independent stack, realized via the "protocol binding" layer, shown here in its generic form (on top) as well as with some popular implementational options.*

correlation, and routing. SOAP assumes that these important networking issues will be handled by the transport layer below it or by the application layer above it.

Part 1 of the SOAP 1.2 specification (i.e., the messaging framework specification) deals with:

1.   The SOAP processing model, which defines the rules for processing a SOAP message.

2.   The SOAP extensibility model, which deals with the concepts surrounding SOAP features and SOAP modules—where "features" in this context are extensions to the base processing model. What the specification does is describe how extensions may be added to the basic model, rather than specify any explicit features.

3.   SOAP's underlying protocol binding framework, which describes the rules for defining a SOAP binding to an underlying transport protocol; this can then be used for exchanging SOAP messages between SOAP nodes.

4.   SOAP message construct, which defines the specific structure of a SOAP message—which in essence consists of one (and only one) SOAP envelope; this in turn may contain an optional header element and a mandatory body element.

Part 2 of the SOAP 1.2 specification (i.e., the so-called "adjuncts") deals with optional functions that may be used with the messaging framework specified in Part 1. The optional adjuncts dealt with in Part 2 are as follows:

1.   A SOAP "data model" for representing application-defined, non-XML-based data structures and values by using a concept that relies on XML-qualified names and namespaces—referred to by a rather cumbersome and misleading turn of phrase that talks about a "directed, edge-labeled graph of nodes."

2.   The SOAP encoding scheme, which can be used with the data model for representing application-defined data that are to be included within SOAP messages.

3.   The ever-so-important RPC encapsulation mechanism, which shows how SOAP can be used as a means to transport and remotely invoke the RPC calls of contemporary programming languages.

4.   A description of how "features" (i.e., extensions) and bindings can be shared between specific SOAP nodes by using "message metadata," which, in this instance, are known as "properties" and property values.

5.   A description of SOAP-Supplied Message Exchange Patterns (MEPs) for two specific "request-response" scenarios, where the first involves a SOAP request that results in a SOAP response, whereas the second deals with a non-SOAP request (i.e., one that does not include a SOAP envelope) that nonetheless results in a SOAP response being sent back.

6.   How a small set of Web server–related "methods" (referred to in the specification as SOAP Web methods), such as GET, PUT, POST, and DELETE, which could be used with HTTP and possibly other protocols, supports SOAP messaging over the Web (e.g., SOAP over HTTP).

7.   The oft-mentioned SOAP HTTP binding, which defines how SOAP can be gainfully deployed over HTTP—particularly for RPC applications.

The adjunct part of the specification appears to be somewhat esoteric and obtuse. This, unfortunately, is a growing problem with today's egalitarian, Web-oriented "standards." Everybody within reason, gets a say, and too many agendas and views, however well intentioned, come into play. The SOAP 1.2 adjuncts are a compromise of sorts. These adjuncts try to provide optional extensions, within the overall SOAP messaging framework specified in Part 1, that satisfy as many groups as possible.

At this juncture, it is worth recalling once again that SOAP's overarching goal is to provide a simple, stateless, one-way message exchange model. A SOAP message is the basic unit of communication within this context. A SOAP message is fundamentally a one-way transmission between SOAP nodes, from a SOAP sender to a SOAP receiver—where a SOAP node is an implementation of the necessary processing logic to transmit, receive, process, or relay a SOAP message. The SOAP nodes enforce the protocols that govern SOAP message exchanges. SOAP permits and expects SOAP messages to be combined by applications to realize complex interaction patterns that involve multiple, back-and-forth "conversational" exchanges. This is where the adjuncts come in. They show how applications can take the basic one-way messaging paradigm and create more complex interaction patterns by exploiting features provided by an underlying protocol or through application-specific functionality.

SOAP, as the specification likes to point out, is also silent on the semantics (i.e., meaning or intent) of any application-specific data it conveys, as it is on issues such as the routing, reliable data transfer, and firewall traversal, as mentioned earlier. SOAP, however, particularly via the adjuncts, provides the framework by which application-specific information may be conveyed in an extensible manner (e.g., the SOAP data model). Thus the adjuncts, though optional, ensure that SOAP can satisfy the requirements of contemporary Web-related applications—in particular, Web services.

5.2.1   SOAP processing model

The SOAP processing model, which sets out to define a distributed processing environment, revolves around the concept of SOAP nodes. A SOAP node, specific to a given SOAP message, can be:

1.   The initial SOAP sender

2.   The ultimate SOAP receiver

3.   A SOAP intermediary

A SOAP node, on receiving a SOAP message, must perform processing on that message per processing model "protocols" set out in the SOAP specification. When processing a SOAP message, a SOAP node is said to act in one or more SOAP "roles"—where each such role is clearly identified by a specific URI, which is known as the SOAP "role name." Each node can determine the set of roles in which it proposes to act when handling a given message. The role or roles assumed by a node, however, have to remain constant during the processing of a given message.

A node identifies the role or roles that it can play for a given message via the URIs that specify the role names. Such role names will be stated via a "role=" attribute, which can be included in a SOAP header block—where a header block constitutes a single "computational unit" within a SOAP header. (This "role=" attribute used to be the "actor=" attribute in SOAP 1.1.) Thus, for example, you could have a role name that indicates "audit" or "journal"—as shown in this SOAP extract:

```
<soap:Envelope xmlns:soap=http://www.w3.org/2003/05/
soap-envelope
        xmlns:rl="http://examples.org/app-roles">
 <soap:Header>
  <rl:track soap:role= "http:// examples.org/journal">
  :
  :
```

```
</soap:Header>
<soap:Body>
   :
   :
   :
   :
</soap:Body>
</soap:Envelope>
```

Nodes that recognize the indicated role name and are capable of playing that role would perform the necessary actions—which in this case might be to journal the forwarding of the message so that there is an audit trail of its passage. A header block is deemed to be targeted at a SOAP node if a role name in a header block corresponds to a name of a role in which that node is capable of operating. Though the specification does not prescribe how implementations may exploit the role "function," it is easy to see how this attribute could be used to realize node-specific routing capabilities or to indicate whether certain messages could be cached for subsequent "replay" from an intermediary node.

The SOAP 1.2 specification defines three role names that have special significance. These, with their corresponding URIs, are as follows:

- *next*—"http://www.w3.org/2003/05/soap-envelope/role/next"

- *ultimateReceiver*—"http://www.w3.org/2003/05/soap-envelope/role/ultimateReceiver"

- *none*—"http://www.w3.org/2003/05/soap-envelope/role/none"

Each node that is expected to act as an ultimate receiver (i.e., intended recipient) or as an intermediary must be able to perform the "*next*" role. Those that will be an ultimate receiver have to be able to perform the "*ultimateReceiver*" role. The "*none*" role is somewhat incongruous but is there to ensure total architectural completeness and integrity. It indicates a role that is not to be performed by a SOAP node. SOAP header blocks that are targeted at "http://www.w3.org/2003/05/soap-envelope/role/none" are not supposed to be processed by SOAP nodes. It thus provides a kind of out-of-specification mechanism to convey data in a header block that may be of use when processing other valid header blocks. While an intermediary node may have the option of removing a header block that is tagged with a "*none*" role, it is typically assumed that such header blocks are relayed, unchanged, to the ultimate receiver.

Much of the "free-form" extensibility associated with SOAP is derived from the implementation-specific flexibility that nodes have in processing

SOAP header blocks. In addition to the "role=" attribute, the other attribute that controls how a header block is processed by a node is the "mustUnderstand=" attribute. The "mustUnderstand=" attribute is Boolean and as such can only have the values "true" and "false." The "mustUnderstand=" attribute can be used, elegantly and effectively, to segregate header blocks into those that are mandatory (relative to a given node) and those that are optional.

The following example, directly from the *SOAP 1.2 Primer*, shows the use of the "mustUnderstand=" attribute, as well as that of "role=," albeit in this instance in the rather innocuous "next" mode:

```
<env:Envelope xmlns:env="http://www.w3.org/2003/05/soap-
envelope">
 <env:Header>
 <m:reservation xmlns:m=http://
travelcompany.example.org/reservation
     env:role=http://www.w3.org/2003/05/soap-envelope/
role/next
       env:mustUnderstand="true">
  <m:reference>uuid:093a2da1-q345-739r-ba5d-
pqff98fe8j7d</m:reference>
  <m:dateAndTime>2001-11-29T13:20:00.000-05:00</
m:dateAndTime>
 </m:reservation>
 <n:passenger xmlns:n=http://mycompany.example.com/
employees
     env:role=http://www.w3.org/2003/05/soap-envelope/
role/next
       env:mustUnderstand="true">
  <n:name>Åke Jógvan Øyvind</n:name>
 </n:passenger>
 </env:Header>
 <env:Body>
  :
  :
  :
  :
 </env:Body>
</env:Envelope>
```

A SOAP node is said to understand a given SOAP header block if the software implementation of that node is capable of understanding the namespace "qualified" outermost XML element name associated with that header block (i.e., "m:reservation" and "n:passenger" in the previous example). Mandatory header blocks, by definition, are deemed to be "significant" vis-à-vis the rest of the SOAP message in that they are considered to impart some level of additional meaning that could affect the processing of other header blocks or even the "payload" contained in the body of the message.

Thus, a mandatory header block targeted at a node either has to be completely processed by that node or has to be rejected by that node, without any processing, with the appropriate SOAP fault "code." In this context, the targeting of a header block to a particular SOAP node is achieved by using the "role=" attribute. Thus "role=" and "mustUnderstand=" work in tandem—as indicated by the previous example. SOAP faults are represented by SOAP fault messages. A fault message contains a standard SOAP body with a subelement called "fault," which in turn contains two mandatory subelements known as "code" and "reason." There is the option of inserting a further application-specific subelement known as "details." Figure 5.4 shows an example of a SOAP fault message, as shown in the SOAP 1.2 Primer, that relates to the unsuccessful processing of a credit card transaction, invoked in the form of an RPC, via a SOAP-oriented travel reservation application.

```xml
<?xml version='1.0' ?>
<env:Envelope xmlns:env="http://www.w3.org/2003/05/soap-envelope"
              xmlns:rpc='http://www.w3.org/2003/05/soap-rpc'>
  <env:Body>
    <env:Fault>
      <env:Code>
        <env:Value>env:Sender</env:Value>
        <env:Subcode>
         <env:Value>rpc:BadArguments</env:Value>
        </env:Subcode>
      </env:Code>
      <env:Reason>
       <env:Text xml:lang="en-US">Processing error</env:Text>
       <env:Text xml:lang="cs">Chyba zpracování</env:Text>
      </env:Reason>
      <env:Detail>
       <e:myFaultDetails
         xmlns:e="http://travelcompany.example.org/faults">
         <e:message>Name does not match card number</e:message>
         <e:errorcode>999</e:errorcode>
       </e:myFaultDetails>
      </env:Detail>
    </env:Fault>
  </env:Body>
</env:Envelope>
```

Figure 5.4   *An example of an actual SOAP fault message, in this case indicating the failure to process an RPC request, as shown in the* SOAP 1.2 Primer, *illustrating the possible use of fault codes, a fault reason, and a detailed description of the fault.*

The appropriate processing of a header block by a SOAP node could involve the removal of the header block from that message, modification of the header block, or the insertion of a new header block. Per SOAP conventions, a targeted intermediary that does not process a header block is expected to remove it from the message prior to the message being forwarded. There is, however, a new and optional attribute known as "relay=" that may also be included in a header block to override this somewhat counterintuitive behavior. A header block in which the "relay=" attribute is set to "true" will be forwarded by intermediary nodes whether they process that block or not.

If a targeted node cannot process a mandatory header block, all further processing of that SOAP message ceases, and the message will not be forwarded any further. Though a "mustUnderstand=" attribute is not associated with the body (i.e., payload) of a SOAP message, it is a given that it has to be processed by the ultimate recipient (i.e., the node that plays the "ultimateReceiver" role). The ultimate recipient may also process any header blocks targeted at it.

5.2.2   Security considerations with SOAP

The SOAP specifications, 1.1 or 1.2, do not explicitly address SOAP-related security issues. Thus, there are no SOAP-defined mechanisms for dealing with access control, confidentiality (e.g., encryption), integrity (i.e., validity), and nonrepudiation (i.e., disowning a message). The specification, while acknowledging the need for such security measures, nonetheless expects these to be handled with the SOAP extensibility model—in particular, SOAP protocol bindings. The SOAP bindings are the conventions for encapsulating a SOAP message within or on top of another protocol (i.e., the underlying protocol) for the purpose of transmitting these messages between nodes with SOAP messages. Typical SOAP bindings include carrying a SOAP message within an HTTP message or an e-mail (e.g., MIME) or simply on top of TCP.

SOAP security is thus very implementation specific. This is not entirely a bad thing. As previously mentioned, in the context of firewall traversal, a SOAP message by itself cannot typically harm a system without the active involvement of SOAP message processing software at a node. The one noteworthy exception here is that a flood of malicious SOAP messages, though not harming the system or network, could grind things to a halt so as to constitute a denial-of-service attack. In this context a SOAP message is very much like an e-mail attachment (and it is worth noting that it is possible to send SOAP messages by using SMTP in conjunction with MIME).

Receiving a malicious e-mail attachment (e.g., virus or worm) in itself does not generally harm a system. The damage occurs when one opens (or "activates") such a rogue attachment. The same "inert-until-processed" is true when it comes to SOAP message processing. A SOAP message can damage a SOAP node and bar the denial-of-service scenario only with cooperation of the SOAP message processing software, so what is crucial is to ensure the integrity, veracity, and reliability of the SOAP software—before worrying too much about the potential rogue contents of SOAP messages.

Given that a SOAP message, by definition, may be processed by multiple intermediaries, it is vital to have trust in all SOAP nodes that are likely to come in contact with a SOAP message—as opposed to just thinking about the credentials of the ultimate receiver. Since it may not be possible, in many cases, to know about all the SOAP intermediaries that may be involved, it is imperative that all sensitive information is safeguarded within a message with suitable end-to-end application-level encryption. Depending on the transport being used, it may be possible to realize some level of point-to-point encryption at the transport layer (e.g., using SSL with HTTP). However, transport-level security alone may not be sufficient if one does not want the information in a message disclosed until it reaches the ultimate destination application.

The first priority when it comes to SOAP-related security is to ensure the credentials, capabilities, and validity of the software that will be processing the SOAP message. In this context, particularly given the Microsoft Windows–related security attacks that exploit unintended "holes" in the software, it is important to try, as much as possible, to make sure that the software does not have any weaknesses that could be pried open by a message created by an author aware of this soft spot in the software. The main thing, as repeatedly stressed here, is to ensure that the SOAP software is only capable of doing things that it is supposed to do—and that one is aware of what it can do, should do, and furthermore what it really cannot do (e.g., secretly transcribe the contents of a message or delete random files).

Once the trustworthiness and reliability of the SOAP nodes involved have been established, one can then concentrate on ensuring the actual bona fides of SOAP messages and authenticating the purported originators of these messages. This again becomes an application-level function. Basically, the SOAP message processing software could be written so that it processes messages only from known and authenticated sources—and moreover processes only individually authenticated messages that contain data per presubscribed encoding schemes. This could be realized by including an application-specific user ID/password mechanism on each message. The privacy of such an authentication scheme can be achieved by using end-to-end encryption. The bottom line here is that the only true SOAP-related security safeguard you can have is to use only trusted (and well-behaved) software that processes only valid messages from authenticated sources.

SOAP permits application-specific data, which could include authentication data and other security measures, to be carried within either SOAP header blocks or the SOAP body. If security-related items are being placed in a header block, one needs to realize that header block processing may involve the removal or modification of that header by an intermediary node, so where necessary the "role=" and "mustUnderstand=" attributes need to be rigorously used to ensure that any security measures placed in a header block are processed appropriately.

5.3   SOAP messages

A SOAP message is the basic unit of communications between SOAP nodes. A SOAP message is made up entirely of a SOAP envelope, as shown in Figure 5.5. In other words, a SOAP message "document" starts off with a definition for an envelope, and you can only have one envelope definition per SOAP message. The "envelope" is thus the top (and thereby the outer-

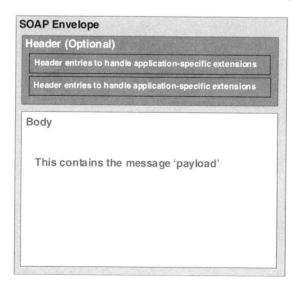

Figure 5.5   *The overall structure of a SOAP message highlighting that the entire message is made up of a SOAP envelope that consists of an optional header and a mandatory body, which contains the actual "payload."*

most) element of any SOAP message. This can be clearly seen in all of the SOAP message examples shown in this chapter—with the XML definition for the "envelope" occurring very near the top. In the case of SOAP, the envelope is the message.

A SOAP envelope may contain two subelements—namely, an optional header and a mandatory body. The envelope thus defines an overall framework for expressing what is in a message. Figure 5.6 shows a relatively long

```
<?xml version='1.0' ?>
<env:Envelope xmlns:env="http://www.w3.org/2003/05/soap-envelope">
 <env:Header>
  <m:reservation xmlns:m="http://travelcompany.example.org/reservation"
          env:role="http://www.w3.org/2003/05/soap-envelope/role/next"
           env:mustUnderstand="true">
   <m:reference>uuid:093a2da1-q345-739r-ba5d-pqff98fe8j7d</m:reference>
   <m:dateAndTime>2001-11-29T13:20:00.000-05:00</m:dateAndTime>
  </m:reservation>
  <n:passenger xmlns:n="http://mycompany.example.com/employees"
          env:role="http://www.w3.org/2003/05/soap-envelope/role/next"
           env:mustUnderstand="true">
   <n:name>Åke Jógvan Øyvind</n:name>
  </n:passenger>
 </env:Header>
 <env:Body>
  <p:itinerary
    xmlns:p="http://travelcompany.example.org/reservation/travel">
   <p:departure>
     <p:departing>New York</p:departing>
     <p:arriving>Los Angeles</p:arriving>
     <p:departureDate>2001-12-14</p:departureDate>
     <p:departureTime>late afternoon</p:departureTime>
     <p:seatPreference>aisle</p:seatPreference>
   </p:departure>
   <p:return>
     <p:departing>Los Angeles</p:departing>
     <p:arriving>New York</p:arriving>
     <p:departureDate>2001-12-20</p:departureDate>
     <p:departureTime>mid-morning</p:departureTime>
     <p:seatPreference/>
   </p:return>
  </p:itinerary>
  <q:lodging
    xmlns:q="http://travelcompany.example.org/reservation/hotels">
   <q:preference>none</q:preference>
  </q:lodging>
 </env:Body>
</env:Envelope>
```

Figure 5.6   *Example of a representative and complete SOAP message—in this case a travel reservation example, as included in the* SOAP 1.2 Primer.

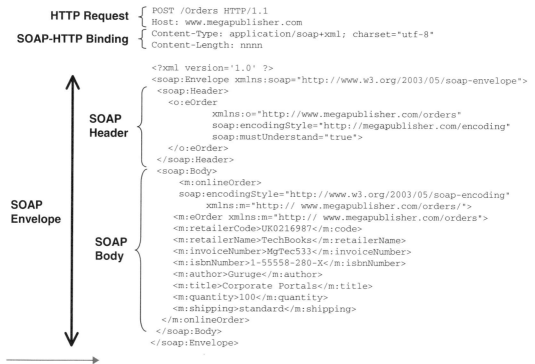

```
HTTP Request ⎰ POST /Orders HTTP/1.1
             ⎱ Host: www.megapublisher.com
SOAP-HTTP Binding ⎰ Content-Type: application/soap+xml; charset="utf-8"
                  ⎱ Content-Length: nnnn

<?xml version='1.0' ?>
<soap:Envelope xmlns:soap="http://www.w3.org/2003/05/soap-envelope">
 <soap:Header>
   <o:eOrder
          xmlns:o="http://www.megapublisher.com/orders"
          soap:encodingStyle="http://megapublisher.com/encoding"
          soap:mustUnderstand="true">
   </o:eOrder>
 </soap:Header>
 <soap:Body>
     <m:onlineOrder>
      soap:encodingStyle="http://www.w3.org/2003/05/soap-encoding"
          xmlns:m="http:// www.megapublisher.com/orders/">
      <m:eOrder xmlns:m="http:// www.megapublisher.com/orders">
      <m:retailerCode>UK0216987</m:code>
      <m:retailerName>TechBooks</m:retailerName>
      <m:invoiceNumber>MgTec533</m:invoiceNumber>
      <m:isbnNumber>1-55558-280-X</m:isbnNumber>
      <m:author>Guruge</m:author>
      <m:title>Corporate Portals</m:title>
      <m:quantity>100</m:quantity>
      <m:shipping>standard</m:shipping>
     </m:onlineOrder>
   </soap:Body>
 </soap:Envelope>
```

Labels on figure: **SOAP Header**, **SOAP Envelope**, **SOAP Body**

Figure 5.7   *The composition of a real SOAP message—in this case the "eOrder" message used at the start of this chapter.*

travel reservation–related SOAP message, as included in the *SOAP 1.2 Primer,* to highlight the composition of a real SOAP message, while Figure 5.7 takes the "eOrder" book ordering SOAP example used at the start of this chapter and demarcates it to show the various components of a SOAP message.

It should be clear from all of the SOAP message examples included in this chapter that the envelope element is always qualified with a namespace of:

"http://www.w3.org/2003/05/soap-envelope"

where the "2003/05" is essentially a timestamp. The inclusion of this namespace is not an affectation. This namespace, whose contents are shown in Figure 5.8, contains a formal, unequivocal specification of all the elements and attributes that can occur within a valid SOAP message. SOAP messages that do not subscribe to this namespace are construed to be invalid and SOAP nodes are thus expected to reject them with a "fault." (SOAP messages constructed before 1.2 would typically refer to

```
<!--
Schema defined in the SOAP Version 1.2 Part 1 specification
  Proposed Recommendation:
  http://www.w3.org/TR/2003/PR-soap12-part1-20030507/
  $Id: soap-envelope.xsd,v 1.1 2003/04/17 14:23:23 ylafon Exp $

  Copyright (C)2003 W3C(R) (MIT, ERCIM, Keio), All Rights Reserved.
  W3C viability, trademark, document use and software licensing rules
  apply.
  http://www.w3.org/Consortium/Legal/

  This document is governed by the W3C Software License [1] as
  described in the FAQ [2].

    [1] http://www.w3.org/Consortium/Legal/copyright-software-19980720
    [2] http://www.w3.org/Consortium/Legal/IPR-FAQ-20000620.html#DTD
  -->
<xs:schema xmlns:xs="http://www.w3.org/2001/XMLSchema"
    xmlns:tns="http://www.w3.org/2003/05/soap-envelope"
    targetNamespace="http://www.w3.org/2003/05/soap-envelope"
    elementFormDefault="qualified">
 <xs:import namespace="http://www.w3.org/XML/1998/namespace" />
  <!--
  Envelope, header and body
  -->
 <xs:element name="Envelope" type="tns:Envelope" />
 <xs:complexType name="Envelope">
 <xs:sequence>
 <xs:element ref="tns:Header" minOccurs="0" />
 <xs:element ref="tns:Body" minOccurs="1" />
    </xs:sequence>
 <xs:anyAttribute namespace="##other" processContents="lax" />
    </xs:complexType>
 <xs:element name="Header" type="tns:Header" />
 <xs:complexType name="Header">
 <xs:annotation>
 <xs:documentation>Elements replacing the wildcard MUST be namespace qualified,
    but can be in the targetNamespace</xs:documentation>
    </xs:annotation>
 <xs:sequence>
 <xs:any namespace="##any" processContents="lax" minOccurs="0"
    maxOccurs="unbounded" />
    </xs:sequence>
 <xs:anyAttribute namespace="##other" processContents="lax" />
    </xs:complexType>
 <xs:element name="Body" type="tns:Body" />
 <xs:complexType name="Body">
 <xs:sequence>
 <xs:any namespace="##any" processContents="lax" minOccurs="0"
    maxOccurs="unbounded" />
    </xs:sequence>
 <xs:anyAttribute namespace="##other" processContents="lax" />
    </xs:complexType>
    <!--
    Global Attributes.  The following attributes are intended to be
    usable via qualified attribute names on any complex type referencing
    them.
    -->
 <xs:attribute name="mustUnderstand" type="xs:boolean" default="0" />
```

Figure 5.8   *The contents of "http://www.w3.org/2003/05/soap-envelope" showing the formal specification of all the elements and attributes that can occur within a valid SOAP message.*

```xml
  <xs:attribute name="encodingStyle" type="xs:anyURI" />
  <xs:element name="Fault" type="tns:Fault" />
- <xs:complexType name="Fault" final="extension">
- <xs:annotation>
  <xs:documentation>Fault reporting structure</xs:documentation>
     </xs:annotation>
- <xs:sequence>
  <xs:element name="Code" type="tns:faultcode" />
  <xs:element name="Reason" type="tns:faultreason" />
  <xs:element name="Node" type="xs:anyURI" minOccurs="0" />
  <xs:element name="Role" type="xs:anyURI" minOccurs="0" />
  <xs:element name="Detail" type="tns:detail" minOccurs="0" />
     </xs:sequence>
     </xs:complexType>
- <xs:complexType name="faultreason">
- <xs:sequence>
  <xs:element name="Text" type="tns:reasontext" minOccurs="1"
    maxOccurs="unbounded" />
     </xs:sequence>
     </xs:complexType>
- <xs:complexType name="reasontext">
- <xs:simpleContent>
- <xs:extension base="xs:string">
  <xs:attribute ref="xml:lang" use="required" />
     </xs:extension>
     </xs:simpleContent>
     </xs:complexType>
- <xs:complexType name="faultcode">
- <xs:sequence>
  <xs:element name="Value" type="tns:faultcodeEnum" />
  <xs:element name="Subcode" type="tns:subcode" minOccurs="0" />
     </xs:sequence>
     </xs:complexType>
- <xs:simpleType name="faultcodeEnum">
- <xs:restriction base="xs:QName">
  <xs:enumeration value="tns:DataEncodingUnknown" />
  <xs:enumeration value="tns:MustUnderstand" />
  <xs:enumeration value="tns:Receiver" />
  <xs:enumeration value="tns:Sender" />
  <xs:enumeration value="tns:VersionMismatch" />
     </xs:restriction>
     </xs:simpleType>
- <xs:complexType name="subcode">
- <xs:sequence>
  <xs:element name="Value" type="xs:QName" />
  <xs:element name="Subcode" type="tns:subcode" minOccurs="0" />
     </xs:sequence>
     </xs:complexType>
- <xs:complexType name="detail">
- <xs:sequence>
  <xs:any namespace="##any" processContents="lax" minOccurs="0"
    maxOccurs="unbounded" />
     </xs:sequence>
  <xs:anyAttribute namespace="##other" processContents="lax" />
     </xs:complexType>
  - <!--
  Global element declaration and complex type definition for header entry returned due to
    a mustUnderstand fault
    -->
```

Figure 5.8   *(continued)*

```
<xs:attribute name="qname" type="xs:QName" use="required" />
  </xs:complexType>
<xs:element name="Upgrade" type="tns:UpgradeType" />
<xs:complexType name="UpgradeType">
<xs:sequence>
<xs:element name="SupportedEnvelope" type="tns:SupportedEnvType"
  minOccurs="1" maxOccurs="unbounded" />
  </xs:sequence>
  </xs:complexType>
  </xs:schema>
```

Figure 5.8   *(continued)*

the envelope namespace used with 1.1, which was http://schemas.xml-soap.org/soap/envelope.)

The consistent use of this envelope defining namespace within SOAP messages ensures that there will be no conflicts between the elements that make up a valid SOAP message and application-dependent elements included in the payload of a message. This is why SOAP puts so much stock in namespaces. Proper use of namespaces guarantees that there is no ambiguity anywhere along a chain of SOAP nodes, from the originator to the ultimate destination, as to what all the elements of a SOAP message are supposed to represent.

The set of rules used to represent the data included within a SOAP message is referred to as the "encoding style" for that message. SOAP provides an attribute called "encodingStyle=," which can be used with the usual reference to a URI, to specify the data encoding rules in play at any given time. This attribute could be specified on the envelope level. It could also be specified against any element within the message. Since SOAP does not define a default encoding scheme, it is important that an appropriate encoding scheme is specified in each SOAP message to ensure that nodes are not forced to either reject the message or rely on capricious, implementation-specific assumptions.

SOAP 1.1 advocated as its encoding scheme a simple type system similar to that used by programming languages and databases. With this scheme, which was modeled on the XML schema, an encoding type is either a simple (scalar) type or a compound type constructed as a composite of several parts, each with its own type. The encoding rules thus defined a serialization mechanism that can be used to readily and unambiguously exchange instances of application-defined data types in a platform-independent manner.

The optional SOAP header serves in a message extension capacity. Since SOAP does not deal with message routing, SOAP headers should not be considered in the conventional networking sense of being there to convey addressing- and routing-specific details. SOAP headers enable auxiliary information to be conveyed outside the actual message payload—particularly information of relevance to any intermediary nodes. Headers are thus typically used to pass application-specific "control" information that pertains to how a message should be processed. In this context what is important to note is that SOAP intermediaries can and are expected to inspect, modify, insert, reinsert, or delete SOAP headers. The use of headers thus permits intermediate nodes to provide value-added services to a message as it is being forwarded from its initial sender to the ultimate recipient.

The SOAP header, as shown in Figures 5.6 and 5.7, can consist of individual header blocks. A header block is a logical and discrete set of application-defined data—with it being possible for each header block to be associated with a different namespace. Each such header block can be explicitly targeted at specific nodes, whether they are intermediaries or the ultimate receiver, via the "role=" attribute. This affords even greater application-level flexibility and extensibility, given that different header blocks can be used to convey different types of directives to different nodes. The SOAP specification does not specify the content or actual composition of a header block element.

The SOAP body is the mandatory element within a SOAP envelope—and thus in a SOAP message. There is an implication that this is where the main information conveyed in a SOAP message should be included. However, the choice of what data are included in header blocks and what is included in the body of the message is left entirely to the actual application designers. The one distinction here, however, is that information in a header block can be inspected and processed by intermediary nodes as well as the ultimate receiver, while the information included in the body, which may include subelements, can be processed only by the node designated as being the ultimate receiver.

5.4   SOAP implementations

To be able to use SOAP in the real world, irrespective of whether it is for use with Web services or with non-Web services–related software, an actual software implementation of the SOAP specification is needed. This is not going to be an impediment, given that more than 70 SOAP implementations at present cover all popular hardware and software permutations—though many of these, as of mid-2003, were still based on the 1.1 specification rather than the full 1.2 specification. Implementations of the 1.2 specification should nonetheless be commonplace by early 2004, given that most of the major SOAP implementations (e.g., Apache Software Foundation's Axis V1.1) already have included support for 1.2 at the prerecommendation level (i.e., the so-called 1.2 "candidate recommendation"). A relatively comprehensive list of current SOAP implementations can be found at http://www.xmethods.net.

In general, developers will not set out to directly generate and receive SOAP messages. Instead, when developing Web services that will use SOAP for their I/O operations, they would typically opt to use a SOAP Toolkit, an application development "studio" product (e.g., IBM's WebSphere Studio Application Developer, BEA WebLogic Workshop, and Microsoft's Visual Studio .NET 2003), or a Web services–specific toolkit (e.g., IBM's Web Services Toolkit [WSTK] or Microsoft's WSTK) to help them create, parse, and manage the necessary SOAP messages. Figure 5.9 shows the overview for IBM's WebSphere Studio Application Developer product, which shows as its third item that one of its primary uses is to "Build new applications or enable existing assets quickly that are consistent with the WS-I Basic Profile 1.0 using open standards such as Universal Description Discovery and Integration (UDDI), Simple Object Access Protocol (SOAP), and Web Services Description Language (WSDL)."

SOAP-based Web services (or other applications), once developed with a toolkit or a "studio," will typically be deployed, at least on the server side, on top of application servers (e.g., IBM's WebSphere Application Server, BEA's WebLogic Server, Microsoft's .NET Framework, Apache Tomcat, Sun ONE, and the open-source JBoss), which in turn will support SOAP-based messaging over a variety of different transports. On the client side, SOAP support can generally be obtained in two distinct ways depending on the platform in question. Microsoft's .NET Framework, which is available for Windows XP, Windows CE .NET 4.2, and Windows Mobile 2003, as discussed in Section 3.2.1, true to its goal of being a strategic software environment for running XML Web services, includes built-in support for SOAP. To this end, Microsoft's technology overview for .NET Framework 1.1 starts off with the statement "The .NET Framework 1.1 is used for building and running all kinds of software, including Web-based applications, smart client applications, and XML Web services—components that facilitate integration by sharing data and functionality over a network through standard, platform-independent protocols such as XML (Extensible Markup Language), SOAP, and HTTP." If, instead, Java- or C++–based support is required for a client, one would typically include the necessary

SOAP libraries, which would be provided by the original development tool as an overall part of the Java or C++ code that would be downloaded to the client.

Figure 5.9   *IBM's high-level description of its highly promoted, Java-oriented, WebSphere Studio Application Developer, showing the built-in support for SOAP and other Web services–related protocols.*

Some of the best-known and most widely used SOAP implementations include:

- Microsoft's SOAP Toolkit 2.0
- IBM's Java-based SOAP4J, which later became the Apache SOAP project
- SOAP::Lite for Perl
- EasySOAP++
- GLUE

Given its pioneering work on SOAP, it is not surprising that Microsoft was one of the first to offer a SOAP implementation. This was the so-called SOAP Toolkit 1.0, which was available in summer 2000, shortly after SOAP 1.1 had been formulated and submitted to the W3C. This initial toolkit did not support WSDL (which was at that juncture still being formulated) and accommodated only RPC-mode transactions over HTTP. Version 2 of this toolkit, which received widespread publicity within the software development community and as such became a de facto standard for this genre, was officially available as of April 2001. Though Microsoft came out with a Version 3 in July 2002, even today it is Toolkit 2.0 that comes to the mind of most developers when they think about SOAP-specific development options from Microsoft.

The SOAP Toolkit permits developers to easily add XML Web Service functionality to existing Microsoft COM-oriented applications and components. The Toolkit is heavily WSDL-centric. It includes a WSDL generator that will automatically generate WSDL descriptions of existing COM libraries. It can be used by itself or in conjunction with Microsoft Visual Studio .NET. The primary features of the 2.0 Toolkit include:

- A client-side component, which permits applications to invoke SOAP-based Web service operations as described by the WSDL definition for that service
- A server-side component, which generates SOAP message from COM object method calls per the WSDL description—albeit only when augmented with Microsoft-specific Web Services Meta Language (WSML) files
- The necessary code to transmit, read, "serialize," and process SOAP messages

The 3.0 Toolkit included support for sending and receiving attachments (e.g., pictures). Remember that this type of attachment handling essentially falls into the realm of SOAP bindings (e.g., SMTP with MIME), SOAP extensibility, and SOAP encoding. Thus, it is a legitimate implementation-related option. Microsoft sets out to further extend this capability by adding support for Direct Internet Message Encapsulation (DIME)–based attachments. DIME is a new proposed standard for use with SOAP that, similar to MIME, will allow any file of an arbitrary type to be attached to a SOAP message. There is also a generic-type mapper to facilitate the mapping of complex data types to the necessary WSDL and WSML descriptions.

On the Java side, Apache Axis, from the Apache Software Foundation (http://www.apache.org), the doyen of Web-oriented open software, is now the gold standard when it comes to SOAP implementations. Apache Axis, which includes support for WSDL as well as XML-RPC, supersedes the well-known Apache SOAP project. This project, in turn, got its impetus when IBM magnanimously donated its SOAP4J implementation to Apache. Axis, which is positioned as a SOAP engine that is 1.2 compliant, can in effect be thought of as Apache SOAP 3.0. In addition to the inclusion of new features such as WSDL and XML-RPC, Axis represents a total rewrite of the original SOAP4J code as well as a move, within this code, from the display-oriented XML DOM API to the more appropriate inter-program-oriented SAX API. The Axis implementation is credited as being much faster than the Apache SOAP version, which was often criticized for being somewhat slow.

The Axis SOAP engine is available as a simple, small footprint, stand-alone server. It is also available as a plug-in, which can be seamlessly integrated into application (or servlet) servers. The Axis SOAP implementation is already in use by IBM, Apple, Borland, Macromedia, and JBoss, among others. IBM's market-leading WebSphere Application Server 5.0 has the Axis software built in. IBM's WSTK also uses the Axis software. Axis, like the Microsoft SOAP Toolkit, provides support for attachments. Whereas the Microsoft Toolkit is COM-centric, Axis understandably is JavaBean oriented. For example, it will automatically "serialize" JavaBeans, with the added option of customizable mapping to specific XML fields or attributes.

Interoperability, as mentioned earlier, was an issue with SOAP 1.1 implementations. Consequently there are various efforts afoot to ensure that this will not continue to be a stumbling block down the road—particularly with 1.2-based implementations. Obviously the "Assertions and Test Collection" test suite is pivotal in this respect. Then there is also the Web Services Interoperability (WS-I) organization, which was founded by Accenture, BEA, H-P, IBM, Intel, Microsoft, Oracle, SAP, and Fujitsu in

February 2002. Since then, Sun and Cisco, among many others, have joined WS-I in various capacities.

WS-I is an open industry organization whose goal is to promote Web services interoperability across platforms, operating systems, and programming languages. WS-I set out to work across the industry and standards organizations as an end-user-focused advocacy that would provide guidance as to best practices when it came to Web services and the standards upon which they were based. One of its explicit charters is that of creating, promoting, and supporting generic protocols for interoperable exchange of messages between Web services. Thus, SOAP comes under its purview, whichever way one looks at it. In addition to the WS-I efforts and the W3C 1.2 test suite, individual implementers such as Apache are also doing their part to foster interoperability. The Axis SOAP engine, for example, has been subjected to Java-related interoperability tests specified by the Java creator and mentor Sun.

The bottom line is that Web services development, deployment, or exploitation is in no way going to be hindered by the paucity of SOAP implementations. The fact that the SOAP specification currently does not address the needs of transaction processing scenarios could be an issue as more and more organizations opt to start exploiting Web services for production applications. These issues, however, for the time being, can be very effectively and elegantly addressed by using SOAP over a transport scheme that does offer the necessary transactional processing-oriented features (e.g., a cross-platform, message queuing scheme such as IBM's WebSphere MQ).

Most major toolkits and studios targeted at Web service developers offer SOAP functionality to the application servers that will be used as the execution environments for Web services. Thus, the choice of exactly which SOAP implementation an organization will use will invariably be dictated by the overall software development preferences and dictates of that organization. If it favors .NET-based software development, then it will most likely start by reviewing Microsoft's Visual Studio .NET 2003, SOAP Toolkit 3.0, and WSDK options. If, on the other hand, it happens to be a Java shop, it will most likely start with one of the popular Java studios and application servers (e.g., IBM's WebSphere or BEA's WebLogic). There are also other language-specific options for C++, Perl, and so forth.

5.5   Q&A: A time to recap and reflect

Q: What does SOAP stand for?

A: SOAP, up until mid-2003, was an acronym that stood for Simple Object Access Protocol. However, with the SOAP 1.2 specification, the term "SOAP" ceased to be an acronym. The introductory section 1.0 of the *SOAP Version 1.2 Part 1: Messaging Framework* includes this terse, one-line note at its very end: "In previous versions of this specification the SOAP name was an acronym. This is no longer the case." There are two overriding rationales for this change in name. SOAP never was an object access mechanism, like Internet Inter-Object Request Broker Protocol (IIOP), in the conventional sense. It was always a messaging scheme. Moreover, whether it was simple or not was subjective and open to debate. Consequently, it was best to do away with the acronym and just think of it as SOAP.

Q: What is SOAP?

A: SOAP is a totally XML-centric messaging scheme that can be formally characterized as a lightweight communications protocol for exchanging XML-based information between applications in a decentralized, distributed environment. If you need a thumbnail sketch, you can think of it as "XML datagrams," albeit with a powerful capability that enables RPCs, irrespective of programming language, to be encapsulated within the SOAP messages.

Q: Is SOAP a standard?

A: Yes. SOAP 1.2 was accepted by the W3C as a recommendation as of June 24, 2003. That makes it a bona fide industry standard for the Web community. The SOAP 1.1 specification had also been submitted to the W3C in May 2000. It was, however, never formally ratified. Thus SOAP 1.1 at best was but a de facto standard.

Q: What is SOAP's role in relation to Web services?

A: SOAP is the underlying XML-based communications mechanism for conventional XML Web services. It is what is used to send input to and receive output from Web services—given that XML Web services operate via exchanging XML documents. Since a Web service requires input parameters in order to be activated, SOAP is also considered to be what invokes a Web service—given that it is what delivers the input parameters. While it is theoretically possible to have Web services that do not use SOAP, today's conventional wisdom is that SOAP is a mandatory prerequisite for XML Web services at least for the next 4 to 5 years.

Q: Is SOAP just an RPC mechanism?

A: No. SOAP is much more than just an RPC mechanism, though it is seen as a nifty, platform-independent, and programming language–independent RPC invocation scheme. In addition to invoking RPCs via an RPC encapsulation methodology, SOAP can also be used to send request-response-type messages in client/server, multicast, or workflow-type scenarios.

Q: Will SOAP work only over HTTP?

A: SOAP, by and large, is transport agnostic. HTTP is just one of the transport protocols on top of which it can be layered. SOAP also can be used on top of TCP, SMTP, FTP, message queuing, BEEP, or even other programming language–specific RPC mechanisms. HTTP, however, is the preferred and most widely used transport scheme for SOAP—in the context of Web services as well as other scenarios. The SOAP specifications (i.e., 1.1 and 1.2) categorically state that SOAP is not tied to any one particular transport protocol, though the only SOAP binding examples shown in these specifications are those for HTTP.

Q: With what network configurations can SOAP be used?

A: SOAP can be used in any distributed networking environment consisting of two or more logical SOAP nodes. Since SOAP nodes are implemented in software, it would be possible to have a multinode SOAP network implemented on a single physical machine—especially if it is a machine such as a mainframe or UNIX server that can be readily partitioned into multiple virtual machines. SOAP messages flow from an original sender to an ultimate recipient. It is possible to have configurations that do not have any intermediaries between the sender and the receiver, as well as those that have one or more intermediaries. Within this overall, unconstrained framework it is possible to have any conceivable network configurations, including point-to-point, multipoint, meshes, and loops.

Q: What is the composition of a SOAP message?

A: A SOAP message is made up entirely of a SOAP envelope. Thus in the case of SOAP, the envelope is the message. A SOAP envelope may contain two subelements—namely, an optional header and a mandatory body. A SOAP header, in turn, can consist of individual header blocks. A header block is a logical and discrete set of application-defined data—with it being possible for each header block to be associated with a different namespace. Each such header block can be explicitly targeted at specific nodes, whether they are intermediaries or the ultimate receiver, via the "role=" attribute.

Q: Why does SOAP appear to be so dependent on XML namespaces?

A: XML namespaces are the standard XML mechanism to ensure that there will be no ambiguity when it comes to the meaning or intent of elements used in an XML document—especially with documents exchanged between different organizations or individuals. Namespaces guarantee the uniqueness and integrity of XML elements across documents, organizations, businesses, and industries. Since SOAP is a messaging scheme for XML-based documents, it is taken as a given that XML documents used with SOAP will in general be read and processed at a site different from that in which the document was originally created. Use of namespaces ensures that there is no ambiguity between the sender and receiver. Moreover, using a namespace to describe the elements that make up a SOAP message (e.g., the envelope) ensures that no restrictions have to be placed as to the contents of a SOAP message to preclude conflicts with the SOAP message structure. Thus namespaces in relation to SOAP provide overall flexibility and extensibility and guarantee that the contents of XML documents delivered via SOAP can always be clearly and consistently interpreted.

Q: Are there any known security issues related to SOAP?

A: SOAP messages when used with HTTP can typically go through firewalls, since they are treated as HTTP transmittals. This by itself is not a major security threat—though it is fair to point out that, as with anything that can get through a firewall, this capability could potentially be exploited to cause a denial-of-service-type attack. However, SOAP messages can be processed only by actual implementations of SOAP nodes—which furthermore have to be explicitly programmed to accept designated SOAP messages and process them (per different roles). If a SOAP node does not process a given message, the contents of that message cannot generate any harmful behavior at the receiving system—bar clogging it up with spurious messages. When it comes to SOAP, the key thing to ensure when it comes to security is that SOAP messages are accepted and processed behind the firewall only by trusted, proven, and reliable software. This is because whatever SOAP-related security exposures that can happen behind the firewall have to be done via collusion with the SOAP message processing software. A SOAP message by itself is on the whole harmless—in much the same way that today's e-mails, other than clogging up mailboxes and servers, cannot typically cause damage until someone executes a malicious piece of code attached to an e-mail. However, given that it is possible to have rogue SOAP messages sent by somebody other than who is claimed on the message that may ask the recipient to perform certain tasks, it is important to validate and authenticate SOAP messages. The privacy of SOAP messages, especially when they flow across the Internet, is another matter. The content of SOAP messages could be intercepted by SOAP and non-SOAP intermediary nodes. Thus, any sensitive information conveyed with SOAP should always be adequately encrypted on an end-to-end basis.

6

Java and Web Services

If I had six hours to chop down a tree,
I'd spend the first four sharpening the axe.

—Abraham Lincoln

Java, a technology created by Sun Microsystems, should be the ideal partner for Web services. In addition to having much in common, they complement each other. One could even say that they are synergistic. One could go on to claim that Java applets were a kind of precursor to today's XML Web services. It is worth noting that Java applets are defined as being "small applications" that are delivered over the Web. The similarity of this definition to the one for Web services is inescapable and irresistible. But there are also some obvious and fundamental differences between these two highly Web-centric methodologies.

Java applet methodology, which predates XML by 2 to 3 years, is not XML-based in any way or shape. On the other hand, applets, though they do not deal in HTML, are inextricably associated with HTML because they can be invoked via the HTML <applet> tag. Java applets are a mechanism to add dynamism and flair to HTML Web pages. In this context, there is also an interesting and profound difference as to what actually gets delivered across the Web in the case of these two methodologies. With Java applets, the actual and complete Java mini-application is delivered to the invoker of the applet, which typically is an HTML Web page being rendered by a Web browser. The applet will then be executed within the Web browser's Java Virtual Machine (JVM).

In marked contrast to applets, Web services use the remote execution model. The application software is not sent to the invoker. Instead, the invoker gets back the results of the remotely executed Web service. Despite these basic differences, one should be able to readily perceive and appreciate the commonality of the motives involved. Both of these methodologies set out to exploit the Web as an unparalleled and universal mechanism for delivering application functionality in an object-oriented manner. Object orientation is another big and important feature that Java and Web services have in common. Just as object-based modularity is a defining attribute of Web services, Java is innately object oriented.

The other major attribute that they are said to have in common is platform independence. There is, however, a beguiling but key difference as to the connotation of "platform independence" in relation of these two methodologies—and ironically it is this discrepancy in meaning that makes Java so important and enticing when it comes to Web services. In the context of Web services, platform independence, as discussed in Chapters 1 and 3, means that Web services are not specific to a particular platform (or for that matter programming language). Web services can be implemented on any platform, and Web services running on any platform can be readily invoked and exploited by applications running on any platform. But Web services–related platform independence does not mean that Web services are portable across platforms. This lack of portability is the crux of the issue here.

A Web service, unless it is written in C, C++, or Java, will typically be restricted to a particular platform—for example, Windows, an IBM mainframe running MVS, an AS/400 with OS/400, or a Sun server running Solaris. Let's start off by looking at Web services developed with any of Microsoft's popular software development tools, such as the current flagship offering, Microsoft Visual Studio .NET 2003. As shown in Chapter 3, software developed with such Microsoft tools, including all of those that fall under the .NET umbrella, can be deployed only (per Microsoft) on Windows platforms.

A similar platform dependency would also be true if one wrote a Web service in PL/I to run on an IBM mainframe or in RPG to run on an AS/400. Though one could persuasively argue that any piece of software, given enough effort, could be reengineered to work on any platform, the rub, as ever, is the exact scope of the effort, both in terms of time and money. Software ports, as anybody who has been involved with them will testify, usually with a shudder, are never as straightforward as they first appear.

Even C and C++ applications are portable only at the source-code level. They need to be compiled and linked on each new platform that they need to be executed upon. Software written in Java, in marked contrast, is portable across all of today's popular computing platforms in compiled binary form (i.e., in object-code form) as well as in source-code form. Hence, Java's famous, trademark catchphrase: "write once, run anywhere." With Java, platform independence does mean bona fide, cross-platform software portability.

Hence, a Web service developed in Java could in theory be effortlessly moved from one platform to another without any need for recompilation, let alone any rework of the code. This portability is the key value proposition vis-à-vis Java and Web services, though some would rightly point out that such portability, though invariably assured, may in some cases still require some amount of tweaking, not to mention diligent testing. Figure 6.1 sets out to highlight how platform independence in the case of Web services is markedly different from what Java means by that expression, and

Figure 6.1

Platform independence à la Web services is different from the genuine software portability across platforms offered by Java.

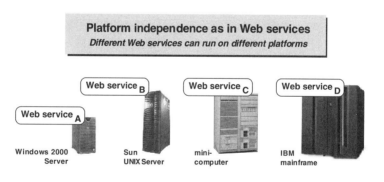

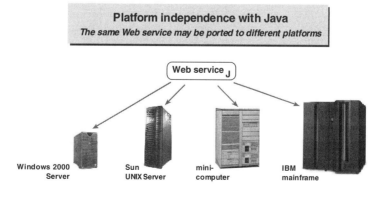

why Java's flavor of platform independence can be very important when considering the use of Web services for mission-critical, enterprise-class application scenarios.

Ensuring that one has the option of being able to readily port enterprise-class, production-level software from one platform to another is no longer a frivolous indulgence or an uncalled-for affectation. It can actually be advantageous for career advancement. The dynamics, politics, economies, and viability of enterprise computing platforms are in a state of unprecedented flux. The remorseless, unending security attacks on Windows, prompted by the steady stream of software holes being routinely discovered in Windows software, including in the supposedly trustworthy Windows Server 2003, persist in undermining the credibility of Windows as a true, enterprise-class platform for any mission-critical-related applications. At the same time, partly in response, the popularity of and acclaim for Linux continues to grow, with Sun now promoting a Java/Linux-based desktop and Office alternative to Windows. The fundamental economics of the hardware platforms are also changing—markedly for the better.

Thanks to the vicious battle for market leadership between Sun and IBM, the pricing of UNIX servers, across the board from the utilitarian low end to the ultra-sophisticated high end, is in a steep downward spiral. From a true, total cost of ownership standpoint, especially when one factors in the potential lost opportunity costs of security breaches or system crashes, today's UNIX servers stack up extremely favorably against multiprocessor WinTel platforms. Mainframes and AS/400s (now referred to as iSeries machines) are also more affordable and cost competitive than ever before. Moreover, true to IBM's unstinted commitment to Linux, these proven, mission-critical servers support Linux, as well as Java, alongside the proprietary operating systems. In reality, if an enterprise has a need for a large number of Linux servers, then one of IBM's new mainframes (e.g., z800) might in practice be the optimum solution. Given these dynamics, not striving for software portability, especially in the realm of Web services, could prove to be short-sighted and career limiting.

The bottom line here is that a Web service's security, scalability, performance, and availability characteristics can be profoundly impacted by the platform on which it is running, as was discussed at length in Chapter 3 relative to Web services that might be deployed on Windows servers. Given this, there will be many scenarios in which an enterprise wishing to make use of a Web service from an external organization will want to have that Web service running on a particular platform. In some cases the enterprise may actually want to acquire the Web service and bring it in house so that it can run on a server of its choice, behind its firewall. Such attempts will be thwarted by platform-specific Web services. Hence, the motivation to have Java-based, cross-platform Web services.

Java, as patently testified by the java.sun.com URL for its home site, is not an industry standard in the conventional sense. Sun, at least for the time being, controls the Java specification and the Java trademarks, including the well-known steaming cup of coffee logo and administers compliance testing. In December 1999, Sun somewhat surprisingly backed away from its previous work to make Java, or to be more precise, Java 2, into a genuine, vendor-neutral standard in conjunction with the European Computer Manufacturers Association (ECMA)—a recognized and respected standards body in Europe.

Despite Sun's ongoing stewardship of Java, it is still accepted by a very large segment of the computer industry, including the influential open-software advocate, the Apache Software Foundation, as a de facto industry standard. To be fair to Sun, it does have an egalitarian, open-to-all, low-cost (i.e., free for individuals) mechanism known as the Java Community Process (JCP), whereby developers and Java licensees can participate in the evolution of Java. Visit http://jcp.org/en/home/index for details on the JCP. In addition, though many think of enterprise Java in terms of high-profile Java application servers such as IBM's WebSphere, BEA's WebLogic, Oracle's 9i, and Sun's ONE, there are at least two mature, no-cost, widely used, open-source Java application servers: Apache's Tomcat and JBoss. In addition, and to afford further legitimacy to this Java freeware concept, Sun provides an entry-level version of its Sun ONE Application Server 7, known as the platform edition, for free in parallel to the no-cost Java reference implementations available from java.sun.com. Thus, in effect, Java is to application development and deployment what Linux is to operating systems.

So all in all, though Java is not a true standard, it certainly acts and quacks like one. Consequently, those who endorse and actually license Java technology from Sun read like the "Who's Who" of the computer industry—with Microsoft being the one conspicuous, but obvious, exception. The major industry luminaries that are actively behind Java include IBM, Oracle, SAP, BEA, H-P, Borland, Macromedia, NEC, Nokia, Hitachi, and Fujitsu. Given this huge backing, Java is obviously a credible, worthy, and formidable competitor to Microsoft's .NET. Figure 6.2 shows how the significance of Java as a server-side IT technology has a direct correlation to a company's size.

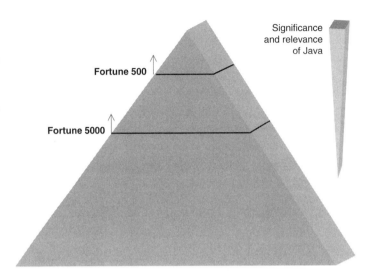

Figure 6.2
The significance and relevance of Java to an enterprise is usually related to the size of the enterprise.

When it comes to Java and Web services, the battle lines in relation to .NET get drawn along these lines:

- Cross-platform portability against Windows-specific solutions

- Open standards versus proprietary

- No danger of vendor lock-in (given that Java solutions are available from multiple sources) as opposed to being always dependent on Microsoft

- Free (e.g., Tomcat, JBoss, or Sun's ONE 7 platform edition on a Linux server) versus the inevitable cost of a Microsoft server solution

- Industrial strength as opposed to "departmental"

- UNIX (as in Sun) against Windows

- IBM against Microsoft

- Resource hog versus lean and mean

- Good for selling more hardware against scalability

- Microsoft versus the rest

6.1   Java: An overview

Java is a high-level, third-generation, object-oriented programming language developed by Sun. It resembles C and C++ to an extent, given that it was created to be a better C++ by James Gosling, Patrick Naughton, and

Mike Sheridan as part of a so-called "green project" at Sun toward the end of 1990. It was originally intended for use in embedded systems included in smart consumer electronic devices such as TV set-top boxes, game consoles, and PDAs. Its original name was "Oak." The hackneyed, "hello world" program written in Java, per Sun, would look like this:

```
class hello {
public static void main(String argv()) {
System.out.println("Hello!");
}
}
```

Java, as it is known now, came to be in 1995 when Sun unveiled it as a platform-independent technology for enhancing what could be done on the Web—particularly in terms of dynamic, highly interactive Web pages with lots of animated graphics, as well as other value-added functionality from locally executed code. Netscape Navigator 2.0, released in March 1996, at that juncture the undisputed top-dog of Web browsers, included ground-breaking support for both Java and JavaScript. Java had been propelled onto the Web by two of the then most influential and respected players vis-à-vis the Web: Sun and Netscape. Java has not looked back since.

Though Java has a syntax modeled on that of C, it is neither C nor, as in the case of C++, a superset of C. A Java compiler will thus not accept C code, and most nontrivial C programs typically need to be significantly reengineered before they can be treated as Java applications. Knowing C or, better still, C++ will certainly shorten a programmer's learning curve when it comes to Java, though it should be stressed that familiarity with C or C++ is in no way a prerequisite for mastering Java. What truly distinguishes Java from C and C++ as well as from all prior programming languages, however, is the concept of applets—the small, platform-independent applications that can be dynamically downloaded to a target system over the Web.

In the early days there were essentially two main types of Java programs: applications and applets. Java applications are conventional, stand-alone programs, installed and executed off a system's hard drive in the same way as applications developed with other languages—with one distinguishing feature: Java applications can be readily ported between vastly disparate systems. Java applications, in common with applications developed with other popular languages, will typically be invoked via a command line (e.g., Windows Run prompt) instruction. Java applications, as with other applications, will normally also have unfettered access to the host system's resources (e.g., data files)—though it is important to note that Java software does not support, in any way, the concept of pointers. Consequently, at least in theory, Java programs can be considered to be more secure and well-behaved than most others in that they cannot access arbitrary addresses in memory—always keeping in mind that unauthorized and unintended memory access is one of the major causes of application or system crashes (or hangs).

Applets, though similar to applications, are not considered to run in stand-alone mode. Instead, an applet is a program that runs within a Web browser or an applet viewer and, moreover, has strictly limited access to host resources, in particular any kinds of files. An applet, as such, is meant to be nonmalicious, at all costs. This intentional restricted access to host resources precludes the danger of applets being used to propagate viruses or worms. The ongoing popularity of Java applets owes much to this "applets are benign" claim and reputation. In today's security-conscious culture, Java would already be dead and buried if there were even the slightest suspicion that Java applets could be used maliciously. Microsoft, for one, would have gone all out to make sure of that! But Java applets, which in the main typically run within the confines of Web browsers, including Microsoft's Internet Explorer (IE), are considered by most to be safe—though one always has the option of disabling Java applet execution by a browser.

In the context of applets, there used to be the concept of a Java "sandbox." Applets could play only within the strict and highly controlled confines of the sandbox, and the safeguards in place ensured that applets could not pry, prod, or poke. To start with, an applet could not even communicate with another server, other than the one that had originally downloaded it to its present target system. Though the scope of what an applet can now do has been slowly extended through the use of Java SecurityManager objects, it is still safe to say that applets cannot easily misbehave, particularly when it comes to reading and writing files. Even if authorized to do so, an applet will typically request explicit permission each and every time it wants to access a host file.

6.1.1   Virtual machines, containers, and developer kits

Java applications, as well as Java applets, were said to execute on Java Virtual Machines (JVMs). A Java VM was a virtual platform that executed the instructions that were generated by a Java compiler. A JVM is thus a runtime (or execution) environment. JVMs are implemented on various computing platforms—in particular, Web browsers and all popular operating systems, ranging from mainframe z/OS to the Mac OS with all flavors of UNIX, Linux, and Windows being more than adequately catered to in

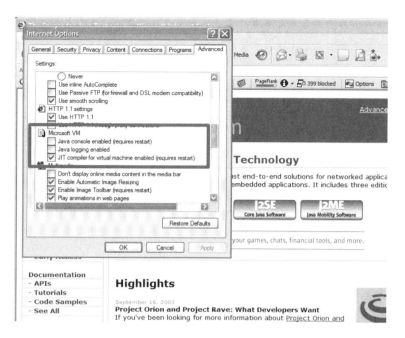

Figure 6.3

Screen shot of the Internet Options for Microsoft's Internet Explorer (IE) 6.0 showing the reference to Microsoft's version of the virtual machine for running Java— including mention of a JIT compiler.

some way or another. Sun generally provides JVMs for Solaris, contemporary Windows releases, and one or more versions of Linux, while the JVMs for other platforms are developed by other entities (e.g., IBM, Apple) with vested interest in a particular platform. Figure 6.3 shows a screen shot of Microsoft IE 6.0's Internet Options, which refer to Microsoft's version of the VM for running Java.

The ongoing acrimony between Microsoft and the Java camp, as discussed at the start of Chapter 3, is likely to result in Microsoft refusing to include a JVM in future releases of Windows as well as IE (though even now the JVM for IE 6 is only installed the first time it has to render a Web page that invokes a Java applet). This is not a show-stopper in any way, since JVMs for all releases of Windows, starting with Windows 98, are readily and freely available for download from java.sun.com and www.java.com.

The concept of a JVM is still very much an integral part of the Java landscape. Today, with the so-called Java 2 technology and in particular Java 2 Enterprise Edition (J2EE), the term *container* is preferred—where a container is a Java execution environment replete with a number of key built-in services such as database access, directory and naming, messaging, transaction management, and CORBA interoperability. The term *Java 2 Runtime Environment* (J2RE) is also sometimes used to describe a JVM in the context of Java 2. It is the availability of JVMs (or containers or J2REs in the case of Java 2) on all major platforms that makes it possible for Java to have its trademark portability. It goes without saying but is still worth mentioning just to be on the safe side that it would not be possible to execute a Java application or applet on a platform that did not contain the appropriate JVM (or container).

Java's JVM-based platform independence is realized through the use of an intermediary pseudocode known as "bytecode." A Java compiler, in marked contrast to other compilers, does not convert Java code to a specific, directly executable machine code. Instead, Java compilers turn all Java code into Java-dictated, platform-neutral bytecode (i.e., the bytecode corresponding to a Java program is always the same, irrespective of which platform it was compiled on or which platform it is going to be executed on). JVMs in general will interpret this bytecode to execute the Java program—whether it be an application or applet. Figure 6.4 illustrates the Java concept of first compiling code into bytecode and then having that bytecode interpreted by JVMs on different platforms.

Interpreting involves processing a line of code each time it has to be executed, even if that line of code had been previously processed. BASIC, highly popular with PC users during the 1980s, similar to Java, was typically interpreted. List-processing LISP and object-oriented SmallTalk are other well-known examples of interpreted, as opposed to compiled, languages. Interpreting code can be inefficient and result in less-than-optimum performance, since the original code is continually being reprocessed line by line without any use being made of previously processed code. With interpreted code, Java would sometimes run into situations where its performance would be characterized as being sluggish. To avoid this, various JVM implementers, led by Sun and IBM, developed so-called "Just-in-Time" (JIT) Java compilers.

When JIT is available with a JVM, it obviates the need for the JVM to interpret Java code. Instead, the JIT takes the previously produced bytecode and recompiles it into a native machine code that can be directly executed by the platform on which the JVM is implemented. A JIT thus takes platform-independent bytecode and makes it platform specific. Since Java is a highly object-oriented, dynamic language, it is not typically possible to compile all of a Java program until the various object-based classes within it are invoked. Hence, the term *just-in-time*, since JIT compilers compile the necessary Java code as and when the various classes are invoked. Having a JIT compiler on a JVM does not preclude the JVM from still being able to interpret bytecode. Thus, it is possible to have scenarios in which a JVM

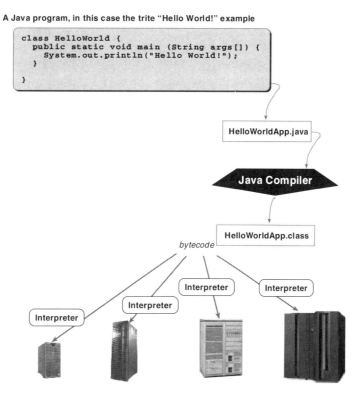

A Java program, in this case the trite "Hello World!" example

```
class HelloWorld {
  public static void main (String args[]) {
    System.out.println("Hello World!");
  }

}
```

HelloWorldApp.java

Java Compiler

HelloWorldApp.class

bytecode

Interpreter

Interpreter

Interpreter

Interpreter

Figure 6.4 *The cross-platform portability of Java is realized by first having all Java programs compiled into a platform-independent bytecode and then using interpreters within the Java virtual machine on a specific platform to interpret the bytecode.*

interprets some Java programs while relying on a JIT compiler to produce natively executable code of other Java programs.

In the 1996 to 1998 time frame, JVMs and Java compilers were made available via what used to be referred to as the Java Developer Kit (JDK). There were different JDKs for each of the platforms that supported Java, with Sun initially supplying JDKs for Sun Solaris, Windows 95, Windows NT, and the Mac. IBM, for example, had a JDK for mainframe OS/390 V1 and V2 by late 1998. A JDK, at a minimum, consisted of:

1. A JVM for that particular platform

2. A Java compiler to convert Java applications and applets to byte-code

3. A set of standard "foundation" Java class libraries (including the source code) to facilitate the development of new Java applications and applets

4.   An applet viewer to preview and run applets in case an applet-enabled Web browser is not available

5.   A debugger for testing and fixing new Java code

JITs were optional and were only available with some JDKs. Sun came up with the term *Java 2* in December 1998. Java 2 corresponded to a new level of the Java specification, which was referred to as Java 2 Platform, Standard Edition V1.2. The JDK corresponding to this 1.2 version of Java was called JDK 1.2. However, with the introduction of the overarching umbrella term *Java 2* to describe the latest Java technology, JDK 1.2 became renamed Java 2 Software Developer Kit, Standard Edition (J2SDK) V1.2. Since then the term *SDK*, as in J2SE 1.4.2 SDK, has superseded the use of the term *JDK*. In today's Microsoft world, .NET Framework is the .NET equivalent of a Java JDK.

6.1.2   The basic Java argot

Given the impetus of all the major players with a vested interest in Java, as well as its pivotal and pioneering role in helping make the Web that much more dynamic and interactive, Java has expanded and evolved significantly faster than any prior programming methodology. This rapid growth has, as is to be expected, resulted in a rich and varied array of Java-related terms and concepts. This section attempts to address the most important of these so as to provide readers with enough navigational aids to be able to chart a meaningful path through contemporary Java technology.

Anybody involved with Web page development would invariably encounter the term *JavaScript* and possibly even *JScript*. Despite the similarity in their names, JavaScript is not a direct offshoot of Java. While Java and JavaScript, to be fair, are not as distinct as chalk is from cheese, their relationship is akin to that of cheese to cheesecake. For a start, JavaScript was not developed by Sun. Instead it was created by Netscape. Though JavaScript, like Java, is object oriented, it is at best a smaller and much simpler version of Java. Unlike Java, with JavaScript it is not possible to have stand-alone applications. Instead, JavaScript, which always remains in text form, only works inside an HTML-based document. JavaScript is enacted in text form by a Web browser as it is rendering standard HTML.

Unlike Java, which is always first compiled into bytecode, there is never a compilation step with JavaScript. Rather, JavaScript, which will be contained within an HTML document, is interpreted by a Web browser. Hence, Java-Script is not executed by a JVM. Neither is there any other virtual machine associated with JavaScript. JavaScript in many ways is a Java-inspired script-ing extension to HTML. Despite these differences, both Java and JavaScript can be used more or less interchangeably to add dynamism, the so-called "events," to a Web page. Java, however, is more powerful and extensible, whereas JavaScript is simpler to master and easier to use. Within this con-text, JScript is a Microsoft version of JavaScript for Internet Explorer.

In addition to JavaScript, the Java programming space now also includes servlets, JavaBeans, Enterprise JavaBeans (EJBs), and JavaServer Pages (JSPs). All of these, in marked contrast to JavaScript, are direct derivatives of Java. These technologies were also developed under the auspices of Sun. Java servlets provide Web developers with a relatively easy-to-use, Java-based mechanism for extending Web server functionality and for creating back-end connections for integrating business logic from existing business applications into new Web-based applications. A servlet is essentially a server-side applet—albeit without a user interface. As with applets, servlets are downloaded on demand when invoked. Consistent with the Java creed, they are meant to work on any platform with any Web server.

In this respect, note that an absence of a user interface was also one of the original criteria associated with Web services until IBM postulated the concept of WSRP. Suffice to say, servlets are an ideal means for implement-ing Java Web services. They can also be used to create complex, platform- and server-independent applications, which could rely on Web services for some of their functionality. Servlets, per the new Java terminology, run within the context of Java containers (i.e., JVMs replete with key services). Containers for running servlets are readily available for all relevant plat-forms, including Microsoft's widely used IIS Web server. The freely avail-able, open-software Apache Tomcat, for one, is a highly proven and popular container for running servlets that works with most commercial Web serv-ers. In addition, all major Java application servers (e.g., IBM's WebSphere, BEA's WebLogic, and so on) support servlets, since they are a strategic means for developing new Web applications.

JSPs are built on top of servlets. They are somewhat analogous to the now relatively common Microsoft Active Server Pages (ASPs). The big dif-ference is that ASPs are Microsoft IIS–centric, whereas JSPs are meant to work with any Web server. The underlying rationale for JSPs is to neatly demarcate HTML from servlet code. It enables Web developers to keep HTML separate from servlets. It is thus a technology to simplify and expe-dite the creation of dynamic Web content, particularly in the context of developing new Web-based applications. Given that they are built on top of servlet technology, JSPs are now often positioned as the strategic way to develop Java-based, platform-neutral, server-side applications.

JSP decouples the user-interface aspects of Web applications from those of content generation. It thus enables Web developers to change the presentation layout of a Web page or the contents of that Web page independently of each other. This separation, as should be readily appreciated, greatly simplifies the design and maintenance of complex Web applications that deal with lots of Web pages. This separation is realized through the use of XML-like tags, which typically start with "<%" and end with "%>". These tags are used to encapsulate the content-generating program logic of a particular page and keep it separate from the HTML. In addition, these tags can be used to invoke object-based, server-side, application logic—in particular, JavaBeans. Behind the scenes, the program logic part of a JSP is often converted to a servlet by the container that has to run it. This makes JSP processing even more efficient and expedites end-user response times.

JavaBeans are Java's powerful component architecture for designing and exploiting reusable, platform-independent software components. The JavaBeans specification defines a set of standard software APIs for the overall Java platform. It is thus the component architecture recommended for use when developing client-side Java applications or applets. JavaBeans components, often referred to as "beans," can be developed and manipulated by using visual development methodology—such as the Bean Builder tool available with the Java platform.

As a component methodology, beans can be gainfully used to develop any frequently used software entity, whether it be something as relatively simple as a button for a Web page or something more sophisticated such as a database access mechanism. JavaBeans were developed to ensure ready interoperability with Microsoft's ActiveX component architecture. Interoperability with ActiveX and other component schemes is realized through the use of bridges.

Enterprise JavaBeans are server-side, reusable beans ideally suited for implementing middleware business logic for *n*-tier (and, in particular, data, business logic, and client layer–oriented 3-tier) application scenarios. EJBs take the component model of JavaBeans to the next level, so to speak, by providing a built-in, automated repertoire of server-side services. EJBs are considered to reside and run in EJB-ready containers. These containers include a standard set of EJB-related services, which include database connectivity, security, transaction management, messaging, persistence (i.e., maintenance of certain data or relationships), and concurrency (i.e., performing multiple parallel tasks). The major Java application servers include comprehensive support for EJBs. Applications developed with EJBs, in addition to being platform independent, are normally expected to be scalable, transactional, and secure for concurrent use by multiple users.

An EJB consists of three major components:

1.   Bean class

2.   Home interface

3.   Remote interface

The bean class is what is used to implement the business logic that will be performed by an EJB. The home interface can then be used by clients to find, create, and delete instances of that EJB. Clients access the business logic of an EJB via the remote interface. There are four distinct types of EJBs: stateless session EJBs, stateful session EJBs, entity EJBs, and message-driven EJBs. The first two differ in terms of whether they are session oriented or asynchronous when it comes to transaction processing. Entity EJBs are typically used to provide an object-oriented view of database records. They can also be used to represent data accessible via existing legacy applications. Message-driven EJBs, as indicated by the name, are used in Java Message Service (JMS)–based message processing scenarios.

An overriding goal of the new EJB V2.1 specification, which was finalized in June 2003, was to position EJBs as an optimum technology for developing, deploying, and consuming Web services. Thus, it is now possible to implement a Web service as stateless session EJB. It is also now possible for EJBs to invoke and use external Web services. There is also support for WSDL.

Two other important Java programming–related terms that one is likely to encounter are AWT and Swing. Both of these refer to the user-interface aspects of Java software. AWT, which, according to Sun, stands for Abstract Windows Toolkit (though there are other variants such as Advanced Windows Toolkit), is a standard library of user interface development–related classes. AWT includes components that can be used by applets or applications for displaying and using presentation-related constructs such as buttons, menus, and scroll bars. Swing, whose official name is "Project Swing," is another standard library of classes that can be used by applets or applications to create and manage sophisticated GUIs. With Swing a developer can opt for a platform-dependent look and feel or elect to have a consistent look and feel across all platforms.

Java-centric distributed computing, where necessary across disparate platforms, is facilitated by RMI—Java's Remote Method Invocation methodology. With RMI, programmers can readily and safely invoke Java objects on remote systems—across a network or the Web. RMI eliminates the distinction between local and remote Java objects. With RMI it is possible to access a remote object as easily as it is to access a local one.

6.2   The Java 2 platforms

The trademark "write once, run anywhere" platform independence of Java is not restricted to conventional computing platforms. Java technology, reflecting its roots as an embedded system for consumer electronics, even today is carefully positioned as a powerful, full-function software methodology that can be made to work on just about any electronic device. Java is already poised to be a major player in next-generation, multimedia, intelligent phones. It can be used in PDAs, and, given its symbiotic relationship with Windows, can be readily used with tablet PCs as well as Pocket PCs. It is yet again being considered for TV set-top boxes. Java-based smart cards, as shown in Figure 6.5, have been available since October 1996. These are known as Java cards, and information about them can be found at http://java.sun.com/products/javacard/.

Given this wide spectrum of hardware and software permutations it is intended to work on, Java itself is thought of as a self-contained platform in its own right. Thus, there is the concept of a Java platform. The original Java platform had two key components: the JVM and the Java API.

Figure 6.6 depicts a Java platform vis-à-vis a specific computing or consumer electronic environment. The Java API is an extensive collection of predefined, ready-to-run software components for facilitating and expediting Java application or applet/servlet development. This API is grouped into standard libraries containing related sets of functional entities known as classes. Thus, there are libraries for GUI creation, database access, and so on. These libraries are known as a package. This overall Java platform is then ported onto a specific target system, whether it be a PC, mainframe, handheld, phone, or TV set-top box. Though this original premise that a

Figure 6.5
A picture of a Java-based smart card from the java.sun.com Web site.

Figure 6.6
The concept of a Java platform, consisting of a JVM and a Java API, on a specific computing platform.

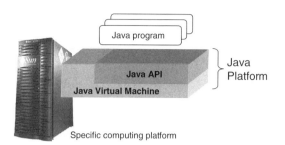

Java platform consists of a JVM and a Java API set is still conceptually sound, Java technology and terminology, as is to be expected, have expanded and evolved. For a start, the term *container* is now preferred to that of JVM.

Since the introduction by Sun of the term *Java 2* in December 1998, the current Java platform is known as the Java 2 platform. The Java 2 platform is billed by Sun as providing robust, end-to-end solutions for networked applications as well as being a trusted standard for embedded applications. Today's Java 2 platform consists of three editions. These are known as:

1.   Java 2 Platform, Standard Edition (J2SE)

2.   Java 2 Platform, Enterprise Edition (J2EE)

3.   Java 2 Platform, Micro Edition (J2ME)

Figure 6.7 shows Sun's depiction of how these three editions stack up against each other. Also note that Sun, for the sake of completeness, includes the Java Card APIs. The optional packages, shown with J2EE and J2SE, are libraries of value-added services—which in practice will typically be provided by an application server implementation.

Figure 6.7
Sun's depiction of the three Java 2 editions, J2EE (at left), J2SE, and J2ME, and how they stack up against each other.

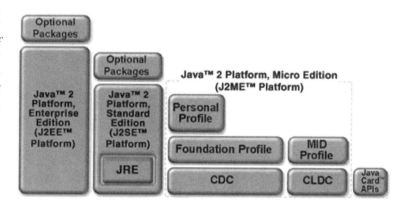

J2SE, known as the core Java software, came about from what was known in early 1998 as Java 1.2. Today, J2SE, which is at Version 1.4, is positioned as a fast and secure foundation for building and deploying mission-critical enterprise applications—albeit primarily for client-side (i.e., desktop) applications, whether they be in the form of applets or applications. J2SE provides the necessary Java APIs; compiler; tools; and run times for writing, debugging, deploying, and executing Java applets and applications. The J2SE JVM in this instance, as shown in Figure 6.7, is known as the Java Runtime Environment (JRE). J2SE supports JavaBeans but not EJBs.

The standard built-in repertoire of services offered by J2SE includes database access (i.e., JDBC), directory, and security. The security-related functions include Java authentication and authorization service (JAAS) for imposing access control; Java secure socket extension (JSSE), which is a Java version of SSL; and Java cryptography extension (JCE), which facilitates encryption. J2SE 1.4, in addition, includes support for key industry standards including XML, XML's DOM API, Kerberos, LDAP, and CORBA. It supports 64-bit addressing and thus gives Java applications the option of accessing hundreds of gigabytes of RAM for highly memory-intensive scenarios such as memory-resident table (i.e., database) processing. It is also claimed to be highly scalable and nimble.

Though J2SE, with its support for XML, can be used as a basis for developing Web services or applications that consume Web services, in reality it is the server-side-oriented and highly component-based J2EE platform that is invariably targeted for most Web services–related uses. This makes sense. As stated in its name, this is the Java platform intended for use by enterprises. J2EE includes support for servlets, JSPs, and EJBs. It is also the platform implemented by all of the major commercial Java application servers. Given its relevance to Web services, the next subsection focuses entirely on J2EE.

J2ME, the Java counterpart to Microsoft's Windows CE, is a highly optimized, low-resource consumption Java run-time environment targeted at small footprint consumer devices. In addition to being aimed at cell phones and TV set-top boxes, it is also positioned for use on pagers and smart cards. As with all things Java, the mantra, yet again, this time in the context of consumer devices, is "write once . . . for potential use on a wide range of devices." J2ME includes a flexible user interface, a robust security model, and support for a wide range of networking protocols. Recognizing that the MO of consumer devices can be very different from that of contemporary, Internet-dependent computers, J2ME caters to both network-connected and off-line (i.e., disconnected) applications—though always ensuring that the necessary Java applications can be dynamically downloaded onto a device when it has a network connection.

J2ME, as shown in Figure 6.7, comes in two distinct configurations. The so-called "CDC" configuration, which includes a foundation profile as well as a personal profile, is for connected devices—where CDC refers to connected device configuration. The other configuration is called "CLDC." CLDC stands for "connected limited device configuration." CLDC is for devices that are expected to work in off-line mode for extended periods of time. On this basis, CDC is targeted at TV set-top boxes, networked embedded devices (e.g., medical equipment), and high-end PDAs. CLDC, on the other hand, is for cell phones, pagers, and low-end PDAs. Each configuration includes a virtual machine and a minimal set of Java class libraries applicable to the range of devices being addressed by that configuration. Similarly, each configuration is carefully tailored to work optimally with the processor, memory, and I/O capabilities likely to be available on the target devices.

The profiles included with the J2ME configurations cater to the specific, run-time requirements of different device categories. Thus, the personal profile is for devices such as PDAs and high-end cell phones that require a GUI as well as the option for executing standard Java applets invoked from Web pages. This profile includes the full AWT library and ensures that standard Web applications, originally developed for desktop use, can be executed on devices running the CDC configuration. On the other hand, the foundation profile is a lower-level functional set, without a user interface, for use in networked embedded systems.

6.2.1   Java 2 Platform, Enterprise Edition (J2EE)

Whenever Java is being discussed, in earnest, within the context of Web services, it would typically be the capabilities offered by J2EE that are most likely being considered—implicitly or otherwise. From a Java standpoint, J2EE is, indubitably, the obvious foundation technology for developing and deploying Web services. J2EE, from ground up, is a component-based methodology. It is built on top of J2SE and in essence adds enterprise- and server-related functionality to the J2SE core—in particular, support for EJBs, servlets, and JSPs.

J2EE is a service-rich, distributed application model that places much emphasis on modularity, security, transaction processing, messaging, and interoperability with legacy applications. Its express purpose is to facilitate the development and use of platform-independent, server-side software for Web-oriented, *n*-tier applications—including those that require either back-end data interchange connections to existing applications or those that leverage business logic from legacy applications that have been isolated and modularized into reusable components (e.g., JavaBeans).

J2EE's basic premise is that it will deliver a complete set of easy-to-access backbone services for component-based software so that the software developers can concentrate on the business logic aspects of the software without getting sidetracked trying to work out how they obtain necessary functionality such as directory lookup, authentication, and messaging. The component model advocated by J2EE is EJBs. J2EE, however, offers interoperability with CORBA. With the J2EE software model, business logic is encapsulated within EJBs. EJBs, which can be used by servlets and JSPs, run in a Java container. This container provides the EJBs with all of the necessary backbone services.

Figure 6.8, from Sun's "BluePrint Design Guidelines" for J2EE, clearly demonstrates the highly component-oriented role envisaged for J2EE in an *n*-tier application scenario. In this figure, J2EE is the basis for both of the central columns—one of which provides the server-side business logic, exploiting EJBs, while the other, in conjunction with a Web server, handles the server-side data presentation aspects, leveraging the Web page design flexibility afforded by JSPs. It is the functionality associated with these two central columns that is implemented and leveraged by Java application

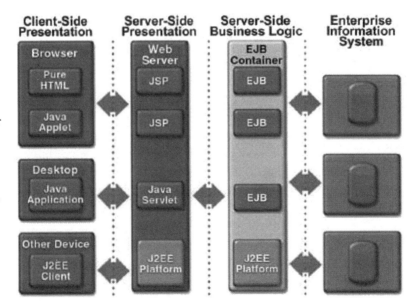

Figure 6.8

Sun's representation of a possible J2EE-based n-*tier model, highlighting the component-oriented nature of J2EE as well as the fact that in such a model it is possible to have Java on both the client and server sides.*

servers. This figure also shows the possibility that J2EE-based clients, through standard Web browsers and where necessary augmented by applets or desktop J2SE-level Java applications, will in general be the norm for the client tier of J2EE applications.

The application model envisaged for J2EE divides enterprise applications into three fundamental parts:

1.   Components

2.   Containers

3.   Connectors

The components (i.e., EJBs) are the end-user consumables that developers create using Java. Java developers creating components do not have to worry about also having to create containers and connectors. Containers and connectors are implemented and delivered by system vendors—typically in the form of application servers. Containers are in essence the hosts for the components. Containers provide the necessary backbone services to the components—as well as the end users making use of those components. Since containers are implemented on specific platforms, the exact run-time services they provide can typically be specified and customized for a particular set of components at the time the components are deployed on that platform. For example, containers could provide transparent load balancing and automatic failover capabilities.

The connectors in this model are external to the J2EE platform. They are located beneath the J2EE platform in the form of a portable API. They enable system vendors to provide seamless Java-based interoperability with specific system services or existing applications. Figure 6.9 shows the relationship between the three Cs of the J2EE application model. Figure 6.10 goes on to illustrate the overall J2EE architecture per Sun.

The fundamental value proposition of J2EE revolves around its provision of a comprehensive set of services. The prime services available with J2EE can be summarized as follows:

■   Relational database access with the Java Database Connectivity (JDBC) API

■   Directory and naming services, which enable J2EE components to look up other objects they require to access, provided via the Java Naming and Directory Interface (JNDI) API

■   A mail service to facilitate e-business application development (e.g., order confirmation via e-mail) via the JavaMail API

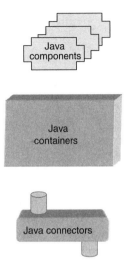

Figure 6.9
*The Java
application model
divides enterprise
applications into
components,
containers, and
connectors.*

- A powerful messaging mechanism, known as the Java Message Service
  (JMS), to enable components to send and receive messages asynchro-
  nously

- While J2EE provides built-in transaction support, the Java Transaction API (JTA) provides J2EE components and clients with further
  control to fine-tune their transactions, including the ability for multiple components to participate in a single transaction

- CORBA compliance via the JavaIDL, which enables Java compo-
  nents to interact with CORBA-compliant software resources, and the
  RMI-IIOP interface, which bridges the Java Remote Method Invoca-
  tion API (RMI) with CORBA's equivalent Internet ORB Protocol
  (IIOP) to facilitate the integration of legacy business logic into new
  Java applications

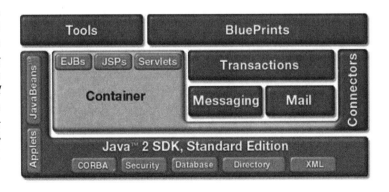

Figure 6.10
*The J2EE platform
per Sun showing
how it provides a
set of standard
services built upon
the basic services
provided with
J2SE.*

Then there is also the tight integration with XML, along with the support for the XML DOM and SAX APIs via the Java API for XML Parsing (JAXP).

J2EE consists of four specific deliverables:

1. J2EE specification

2. J2EE reference implementation

3. J2EE Sun BluePrint

4. J2EE compatibility test suite

The specification spells out the J2EE architecture and the nature of the services that are associated with a given version of J2EE in terms of the J2EE API set. The specification is totally implementation agnostic. The various Java application servers provide specific implementations of this specification on various platforms. The reference implementation, per its name, provides a tangible interpretation of the J2EE specification for Windows (currently Windows 2000 Professional and Windows XP Professional versions), Sun Solaris, and Linux (typically RedHat) platforms. It includes software developed by the open-source Apache Software Foundation—in particular, the Tomcat servlet engine. These days Sun, to the chagrin of the other application server vendors, also throws in the no-charge Sun ONE Application Server Platform Edition as another reference model.

The reference implementation also includes sample applications, tools (e.g., compilers and a debugger), and documentation. The reference implementation serves two key purposes. First, it provides those developing platform-specific implementations with a concrete, readily recreatable benchmark of how the J2EE services should operate and how they can be accessed. They can thus use the reference implementation to compare their implementations with what has been sanctioned, as the norm, by the Java community process (JCP). It thus takes the guesswork out of J2EE implementations. In addition, the reference implementation also serves as a fully functional, no-charge, easily Web-downloadable J2EE product that can be freely used without any caveats by developers who may want to develop Java applications or evaluate Java without incurring the cost of purchasing a commercial Java application server. Though only available on a limited but popular set of platforms, the reference implementation does, nonetheless, fulfill the open and free-of-charge credentials for Java.

The reference platform, along with the compatibility test suite, ensures that J2EE implementers should be able to guarantee a base level of consistency and interoperability between different implementations on different platforms. In the early days of Java, implementations of different platforms were not as consistent as they should have been. Thus, for example, an applet that would work immaculately on a browser running on Windows 98 might not work as well on Netscape running on a Mac. This led to software developers twisting the Java "write once, run anywhere" catchphrase to: "write once, test everywhere." But now with the compatibility test suite, implementations are more consistent and predictable. A Java Application Verification Kit (AVK) is also available to validate Java software portability. The BluePrints, the final part of the J2EE deliverables, consist of both documentation and Java coding examples. They set out to serve as a best practices design guide for developing and deploying J2EE component-based enterprise applications.

J2EE is at version 1.4 (final draft 3) as of April 15, 2003. Catering for Web services was an overarching goal for J2EE 1.4. Consequently it is billed by the Sun camp as the most complete Web services platform ever. A key Web services–related feature in 1.4 is the new JAX-RPC 1.1 API—where JAX stands for "Java API for XML-based RPC." JAX-RPC enables Java developers to create SOAP-based, Web services–related, platform-independent software. With SOAP capability provided by JAX-RPC, Java software can act either as a Web service or as applications that make use of other Web services. JAX-RPC also supports Web service invocation parameters defined with WSDL. JAX-RPC can be used by servlets or EJBs. In addition to offering other XML Web services–related APIs, which are discussed in Section 6.3, J2EE 1.4 also features ground-breaking support for the WS-I basic profile 1.0 to guarantee a specific level of Web services–related interoperability with other non-Java software.

The J2EE 1.4 also includes the J2EE Management 1.0 API. This new API defines the information model for J2EE management, including the standard Management EJB (MEJB). It includes the Java Management Extensions (JMX) API, which is used to log statistics of resource usage. In addition, 1.4 also introduces the J2EE Deployment 1.1 API, which provides a standard platform-independent API for the deployment of software on any target platform. There are also enhancements to the J2EE connector architecture, which now includes support for integration with JMS.

6.3   Java support for Web services

The Java camp, albeit after a slightly stuttering start, is determined to make sure that Microsoft does not hijack the Web-services market with .NET. As far as the Java camp is concerned, Web services offer a golden opportunity to level the playing field between proprietary (i.e., Microsoft) and open (i.e., Java) when it comes to application software. XML and Web services are platform independent and that is also Java's claim to fame—though Java's platform independence, as discussed at the start of this chapter, is broader and more meaningful than what XML Web services set out to achieve. However, developing XML Web services and the applications that intend to use them in Java does ensure that one has the best of all worlds— platform-independent solutions that can be easily ported across vastly disparate platforms (e.g., mainframes and PCs).

Since at least early 2002, it has been possible to develop Web services or applications that invoked Web services by using Java—albeit typically with a high-end, commercial application server such as BEA's WebLogic or IBM's WebSphere. This was because total built-in support for SOAP etc. was not available in J2EE 1.3. Thus, one had to rely on implementation-specific Web services–related extensions. But all of this has been rectified with J2EE 1.4, which sets out not just to be Web services savvy but to be a preferred platform for Web services–related solutions. To this end many XML-related APIs have now been included in Java—in particular, J2EE. This repertoire of APIs is known as the Java APIs for XML (JAX). The goal of JAX is to ensure that any and all Web services–related software, on either side of the invoker-provider model, can be created entirely in standard Java without recourse to tools written in other languages or implementation-specific extensions.

The Java APIs for XML fall into two broad categories: those that deal explicitly with the processing of XML documents and those that deal with the procedures used to interchange XML-oriented documents. There are three XML document-oriented Java APIs:

1.   Java API for XML Processing (JAXP)

2.   Java Architecture for XML Binding (JAXB)

3.   SOAP with Attachments API for Java (SAAJ)

There are two APIs that deal with the procedures used to interchange XML-oriented documents:

1.   Java API for XML-based RPC (JAX-RPC)

2.   Java API for XML Registries (JAXR)

JAXP is invaluable for processing XML documents. It is a powerful and extensible API based on the concept of using external plug-in modules. JAXP supports SAX, DOM, and XSLT—replete with full XML namespace processing. SAX and DOM, as mentioned in Chapter 2, are the two most popular APIs associated with XML. They both work by using a document parsing model—in this case the accepted XML document parsing methodology. All XML parsers verify that an XML document is well formed (e.g., check that there are no missing tags).

Some XML parsers are known as validating parsers. Validating parsers, in addition to verifying the structure of an XML document, go a step further by validating the contents of a well-formed XML document against the appropriate DTD or schema. Xerces, which is available from Apache in both Java and C++ versions, is a widely used example of a quintessential XML validating parser that supports both the SAX and DOM APIs.

JAXP does not implement either the SAX or DOM APIs. Instead, it allows any Java application to invoke a suitable XML parser from within the Java application. JAXP in essence allows XML parsers to be plugged in to a Java application via what Java refers to as the plugability layer. Xerces, which is comprehensive and all inclusive, is rapidly becoming the gold standard within the Java community for XML parsers. But other XML parsers are available from Oracle and others. There is also a very nimble, Java-based, nonvalidating XML parser known as Piccolo (piccolo.sourceforge.net).

SAX is an event-based parser best suited for interprogram interactions associated with Web services, while DOM is targeted at XML presentation-oriented applications such as XML editors or XML browsers. An event-based parser, when parsing a document, triggers an event each time it encounters a document construct it recognizes. Thus, in the example of an XML parser, an event could be triggered each time the parser encounters the "<" symbol, the "</" string or whitespace characters. In the case of Java, the event triggered by SAX would be a previously defined method within the application. Thus, you would typically have a method to handle the start of an element that would be invoked each time the SAX parser encountered the "<" symbol. DOM, on the other hand, takes an XML document, parses it, and creates an object representation of that document—in the form of a tree (e.g., the XML representation of an XML spreadsheet, as shown in Figure 2.3[b]).

The current version of JAXP also includes support for XSLT. Consequently, programmers can convert XML content obtained via a parser to other formats, including HTML. JAXP, very much in tune with XML trends, makes sure that there is full support for XML namespaces. Thus, the bottom line here is that JAXP ensures that Java applications have unconstrained access to the structure and content of any XML document through the use of an appropriate XML parser and moreover ensures that XML-defined data extracted in this manner can be easily converted to any other format by using XSLT.

JAXB is another way by which Java applications can process XML docu-mets. It is a Java technology that enables developers to easily generate Java classes (i.e., templates for creating objects in the form of JavaBeans) from an XML schema. Thus, you can use JAXB to create a representation of an XML schema in terms of Java code. It provides an easy and convenient way by which Java developers can incorporate XML data and XML-related processing functionality into Java applications without even having to know much about the intricacies and mechanics of XML.

SAAJ, though categorized by the Java camp as an XML document-related API, is very different from the other two APIs. Rather than being an API related to processing XML documents, as is the case with JAXP and JAXB, SAAJ is in reality a SOAP-related API. It provides a standard means by which Java applications can send XML documents by using SOAP. SAAJ is obviously targeted at Web services–related scenarios. The current SAAJ API is based on the SOAP 1.2 specification.

As with SAAJ, JAX-RPC is another Web services–oriented API—albeit this time on the procedural side rather than on the document-related side. JAX-RPC is the pivotal API when it comes to developing and deploying Web services on a Java platform. It is a featured highlight as well as a corner-stone of the J2EE 1.4 initiative. JAX-RPC, as implied by the name, is an RPC invocation mechanism. It enables Java applications to invoke XML-based RPC functionality per the SOAP 1.2 specification. It firmly aligns Java software with accepted Web services modus operandi for I/O, as discussed in the previous chapter. JAX-RPC enables Java software to participate, with aplomb and ease, anywhere within a Web services–related programming scenario—either as Web services being invoked by other applications or as applications invoking Java or non-Java-based Web services.

JAXR, from a Java perspective, puts the icing on the cake vis-à-vis Web services. It is a uniform and standardized API for accessing and querying different kinds of XML registries—with UDDI and the OASIS-sponsored ebXML registry being key among these. It provides Java applications with a unified information model that describes the content and meta-data included within XML registries. With JAXR, Java developers can write powerful and versatile registry client software—for example, for UDDI reg-istration, update, and query. With this set of APIs, all of which are integral parts of J2EE 1.4, the Java camp has indeed gone all out to make sure that it has left no bases uncovered when it comes to unstinted support for Web services. But it did not stop there. It raised the ante, obviously against .NET, by packaging all of these XML-related APIs and more into what is called the Java Web Services Developer Pack (Java WSDP) 1.2.

Java WSDP is a free integrated toolkit to help Java developers create any type of XML-related software with the latest Java APIs. It can be downloaded at will from java.sun.com, for the four traditional reference platforms supported by Java: Sun Solaris, Windows 2000, Window XP, and RedHat Linux. Consistent with the fact that the current J2EE 1.4 support for the core Web services–related technologies is highly standards compliant, Web services–related software developed with WSDP is assured to conform to WS-I's basic profile 1.0. In addition to offering JAXP, JAXB, SAAJ, JAX-RPC, and JAXR, WSDP also includes additional value-added capabilities, such as JavaServer Faces (JSF) and access to all of the J2EE security features (including authentication and encryption). JSF is a technology for simplifying the building of user interfaces for server-side Java software. JSF enables Java programmers to quickly and easily assemble reusable UI components into a displayable page, connect these components to the appropriate application data sources, and then correlate client-generated events to server-side event handlers.

The bottom line here is that with J2EE 1.4, all of the XML-related APIs, and the free WSDP it is difficult for anybody to cogently argue that Java does not provide adequate support for developing and deploying Web services or applications that invoke Web services. One has to agree that at least on paper, J2EE 1.4 is indeed an extremely complete, and as such compelling, platform for Web services. Furthermore, it is worth remembering that all of this, at least for the Solaris, Windows, and RedHat Linux platforms, is available for free on an open-source basis.

This is obviously a boon for those who want to develop Java-based Web services (maybe on a low-overhead, cottage-industry basis)—keeping in mind that per the Java mantra, Java software developed on a Windows or Linux platform can still be deployed on any other platform that includes a suitable run-time environment. Then there are the commercial Java-based studios and application servers, discussed in Section 6.4, that set out to make development, testing, and deployment even easier, more flexible, and global in terms of platform permutations. So when it comes to Java and Web services, no person, at least with a rational frame of mind, can claim that there is a shortage of germane technology and tools.

6.4   Web services–related Java implementations

Not counting the actual Web services and Web services–dependent applications written in Java, the three most important categories of Java implementations in relation to Web services are:

1.   Java application servers (e.g., Sun's ONE Application Server)

2.   Java software development studios (e.g., BEA WebLogic Workshop)

3.   Java-based legacy integration tools (e.g., IBM's WebSphere Host Publisher)

While the availability of the free reference implementations and open-source offerings (e.g., Apache Tomcat and the Eclipse Web tools from eclipse.org) tends to sometimes cloud and confuse the picture, the Java platforms (e.g., J2EE 1.4) are also implementation-agnostic specifications like industry standard or an IETF RFC. This is where the commercial Java application servers, led by the market leaders from IBM, BEA, Sun, and Oracle, come into the picture. Their express charter is to deliver reliable, value-added, platform-specific implementations of a particular J2EE specification. Consequently, the level of J2EE supported by the commercial application servers will, and should, lag behind (typically from six to nine months) the release of a new version of the specification. Thus, toward the end of summer 2003, all the well-known application servers, including Sun's own ONE Application Server 7, were still based on J2EE 1.3—albeit with ahead of the spec, value-added support for SOAP, WSDL, UDDI, and WS-Security.

The overriding value propositions offered by commercial Java application servers, over and above the basic functionality available with a no-charge reference implementation, are:

■ Platform-specific availability and performance-related features—in particular, support for load balancing, system clustering, failover, multithreading (i.e., concurrent execution of different instances of the same Java code, with each instance serving a different user or sets of users), and object/content caching

■ JDBC drivers optimized for specific, platform-dependent database offerings (e.g., DB2, Oracle, SQL Server, and so forth)

■ Extensive back-end connectors (or adapters) to existing application systems (e.g., ERP, CRM, legacy, and so on), typically per the J2EE Java Connector Architecture (JCA), to facilitate the integration of existing software resources with new Java-based applications

■ Graphical, easy-to-use and master, point-and-click deployment, monitoring, and management capabilities

■ Support for additional platforms, in particular mainframes, mini-computers (e.g., IBM AS/400), non-Solaris versions of UNIX (e.g., AIX), and non-RedHat versions of Linux

- Tight integration with other pertinent enterprise-class server functionality, such as message servers, Web servers (also referred to as HTTP servers), portal servers, and e-commerce servers

- Bidirectional tie-in with selected application development studios, workshops, or IDEs

The best way to think of this is that commercial application servers deliver feature-rich, highly interoperable, industrial-strength Java run-time environments for enterprise-class, mission-critical applications. The intense competition for market share between IBM, BEA, Sun, and Oracle, for a start, ensures that each tries to outdo the others, especially when it comes to ease-of-use, security, manageability, scalability, and RAS (i.e., reliability, availability, and serviceability) issues. Much effort is devoted to offering incisive and tangible load balancing, failover, and server clustering capabilities.

At the very basic level, they all enable you to install multiple versions of the application server (or the virtual machine part of it) on the same system—with dynamic load balancing (based on actual workload, round-robin, or application/user type criteria) and failover. This type of simple, run-time multiplicity is usually referred to as clustered Java VMs on a single CPU/system. The next step up from there is horizontal load balancing, where you run one or more Java VMs on separate CPUs—with transparent, cooperative workload sharing and failover support between them.

A variation of this, known as vertical load balancing, is possible on parallel-architecture, high-processor-content server machines available from IBM (e.g., mainframes, iSeries, and UNIX pSeries), Sun (e.g., Sun Fire family), and so on. With this type of setup, one or more Java VMs are run as a cluster, each in a virtual partition powered by multiple CPUs and a pre-allocated set of memory and I/O resources. The end goal of all such load balancing and failover options is to ensure that server-side, mission-critical Java applications, when deployed on suitable hardware systems, are able to handle very large workloads, possibly serving hundreds of thousands of concurrent online users, without performance degradation or instability. This is a key area where Java on a non-WinTel platform (e.g., UNIX server) can really demonstrate irrefutable superiority when it comes to performance, capacity, and scalability over .NET.

The bottom line here is that commercial Java application servers of the WebSphere, WebLogic, and Oracle9i (soon to be 10g) ilk are essentially synonymous with enterprise-class, mission-critical Java deployment. If you are seriously considering Java-based e-business applications (with or without Web services) for an enterprise that is deemed to be mid-size (let's say

250 employees) or greater, it would border on gross irresponsibility not to seriously evaluate one or more of the popular commercial application servers. If your enterprise is already using Java on an enterprise scale, then the chances are relatively good that you already have an application server or servers in place—or a well-stated strategy as to how and when you are going to start using application servers. Basically, trying to run large-scale, high-volume Java applications without the aid of an application server is bound to be counter-productive—akin to trying to drive a large truck cross-country in the middle of the summer without power steering and air conditioning.

An enterprise's IT platforms of choice could also dictate the need for a commercial application server—and possibly even a specific application server from a particular vendor. The issue here is that the free Java servers from the Java camp do not support non-UNIX high-end systems—in particular mainframes and AS/400 systems—though it is estimated that the installed base for AS/400s is in excess of 600,000 systems. However, to be fair, IBM does offer no-charge, no-frills JDKs for these platforms—though they do not set out to offer platform-specific exploitation capabilities (e.g., integration with workload management). Commercial application servers are also usually required for some non-Solaris versions of UNIX (e.g., AIX)—though it should be noted that some vendors (e.g., H-P) take the Java reference implementation, customize it to their flavor of UNIX, and then make it available for download from their Web sites. Note that such platform-customized, redistributable versions of J2EE, though optimized for a particular vendor's platform(s), will typically not include all of the value-added features offered by commercial application servers.

If your preferred IT platform for mission-critical applications still happens to be IBM mainframes running MVS (e.g., OS/390 or z/OS) or AS/400s with OS/400, then you will most likely have to opt for IBM's own WebSphere Application Server (WAS)—which is now at Version 5 (though it should be noted that z/OS does also include a no-charge JDK). Given how specialized these systems are and the considerable expense associated with testing, maintaining, and supporting mainframe software, as well as IBM's hold of this segment of the market, mainframes and AS/400s are no longer supported by the non-IBM application servers. This in itself should not be considered a grave imposition, given that WAS is the current market leader in this field and has over the years invariably set the standard for the value-added capabilities offered by application servers.

Figure 6.11, from IBM, highlights the key features of WAS 5.0.2. For comparison, as well as to keep the playing field as level as possible,

Figure 6.11
*The key features of
the latest
WebSphere
Application Server,
V5.0.2, per IBM.*

WebSphere Application Server Enterprise

Overview

- Employs a service orientation to dynamically integrate IT assets within and across enterprises.

- Choreographs interactions between reusable services with a fully integrated Web services workflow engine.

- Enables advanced transactional connectivity to coordinate interactions with multiple back-end systems across the network.

- Provides intelligent, out-of-the-box compensation capabilities to rollback multiple transactions in reverse order if a failure should occur later in a business process.

- Leverages business rules to create adaptive applications that can quickly respond to changing business conditions.

- Allows the development of flexible applications with which users can dynamically interact by building and submitting queries at runtime.

- Works with a highly integrated, Eclipse-based application development environment for building workflows, J2EE artifacts, Web services and sophisticated application adapters.

- Delivers J2EE and Web services innovations to tackle some of today's toughest coding challenges.

- Reduces time to market by promoting the reuse of services in new applications and by minimizing the disruption in existing applications when changes to individual services are required.

- Includes agile deployment capabilities offering developers the tools to optimize performance without impacting source code.

- Provides the ability to insatiate back-up server clusters autonomically without writing code.*

- Increases application performance and flexibility with Dynamic workload management. This capability allows the system to monitor the workload on each server in a cluster and automatically route the work to a server with the lightest workload.*

- *Denotes new capabilities available in WebSphere Application Server Enterprise, V5.0.2

Figure 6.12 shows the first page of BEA's equivalent marketing material for its WebLogic Server—claimed by BEA to be the world's leading application server. To be fair to both IBM and BEA, the exact market share numbers for WebSphere and WebLogic are contentious at best, and WebLogic, a couple of years ago, was the market leader—though the consensus is that IBM is now ahead, even if only by a nose.

Figure 6.12
Some of the key features of the latest BEA WebLogic Server 8.1 per BEA.

BEA WebLogic® Server 8.1
The Enterprise-Class Foundation for
Services-Oriented Applications

Easy to Use
- Unified, Easy to Use Development Environment and Programming Model
- Auto Configuration and Whole Application Monitoring

Enterprise Strength
- Secure and Reliable Web Services
- Industrial Strength Foundation Hardening

Massive Gains in Developer Productivity

    – *Reduced skill requirements through unified development environment*
    – *Shortened project cycles through more tools, iterative development, and faster start-up*

Unified application development environment for J2EE and non-J2EE developers that highly simplifies development of application components such as JSP, EJB, Web Services, and offers powerful built-in integration capabilities through messaging, Java Connector Architecture, and Web Services.

EJBGen – rapid EJB development tool fully integrated with BEA WebLogic Workshop IDE. Simplifies and speeds up EJB development by removing the need to work with multiple source files, requiring less or no code to write, with automatic database mapping.

More ANT-based Web Services configuration tools – built-in validation and compliance checks.

Thin client – for accessing BEA WebLogic Server-based applications and components from limited resource environments like mobile, embedded, or Web-based applets while providing full transactions and failover support, load balancing, security, and high performance.

New end-to-end sample application – illustrating best practices in J2EE and Web Services application development utilizing major features of BEA WebLogic Server.

More Power and Flexibility for the Administrator

    – *Simplified configuration, deployment*
    – *Powerful administration*
    – *Ease operations*

More tools for administrators for easy configuration, deployment, operations and troubleshooting.

Enhanced Domain Configuration Wizard – automates and accelerates cluster configuration, removing tedious steps and error prone manual settings.

New administration assistants (wizards) – help with configuration tasks like database pool configuration, writing security policies, and setting up a cluster or application domain.

New performance and monitoring options – including BEA JRockit JVM and real-time Java code execution visibility, and new application life cycle events.

New flexible deployment options – partial application update, hot deployment for JSP and EJB, real-time update of a deployed application.

Download: *http://commerce.bea.com/downloads/*
Documentation: *http://e-docs.bea.com/wls/docs81/*

This discussion has focused on the desirability of using application servers for running enterprise-class Java applications. However, from a Web-services perspective, it is indeed conceivable that enterprises of all sizes and shapes may also start looking at Java as an attractive platform on which to offer Web services—particularly with Windows servers now under siege due to their apparently never-ending stream of security vulnerabilities. While commercial application servers will still provide better manageability, RAS, performance, and scalability, it is indeed possible for one to consider offering Java-based Web services on a UNIX or Linux platform by using just reference implementation or JBoss, at least to begin with, if cost is an issue and the usage levels for these Web services are expected to be light to moderate.

Next to the application servers, the most important Java implementations in relation to Web services are the application development studios such as BEA's WebLogic Workshop, IBM's WebSphere Studio Application Developer, and Sun ONE Studio. The express goal of these highly visual

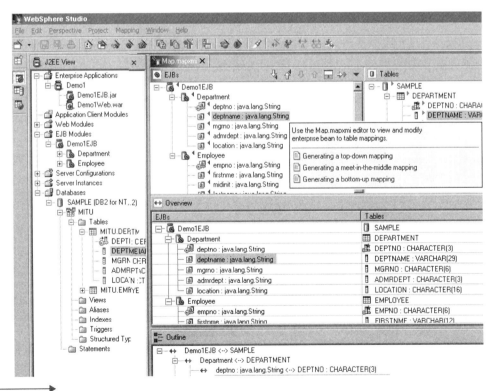

Figure 6.13(a)   *A representative screen shot from IBM's WebSphere Studio Application Developer, high-lighting its highly visual, drag-and-drop software development paradigm—in this instance, manipulating EJBs.*

IDEs is to compress the software development cycle and thus enhance, by hook or by crook, programmer productivity—that ever-elusive, Holy Grail of the software community. Figures 6.13(a) and 6.13(b) show representative screen shots from WebSphere Studio Application Developer, while Figure 6.14 shows one from BEA's WebLogic Workshop.

In much the same way that one, given enough time, patience, and skill, can still develop sophisticated HTML Web pages just using a no-frills text editor (e.g., Windows Notepad), it is also possible to develop Java code of any complexity by using a straight text editor and the JDKs available with the Java platform. It should also be remembered that when it comes to Web services, there is also the new Java WSDP 1.2. Furthermore, as is the case with Java servlet servers, there are also some no-charge, open-source Java IDE initiatives—most notably the IBM-encouraged Eclipse platform, which continues to gain vendor sponsorship and market visibility. To this

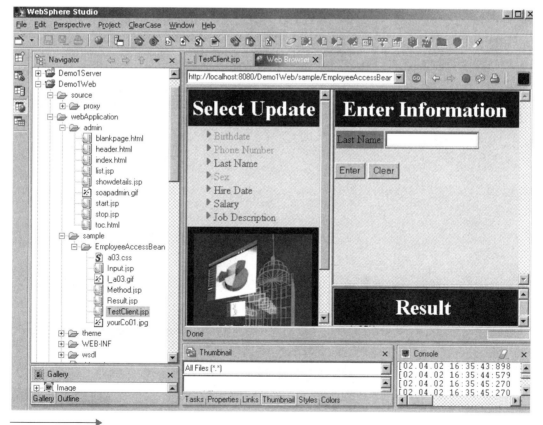

Figure 6.13(b)   *Another screen shot from IBM's WebSphere Studio Application Developer, in this case showing the dynamic creation of a user interface for a Java application using JSPs.*

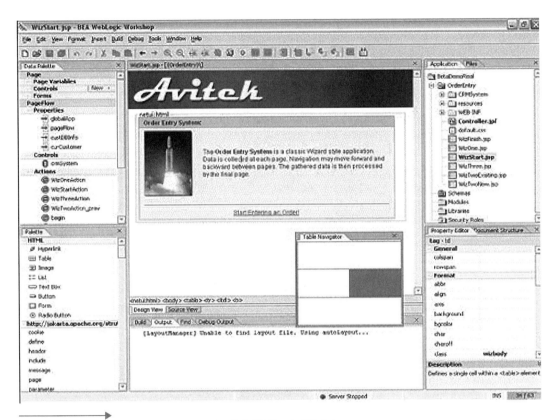

Figure 6.14   *Creating JSPs with BEA's WebLogic Workshop.*

end it should also be noted that IBM's high-profile WebSphere Studio
products are now based on this open-source, readily extensible, Eclipse platform, thus making this product family even more attractive.

But as is the case with Web page design, using a visual, drag-and-drop
IDE, rather than coding everything laboriously by hand, is invariably more
convenient, more efficient, faster, and prone to fewer errors—though there
will always be an initial learning curve associated with using any IDE. Ease-
of-use, convenience, and potential productivity enhancements are, nonetheless, the primary value propositions for using a studio for developing
Java-based Web services or applications. In many ways this is another pivotal enterprise IT strategy, philosophy, and standards-related issue, which
invariably becomes intertwined with the enterprise's stance on using an
application server—given that the leading application servers have compan-
ion, complementary studios with tight, single-image integration between
the two. However, whereas an enterprise may be forced to use a Java application server because of the server platforms it uses (e.g., mainframes), the

need for a studio product is unlikely to be dictated by platform preferences alone, given that Windows, UNIX, and Linux (in that order) will continue to be the platforms of choice used by Java programmers.

The bottom line here is that today's studio offerings are proven, flexible, and include an extensive repertoire of capabilities—particularly in the areas of Web services–related technologies such as SOAP and WSDL. Once programmers have circumvented the inevitable, initial learning curve, these studios, by their very design, should accelerate software development, integration, testing, and deployment. In general, they should deliver a positive

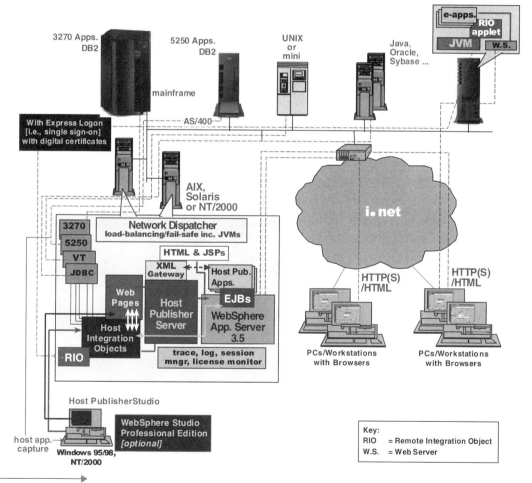

Figure 6.15   *High-level architecture of IBM's Java-based host integration product, WebSphere Host Publisher (at the V3.5 level), showing where EJBs, JSPs, XML, and the WebSphere Application Server come into play.*

ROI in relatively quick time. So the moral here is that if an enterprise is serious about using Java as its strategic, long-term software development methodology, then it would behoove the enterprise to carefully evaluate some of the leading studio offerings to determine the potential benefits of standardizing its development framework on one of these visual IDEs.

Java-based legacy integration tools, the so-called "host integration" category within the Web-to-host genre of offerings, round off the Web services–related Java implementations. The significance of these products, with IBM's WebSphere Host Publisher being the quintessential example, is that they enable enterprises to gainfully extract and reuse business logic fragments from mission-critical applications—with each fragment now represented as an EJB. One or more of these EJBs could then be packaged as a Java-based Web service, using either a tool such as the Java WSDP or a studio product. Figure 6.15 shows the high-level architecture of the WebSphere Host Publisher product. In some cases this type of integration may also be realized by using one or more of the connectors (or adapters) available with application servers. One way or another, these legacy integration tools enable enterprises to maximize their considerable investment in mission-critical applications. The bottom line here is that Java is extremely enterprise savvy. There is no shortage of competitive and compelling industrial-strength Java implementations to enable enterprises to safely pursue a Java-centric Web-services strategy with confidence and panache.

6.5   Java in relation to .NET relative to Web services

By now it should be obvious that despite the massive onslaught of security attacks against Windows systems, the global Web-services stage will have to be shared by Java and .NET over the coming years. While larger corporations will continue to gravitate toward Java initiatives because of security concerns, as well as their need for larger, mission-critical servers, small enterprises and individuals, thanks to inertia, will persevere with Windows. Microsoft's desktop monopoly alone is such that even if Microsoft stopped marketing Windows in the near future (given the security flaws), it would still take quite a few years for any other system to make a perceptible dent in market share. But let's face it, despite the ignominy of the Blaster and LovSan worms, which showed more than ever that the secure by design Windows 2003 Server is vulnerable, Microsoft is not going to abandon its holy cash cow.

Java and .NET will thus continue to have a ying-and-yang role when it comes to Web services even if it is just at the intranet or extranet level. Consequently, one cannot rule out scenarios that involve Java applications running on UNIX servers invoking .NET Web services running on Windows 2000 servers, or that of .NET applications running on Windows 2003 servers invoking Java Web services deployed on an IBM mainframe. As discussed in Chapter 3, an enterprise that discovers that the exact functionality it seeks is available only as a .NET Web service may elect to acquire or license that Web service and run it on a secure, stand-alone Windows server behind its firewall rather than trying to rewrite it in Java or C++.

Hence, one should not jump to the conclusion that there will always be a clear demarcation between Java and .NET based on the size of an enterprise, with the large enterprises standardizing on a Java-only strategy. The flip side of this is that a relatively small company having only Windows 2000 servers may acquire an application (e.g., e-commerce or SCM) that relies on Web services (e.g., credit authorization, shipment status, or tax calculation) invoked across the Web that are in fact Java based and running on high-end, UNIX servers.

At this juncture it is also salutary to note that despite Microsoft's antagonism toward Java, it is still eminently possible to have Java Web services or applications running on a Windows platform, either by using a free download from the Java Web site (e.g., reference implementation), a free Java server (e.g., Sun ONE Platform Edition or JBoss), or a commercial application server. However, just running a Java platform on a Windows machine does not by itself obviate security, scalability, and reliability issues. For a start, and most disturbingly, the underlying Windows machine could continue to be vulnerable to attacks that intercept, modify, or destroy data or files on that machine even if the Java portion of the system continues to be above reproach. In addition, the extra processing and resource consumption involved with running the feature-rich Java platform on top of Windows could potentially exacerbate performance and scalability issues. Consequently, Java on top of Windows, though this will continue to be a popular permutation, is not a panacea for the security, availability, and scalability issues that currently beset Windows solutions.

Java's irrefutable strengths are that of software portability across multiple platforms and its open-source status. On the other hand, Windows is ubiquitous and this makes it attractive to small enterprises and individuals who want to actively participate in the coming Web-services phenomenon. It would be shortsighted and unrealistic to write off this segment of potential

Web-services creators just because of their dependence on Windows since, given the numbers involved, the chances are high that this group will develop some much-sought-after Web services.

The best way to put all of this into proper perspective is to quote Steve Ballmer, Microsoft's CEO, who had this to say on September 15, 2003, in a speech at the Churchill Club, a Silicon Valley business networking group: "Windows (operating system) is the most popular platform in the world, so every security incident with it is just magnified and magnified and magnified across so many more systems than with any other platform. We know that the bad guys are going to keep writing viruses; we know that. Our goal has to be to block them before they can ever get onto those PCs."

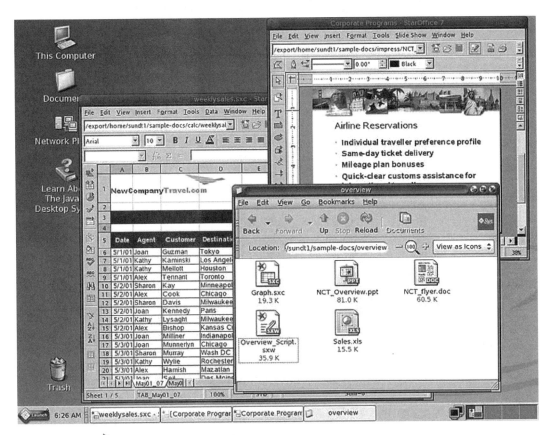

Figure 6.16   *A screen shot of Sun's Java Desktop, replete with productivity software akin to those offered by Microsoft Office, which is now being positioned as an obvious, cost-competitive, and secure alternative to Windows.*

Linux is the wild card in all of this. IBM is already a huge Linux fan and supports Linux on all of its hardware platforms, whether they be mainframes, UNIX servers, iSeries mini-computers, or Intel machines. Sun, trying to exploit the security-induced vulnerability of Windows, has jumped on the bandwagon with the open-source, Linux-based Java Desktop System, which sets out to be an alternative to Windows desktops, Microsoft Office applications, and even Internet Explorer (IE). Figure 6.16 shows a screen shot, provided by Sun, of the Java Desktop System. While Sun and others will have to go a long way and do so for a long time to displace Windows from the corporate desktop, initiatives such as this will indubitably garner some market share as enterprises and individuals despair of continually being in the cross-hairs when it comes to worms, viruses, and system takeover threats.

Rather than just compare the pros and cons of Java and .NET, what is more germane at this stage of the game is to do what is referred to as SWOT analysis of these two technologies—where a SWOT analysis looks at the strengths, weaknesses, opportunities, and threats of a particular technology or enterprise. A SWOT analysis for Java is shown in Table 6.1 and for .NET in Table 6.2. These tables sum up the whole story as to how these two methodologies will continue to stack up against each other in the light of current developments.

Table 6.1   *SWOT Analysis of Java*

Strengths:	Weaknesses:
■ Java software is portable across all popular computing platforms ■ Considered to be an open-source standard ■ Has the backing of IBM, Sun, Oracle, BEA, and H-P to name just a few	■ Disparaged by Microsoft ■ Considered by some developers to be complex, sluggish, and resource hungry ■ Effective, industrial-strength deployment, with load balancing and more on some high-end platforms (e.g., mainframes) only feasible with relatively costly commercial Java application servers
Opportunities:	**Threats:**
■ Tighter Java-centric alliance between IBM and Sun, resulting in less product-specific competition (e.g., UNIX server hardware and application servers) and more software-related collaboration ■ Continuing promotion of viable Java/Linux-based alternatives to Windows and Microsoft Office ■ Hackers continue to expose major security vulnerabilities in Windows	■ Reduced IT budgets curtail development of new e-business applications ■ Enterprise-level standardization on UNIX/Linux minimizes the need for cross-platform portability, opening the door for a resurgence of C or C++ ■ Microsoft with Windows 200x Server finally delivers a trustworthy, high-availability, scalable platform supported on Intel's new 64-bit processors

Table 6.2   *SWOT Analysis of .NET*

Strengths:	Weaknesses:
■ Unprecedented market reach thanks to the popularity of Windows ■ Microsoft's active involvement in Web services technology, from day one, has resulted in .NET always being at the forefront when it comes to the necessary support for Web-services development or deployment ■ Huge base of developers highly comfortable with Microsoft development methodology	■ Security exposures on Windows has reached epidemic proportions ■ .NET solutions confined to Windows platforms ■ Windows servers not considered by many IT professionals to be rugged, reliable, and scalable for data center–type, large-scale, mission-critical applications
Opportunities:	**Threats:**
■ Make a concerted attempt to deliver a secure and robust version of Windows ■ Collaborate with Intel or H-P to deliver high-end systems that could credibly compete against the top-end UNIX servers ■ Invest heavily in small software companies and individuals to generate an irresistible portfolio of .NET Web services	■ Hackers continue to expose new security weaknesses—especially in future releases of Windows ■ Companies and households exasperated by Windows-related worms and viruses turn to Linux ■ Sun and IBM join forces to further promote Java/Linux

6.6   Q&A: A time to recap and reflect

Q: What exactly is Java?

A: Java is a platform-independent, highly object-oriented, third-generation programming language and software development methodology developed by Sun. Though its origins predate the advent of the Web, Java was introduced to the world in 1995 as a strategic technology for realizing dynamic, interactive Web applications.

Q: Is Java a true standard?

A: Yes and no. It is not a bona fide industry standard maintained by a recognized standards organization. Instead, Sun still controls much of what happens to and with Java, though there is an egalitarian, open-to-all mechanism, known as the Java Community Process (JCP), where anybody can participate in the evolutionary process of Java. The Java specifications are also freely open to all and there are free, open-source reference implementations of these specifications. Consequently, a large and influential segment of the software development community, including those associated with powerful open-source movements such as Apache, is willing to treat Java as at least a de facto standard despite Sun's stewardship of it.

Q: Does Java have built-in support for Web services?

A: Yes. The latest version of the server-side Java specification, J2EE 1.4, includes extensive support for XML and Web services via a series of APIs for XML document parsing, SOAP-based XML document transmission, UDDI access, and RPC invocation with SOAP. All of these Web services–related APIs are packaged and available for free, along with other complementary software, such as user-interface creation technology JavaServer Faces (JCF), with the Java Web Services Developer Pack (Java WSDP) 1.2.

Q: What is an applet and how does it differ from an application?

A: Java applications are conventional, stand-alone programs, installed and executed off a system's hard drive in the same way as applications developed with other languages—with one distinguishing feature being, however, that Java applications can be readily ported between vastly disparate systems. They could typically be invoked via a command-line instruction and, in common with other applications, will normally have unfettered access to the host system's resources (e.g., data files). Applets, though similar to applications, are not considered to run in stand-alone mode. Instead, an applet is a program that runs within a Web browser or an applet viewer and, moreover, has strictly limited access to host resources, in particular any kinds of files. An applet, as such, is meant to be nonmalicious at all costs. This intentional restricted access to host resources precludes the danger of applets being used to propagate viruses or worms.

Q: What is a JVM?

A: Java applications as well as Java applets were said to execute on Java Virtual Machines (JVMs). A JVM is thus a run-time (or execution) environment. JVMs are implemented on various computing platforms, in particular Web browsers, and all popular operating systems ranging from mainframe z/OS to the Mac OS. Though the concept of JVMs is still very much a part of the Java culture, today JVMs are referred to as containers.

Q: What is J2EE?

A: J2EE is the Java 2 Platform, Enterprise Edition. A Java platform is said to consist of a JVM (or container) and a series of standard libraries, which are referred to as the Java API. Today there are three Java 2 platforms, with J2EE being one of them. The other two are J2SE, the standard edition of the platform targeted at client-side implementations, and J2ME, a micro-edition meant for embedded applications in devices such as cell phones and TV set-top boxes.

Q: Is Java supported on Windows platforms?

A: Most certainly. Though Microsoft, in a fit of pique with Sun related to Java licensing, has claimed that it would no longer be including a built-in Java run-time environment within Windows, starting in early 2004, free versions of the necessary Windows software are readily and conveniently available from java.sun.com and www.java.com.

Q: What is JSP?

A: JavaServer Pages (JSPs) decouple the user-interface aspects of Web applications from that of content generation. JSP thus enables Web developers to change the presentation layout of a Web page or the contents of that Web page independently of each other. JSPs are somewhat analogous to the now relatively common Microsoft Active Server Pages (ASPs). The big difference, as ever, is that ASPs are Microsoft IIS–centric, whereas JSPs are meant to work with any Web server. JSPs are built on top of Java servlet technology—where a servlet is in essence a server-side applet. JSPs neatly demarcate HTML from servlet code.

Q: Are there free, server-side implementations of the Java platform?

A: Most definitely. So-called "reference implementations" of the Java platforms are available from java.sun.com for Windows, Solaris, and RedHat Linux platforms. Other vendors, such as H-P and IBM, provide platform-specific implementations for their particular systems. In addition, Sun provides an entry-level version of its Sun ONE Application Server on a no-charge basis, as does a company called JBoss (www.jboss.org). No-charge, open-source Java-related software is also readily available from Apache.

Q: What is a Java application server?

A: A Java application server, which typically refers to a commercial product, though the no-charge JBoss offering is also called an application server, is a value-added, platform-specific implementation of a particular J2EE specification. Commercial application servers offer extensive load-balancing, failover, and system clustering support as well as optimized drivers for specific commercial database systems. They include back-end connectors (or adapters) to existing applications as well as graphical application deployment and management capabilities.

7

Deploying and Managing Web Services

Deployment- and management-related concerns, in practice, will circumscribe all the real-world operational issues currently facing those trying to use or offer production-grade Web services for enterprise-level applications. This, as the saying goes, is when the rubber really hits the asphalt when it comes to Web services, or when one quite literally has to start reconciling the hype with the hardware. The real problem here, to immediately cut to the chase, is that the dynamics surrounding Web services have been dramatically undermined by circumstances outside the scope of Web-services technology and industry.

It is fair to say that the world—socially, economically, and technologically—has changed quite a bit and unexpectedly between mid-2000, when Web services were first being postulated, and now. First, there was the crash and burn of the dot.coms that tarnished the credibility, even if it was subliminally, of e-business. Then there was 9/11!

While the repercussions of 9/11 were still reverberating, there was the anthrax scare. The threat of terrorism, in all forms, including that of cyberterrorism, started to impact all forms of decision making, whether corporate or personal. A siege mentality set in. In big cities such as New York people wait for another shoe to drop. The relentless attacks by the hacker community continue to add insult to injury. Pantophobia, a fear of everything, is rife. There are people who have stopped opening regular mail and others who have stopped using e-mail.

It is against this pervading climate of uncertainty and fear, where trust is in short supply, that one now tries to promote Web services—a brand new, unproven, iconoclastic technology that advocates information sharing and collaborative processing over the Web. Suffice to say that the original, somewhat utopian model of Web services being dynamically located (using UDDI and WSDL) and then automatically exploited—in a free-wheeling, "take it for a test spin," plug-and-play manner—is now passé, especially when it comes to enterprise-class applications. There is an evocative analogy here pertaining to the free love culture of the mid-1960s and what happened to all of that with the advent of the deadly STDs.

The concept of glibly sourcing software functionality over the Internet from previously unknown service providers is no longer viable at the enterprise level—despite all protestations from the cognoscenti that it is indeed possible to have safe and secure scenarios. While the standards-based technology offered by Web services still has tremendous potential and appeal, for the time being, the purveyors of Web services will have to be carefully vetted by using the traditional due-diligence methods involving reference checks, credit ratings (e.g., Dun & Bradstreet rating), installed base, financial reports, and testimonials. UDDI—which already includes the Publisher-Assertions structure, which can be used to enumerate certifications, memberships, relationships and so on—could still help in providing initial (and moreover programmatic) first-cut validation. There can even be WSDL-centric service contracts. But most enterprises will want some level of face-to-face interaction with potential Web-service providers—even if it is via videoconferencing.

In addition to wanting traditional validation of providers, there is also an understandable preference by most corporations, at present, for acquiring or licensing required Web services from their providers and then deploying them on in-house servers, behind the corporate firewall. This obviously eliminates the uncertainty and risk of relying on a Web service being run by a third party at a remote location. It all boils down to control. In today's climate of uncertainty and distrust, enterprises want to have as much control as possible of their destinies—and that means controlling as much as possible of their IT systems, resources, and dependencies. This does not preclude outsourcing, but outsourcing done with control, contracts, and commitments. Web-service use, rather than being Internet oriented, has, for the time being at least, become intranet/extranet focused.

These concerns about trust, security, and thus control have in essence changed the fundamental Web-services paradigm in the eyes of corporate IT professionals. There is now an added level of complexity and expense.

Bernard Borges, an IBM Web-services architect, was quoted in the September 8, 2003, issue of *InfoWorld* as saying, "People in general thought Web services were simple and cheap, and it turns out they are complex and not so cheap. I think the whole notion of a Web service was using them as a simple integration tool. [But] it painted a rather rosy and low-tech picture compared with proprietary EAI products." And, as *InfoWorld* notes, somewhat tongue in cheek, IBM, as a Web-services pioneer, was one of the parties instrumental in propagating the "Web services are simple" picture. But life in general was simpler prior to 9/11.

The bottom line here is that the Web services-in-practice paradigm has changed between what was first thought when the XML Web-services

Table 7.1   *Web Services Usage Model from an Enterprise Usage Perspective*

Initial Expectations	Reality, mid-2003
■ Dynamic, on-the-fly location and invocation ■ Invoke and use across the Internet ■ Mechanism to facilitate exploitation of external, third-party software functionality ■ Focus on functionality and results rather than the platform ■ Distributed, trust-based control ■ Usage-based payment model ■ Distributed management across domains ■ Simplicity is the byword ■ Inexpensive means of obtaining software functionality ■ Service provider can update Web-service software provided I/O model and promised results stay the same ■ Standard Web-centric security measures based on authentication, digital certificates, digital signatures, SSL, firewalls, etc., will suffice ■ New distributed, decentralized software model ■ Standards based and simple—no need for expensive consultants ■ Simplify and expedite application integration	■ Dynamic location (using UDDI) but careful evaluation of providers' credentials prior to trying out the Web service ■ Usage restricted to intranet/extranet behind firewalls ■ Methodology for in-house software development and software functionality sharing between selected partners ■ Need to know about the platform, because the platform could be an issue ■ Tight, in-house control ■ Acquire or license Web service so that it can be deployed in-house ■ Centralized, in-house management ■ Not as simple as hoped—security concerns alone make it much more complex and convoluted ■ Not as inexpensive as initially hoped but still attractive ■ Any and all changes to the Web-services software or infrastructure need to be carefully vetted, regression checked, and monitored ■ Security concerns will continue to dampen all out exploitation of what Web services can offer ■ XML-based extension to intra-enterprise object-oriented programming ■ Better hire some consultants to determine optimum strategy, options, and action plan ■ Jury is still out

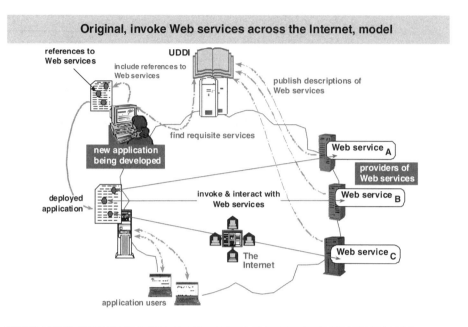

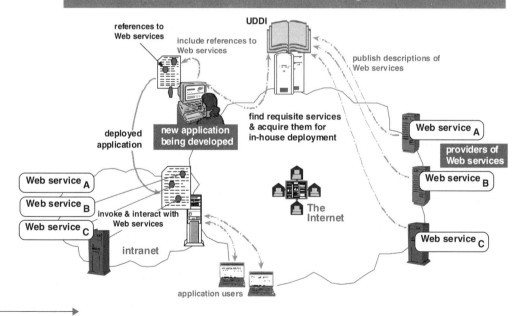

Figure 7.1   *While the original Web-services model envisaged Web services being freely invoked across the Internet, the current corporate preference is the intranet/extranet model.*

vision was postulated in mid-2000 to what is thought now as enterprises wrestle with how best to exploit Web services in a safe and secure manner. The intelligentsia faction of the Web-services community continues to try to address some of these deployment-related issues with new standards. To this end there is the nascent Web Services Manageability 1.0 specification, as well as a raft of security-related specifications such as Web Services Policy Attachments, Web Services Policy Assertions, Web Services Trust Language, Web Services Secure Conversation Language, Web Services Security Policy Language, and Web Services Policy Framework, as shown in Table 1.1. These emerging standards, however, have a long way to go and need to be bolstered with other identity and trust management standards before enterprises will be willing to again explore the dynamic, free-wheeling model first espoused for Web services.

Table 7.1 summarizes how the Web-services usage model has changed since its inception, while Figure 7.1 depicts this change graphically.

7.1   Web services: The risk assessment

This candid assessment of how Web services are currently being viewed and used by enterprises should not be construed in any way as portending the demise of Web services or as an indictment of the enabling technologies associated with Web services. Much of what has transpired has to do with a climate of uncertainty and fear that came to be independent of Web services. At the time of writing, I am unaware of any security breaches that have been attributed to Web services. This could, however, be attributed to the prudence shown to date when it comes to the use of Web services.

At this juncture it is worth reiterating that when everything is said and done, the basic Web-services model, which is based entirely on the exchange of XML documents, does protect users from viruses and worm-like security threats. Even the potential danger from the optional SOAP attachment capability can be negated by ensuring that the application invoking Web services does not automatically open any attachments without explicit authorization from a designated systems operator. This type of control, which can be enforced via the calling application, should not be underestimated or ignored. The calling application, which would typically be written in-house or developed specifically for an enterprise, does have total control over all of the interactions that take place with invoked Web services.

When a Web service sends information back to the application, in the form of one or more documents conveyed using SOAP, it is still up to the application as to how it processes those documents. Enterprises could insist that developers design applications like the Java applet "sandbox" model—that is, information sent back from a Web service cannot in any way cause the application to perform any malicious or unexpected actions. In other words, the application developers have to do their utmost to prevent scenarios similar to the unpredictable but inevitably dangerous results in the event of buffer overflow security exposures that are currently plaguing Microsoft's Windows software. One of the key things to remember in this context is that the calling application can play a pivotal role in ensuring that Web services can't compromise enterprise resources.

In practice, the real dangers with Web services relate to bait-and-switch or Trojan horse scenarios that set out to deceive the calling application. This is where a Web service is not what it claims to be—particularly when it is dealing with sensitive information (e.g., credit card details, medical records, financial data). For example, the Web service, in addition to performing what it is supposed to do and thus satisfying the requirements of the calling application, may also be performing nefarious actions with the information it receives—unbeknownst to the users of that application. A Web service being provided at a remote site, by an unknown third party, unfortunately, has plenty of scope and opportunity to engage in such unauthorized and unethical behavior. For example, an unscrupulous Web-service provider is likely to be able to intercept incoming or outgoing data at multiple points within the processing stack and make unauthorized copies of the data.

There are multiple scenarios that pertain to such rogue Web services. The key scenarios that one needs to be on the guard against include:

1.   A Web service that is corrupt from inception despite masquerading as being above board and respectable—that is, one that has been developed from scratch to scam unsuspecting users. This can be thought of as a Trojan horse setup.

2.   A legitimate, bona fide Web service that gets swapped out, with or without the knowledge and concurrence of its provider, by a rogue Web service that emulates all the functions of the original but in addition performs illegitimate operations behind the scenes. This is a bait-and-switch scenario. A variation of this would be for the calls to the genuine Web service to be intercepted and diverted to a rogue Web service.

3.   The platform on which a bona fide Web service is being run on is compromised, unbeknownst to the service provider, and thus enables a hacker to intercept or alter the data that is being processed by the Web service. This is the concern people currently have with Windows platforms, given the various documented security vulnerabilities that could enable a hacker to surreptitiously take control of a Windows machine. This is a platform vulnerability–related issue, which, at present, is focused mainly on Windows platforms—though other platforms could also, in theory, be compromised by a relentless hacker.

4.   A bona fide Web service offered by a respected provider that has, nonetheless, been compromised, covertly, by one or more members of the development team. This is another variation of a Trojan horse scenario.

5.   A rogue or compromised Web service could flood the calling application with spurious or continually duplicated data, thus creating a denial-of-service (or replay attack in the case when duplicated data is being used) scenario at the application end.

Note that having service contracts or service-level contracts per se will not safeguard an enterprise from such rogue or compromised Web services that intend to deceive the calling application. There are tools being developed that will enable a Web-service evaluator to determine the various actions that will be performed by a Web service, depending on the types of XML input parameters it receives. These types of tools will supplement and simplify the source-level review of Web services to determine their integrity.

WebInspect 3.0 from SPI Dynamics (www.spidynamics.org) is one such tool. It sets out to assist in assessing the fidelity of a Web service by exploring all of the XML input parameters it claims to accept and then performing various parameter manipulation on each XML field, looking for vulnerabilities within the service itself. There are multiple advantages to using these types of automated execution path mapping tools. If well conceived, as WebInspect 3.0 indeed appears to be, such tools can be thorough and systematic—thus ensuring that all potential paths have been adequately explored. They could also bypass the need for source-code-level review—especially if, for intellectual property reasons (if nothing else), the Web-service owner is unwilling to share source code with any potential evaluator, particularly if there is no financial commitment already in place.

But here, however, is the rub. Even a line-by-line source-code review of a Web service is not a safeguard against rogue or compromised Web services.

That is the problem. There could be a bait-and-switch or data interception outside the Web service. Moreover, the platform could be infiltrated at a later date. The bottom line is that safeguarding against rogue Web services is a convoluted challenge that has to be carefully pursued, in the case of remotely-invoked Web services, on a case-by-case basis.

In addition to these dangerous rogue Web-services scenarios, there is also the ever-present concern that information exchanged with a remote Web service, over the Web, can be intercepted or diverted during transmission. Encryption such as 128-bit SSL, obviously is the first-cut protection against such unauthorized access, though one can always argue, quite cogently, that given enough time and processing power this type of encrypted data can be eventually deciphered. However, the real key here is obviating any meaningful ROI of trying to intercept and deencrypt the data in question. The bottom line here has to do with making realistic determinations as to the types of data that are to be transmitted. If the data are extremely sensitive or valuable, then maybe they should not be sent across the Web. Figure 7.2 takes the standard remote Web-services model introduced in Figure 1.2 and annotates it to show how and where this model may be compromised.

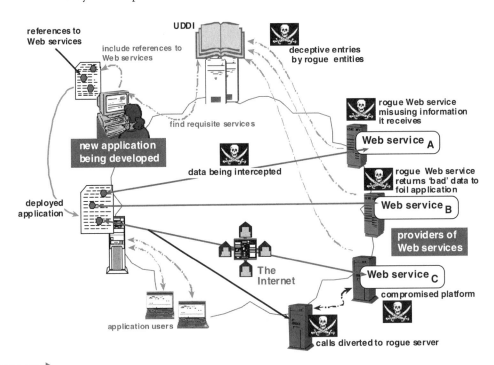

Figure 7.2   *Areas where security in a Web-service configuration may be compromised.*

7.1.1 Growth scenarios for external Web services

All of this said, one can come up with the following examples of how and when enterprises may still be able to safely and gainfully use the originally postulated remote Web-services model in the context of new applications:

- If the remote Web service is being used to process relatively innocuous data—for example, sending a zip code to receive mapping, weather, or traffic data; sending a flight number to ascertain the estimated time of arrival for that flight; sending unqualified numeric strings for currency conversion or sales tax computation.

- Web service has been thoroughly vetted, at the source-code level, and is being hosted by a trusted provider that offers audited, collaborative change control (i.e., Web service cannot be updated without documented permission) as well as continuous remote monitoring to ensure that no changes have been made to the Web-service software or infrastructure.

- Web service dealing with scientific data (e.g., material strength coefficients, chemical properties, etc.) offered by academic or nonprofit organizations.

- Web services that deal with potentially sensitive but nonetheless overtly public-domain information (e.g., property tax records from local authorities, voter registration records, court rulings, etc.).

- Required Web service, possibly dealing with sensitive information, is only available on a remote invocation basis from a specific organization, albeit with elaborate access control, authentication, and encryption mechanisms in place (e.g., a tax-related service from a federal or state tax authority, employment eligibility–related data from an immigration authority, homeland security–related updates from the pertinent authority).

There can be exceptions to this list. For example, management of a company in a highly cut-throat, competitive market sector (e.g., car rental, hotel reservation, stock brokerage) may argue persuasively that even apparently innocuous data related to its business operation could be used by the competition to gain a market edge. In such situations even zip codes, flight numbers, or unadorned numerical strings can be construed as constituting vital corporate data that has to be carefully safeguarded.

To be fair, in today's highly competitive global market, with the data mining tools that are readily available, information such as zip codes, flight numbers, currency conversions, and sales tax calculations could be dissected, analyzed, and reanalyzed to determine what or how a company is doing. Even the number of calls to a specific Web service (e.g., shipping rate calculation, sales tax calculation) over a given period of time could be used to determine the health and vitality of a company. Therefore, depending on the specifics, there can always be valid reasons as to why an enterprise may determine that using an external Web service is just not the prudent thing to do—despite all assurances of Web-service integrity, end-to-end encryption, and the innocuousness of the data.

At this juncture it should also be noted that enterprise-level applications, though a key and potentially highly lucrative market, are by no means the only market for Web services. There is still a huge market for Web services in the nonenterprise application arena. One could even argue that from a Web-services perspective, this personal-use market, with some overlap with the small office, home office (SOHO) market, could be as large and important as the enterprise market.

Remind yourself of all the ingenious, incisive, and magnanimous freeware and shareware software that is readily available on the Web and outside of it. The creators of all such software, as well as their successors, are prime candidates to create a whole new genre of freeware and shareware software based on the original, mix-and-match, plug-and-play Web-services paradigm. This market, which is not as susceptible to or concerned about information pilferage, is ideally suited to truly exploit the platform-independent, dynamic invocation promise of XML Web services. The bottom line here is that the scope and applicability of Web services are not restricted purely to the enterprise market. Even if enterprises persevere in using Web services predominantly on an intranet/extranet basis, remotely invoked Web services, running on third-party platforms, can still flourish within the nonenterprise sector.

Noncorporate portals (e.g., public portals or specialized content portals), are another growth area for externally invoked Web services. As mentioned in Section 1.2, Web services complement portals. This was why IBM felt compelled to institute the concept of Web Services for Remote Portals (WSRP)—where the term *remote* in this instance alludes to remotely invoked Web services, in this instance, Web services with integrated GUIs. Remotely invoked Web services from diverse third parties are the ideal, cost-effective way for a portal provider to offer customized, value-added functionality.

To begin with, most portals will want to use Web services for much of the de rigueur but nonproprietary utility functions users expect from a public portal: weather, sunrise/sunset times, phases of the moon, top news stories, horoscopes, and so on. Web services also provide portal providers with an enormously powerful, flexible, and standards-based mechanism for integrating external functionality. Consequently, it is safe to say that remotely invoked Web services will certainly flourish within the continually expanding portal market.

Another nascent but potentially burgeoning market for Web services is the voice and smart phone arena. There is already considerable momentum around VoiceXML (i.e., Voice eXtensible Markup Language) fostered through the VoiceXML Forum (voicexml.org) an industry organization founded by industry titans AT&T, IBM, Lucent, and Motorola. VoiceXML is a standard essential to making Internet content and information accessible via voice and phone. Given that it is a bona fide XML derivative, it can be easily adapted for use with existing Web-services technology. In addition to voice-based applications, there is an insatiable demand for value-added functionality for the increasingly powerful and versatile cell phones—some of which already support Java virtual machines. Web services are well poised to help developers exploit this new and exciting market for sophisticated software, interactive voice applications, and smart phones.

The final point that should be noted is that the software vendor community, with IBM in the lead, recognizes that there is a huge pent-up market for security and management tools that would make remotely invoked Web services more palatable for enterprise use. IBM's Web-service gateway, which was introduced in the spring of 2002, along with SPI Dynamics WebInspect 3.0 and other software vulnerability assessing software such as Sanctum's AppScan (www.sanctuminc.com), are precursors of things to come.

The express goal of IBM's proxy capability for Web services is to enable the externalization of Web services beyond the boundaries of an enterprise network. This gateway, which serves as a wonderful prototype for subsequent offerings, can act as a bidirectional proxy for services outside an enterprise firewall as well as for those within. It is, in effect, an XML application firewall for Web services; it ensures, per the now-accepted firewall model, that there are no unguarded end-to-end connections into an enterprise network that can be exploited by hackers. This gateway does not safeguard users from rogue or compromised Web services. However, if you do plan to use an adequately vetted and thus trusted external Web service, doing so through this gateway will ensure that all the Web services–related interactions are controlled, deterministic, and protected (as far as possible) against abuse by hackers.

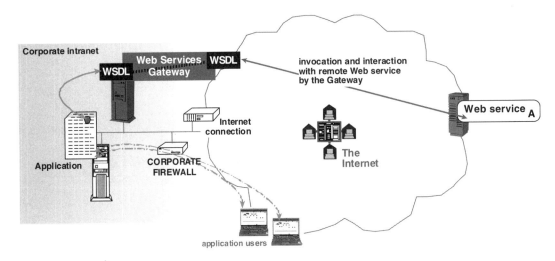

Figure 7.3   *Using a Web-services gateway to act as an XML application-level firewall between the calling application inside the corporate firewall and an externally invoked Web service.*

When an enterprise application wishes to use external Web services, this gateway, using the WSDL definitions for the required service, will import its functionality into the gateway—albeit in the form of an outbound remote call to the original Web service. However, the calls from the enterprise application to the Web service now get terminated at the gateway. There is no end-to-end connection between the calling application and the original Web service. Instead, calls to that external Web service are intercepted and serviced by the gateway, as shown in Figure 7.3.

The gateway in essence acts as an application-level Web-service firewall. It performs a corollary function when applications outside the enterprise firewall wish to invoke a Web service that is deployed inside the firewall.

7.2   Security considerations for Web services

There are three very distinct sides to Web-services security if one looks at this pivotal issue from a holistic, all-inclusive standpoint. Web services by design only work per a strict client/server model (albeit within a larger *n*-tier architecture)—where, depending on one's perspective, the calling application can be considered to be the server while the Web service being invoked becomes the client, or vice versa, where the calling application is deemed to be the client of a Web service. In reality it does not matter which is the server and which is the client, as long as one recognizes that there will always be two independent software components at play—with

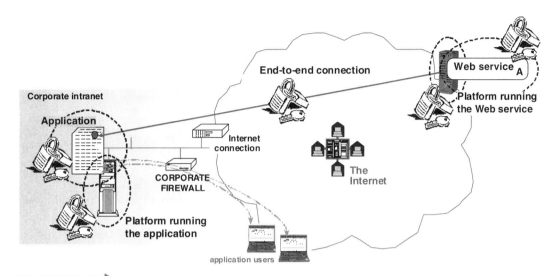

Figure 7.4   *All of the Web services–related entities that need to be protected to guarantee adequate end-to-end security.*

asynchronous (i.e., not session based) communication between them. Thus, from a security standpoint, to guarantee total coverage one has to look at both software components and the connection between them. It means that it can be counterproductive to focus on just one side of the model only to discover down the road that the other side is relatively exposed. Figure 7.4 highlights all of the perimeters that have to be safeguarded when it comes to Web services.

Enterprises already have policies and technology in place to protect their networks (e.g., firewalls, SSLs, virus scans, intrusion detection alarms) and applications (e.g., authentication). Web services–related security measures do not in any way displace any of the existing security policies, procedures, and technologies in use by enterprises. That is a given. Instead, they require that existing technology (e.g., authentication, digital signatures) be extended, as well as the addition of a whole new Web services–specific layer of safeguards (e.g., XML application gateways and software validators such as WebInspect), if one wants to deal with remotely invoked services.

Given that enterprises have now relied on computerized, mission-critical applications for over four decades, the access control and user validation mechanisms needed to deter unauthorized access are well known. Much of these mechanisms now fall into what is referred to as identity management or the "technology of trust." Stringent authentication, whether it be with user ID/password schemes, digital certificates, or two-factor token-based authentication such as RSA Security's SecurID scheme, is the basis for identity management. New applications that intend to invoke Web services should continue to rely on proven identity management and access control mechanisms to ensure that they can be accessed only by authorized users. This is standard application-level security and is independent of whether an application has any Web-services affiliations or not.

The introduction of Web services, however, mandates that application-specific security has to be extended to encompass the new application Web-services interface—if one intends to pursue the remote Web-service model over the Web. At a minimum, there are at least seven different types of security measures that may need to be enforced at each individual application Web-services interface—though the need for some of them (e.g., nonrepudiation) will depend on the nature of the data and transactions involved. These security measures are as follows:

1.   Stringent service provider/service requester authentication between the application and each Web service it invokes

2.   Access control, possibly at both ends, to determine the functions that may be requested—per invocation, based on the authentication instance

3.   Digital signatures to ensure the validity of contents

4.   Nonrepudiation to preclude either side from disowning a transaction once it has been executed

5.   XML application firewall, such as IBM's Web Services Gateway, to decouple the end-to-end communications connection at the enterprise network boundary

6.   Proven data encryption end to end—most likely with the industry standard SSL or its successor TLS

7.   Denial-of-service/replay attack detection and diversion mechanisms—which typically come with powerful traffic pattern sampling, analyzing, profiling, and reporting tools that will continually monitor the network interface to spot any unusual trends

None of these security measures can or is meant to identify rogue or compromised Web services—though bidirectional authentication could make it harder to surreptitiously hijack transactions being sent to one Web service and divert them to a rogue service. Consequently, it is still of paramount importance to unequivocally establish the credentials, trustworthiness, and technical competence of a Web-service provider by using traditional, time-tested methods before one ever gets around to worrying about implementing any of these measures. One course of action is to consider only Web services from well-known, well-funded entities that can reasonably be expected to run a tight ship with all necessary safeguards to prevent Web services from being hijacked, hacked into, or otherwise compromised.

Once a service provider and the necessary Web services from that provider have been adequately validated and chosen, authentication, particularly in the form of digital certificates, can be used to make sure that calls to a specific Web service are in fact being responded to by the expected service. This authentication will typically be done in both directions: the application authenticating the Web service and the Web service authenticating the application. Depending on the sensitivity of the transactions involved, one could consider multilevel authentication—for example, an initial digital certificate–based authentication followed by a two-factor authentication using RSA's widely used SecurID. (For the record, it is worth noting that at present this RSA SecurID technology is being used by over 10 million Web users around the world for secure application access, VPN utilization, Web server protection, and corporate portal partitioning.)

Proven authentication technology, including digital certificates, existed well before the advent of Web services. The success of corporate portals, e-commerce, and b2b applications was contingent on the availability of relatively impregnable authentication—always keeping in mind that, as with any type of security, total 100 percent infallibility is next to impossible to guarantee. But it is safe to say that this technology is mature, widely used, and well understood by those whose job it is to safeguard corporate assets.

Over the last 2 years there have been considerable effort, led by IBM, Microsoft, BEA, and security stalwarts VeriSign and RSA, to come up with new XML-based standards to more tightly align this prerequisite technology with Web services–related methodology—in particular, SOAP.

The key specifications on this front, spearheaded by the overarching WS-Security initiative, are listed in Table 1.1. This, however, as one should be able to appreciate, is a very dynamic and fluid arena at present, with new specifications being added and many updates to the existing ones. For the latest status on these specifications visit www.xmlweb.org, a new portal committed to promulgating the latest status on Web services–related technology.

The good news is that existing authentication, digital signature, SSL/TLS, and nonrepudiation solutions can be easily used very effectively, at the application Web-service interface ahead and independent of the XML-centric security standards. The goal of the new standards is to facilitate tighter integration. But waiting for these standards and products that comply to them should not be used as an excuse for not exploiting Web services. The exact security measures, from the previous list, that should be implemented on a particular application–Web-service interface will depend on a number of factors, including:

- The nature of the data and the types of transactions involved

- The type of network connection being used (e.g., a VPN connection will already have significant authentication and encryption capabilities built in)

- Whether the Web service is public (i.e., available to a variety of subscribers) or whether it is controlled (i.e., only available to a select set of tightly controlled and licensed users)

- The functionality offered by the Web service, given that access control would be superfluous with a single-function Web service

- Reliable safeguards available at the ISP level—particularly in regard to virus scanning and denial-of-service attack interception

- Safeguards, contractually agreed upon, offered by the service providers (e.g., guarantees against repudiation of transactions)

Suffice to say that determining the appropriate cocktail of security measures for any given application Web-service interface will be a complex and multifaceted exercise that will have to be undertaken on a per-service basis. In addition, there will invariably be pressures to consider optional refinements, such as adopting single sign-on schemes to minimize the amount of individual authentication required each time a service is invoked or when invoking different services offered by the same provider. Single sign-on is always a double-edged sword. Though it simplifies and expedites repeated access to the same provider or the same service, at the same time it lowers your authentication barrier, albeit by a smidge, increasing the chances of it being breached by a determined perpetrator.

The bottom line here is that there are plenty of well-proven security measures to adequately safeguard most enterprise-level Web-services scenarios—but you have to be diligent in working out exactly what you need to implement per interface, and you need to be continually vigilant to make sure that all the security measures are functioning as they are supposed to. In many cases it might be best to work with established enterprise security experts, such as RSA, VeriSign, or IBM/Tivoli, to determine an appropriate security architecture for Web services. Plenty of consulting firms, such as

Accenture, EDS, BearingPoint, Deloitte, and individual consultants, will trip over each other trying to help you formulate Web services–related security strategies for a fee.

7.2.1   Digital certificates and PKI

Digital certificates (DCs) are now routinely and transparently used on the Web for e-commerce, online banking, electronic trading, and corporate portal access applications—so much so that the "properties" option of popular Web browsers now includes a button that will show the DC that is in force at any given time. Figure 7.5 shows the DC details available from

Figure 7.5
Details of digital certificate usage shown by Microsoft's Internet Explorer—in this case, for a secure, authenticated connection with the Charles Schwab portal.

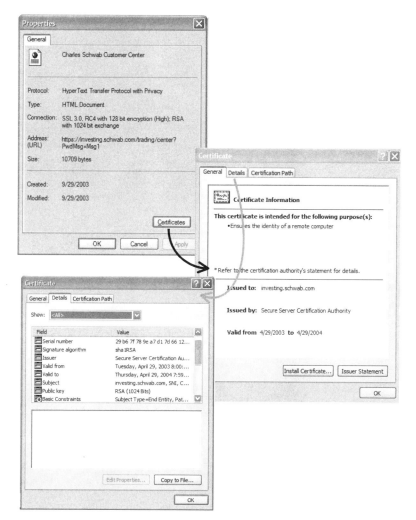

Microsoft's Internet Explorer—in this instance for a secure connection with electronic trading powerhouse Charles Schwab.

Digital certificates are an electronic credential (in the form of a small file) issued by a trustworthy organization such as a large company (e.g., IBM, Microsoft) or a security-specific entity such as VeriSign. Figure 7.6 shows a

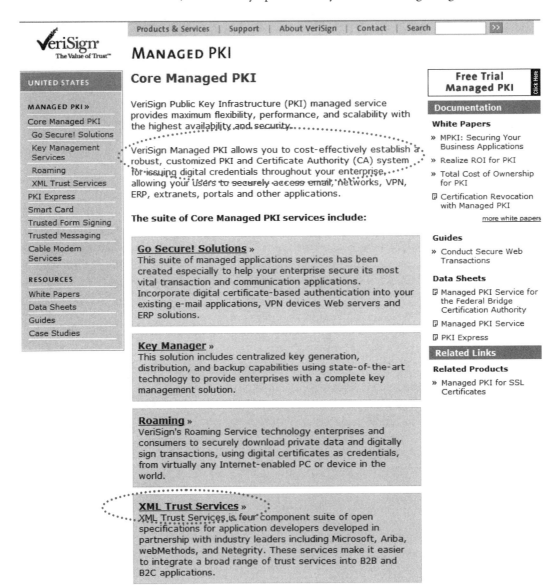

Figure 7.6   *One of VeriSign's public-key infrastructure (PKI)-based digital certificate solutions.*

page from VeriSign's portal providing an introduction to one its public-key infrastructure-based digital certificate programs. A DC vouches for an individual's, a business's, or an application's identity and authority to conduct secure transactions over the Web. DCs are in essence the Internet equivalent of a travel passport. They are a universally accepted means of establishing one's identity and thus gaining entry to a protected resource. DCs are meant to replace traditional user IDs and passwords, which are not as secure or trustworthy—hence, their applicability in the Web-services arena.

The issuing organization of a DC is called a Certificate Authority (CA). Consequently, VeriSign is an example of an existing and well-known CA. Refer to www.pki-page.org for an extensive list of CAs around the world as well as products that can be used to set up a CA. A CA can issue a DC to individual users, a server, or an application—where application in this context will also include a Web service, which is but a mini-application. If your company currently does not have any DCs, you may want to contact a CA and begin the process of acquiring a valid DC for use in Web services as well as other scenarios (e.g., corporate portals).

The acceptance of a DC as a valid credential is totally contingent on the recipient's trust in the CA. Therefore, just having a DC is not enough. You need to have confidence in the CA that issued it, especially since there are no uniform requirements, at least at present, as to what information a CA checks before issuing a DC. Some public Internet CAs may only ask the user for name and e-mail address in order to issue a DC. This is totally inadequate.

Fortunately, DCs today are closely tied in with PKI. CAs that support the PKI Exchange (PKIX) standards typically insist that the requester's identity information is further validated by a Registration Authority (RA) prior to a DC being issued. RAs are an integral part of a public-key infrastructure. There are proven PKI-specific products, such as RSA's Keon and IBM's Tivoli Trust Authority, that can be used by companies so that they can act as RAs. These systems allow companies to set up centralized or distributed electronic enrollment centers that validate user requests for DCs on behalf of the CA. Figure 7.7 shows a section from RSA's portal introducing the PKI capabilities offered by Keon.

The key thing to bear in mind here is that a DC, in the end, is only as good as the CA that issued it. So all DCs are not necessarily equal. If you are going to use DCs as a base-level security measure to establish the ongoing bona fides of a previously selected service provider, then you will have to check which CAs meet your security criteria. For example, you may not want to accept DCs from unknown CAs. Invariably it would be best to for-

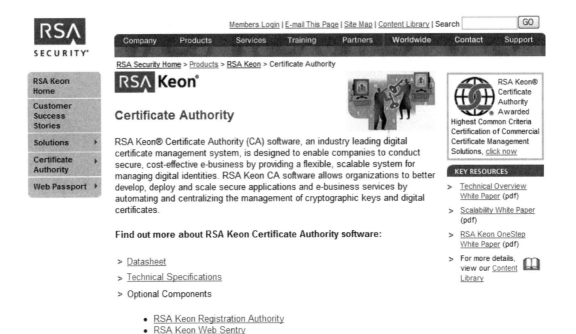

Figure 7.7   *RSA's Keon, one of several products now available that would enable a company to act as a certificate authority (CA).*

mally agree on which DCs you will accept from a provider up front when evaluating and validating the provider.

DCs leverage public-key cryptography. Public-key cryptography relies on the use of a pair of associated keys for encryption and decryption— known as public and private keys. There is a mathematical relationship between these two keys that guarantees that anything encrypted with one key can be cleanly decrypted by using the other key. Which key is made public and which is kept private is totally arbitrary. With public-key cryptography, one can freely distribute the public key without in any way compromising or revealing the nature of the private key. The public key can even be stored in a public directory or a Web page. The private key, true to its name, must, however, be kept guarded and secret.

The public and private keys only work in tandem. That, so to speak, is the key. In other words, a document encrypted with the public key can only be decrypted with the private key. The document cannot be decrypted with the openly available public key, since this would nullify the whole point of encryption. The same applies the other way around. A document encrypted using the private key can only be decrypted using the public key. This

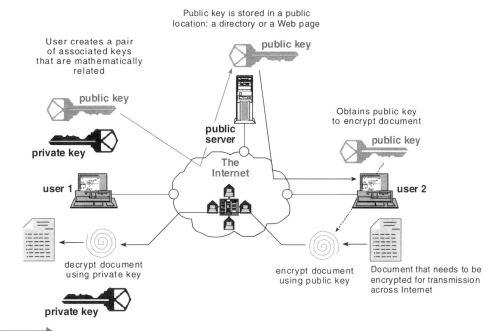

Figure 7.8   *The overall "big-picture" depiction of the dual-key concept of public-key cryptography.*

makes sense because the private key is kept secret and should not be available for use by other parties. Figure 7.8 provides an overview of how public-key cryptography works, and Table 7.2 summarizes which keys are used for which operations. A DC will include the certificate holder's public key.

Digital certificates are defined by the X.509 standard. An X.509 certificate is typically a small file that contains:

- The DC holder's distinguished name (DN) with the identifying information for the certificate holder, which, depending on the identification criteria employed by the issuing CA, can include the common name of the certificate holder, holder's organization (i.e., company name), any organizational units, street address, fully qualified domain name (i.e., company URL), an IP address, and e-mail address

- The certificate issuing CA's distinguished name, which will include the same set of information as that of the holder's DN

- The certificate holder's public key

- The CA's digital signature, which is a hashed (i.e., encoded) code that in turn is encrypted with the private key of the CA and is then used as the seal of authenticity for the DC. A digital signature, which should not be confused with a digital certificate, is the equivalent of a tamper-detection seal on a pharmaceutical product.

- The validity period (i.e., shelf-life) for the DC
- A unique serial number for the DC

Today, there are several different types of DCs, each for a specific security scenario. Some of the main types of DCs include:

1. CA certificates, which digitally validate the identity of the CA; they contain identifying information as well as its public key. CA certificates can be signed (i.e., further validated) by another CA (e.g., VeriSign) or be self-signed if the CA does not require additional validation. A self-signed certificate is referred to as a trusted root for obvious reasons. Self-signed certificates, unless from large corporations, may not be appropriate for Web-service applications.

2. Server certificates to validate a server's identity and provide information as to who owns the server. They will contain the public key of the server's owner. These could be used by both sides to make sure that the servers on which the application and the Web service are running have not been changed without adequate notification.

3. Client or user certificates, which validate the client's identity and contain the client's public key. Authentication of server and client certificates can be used as the basis for encrypted, client/server communications per the SSL protocol.

4. Object signing certificates, which are used as the basis for digital signatures that vouch for the integrity of the accompanying object as well as the originator of that object.

Table 7.2   *Summary of Which Keys Are Used for Which Operations*

Operations	Key Used
Send an encrypted document	Receiver's public key
Send an encrypted digital signature	Sender's private key
Decrypt a received encrypted document	Receiver's private key
Authenticate received digital signature	Sender's public key

The widespread use of DCs as well as digital signatures to validate the authenticity of a document (e.g., XML document) is made considerably easier by PKI. PKI, as indicated by the inclusion of the term *infrastructure* in its name, provides an incisive framework for facilitating secure but at the same time accessible and easy-to-use public-key encryption and digital signatures. The term *public* in the title, however, can be deceptive. PKI is not a centralized, public service for distributing and managing keys. The term *public* in this context refers to the public key in the public-private key combination. Today, PKIs are typically implemented on a corporate basis with PKI facilitating products from a variety of vendors, including IBM, Veri-Sign, and Entrust. IBM now even includes a comprehensive PKI on its flagship z/OS operating system for mainframes.

PKI sets out to hide the intricacies involved in providing a robust public-key encryption system so as not to intimidate users. In the true spirit of an infrastructure sustaining a utility such as that of the electric power grid or the cable TV network, PKI is a nonintrusive, transparent service. You can use PKI without actually knowing or caring that it is there, what it does, or how it does it.

There is a three-way, symbiotic relationship between PKI, digital certificates, and digital signatures. The current use of digital certificates for Internet applications is contingent on PKI. Without PKI, DCs would not be as convenient to use or administer. PKI consists of four primary components:

1.   CAs that issue and validate digital certificates

2.   One or more registration authorities (RAs), which work with the CA to verify a requester's identity prior to the issuance of a digital certificate

3.   One or more public directories (typically based on LDAP), where digital certificates, which will contain the public keys of their owners, can be stored

4.   A comprehensive and foolproof certificate management system

As an infrastructure scheme, PKI is expected to cater to key backup and recovery. Users typically have to enter a password to access their public-key encryption keys. But users forget their passwords or may leave the company. If there is no way to recover encryption/decryption keys in such instances, valuable company information, which has been previously encrypted, may be forever lost. Thus, it is essential to have a secure and reliable way whereby a designated and fully validated security administrator can recover encryption key pairs through the PKI system. Since such recovery will be possible only if the key pairs are properly backed up, it is assumed that the CA will automatically keep a backup of keys that have been issued.

In this context of backup and recovery, it is, however, important to note that recovery is only required for the key used for encryption/decryption. Keys used for digital signatures are not expected to be backed up or recoverable. The reason for this is that having duplicate (i.e., backed up) and thus recoverable signing keys undermines the overall integrity of a PKI. This has to do with something called nonrepudiation.

Repudiate means to disown or reject an action. Thus, denying involvement in a transaction is known as repudiation. Disowning a hotel charge made to a credit card via the signature-on-file scheme favored by North American hotels is an example of a repudiated transaction. Nonrepudiation precludes a person from being able to disown having participated in a transaction. In the digital world this means ensuring the sanctity of digital signatures. A prerequisite for this is the inability of a user to deny using his or her digital signature—hence, the undesirability of having backups of signing keys.

If there are no backups and the user has sole and secure custody of the signing keys, then the latitudes for repudiating a digital signature are considerably reduced. However, just as in the nondigital world, with pen and ink–based signatures, there will still occur situations where users will try to repudiate digital signature–backed transactions. At this point, other electronic logs and traces will have to be used to enforce nonrepudiation.

The loss of a signing key, unlike that of an encryption key, is not catastrophic to business. The user will just have to obtain new keys to use with future signatures. The desirability of keeping backups of encryption keys but not those of signing keys means that users should not be allowed to use the same keys for both purposes because this will again mean that there will be more than one copy of the signing keys. A PKI must support two key pairs per user: one pair for encryption and the other for digital signatures.

Then there is the issue of the longevity of key pairs. To maximize security, key pairs should be periodically updated. A PKI can enforce this based on key expiration thresholds. However, since users may need to go back and decrypt documents encrypted with older keys, the PKI also needs to maintain a history whereby prior keys can be securely recovered. Again, this would not apply to signing keys. The PKI should destroy the old signing key pair each time a new pair is assigned.

Another issue pertaining to PKI and DCs relates to certificate revocation. In the event of a security compromise, DCs may have to be immediately revoked in advance of their built-in expiration setting. This may happen, for example, if the private key corresponding to the public key published in a DC gets into the hands of an unauthorized individual. Another instance would be when a user leaves a company. To cater to certificate revocation, a PKI must maintain a scalable mechanism to publish the status of all certificates, whether they are active or revoked. Application software validating a DC will first make sure that it has not been revoked.

The final topic related to PKI has to do with cross-certification, given the current absence of a global PKI scheme. Cross-certification is also referred to as PKI networking. Cross-certification permits multiple, autonomous CAs to work cooperatively so that they have a mutual trust relationship. One scenario for this might be that of CAs for trading partners having the ability to validate DCs issued by the other CAs. Another scenario might be that of a large multinational enterprise that decides to implement CAs on a geographical basis for scalability and management purposes. Yet again, today's leading PKI solutions are typically able to address all such requirements.

7.2.2   Two-factor authentication

Two-factor authentication, as with DCs, is another powerful and proven authentication system that can be used by itself to authenticate Web services and applications to each other, or in conjunction with another scheme (e.g., DCs). Two-factor authentication gets its name from the fact that it requires users (or applications in this instance) to identify themselves by using two unique factors, one on top of the other. One of the factors would be something users know (e.g., password or PIN), while the other factor would be something they have. Automated teller machine (ATM) cards, though not based on RSA's SecurID, are an easy-to-understand example of two-factor authentication, where your personal PIN is the factor that you know, while the ATM card with its encoded magnetic stripe is the factor that you have.

In reality, RSA does offer an ATM card–type system based on a chip-embedded smart card and a smart card reader connected to the user's PC. Such a smart card–based system, though offering exceptional security, is obviously not applicable for application to Web–service interactions. Fortunately, RSA's SecurID can be and is widely used very effectively by millions of users on a daily basis, without the use of this smart card system.

RSA's SecurID system, in general, works with a user-specific secret password and a token. The password is the factor that a user/application knows, while the token becomes the factor that the user has. The token is a time-synchronized code, which is periodically generated, typically every minute, starting with a unique seed code supplied by RSA. RSA can determine the validity of the token based on the time-sensitive code entered by the user. A valid token proves that the user has access to the factor he or she is supposed to hold. This token in effect becomes the equivalent of the magnetic stripe on an ATM card. To be successfully authenticated, a user/application has to enter this continually updated code (i.e., the token) and the user-specific secret password. RSA tokens can be generated by using RSA supplied software, which can be run on many different platforms. Obviously in a Web-service scenario it is important that this token-generation software and the user-specified passwords are safeguarded to ensure total security.

Since it is essentially an extension to normal password-based security schemes, applications can be modified to use two-factor authentication relatively easily and quickly. Typically a system administrator would have to enter a regularly changed password, as a seed, to activate the token-generation software. If this password is valid, the security software will automatically generate the token, append it to the entered password, and then send this combined key, suitably encrypted, to the security server for authentication. Despite its simplicity from an end-user perspective, two-factor authentication is obviously a significantly more powerful security scheme than a password-only (i.e., one-form) authentication scheme. Large and high-profile high-tech companies such as Cisco have been successfully using two-factor authentication, initially with hardware tokens but with a rapid transition to software tokens, since c. 1995 to partition and safeguard their employee-only intranet portals.

7.2.3 Secure Sockets Layer

SSL, or its successor TLS, should be considered a mandatory prerequisite technology for any Web service that deals with sensitive information. SSL, a client/server-based security mechanism developed by Web browser pioneer Netscape Communications in 1996, is the accepted and trusted basis for most of today's secure transactions across the Web. SSL is so widely used that it appears to be ubiquitous. It is supported by all popular commercial Web browsers and Web servers (e.g., Microsoft's Internet Information Server [IIS], the open software Apache Software Foundation's Apache HTTP Server, IBM's HTTP Server, etc.). In the context of Web servers it is

Figure 7.9   *The locked padlock signifying a secure SSL connection—in this instance, for online banking with the Meredith Village Savings Bank in New Hampshire—along with a superimposed browser properties window showing that SSL 3.0 with encryption is in use.*

used between a browser and the Web server. It can also easily be used in other scenarios—in particular, application-to-application setups.

The little locked padlock icon that gets displayed at the bottom of a Web browser window whenever a secure transaction is being performed (e.g., credit card purchase or online stock trading) indicates that the security in force has been supplied via SSL technology. Figure 7.9 shows an example of the locked padlock icon indicating that SSL security is in force. Whenever the locked padlock icon is on display, the address field at the top of the browser showing the URL invoked is likely to say "https://www. etc. etc.," rather than "http://www. etc. etc." The "s" following the HTTP denotes SSL—in this case HTTP with SSL, or HTTP over SSL. HTTPS transactions are usually conducted across port number 443, while HTTP typically uses port 80. SSL, consequently, is not something new or rare. It is a scheme that most people have already encountered and have successfully used even without realizing that they were doing so. Ports 80 and 443 will typically also be the ports used by Web services if they are relying on SOAP over HTTP/HTTPS as their transport mechanism.

SSL is a Transport Layer (i.e., Layer 4) protocol. As such it provides authentication, integrity, and data privacy for applications running above the TCP Layer (i.e., Layer 3). SSL supports digital certificates. Given its cli-

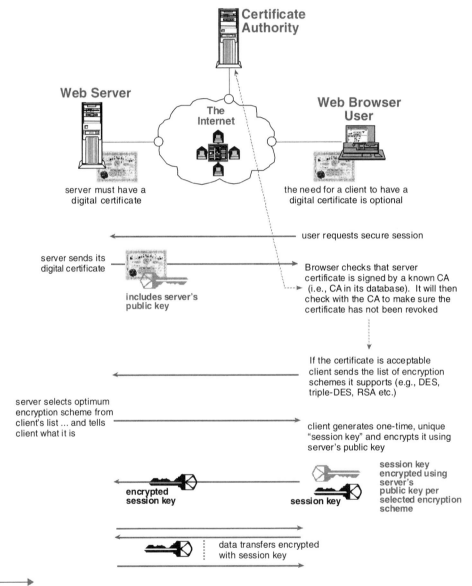

Figure 7.10   *High-level view of the process involved in setting up a secure SSL connection between a Web server and a Web browser user. This process is the same for secure SSL connections between other client/server pairs, including an application and a Web service.*

ent/server orientation, SSL uses digital certificates to authenticate the server and the client—in this case the application and the Web service it intends to invoke. This authentication process, which is achieved via what is referred to as an SSL handshake, typically requires a user ID/password exchange—with the user ID and password being conveyed in encrypted mode with a public key. Following this authentication process, the SSL protocol sets about negotiating a common encryption scheme acceptable both to the client and the server. SSL does not do end-to-end data encryption.

Providing end-to-end client-to-server encryption was never a goal of the SSL protocol. There are well-established industry standards (e.g., 56-bit DES and 168-bit triple DES) and commercial ciphers (e.g., RSA) for enforcing end-to-end security. What SSL does is negotiate an encryption scheme acceptable both to the server and the client (e.g., triple DES)—and then invoke this mutually accepted encryption scheme for encrypting the data flowing between the client and the server. Thus, the security services provided by SSL can be summarized as server authentication via digital certificates, optional client authentication with digital certificates, acceptable encryption scheme negotiation between the server and the client, and invoking the accepted encryption scheme to ensure that the data flowing between the client and the server is indeed encrypted and tamperproof on an end-to-end basis.

The latest version of SSL is called Transport Layer Security (TLS). The two terms will get used interchangeably in the future, with SSL most likely being used more often, even when TLS is being referred to, given its current popularity. Figure 7.10 provides a high-level schematic of how a secure SSL connection is established between a Web server and a browser user.

7.3   A predeployment checklist for Web services

Despite the allure of being considered the latest and greatest in software development methodology and the fleeting fame of once having been hailed as the next big thing on the Web, one should never lose sight of the fact that Web services, in the end, are still nothing more than another incarnation of client/server technology. Consequently, though one may want to believe that things must be different and more difficult, in reality all of the deployment- and management-related issues that pertain to application scenarios involving Web services are no different from those that apply to any other client/server configuration. Distributed computing is not new, and the vanguard of today's systems can be traced back to the mid-1960s. The advent of PCs in 1981 accelerated the interest in client/server in relation to worldwide commerce, and to this end it is worth noting that IBM's SNA-based LU 6.2 advanced program-to-program communications (APPC) was introduced in 1982 for mainframe-to-PC applications around the same time that UNIX distributed computing was making a name for itself.

Control, or to be precise who controls what, is the one area where the Web-services picture differs, in general, from most previous client/server permutations. In the past the client/server model was typically used in what would now be referred to as intranet/extranet configurations. All the software, both on the clients and the servers, would be under the control of one entity. Though the computing was distributed, the control of the software was centralized. Web services offer an alternate model, though corporations at present are opting to ignore this Internet model and are yet again falling back on intranet/extranet deployments. What is important here is that the deployment- and management-related issue in relation to Web services is still the same as for other client/server implementations.

Prior to the emergence of the Web, client/server implementations enjoyed a star-crossed, checkered history. Hindsight has shown that the total reliance on standards contributed much to the success of the Web model. Web services set out to capitalize on that. So at least in the case of Web services, unlike with enterprise-level client/server solutions as recently as the early 1990s, one does not have to wrestle with network protocol (i.e., IPX, NetBIOS, SNA, TCP/IP, OSI) or network topology decisions. Web services, by definition and design, will be standards compliant and as such conform to a consistent networking profile. This means that network compatibility issues, for a change, will not require much debate. One should thus be able to quickly tick off the SOAP, WSDL, etc. related concerns and devote more attention to the other issues.

Given the client/server nature, there will always be two separate sides to be considered for all of the deployment- and management-related issues—with overlap from both sides to cover the network interface as well. As discussed in the preceding sections, most enterprises will already have a firm handle on the issues pertaining to the calling application side, given that this is the driver's side of the equation. Enterprises will already have experience with selecting, deploying, maintaining, and managing applications. It is the external, outside-the-firewall Web-services aspect that will be alien—and as such will demand attention. The issues, as with other client/server software, that one should focus on at this juncture include:

- Pricing and licensing

- Service-level agreement, which covers availability, performance, and scalability (e.g., one-second turnaround time, 20 transactions per minute, etc.)

- Maintenance contract, which deals with how any problems with the software will be handled, including how problems will be reported and escalated, whether there will be a charge for problem resolution, testing of the fix, end-to-end change management, and so on

- Liability protection, particularly against bad data, data interception by employees, unauthorized use of information, and use of unauthorized software (e.g., copyright violations)

- Upgrade policy covering notifications, regression testing mechanisms, and cut-over procedures

- Long-term indemnification, if applicable (e.g., source code deposited in escrow)

- Platform selection

- Assignability—that is, options in the event of a merger or acquisition, and whether the software (i.e., the Web service) or the operation of that software can be sold to another party during the period of the contract

- Privacy policy and guarantee

- Security safeguards, including intrusion detection (especially in the context of a platform being compromised)

- Load balancing and failover configurations

- Disaster recovery scenarios

- Intellectual property issues and waivers

- Marketing and publicity rights—e.g., service providers wishing to publicize that so-and-so uses their *xyz* Web service

- Management of the software covering change management, problem management, performance management, network management, and gateway (e.g., XML application firewall) management

- Usage monitoring and reporting

Of these, the pricing and licensing of Web services are likely to prove to be the most intriguing. Way back when Web services were first being bandied around, there was an implication that many services would be available on a no-charge, freeware-type basis. This could still prove to be the case, though IT professionals have known from the start that most Web services they would wish to use or, conversely, offer to others are likely to have some cost and licensing associated with them. To this end, Microsoft's statement (reproduced here) as to how one can go about purchasing its trend-setting MapPoint Web service offers a glimpse of how the pricing model will evolve:

> *Customers purchase the MapPoint Web Service as an annual subscription direct from Microsoft. There are two primary licensing models:*
>
> 1.   *Per user is for "known" user applications, such as within a call center or fleet tracking applications*
>
> 2.   *Per transactions is for "anonymous" user applications, such as a Web site locator or travel portal*
>
> *Pricing is dependent on the numbers of users and/or transactions you purchase. More information can be found on http://www.microsoft.com/mappoint/webservice/how-tobuy.mspx.*

Suffice to say that the pricing model for Web services is at present in an embryonic stage, with most people, quite rightly, still focusing their attention on the technical side of things. IBM, a major shaker and mover when it comes to Web services and a company that knows a thing or two about complex, usage-based pricing models, has to its credit already started publishing position papers about possible accounting and metering schemes for Web services. Microsoft is already espousing usage-based pricing. What is abundantly clear is that there will be a very wide spectrum, ranging from freeware to expensive, premium offerings coupled with many permutations, in the case of the nonfreeware offerings, as to how the pricing will be structured.

The pricing options available will definitely include one-time charge schemes, periodic licensing (e.g., monthly or yearly), and umpteen usage-based options. In addition, it is likely that there could be third-party Web services distributors—though the inherent dynamic discovery capability of a Web service dilutes some of the potential value that can be offered by a distributor. In the case of Web services the main value that a distributor is likely to provide is that of handling the billing and collection. Indubitably, there will also be syndicated Web services. Figure 7.11 sets out to highlight some of the possible pricing models that will be available for Web services, depending on who is offering the service.

The implications of other items in the preceding list should be self-explanatory, but the management-related issues are elaborated below. As with security, how one would go about addressing each of the items in this

Figure 7.11
Some of the possible pricing models for Web services, depending on their source.

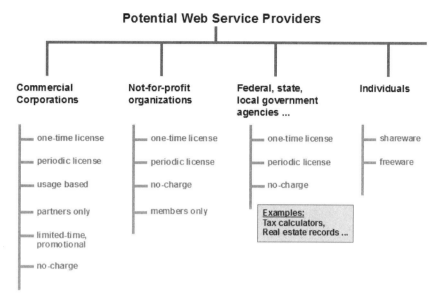

Potential Web Service Providers

Commercial Corporations	Not-for-profit organizations	Federal, state, local government agencies ...	Individuals
one-time license	one-time license	one-time license	shareware
periodic license	periodic license	periodic license	freeware
usage based	no-charge	no-charge	
partners only	members only		
limited-time, promotional		**Examples:** Tax calculators, Real estate records ...	
no-charge			

list will depend and vary on a case-by-case basis. There are no hard-and-fast rules that will cover all instances. Remember that just because we are dealing with a new software methodology does not mean that the famous French adage "plus ça change, plus c'est la meme chose" (the more things change, the more they remain the same) ceases to apply. The software-related issues, such as failures, upgrades, change management, and intermittent slowdowns, will still be the same.

7.4   The platform issue—yet again

It goes without saying, but it has to be said for completeness, that there are two platforms that need to be considered for each Web-service invocation:

1.   The platform on which the calling application is running

2.   The platform hosting the Web service being invoked

Within the context of this duality, one can easily identify the permutations shown in Table 7.3 as being likely candidates,

The platform issues, in the Web services context, as discussed in the context of both .NET and Java, pertain to:

1.   Capacity (i.e., how many concurrent sessions it can handle)

2.   Performance (i.e., delivery of expected response times under normal workloads)

3.   Scalability (i.e., what the upper limits are when it comes to handling increasing workloads)

4.   Overall stability in terms of reliability, availability, and servicability (i.e., the platform can meet the expected uptime criteria, given that mission-critical applications for Fortune 500 corporations require 99.999% uptime over a year)

5.   Vulnerability (i.e., the platform is noted for being safe from hackers)

6.   Manageability (i.e., provides the necessary tools for remote monitoring and management)

Though these concerns have been discussed as they relate to .NET and Java, it is now important to yet again reiterate that both sides of the Web-services model are platform independent in that the calling application for a Web service nor a Web service being invoked need to be restricted to a specific platform. This, as highlighted in Figure 6.1, does not mean cross-platform portability. It does, however, mean that the Web-services model is not confined to any specific platform permutations. Java and .NET are also not the only viable platforms for Web services or the applications that intend to invoke Web services. Any of the traditional platforms (e.g., IBM's CICS, BEA's Tuxedo) can also be used for either side. This is particularly germane in legacy modernization scenarios, as discussed in the beginning of this book, whereby proven business logic from existing mission-critical applications can be isolated and repackaged as Web services using host integration tools such as IBM's WebSphere Host Publisher. The bottom line here is

Table 7.3   *Two Platforms for Web Services*

Calling Application	Web Service Being Invoked
On the same system (i.e., collocated)	
On the same system, on different (but homogeneous) partitions	
On the same system, but on heterogeneous partitions (e.g., z/OS and Linux on a mainframe)	
System$_A$	System$_B$
But System$_A$ and System$_B$ are of the same type (e.g., UNIX servers)	
System$_A$	System$_B$
But System$_A$ and System$_B$ are significantly different	

that any platform, provided it offers an appropriate transport scheme, can be used for Web services–based application scenarios.

The goal when it comes to platform selection, however, is to ensure that the platforms selected adequately meets the performance, uptime, security, and manageability expectations for the overall application in question. The big danger here is ending up with totally mismatched combinations, such as a high-volume, mainframe-resident, mission-critical transaction processing application (e.g., travel reservation system) serving 50,000 concurrent users relying upon a crucial, oft-invoked Web service that happens to be deployed on an old Pentium III server still running Windows NT 4.0. But you cannot make generalizations even with this very uneven combination.

It is indeed possible, depending on the processing involved, that the out-of-date Windows platform may still provide the necessary functionality, with adequate resiliency to meet expectations, especially if the server is located in a data center that is manned 24/7. One assumes that one would not be as concerned if the platforms were reversed, so to speak (i.e., a VB application running on an old WinTel server relying on a Web service deployed on a newly upgraded, multimillion dollar mainframe). However, it is fair to say that mismatched platform combinations invariably warrant particular scrutiny to avoid costly breakdowns in expectations down the road—when the application is in full swing, handling mission-critical production work.

The desirability of cross-platform portability, such as Java, is a contingency against mismatched platform pairing. If a Web service is portable, then one does have the option, albeit at a cost, of having it hosted on a different platform if one has reservations about the platform it is currently being offered on. Given that this platform specificity is primarily going to be an issue if a Web service is limited to Windows, one still could have other options to mitigate the situation. Key among these would be to acquire or license the Web service so that it can be run in-house, behind the corporate firewall, on a carefully tended, dedicated WinTel server—or, per the current trend, on a WinTel blade on a server rack.

The bottom line here is that with all of the debate that has ensued around .NET and Java, enterprises now have enough background and parameters to evaluate the platform criteria for specific Web-service scenarios—independent of whether Java or .NET even comes into the picture. With all of the various platforms and platform options available today, IT professionals, given a set of service-level criteria, should be able to craft appropriate pairings to meet expectations.

7.5   Managing it all

The disciplines and technologies required to incisively manage Web services–based application scenarios fall under the umbrella of what system vendors and system integrators have referred to since the start of the 1990s as total enterprise management, or system management. Total enterprise management goes way beyond just network management to encompass hardware platforms, operating systems, applications, operational procedures, and even business issues (e.g., making sure maintenance contacts were paid in time and kept current). IBM, an early proponent of this strategic field, neatly captured what it was all about by branding it SystemView—to contrast it from NetView, at one point the gold standard for network management in Fortune 1000 companies.

Though many corporations have yet to get around to exploiting the true potential of total enterprise management, the requisite enabling technology

Sun Management Center

Sun Management Center works with accompanying software packages: Service Availability Manager, a set of modules that test and measure the availability of network services, System Reliability Manager, a component that enhances reliability, helping to increase service levels and decrease administrative costs, and Performance Reporting Manager, software that adds analysis, reporting, and graphing capabilities. » More

→ Now Available! Sun Management   → Now available: Sun Management Center ESP Sun Fire
Center 3.5   Supplements - Version 03/03

Product Home
» Features & Benefits
» Data Sheet
» General FAQs

Get the Software »

At a Glance	
Product	**Purpose**
Service Availability Manager	Value added package for Sun Management Center 3.5, increases the availability of network services running locally or remotely on Sun systems. Monitors and confirms the availability of network services such as Web server services, directory FTP, mail, and Solaris Calendar Services.
System Reliability Manager	Value-added package for Sun Management Center 3.5 improves reliability and Solaris software management solutions through four different modules: patch management, file watch, script launcher, and OS crash dump analyzer.
Performance Reporting Manager	Value-added package for Sun Management Center 3.5 adds enterprise wide statistical analysis, reporting, charting, capacity planning, and asset management capabilities to Sun's system management product line.
Change Manager	Stand-alone software product that provides quick and easy deployment of integrated software stacks to multiple managed hosts. Quickly reprovision systems to respond to rapidly changing business environments. Peform software installations or updates on systems while they continue to run. Use auditing capabilities to enable system and file comparisons to detect changes.
Advanced System Monitoring	Value-added package for Sun Management Center 3.5 provides more in-depth monitoring of Solaris and Sun hardware with an enhanced kernel reader, a Solaris health monitoring module and the Hardware Diagnostics Suite. Application monitoring modules are also included with this value pack.

Figure 7.12   *Key features of Sun's Management Center 3.5, which includes Change Manager and Service Availability Manager.*

is well established and readily available from a wide number of bluechip names. Thus, proven total enterprise management solutions, which also encompass the needs of managing Web services, are available from the likes of IBM/Tivoli, Computer Associates (CA), H-P (under the well-known OpenView marquee), and Sun (i.e., Sun Management Center). Consequently, one does not have to be concerned that managing Web services–related software scenarios is going to be hampered by a paucity of appropriate management tools.

The key features of Sun's Management Center, according to Sun, are shown in Figure 7.12, and one should note the management disciplines of particular interest to Web services, such as change management and service availability management. At this juncture it is also useful to see what CA, an acknowledged leader in enterprise management with its Unicenter family of products, has to say about system management of distributed, multivendor environments of the type that will be used in Web-services scenarios. CA's perspective, shown in Figure 7.13, clearly captures what is indeed possible with today's system management tools.

In addition to the holistic total enterprise management solutions that treat Web services as just another software deployment configuration, there

 Enterprise Management

Unicenter Network and Systems Management
NETWORK & SYSTEMS MANAGEMENT AND MORE!

Systems Management software components perform specific tasks to monitor and manage the health and availability across complex, multi-vendor, multi-platform computing environments.

Systems Management solutions reduce the complexity of deployment and use of complex technologies by applying self-managing capabilities to deliver high levels of automation that can relieve the staff

The Unicenter Network and Systems Management product manages the health and availability of operating systems and provides basic status management on all infrastructure elements such as network devices, business applications and database systems. Powerful auto-discovery builds a database with information on system elements and populates 2D and 3D system dynamic visualizations. Historian keeps you informed with past events and object status whereas predictive management capabilities inform you about possible bottlenecks in your systems and applications in future to take automated actions to avoid them. Portal technology provides personalized intuitive information for both technical and business focused administrators.

Figure 7.13 *A composite of material from Computer Associates Web site showing its perspective on system management. Keep in mind that CA has a long and respected track record in the management arena.*

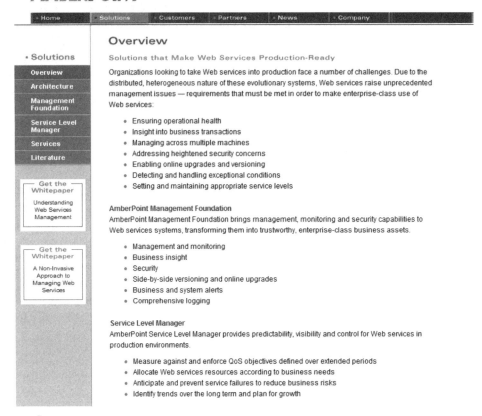

Figure 7.14   *AmberPoint's overview of its Web services–specific management solution.*

are also specific Web-services management offerings from the likes of AmberPoint (www.amberpoint.com). Figure 7.14 shows an overview of AmberPoint's solution, which demonstrates that it recognizes the need to bring management, monitoring, and security capabilities to Web-services systems so that they can be transformed into trustworthy, enterprise-class business assets. Also note that per the repeated themes in this chapter, the AmberPoint offering also targets change management (i.e., enabling online upgrades and versioning), service-level monitoring, and multiplatform management. Yet again the message here is that, as with security measures (e.g., digital certificates, SSL), the necessary knowledge and technology for managing Web services are already in place.

The Web services–related entities that need to be managed with the new application model (Figure 7.15) include:

1.   The calling application

2.   The platform hosting the calling application

3.   The (remote) Web services

4.   The platforms on which the various Web services are running

5.   Web services gateways (e.g., XML application firewall)

6.   Network connection

The need to monitor and manage distant resources owned by third parties, as will be the case with remotely invoked Web services, will be seen by some as adding a whole new dimension of complexity to the overall management challenge. This is not necessarily so. Today's IP-based, Internet-oriented management methodology, by and large, is location and distance independent. Entities are identified and managed per their IP addresses. Thus, the exact location of an entity is immaterial to the management software. As long as the underlying network can locate the required entity (e.g., be able to ping it), the management software will be able to access it irrespective of whether it is located on the same system or halfway around the world. In this context it is also worth remembering that enterprises now have considerable experience managing remotely hosted Web servers. Remotely hosted Web services are but an extension of this model.

Being able to monitor and manage third-party-owned Web services on remotely located platforms should, however, only be possible with the

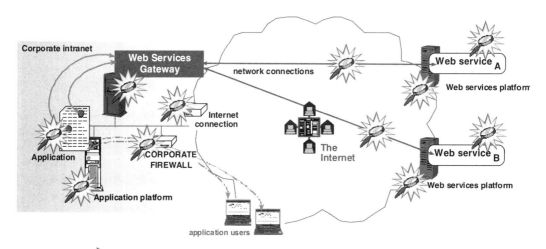

Figure 7.15   *The magnifying glass icons in this diagram signify the Web services–related entities that need to be monitored and managed with the new application model.*

explicit blessing of the Web-service owner—as well as the operator of the remote platform, if the service is being hosted by another. One obviously would want to steer well clear of Web services that supposedly offer an open, unrestricted management interface, given the potential security vulnerabilities of such an unregulated service. Thus, being able to monitor and manage a remote Web service should be contingent on preestablished and validated authentication, access control, and data privacy (e.g., encryption) mechanisms. The management interface should not be a possible point of vulnerability (i.e., the weakest link) in the overall security architecture, since a determined hacker will most likely begin with probing this interface when looking for a way to break into the system.

What is possible and permitted when it comes to the remote monitoring and management of a Web service should be something that is explicitly discussed during the evaluation phase and agreed upon, contractually, prior to production use. It is not something that you would want to tackle on an ad hoc basis after you have already started to use a service. It is also important to remember that this remote management capability, though technically possible and philosophically pleasing, may not always be necessary or practical.

In some instances, depending on the nature of the service or the stature of the provider, one may not want to manage the remote service. Managing software, despite the assistance of the management tools, is a specialized function and should be undertaken only by knowledgeable, trained, and responsible system administrators. Thus, there is a tangible cost component associated with instituting and operating a remote software monitoring capability, especially if it is to be on a 24/7 basis. Consequently, in some instances it may be more practical to leave all the monitoring and management responsibilities with the service provider. A real-time collaborative scheme, based on e-mail, instant messaging, or cell phones, could then be used if any critical issues need to be communicated between the service provider and the service user. There will also be cases where the service provider is unwilling to provide direct monitoring and management capabilities and instead will be willing to offer only a notification mechanism. Proven and incisive technology to facilitate remote management of Web services is readily available, and management is not an impediment when it comes to Web-services exploitation.

The key total enterprise management disciplines that are pertinent when it comes to Web services include:

- Problem management: This obviously applies to all entities, end to end, including the network, and one may want to augment this with filtering and consolidating capabilities to prevent one underlying problem from being reported multiple times, with different flavors, from each of the managed entities.

- Performance management, including workload management and capacity management

- Application management, which embraces resource usage monitoring, user administration, and usage accounting

- Change management, particularly as it applies to the remote Web services

- Security management, which includes intrusion detection notification

- Usage monitoring

- Operations management, which with today's technology can include both automated operations (e.g., backups) and operator tracking (e.g., time taken to respond to an intervention request)

Management portals, where the information streams from multiple management disciplines, can be filtered, correlated, and structured better to aid comprehension, are also now becoming the focal point for total enterprise management. CA's Unicenter Management Portal, as shown in Figure 7.16, is a quintessential example of such consolidated management portals. Another emerging trend, which will in time play a role in Web-services

 Enterprise Management

Unicenter Management Portal
PERSONALIZED SECURE VISUALIZATION OF ENTERPRISE MANAGEMENT INFORMATION

Predictive and historic analysis
for intelligent capacity planning

Portal capabilities – highly
personalized and easy to use

Intuitive visualization – adapts
to unique situations

Focused, high value,
management application add-ons

Enhanced root cause analysis
and advanced event correlation

Figure 7.16   *The concept of a management portal, as exemplified by CA's Unicenter Management Portal.*

management, is that of self-managing software, as epitomized by IBM's ambitious autonomic computing program (née Project eLiza) and Microsoft's new Dynamic Systems Initiative (DSI). The bottom line is that managing Web services–based application environments, though not a simple undertaking, is not going to be hampered by a lack of the necessary tools and expertise.

7.6   Q&A: A time to recap and reflect

Q: Have corporations had a change of heart when it comes to Web services?

A: Yes and no. The technological underpinnings of Web services and their potential when it comes to developing new enterprise applications are essentially beyond reproach and are not in question. However, the overall climate of distrust and security-related paranoia that has permeated North America and Western Europe since 9/11, exacerbated by the unending attacks on security soft spots on Windows platforms, has had a marked impact on how corporations are currently opting to use Web services. Rather than pursuing applicable Web services that may be on offer on the Web from unknown third parties, corporations, for the time being at least, are electing instead to exploit Web-services technology as a new, standards-based component model for software being developed in-house or by trusted partners. In essence the use of Web services is being confined to intranets and extranets.

Q: Is security an insurmountable issue when it comes to Web services?

A: No—most certainly not. While one cannot downplay the need for stringent security in any Web services–related scenario, it is important to keep things in perspective and to objectively evaluate the security implications of using a particular service on a case-by-case basis. Concerns about security need to be proportional to the actual sensitivity of the data involved. Thus, one should not generalize matters in this instance. There will be many Web services that deal in relatively innocuous data—for example, a weather service or even Microsoft's MapPoint Web Service for mapping applications. Some will argue that knowledge of even the invocation of an external Web service, irrespective of the data that was exchanged, may provide a competitor or hacker with some level of insight. Again, it all depends on the application. One should use Web services with portals—particularly public portals. If such a portal routinely invokes Web services dealing with weather, mapping, horoscopes, stock indexes, and so on, one will be hard pressed to argue that knowledge that these Web services are being invoked would provide a competitor with significant intelligence—even though some would counter that knowing the rate at which these services are being invoked could indicate the popularity of that portal. The point here, however, is that it is indeed possible to have scenarios involving remote Web services where security should not be the show-stopper—with the caveat that one always does have the option of still using available and appropriate security measures such as authentication and encryption.

Q: Is adequate security technology currently available to make remotely invoked Web services viable?

A: By and large the answer to this has to be a resounding "yes." At this juncture one should not lose sight of the fact that e-commerce continues to grow and that trillions of dollars worth of financial transactions, including online banking and online trading, take place over the Web on a daily basis. All of the technology used for these types of transactions, such as digital certificates, digital signatures, SSL, and two-factor authentication, are also available to be used in Web services–based applications. A big concern with Web services is that of rogue Web services, where this could be due to an unscrupulous provider or a compromised platform. However, similar rogue trader or rogue Web site scenarios are possible with e-commerce. One minimizes the danger of this by dealing with reputable sites. The same should apply to selecting Web-service providers. Provided you are dealing with a reputable service provider and are using all of the available and pertinent security technology (e.g., digital certificates, SSL) it is indeed feasible to use remotely invoked Web services—particularly if one is dealing with data that is not ultrasensitive.

Q: Is it possible to locate, evaluate, license, and start using a Web service, all on the fly, over the Web, similar to buying and downloading a virus protection subscription online, using a credit card?

A: Yes, this will indeed be possible. This on-the-fly, everything done across the Web, e-commerce-based model, facilitated by UDDI, was the initial and compelling vision for Web services. It was even going to be possible to do all of this programmatically with the UDDI APIs. This original software functionality on-tap, over the Web, paradigm will continue to prosper, and one might check to see that the oft-mentioned Microsoft MapPoint service does indeed pander to this. This model will be the only one of interest to a large portion of the software development community (i.e., the cottage-industry sector made up of talented individual programmers and those who are working for small firms). Large enterprises selecting best-of-breed Web services for mission-critical applications may only espouse this totally dynamic, all-electronic paradigm for Web-service evaluation when the software is being invoked from stringently partitioned test machines. Once they have located a promising service, the norm today is to revert to a traditional, big-ticket purchasing routine involving reference checks, credit checks, background checks, contracts, and so on.

Q: What are digital certificates?

A: Digital certificates are electronic credentials issued by a trustworthy organization such as a large company or a security-specific entity such as VeriSign. A DC vouches for an individual's, a business's, or an application's identity and authority to conduct secure transactions over the Web. DCs are in essence the Internet equivalent of a travel passport. They are a universally accepted means of establishing one's identity and thus gaining entry to a protected resource. DCs are meant to replace traditional user IDs and passwords, which are not as secure or trustworthy. They are thus the preferred means for authenticating users and applications in today's Internet world.

Q: What is the role of SSL in relation to Web services?

A: SSL, a client/server-based security mechanism developed by Web browser pioneer Netscape Communications in 1996, is the accepted and trusted basis for most of today's secure transactions across the Web. SSL is a Transport Layer (i.e., Layer 4) security protocol that works on a client/ server basis. It provides authentication, integrity, and data privacy for applications running above the TCP Layer (i.e., Layer 3). SSL uses digital certificates to authenticate the server and the client of a particular transaction. In the case of Web services, this authentication would be for an application and the Web service it intends to invoke. The authentication can be bidirectional (i.e., both the application and the Web service make sure that they are indeed talking to whom they think they are). Following a successful authentication, the SSL sets about negotiating a common encryption scheme acceptable both to the client and the server. SSL does not do the end-to-end data encryption. SSL relies on well-established industry standards (e.g., 168-bit triple DES) and commercial ciphers (e.g., RSA). What it does is negotiate an encryption scheme acceptable both to the server and the client—and then invokes this mutually accepted encryption scheme for encrypting the data flowing between the client and the server. Thus, the security services provided by SSL in Web-services scenarios would involve bidirectional authentication via digital certificates, acceptable encryption scheme negotiation between the application and the Web service, and invoking the accepted encryption scheme to ensure that the data flowing between the application and the Web service is indeed encrypted and tamperproof on an end-to-end basis.

Q: What are the new security standards being developed for the Web-services arena?

A: There are a raft of new Web services–related security specifications being worked on. In some cases the goal of these specifications is to add XML support to existing technologies (e.g., XML Signature Syntax and Processing as well as XML Key Management Specification [XKMS]). In other cases the goal is to add security measures to SOAP (e.g., WS-Security, WS-Security Addendum, WS-Trust, etc.). A list of these security-related specifications can be found in Table 1.1. For the latest status of these specifications, as well as for news on any new security-related specifications, one should visit www.xmlweb.org.

Q: Is it possible to have Web services that are not deployed on Java or .NET platforms?

A: Yes, most certainly. Java and .NET are today's strategic and popular software development platforms, particularly in the corporate arena. Web services, though truly a technology of the twenty-first century, are not, however, confined to these two new software platforms. Web services can be deployed on any platform that offers an appropriate Web-oriented transport that a calling application is willing and able to support. Web services are programming language and platform independent—as is the case for the applications that wish to invoke Web services. Thus, it is indeed possible to have Web-services scenarios that do not involve Java or .NET. C and C++ on UNIX and Linux platforms are obvious candidates for Web-services scenarios, as are traditional transaction processing systems such as IBM's CICS and BEA's Tuxedo.

Q: What are the potential pricing models for Web services?

A: There will be a wide spectrum of pricing options for Web services, ranging from freeware to expensive, premium offerings, coupled with many permutations, in the case of the nonfreeware offerings, as to how the pricing will be structured. The pricing options available will definitely include one-time charge schemes, periodic licensing (e.g., monthly or yearly), and umpteen usage-based options.

Q: Is management going to be an impediment to the deployment and use of Web services?

A: No.

Taking Stock of Web Services

In every battle there comes a time when both sides consider themselves beaten, then he who continues the attack wins.

—Ulysses S. Grant

One should not deny or try to dodge the fact that the jury, in terms of market penetration, is still out when it comes to Web services—even as we approach 2004. That is a sad and unexpected fact. This is not to say that Web services have not happened. Web services are available and are being used, albeit in the case of corporate deployments, primarily on an intranet/ extranet basis. But there are also publicly available Web services. These adhere to the original vision of the serve yourself software smorgasbord on the Web.

Google, for example, as shown in Figure 8.1, offers its much sought after search capability, now spanning in excess of 3 billion Web documents, as a SOAP and WSDL–compliant bona fide Web service. Then there is the Microsoft MapPoint Web Service—often referred to in this book as a quintessential example. In addition, as shown in Figure 8.2, amazon.com, always at the forefront of Web-centric innovation, now offers the well-known capabilities of its site (e.g., collecting information about a set of products, whether it be books, CDs, or DVDs) in the form of bona fide, SOAP-based XML Web services. These three offerings, by chance, also happen to highlight another, much anticipated feature of Web services—the programmatic delivery of functionality previously available only in interactive form.

The problem with Web services has to do with expectations and predictions. Web services were touted as being the next big thing. This is true from a technological standpoint in that Web services represent a major

Google | Google Web APIs (beta)

Home

All About Google

Google Web APIs
▸ Overview
Download
Create Account
Getting Help
API Terms
FAQs
Reference

Find on this site:

[   ]

[Search]

Develop Your Own Applications Using Google

With the Google Web APIs service, software developers can query more than 3 billion
web documents directly from their own computer programs. Google uses the SOAP
and WSDL standards so a developer can program in his or her favorite environment -
such as Java, Perl, or Visual Studio .NET.

To start writing programs using Google Web APIs:

1   **Download the developer's kit**
The Google Web APIs developer's kit provides documentation and example code
for using the Google Web APIs service. The download includes Java and .NET
programming examples and a WSDL file for writing programs on any platform that
supports web services.

2   **Create a Google Account**
To access the Google Web APIs service, you must create a Google Account and
obtain a license key. Your Google Account and license key entitle you to 1,000
automated queries per day.

3   **Write your program using your license key**
Your program must include your license key with each query you submit to the
Google Web APIs service. Check out our Getting Help page or read the FAQs for
more information.

Google Web APIs are a free beta service and are available for non-commercial use
only. Please see our terms of service.

With Google Web APIs, your computer
can do the searching for you.

Server and developer's kit updates
▸ Example Visual Basic .NET client
▸ Better support for multilingual queries
▸ Java client supports HTTP proxies
See the Release Notes for details.

Program ideas
▸ Auto-monitor the web for new
   information on a subject
▸ Glean market research insights and
   trends over time
▸ Invent a catchy online game
▸ Create a novel UI for searching
▸ Add Google's spell-checking to an
   application

©2003 Google - Home - All About Google - We're Hiring - Site Map

Figure 8.1   *Google's much sought after search capability, now spanning in excess of 3 billion Web documents, is now available as a bona fide Web service that supports SOAP and WSDL.*

breakthrough in self-defining, standards-based component technology. But
the impact of Web services has yet to be felt by software developers on the
whole or by the market in terms of more feature-packed applications.

Right now it all has to do with unfulfilled expectations. Web services are
way behind schedule in regard to living up to their lofty expectations. During their inception in mid-2000, the computer industry as a whole had
gushed, considerably more so than normal, about how Web services would
revolutionize software, e-business, and the entire Web experience. Though
it should be noted that these predictions were made during the exuberantly
heady days when the NASDAQ was trying to defy gravity and logic, there
was nonetheless considerable consensus that Web services were iconoclastic.

Figure 8.2   *Amazon.com, eager to stimulate interest in Web services and to promote its own power-ful brand name, now offers the catalog, search, and e-commerce features of its redoubt-able portal in the form of genuine XML Web services.*

The good news is that the potential is still there and that the apparent leth-argy on the adoption front can be rationalized and justified.

There has been a global economic slowdown since early 2001. High-tech budgets have been particularly hard hit. After allocating funds lavishly for Y2K and Web enablement, senior corporate management understandably have felt obliged to rein in spending, determine the ROI of prior IT investments, and assess the fallout from the dot.com fiasco—especially when they hear that all of the expensive, leading-edge networking gear that they leased a couple of years ago for millions of dollars is now readily available on eBay for 10 cents on the dollar! And that is without factoring in 9/11 and its impact on business around the world.

As 2003 winds down, the software and computer industry is still far from gaining any real traction on a road toward recovery. Sun, the keeper of Java and still a bellwether for strength of the e-business sector despite the corporate interest in Linux, is struggling to maintain revenue momentum and is laying off staff. BEA, a leader in Java application server technology and an aggressive promoter of Web services, also had to lay off staff as the third quarter came to an end. IBM laid off more people earlier in the year. By and large, enterprises around the world are not engaged in developing or acquiring new applications—as had been hoped a few years ago. And it is not just high-tech and Web services that have faced these challenges. Over 200 restaurants have closed their doors in the greater San Francisco area alone since 9/11, and according to locals, the social and entertainment pulse of Manhattan, though it is now 2 years hence, is still not what it used to be.

Web services methodology, as one should always bear in mind, is also not a stand-alone technology. They are very much an enabling technology meant to simplify and expedite software development and reuse. Consequently, the fortunes of Web services are contingent on those of the software industry as a whole. Though Web services, particularly through the repackaging of the business logic contained in legacy applications, can make new application development that much more enticing, particularly in terms of overall costs, they cannot by themselves generate the demand within enterprises for new applications. And that is the rub.

Web services, through no fault of the technology (though some would argue, a tad irrelevantly, that a better job could have been done at the outset to allay security concerns), essentially got caught in a vicious industry-wide downdraft first created by the dot.com collapse and since exacerbated by 9/11, the unremitting security attacks on Windows servers, high unemployment in the United States, and the continuing fragility of the global financial markets. However, when the tide turns, hopefully by the third quarter of 2004, and the software market is rekindled, Web services, by then further bolstered by additional specifications covering security and management, are ideally poised to fulfill what most feel is their rightful destiny. This is the hope.

8.1 Web services: A SWOT analysis

In terms of being just a component technology for facilitating distributed computing, Web services is in no way unique or even that radical. In this field Web services can be thought of as being the latest offspring from strong lineage that has included the Distributed Computing Environment (DCE), Microsoft's DCOM, and CORBA. In the area of remote software functionality invocation, XML Web services, with its ties to SOAP, leverage the tried-and-tested RPC methodology. Despite these ties with the past, XML Web services tangibly raise the ante when it comes to being a powerful and persuasive distributed-component technology. The new capabilities that Web services bring to the table include:

- Consistent self-description mechanism thanks to WSDL

- Expansive and extensible self-advertising capability via UDDI

- Inextricable ties to XML—still considered by much of the computer industry as the best means for facilitating data integration and application interoperability

- Strict compliance to industry standards with bodies such as WS-I validating true, multivendor consistency

- Genuine platform and programming language independence on both sides of the invoker-invokee boundary when it comes to deployment as well as development

- Tight integration with pivotal Web protocols such as HTTP and SSL

Thanks to these capabilities, Web services, in essence, deliver a standardized, programmatic equivalent of the hitherto interactive Web experience. Popular services routinely available to browser users (e.g., Google search, Amazon query for all the books by "Edward Rutherford") can now be packaged and delivered for use within other applications to create even more sophisticated, highly integrated applications for e-business, corporate portals, and intelligent phones.

Cut to the chase, Web services extend the now commonplace Web paradigm to embrace software component technology. With Web services, applications can gain access to software functionality in much the same way, and with the same convenience, that a browser user locates and accesses an

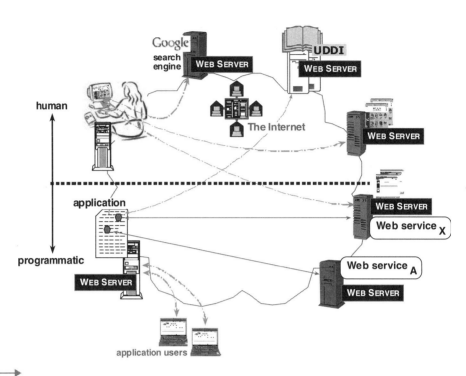

Figure 8.3   *Web services extend the hitherto primarily interactive, people-driven Web experience to now include programmatic access involving applications and software components.*

information retrieval (e.g., stock price quote) or data processing (e.g., loan payment calculation) capability on the Web. Figure 8.3 illustrates how Web services extend the hitherto primarily interactive Web experience to now include applications and software components. This is where the concept of a software smorgasbord on the Web comes in. The software model made available by Web services has the added attraction of being able to support any and all of the payment options that one may desire, ranging from free services to pay-as-you-go subscription schemes, with or without an initial one-time or annual payment.

Obviously, as repeatedly discussed in this book, one of the big factors that has precluded this software smorgasbord on the Web model from really taking flight, as had been hoped by so many, has been prevailing concerns about data security and privacy. But this model for software services across the Web is sound, compelling, and much needed. Thus, it will prevail and prosper—possibly not exactly in the form in which it was originally conceived but as a derivative of it. This potential divergence from the original XML/SOAP/WSDL model is the one danger of the ongoing delay in widescale use of XML Web services.

8.1.1   Web services: Weaknesses and threats

At this juncture, as XML Web services continue to lean more toward theory than practice, one has no choice but to reflect as to whether there have been any pertinent historic precedents, particularly in the distributed computing arena. Unfortunately, there are two that immediately come to mind. Both of these, as with Web services, were widely endorsed by the computer industry; incessantly hyped by the media; were industry standards in their own right; and, as a net result of all of this, had lavish R&D funding behind them.

These two technologies were always behind the curve when it came to living up to their expectations. They flirted with fame for years. But in the end they were unceremoniously swept aside by alternate schemes. These two, "always a bridesmaid, never a bride" technologies, as some of you may recall, were OSI and ATM—where OSI was ISO's seven-layer Open Systems Interconnection model, and the acronym ATM, in this instance, stood for asynchronous transfer mode.

OSI was cherished by the computer industry for over a decade as being the next standard for global, distributed communications. One of its strengths was going to be application-to-application communications via an RPC scheme. Though it was a direct competitor of its then market-leading SNA networking scheme, even IBM, toward the end of the 1980s, endorsed it, set up an OSI-specific development center in Rome, Italy, and spent millions developing OSI-compliant offerings.

Then there was Asynchronous Transfer Mode, which, in the early 1990s, was ardently embraced by the entire computer industry as the only way to realize the bandwidth that was going to be required to support networks that would have to handle data, voice, and video traffic. IBM, a major promoter of ATM from the start, invested well over $4 billion in ATM-specific R&D! Though ATM is still around as a means for realizing broadband WAN bandwidth in some scenarios, including some parts of the North American Internet backbone, it is very much a bit player in today's networking culture (and the pun was intended). There is a danger that Web services, in time, might join this select group—and that is without even pointing out that a decade ago CORBA was widely endorsed and touted as the end-all and be-all of standards-compliant, platform-independent software component technology!

This is why some, including me, who believe that history can repeat itself start to get nervous as months slip by and Web services fail to come of age in terms of commercial success. The problem is that there are some uncanny parallels one can draw between Web services, OSI, and ATM—without even getting bogged down in the debate that object-oriented technology, as a whole, has always lagged behind expectations. OSI and ATM, disconcertingly like Web services, were never out of the news—until they got brushed aside. There was not much, if any, talk about disappointing performance in relation to expectations or that maybe everybody got it wrong about the real promise of these technologies. Vendors and the media kept on acting as if everything were fine and that there was ample justification for the slow ramp-up, until . . . BOOM . . . they were no longer strategic.

September 11 was unprecedented. However, ATM, much like Web services today, came to be just ahead of a global economic slowdown—in that case the one that peaked in 1992 and led to the famous U.S. election catchphrase of: "It's the economy, stupid." Thus, many waited for the economy to turn around so that enterprises would start investing in ATM. Around 1996, spurred by the growth of the Web, the economy did turn around and companies started spending heavily on networking and IT—with Y2K now on the horizon. The problem was that Fast Ethernet, Gigabit Ethernet, Frame Relay, and the Internet as an extremely affordable WAN all conspired to diminish corporate interest in ATM. Then, and this is what is most unnerving, ATM, like XML and Web services, also had a tacit aura of high overhead and thus a somewhat suspect efficiency quotient.

XML, as we all know, is powerful, flexible, and extensible. But these attributes come at the cost of it also being somewhat verbose, complex, and requiring mutual intelligence at both ends. One only needs to look at an XML representation of an Excel spreadsheet, as shown in Figure 2.3(b), to appreciate that there could be developers who believe that there are better and more efficient ways to interchange data between applications—particularly if one only has to worry about a fixed set of applications between a closed group of partners.

ATM had a similar issue. Though its value proposition was all about high bandwidth and speed, ATM insisted that all data had to be sliced and diced into minuscule, 53-byte cells before it could be transmitted over an ATM pipe. Though this slicing and dicing and the reassembly at the receiving end were all done by very fast, ATM-specific hardware chips, there were some, including me in one of my prior books, who agonized that this 53-byte cell architecture was too counterintuitive for technical comfort. The question now is whether XML is bumping up against a similar sentiment, which basically says that the overhead of XML per its intent to be totally unconstraining is too much of a luxury and that it might be more practical to revert back to industry- or application-specific data interchange mechanisms.

To this end, one can already see various camps pushing derivatives of XML Web services. Interestingly, these derivatives fall into two distinct categories: those who like the high-level Web services model but want to use it without XML and those who are totally committed to XML but want to use it directly over HTTP without getting involved with SOAP, WSDL, and even UDDI. In the normal course of events one would treat some derivatives as par for the computer industry and inevitable given the large population of vendors, developers, and end users involved. The problem in this particular instance is that these derivatives could come to pass, over the next few years, at the expense of the original SOAP/WSDL-centric XML Web-services model. But this is not a given. It is but a possibility—a potential threat.

8.1.2 SWOT: Strengths, weaknesses, opportunities, and threats

Table 8.1 presents a SWOT analysis of XML Web services.

Table 8.1 *SWOT Analysis of XML Web Services*

Strengths	<ul><li>Industry-standard, software component technology for use over the Web</li><li>Leverages XML's power as a data interchange and application integration methodology</li><li>Comes with its own specialized and incisive search engine capability—UDDI</li><li>Platform and programming language agnostic</li><li>Unanimous endorsement by all of the major computer and software vendors around the world</li></ul>
Weaknesses	<ul><li>Total dependence on XML for all transactions can make applications cumbersome and complicated</li><li>Public domain, egalitarian control of the specifications (as opposed to control by a single company) means that the effort expended on developing new specifications (at a breakneck pace) is not commensurate with specifications being put to commercial gain</li><li>Delay in cogently addressing all facets of security ran foul of 9/11, denial-of-service attacks, and the security vulnerabilities that keep getting exposed on Windows</li><li>The split between the .NET and Java camps blurs the fact that both are promoting the same Web-services technology—which, moreover, is interoperable</li></ul>

Table 8.1   *SWOT Analysis of XML Web Services (continued)*

Opportunities	<ul><li>A marked up-tick in the global economy in 2004, which will result in a demand for new e-business applications to adequately address Web-centric, global consumer markets and SCM that span the globe</li><li>Developers of next-generation software for smart phones and voice applications standardizing on Web services as their preferred component technology</li><li>Linux and Java start to displace Windows servers as the attacks on Windows continue to demoralize companies; Java application developers, emboldened by the unstinted support in J2EE 1.4, embrace Web services as their strategic methodology for software development</li><li>Fortune 1000 companies making a concerted attempt to gain new revenues by offering business logic from some of their legacy applications in the form of Web services</li><li>IBM and Sun, at a minimum, join forces to promote Web services empowered by Java to enterprises of all sizes</li></ul>
Threats	<ul><li>Unabated, heightened concerns about security, in general, diminish the viability of an Internet-centric Web-services model</li><li>Delay in widescale adoption of Web services results in corporations and developers opting for simpler derivatives optimized for specific industries or applications</li><li>Spam and other abuses of the Internet sap the useful bandwidth and clog servers to an extent that corporations are forced to revert to the old, private network approach to get any work done</li></ul>

8.2   What is the real cost of implementing Web services?

The cost one can associate with Web services depends on whether one's interest in Web services lies in being a Web-service consumer or a Web-service provider. There is an underlying (and often overlooked) commonality in relation to cost between these two different sides of Web-services, which is that Web services are an enabling technology for software development.

Thus, those who wish to acquire Web services (i.e., the Web-services consumers) will have that interest because they are in the process of developing new applications or adding new functionality to existing applications. (At this juncture one could ignore the potential small market of Web-service resellers and bundle these in as a specialized instance of Web-service providers.) In this respect, Web services cannot be treated as just another facet of the computer application industry. The consumers of Web services are not application end users. Web-service consumers are application developers. Web services set out to simplify and expedite their task.

Web-service providers are also, by the same token, software developers. In some cases they also may be application developers. But this does not have to be the case. The Google and amazon.com Web-service offerings mentioned at the start of this chapter, in conjunction with Microsoft's MapPoint Web Service, illustrate this case in point. Microsoft is a recognized application provider—which in this instance is offering a Web service in parallel to its other application initiatives (keeping in mind that there is also a boxed MapPoint application available as a standard, Windows mapping application for end users).

Amazon.com and even Google are not conventional computer application purveyors. However, in this instance they are offering Web services. Yes, there would have been a tangible cost to create these Web services—though they are obviously culled from existing mission-critical software that was developed totally independent of any desire to offer a Web service. These are examples of business logic contained in existing mission-critical applications being repacked and marketed as potential revenue-generating Web services.

The cost of developing such culled Web services is in general relatively small, particularly given the studio-oriented tools available on the market to facilitate such endeavors. Typically a company should be able to get a positive ROI on such culled Web services relatively quickly—even if in some cases, as with amazon.com, the return, rather than being in terms of explicit dollars for the Web service, would be in terms of overall increased e-commerce and added competitiveness. In other words, when amazon.com's Web service is embedded in another application, users of that application will be directed to amazon—at the expense of the likes of Barnes & Noble, or Best Buy in the case of electronics.

What should be apparent by now is that with Web services what you are really dealing with is lost opportunity costs as opposed to explicit costs!

Not exploiting Web services when developing applications, or not offering culled Web services from existing applications, could result in higher overall development costs in the case of the former and lost business and diminished competitiveness in the case of the latter. So when it comes to Web services, one really should look at them in terms of obviating lost opportunity costs—rather than as something that has an intrinsic cost associated with it. The bottom line here is that not exploiting Web services, whether as a consumer or provider, is likely to cost you much more than any cost associated with using or creating Web services. It really is as simple as that.

8.3   The last hurrah in terms of the advantages of Web services

As this book draws to an end, it is worth reiterating the advantages of Web services, given that they are manifold and furthermore apply to both the supply and demand side of the computer application market—in addition to those derived by providers of Web services. Moreover, Web services have the ability to make anyone, whether an enterprise or an individual, who owns rights to some application software into a bona fide software entrepreneur. The Google and amazon.com examples attest to this. Thanks to Web services, companies that hitherto never thought of themselves as being in the software industry can now think of marketing software functionality, for profit, over the Web. It is these considerations that make Web services so worthy of interest. Thus, keeping to the SWOT theme used in Table 8.1, one can highlight the key benefits of Web services to different audiences using the information presented in Tables 8.2 through 8.4.

Table 8.2   *Benefits for New Application Developers (Supply Side)*

As Web-Service Consumers	As Web-Service Providers
■ Expedite application development and testing by using best-of-breed, third-party functionality ■ Minimize in-house development costs by utilizing externally developed functionality ■ Deliver more sophisticated and feature-rich applications that exploit value-added functionality from third-party Web services ■ Facilitate enterprise application integration (EAI) with applications from other vendors, using Web services as the data interchange mechanism ■ Gainfully reuse software functionality between different applications	■ Gain new revenue streams by offering certain software functionality, culled from previously developed applications or applications being developed, as Web services (e.g., Microsoft MapPoint model) ■ Minimize any platform-specific dependencies in the application software by offering various functions from such applications as Web services ■ Collaborate with other application vendors or major system integrators by offering sought-after application functionality in the form of Web services

Table 8.3   *Benefits for Owners of Previously Developed Applications (Supply Side)*

As Web-Service Consumers	As Web-Service Providers
■ Rejuvenate the old applications, cost effectively, using functionality derived from third-party Web services ■ Possibly create new applications or application suites by creatively synthesizing culled Web services from old applications ■ Promote EAI with applications from other vendors, using Web services as the data interchange mechanism	■ Gain new revenue streams by offering software functionality, culled from the old applications, as Web services ■ Eliminate any platform-specific dependencies in the application software by offering various functions from such applications or the entire application as Web services ■ Collaborate with other application vendors or major system integrators by offering sought-after application functionality in the form of Web services

Table 8.4   *Benefits for Enterprise-Level Application Consumers (Demand Side)*

As Second-Level Web-Service Consumers	As Web-Service Providers
■ Access to more sophisticated, feature-rich applications ■ Easier in-house application development or enhancement using third-party Web services ■ Faster availability of specialized applications ■ Cross-vendor EAI using Web services ■ Legacy modernization using Web services	■ Gain new revenue streams by offering culled business logic from legacy applications ■ Tighter collaboration with suppliers and partners by sharing application logic in the form of Web services

8.4   Q&A: A final reprise and recap

Q: Can the value proposition of XML Web services be summarized in one pithy sentence?

A: Yes. Web services provide a standards-based mechanism that provides new e-business applications with the programmatic equivalent of the now familiar, explore-and-locate, interactive Web experience—albeit with the sought-after services being delivered by XML-speaking, modular software components.

Q: Is the XML Web services model flawed in any way?

A: No. The core XML model, consisting of XML, SOAP, WSDL, and UDDI, is not technically flawed and by now has been repeatedly validated in multiple ways and in diverse forums by the acknowledged doyens of the computer industry, including IBM, Microsoft, Sun, Oracle, SAP, and H-P—not to mention W3C, the guardians of the Web. The fact that some of the security-, management-, and transaction processing–related specifications that pertain to Web services are still being worked on does not, in any way, mean that the fundamental model is flawed. The new specifications are enhancements. Given that Web services facilitate Web-based distributed computing, the core Web-services specifications will continue to be complemented and augmented with new initiatives as technology and usage trends evolve.

Q: Is there any reason to steer clear of Web services?

A: No, not really. The core Web-services model is technically very sound and becomes even more powerful and compelling as additional functionality is introduced via new versions of the key specifications such as SOAP 1.2 and UDDI Version 3. In addition, the work being done to ensure seamless interoperability by WS-I, as well as the various test suites (e.g., SOAP 1.2 and J2EE 1.4), gilds the lily even further. Yes, there are data security and privacy-related concerns, but these in the end are no different from those already addressed in the realms of e-commerce, online banking, and Web trading. Obviously, if sensitive data is going to be sent or received from a Web service, one must use proven authentication and encryption technology such as digital certificates and SSL. But there is no reason to steer clear of Web services.

Q: Why have Web services been so slow to live up to their expectations?

A: Web services provide an enabling technology. As a software component methodology they simplify and expedite application development. Consequently, the fortunes of Web services are directly tied to the health of the application development industry. The key specifications for XML Web services came to be in September 2000. Thus, realistically, Web services were not ready for prime-time use until mid-2001. But after the billions, if not trillions, of dollars that were spent on Y2K around the globe, enterprises had by then slowed down on their IT spending, partly to take a breather after the Y2K exertions and also to compensate for all the monies spent. However, before IT budgets and spending could be reevaluated and reenergized there was the dot.com implosion, followed by 9/11. Suffice to say that enterprises have not spent lavishly on IT expansion during the global economic slowdown that came on the heels of 9/11. With not too many new applications being developed, the demand for the nascent Web-services technology has, understandably, not lived up to the original predictions and ensuing expectations.

Q: What is a "killer" application for Web services?

A: Portal-related applications, whether for corporate or public portals, continue to be an obvious, fertile field for Web-services exploitation. Portal applications thrive on functionality. A portal, particularly public portals, cannot ever have enough functionality. Portal users demand and devour new functionality. Providing value-added, best-of-breed functionality is the primary raison d'être for Web services. Thus, Web services are ideally poised to provide portal application developers with the value-added functionality that they constantly crave. Portal technology is now being extended to accommodate voice applications as well as specific services for wireless, handheld devices—in particular, smart phones. Web services, yet again, provide an ideal, standards-based mechanism for acquiring some of the required functionality—especially given that there is already a well-established standard, voiceXML, for making Internet content and information accessible via voice and phone.

Q: Is it possible that there will be derivatives of the current XML Web-services model?

A: Yes—and this is already happening. There are some who wish to use the XML model directly over HTTP or a similar transport protocol without resorting to SOAP. There are others who advocate the basic software component invocation model, across the Web, but without XML. Obviously, any move away from XML will limit the global applicability and extensibility of such a service. But non-XML-based, industry- or application-specific schemes could be optimized to be very efficient for designated scenarios. This, however, would be deja vu. But given the dynamics and politics of the Web, such derivatives are inevitable and attest to the inherent innovation within this industry.

Q: What is the real cost associated with Web services?

A: The real cost one needs to be always cognizant of when it comes to Web services is that of the lost opportunity costs one could incur by not exploiting Web services! This lost opportunity cost will, invariably, far outweigh the cost of using or providing Web services. In other words, shying away from Web services could cost you more money than what you spend on embracing them. This is not mere hyperbole. Web services are an enabling technology. Creatively exploiting best-of-breed, third-party Web services when developing new applications will compress development and test schedules—and thus reduce overall development costs. It will also be possible to offer more functionality and get to market faster. Web services will thus enhance competitiveness. If you already own application software, not investigating the possibility of offering some functionality from those applications as possible revenue-producing Web services could also cost you money. So when it comes to Web services, rather than asking "What will Web services cost me," instead ponder on "What will I stand to lose if I don't embrace Web services."

Q: Is there any good reason for procrastinating further in terms of making use of Web services?

A: No. Web-services technology in late 2003 is viable, proven, and powerful. The new specifications that are being worked on, even those related to security and management, are embellishments, as opposed to replacements, for the existing model. The new specifications will provide tighter, XML-centric integration. However, existing security and management solutions, in particular digital certificates, SSL, and total enterprise management, can be used very effectively with Web services, albeit in implementation-specific flavors, irrespective of where the new specifications stand. Thus, there is really nothing to be gained by procrastinating.

Q: Is there a Web site that will provide updates to the material covered in this book?

A: www.xmlweb.org is a new vendor-neutral Web site committed to propagating XML and Web services–related information targeted at an executive-level audience.

Q: What is the bottom line when it comes to XML Web services?

A: XML Web services represent the latest iteration when it comes to contemporary software component technology. It is XML based and geared for use across the Internet, though it can also be used very effectively on intranets and extranets. Web services are modular, self-contained, self-describing, self-advertising software components. Thus, one can build new applications by reusing or assembling components from within and outside of an enterprise. Web services dramatically and positively alter everything related to applications, both on the supply and the demand side. Web services expedite, simplify, and reduce the cost of new application development. They also allow valuable software functionality embedded within existing applications to be isolated and reused. Since they are totally Web-centric, developers looking for sources for best-of-breed software functionality now have ready access to the entire worldwide software community without the hindrance of geographical, political, or trade boundaries. The bottom line is that Web services have the power and reach to revolutionize application development, from ground up, in the years to come. The Web browser opened up hitherto unimagined vistas of information for people. Web services are poised to do the same on a programmatic basis for applications.

Acronyms

AOL	America Online
API	Application Programming Interface
APPC	[IBM's] Advanced Program-to-Program Communications
ASP	[Microsoft's] Active Server Pages
ATM	Asynchronous Transfer Mode or Automated Teller Machine
AVK	Application Verification Kit
AWT	Abstract Windows Toolkit or Advanced Windows Toolkit
b2b	Business-to-Business
b2c	Business-to-Consumer
b2e	Business-to-Employee
BAL	Basic Assembler Language
BEEP	Blocks Extensible Exchange Protocol
BPEL4WS	Business Process Execution Language for Web Services
CA	Certificate Authority
CDC	Connected Device Configuration
CGI	Common Gateway Interface
CICS	[IBM's] Customer Information Control System
CLR	Common Language Runtime
CML	Chemical Markup Language
COM	[Microsoft's] Component Object Model

CORBA	Common Object Request Broker Architecture
CPU	Central Processing Unit
CRM	Customer Relationship Management
CSS	Cascading Stylesheets
CTO	Chief Technical Officer
cXML	Commerce XML
D&B	Dunn & Bradstreet
DC	Digital Certificate
DCE	Distributed Computing Environment
DCOM	[Microsoft's] Distributed Component Object Model
DES	Data Encryption Standard
DIME	Direct Internet Message Encapsulation
DMZ	Demilitarized Zone
DN	Distinguished Name
DNS	Domain Name Server or Domain Name Service/System
DOM	Document Object Model
DTD	Document Type Definition
EAI	Enterprise Application Integration
ebXML	Electronic Business XML
EC	Engineering Change
ECMA	European Computer Manufacturers Association
EJB	Enterprise JavaBeans
ERP	Enterprise Resource Planning
FTC	[U.S.] Federal Trade Commission
FTP	File Transfer Protocol
GUI	Graphical User Interface
GUID	Globally Unique Identifier
HTML	HyperText Markup Language
HTTP	HyperText Transfer Protocol
HTTPR	Reliable HTTP

HTTPS	HTTP Secure or HTTP over SSL
IDE	Integrated Development Environment
IDS	Intrusion Detection System
IE	[Microsoft's] Internet Explorer
IETF	Internet Engineering Task Force
IIOP	Internet Inter-ORB Protocol
IIS	[Microsoft's] Internet Information Server
IKE	Internet Key Exchange
IP	Internet Protocol
IPSec	IP Security
IPX	[Novell's] Internetwork Packet Exchange
IS	Information System
ISO	International Organization for Standardization
IT	Information Technology
J2EE	Java 2 Platform, Enterprise Edition
J2ME	Java 2 Platform, Micro Edition
J2RE	Java 2 Runtime Environment
J2SDK	Java 2 Software Developer Kit
J2SE	Java 2 Platform, Standard Edition
JAXB	Java Architecture for XML Binding
JAXP	Java API for XML Parsing
JAXR	Java API for XML Registries
JAX-RPC	Java API for XML-based RPC
JCA	Java Connector Architecture
JCE	Java Cryptography Extension
JCP	Java Community Process
JDBC	Java Database Connectivity
JDK	Java Developer Kit
JIT	Just-in-Time [Java Compiler]
JMS	Java Message Service
JMX	Java Management Extensions

JNDI	Java Naming and Directory Interface
JPEG	[images formatted per] Joint Photographic Experts Group [standard]
JRE	Java Runtime Environment
JSF	JavaServer Faces
JSP	JavaServer Pages
JSSE	Java Secure Socket Extension
JTA	Java Transaction API
JVM	Java Virtual Machine
KM	Knowledge Management
LDAP	Lightweight Directory Access Protocol
LU	Logical Unit
MAC	Media Access Control
MEJB	Management EJB
MEP	Message Exchange Pattern
MIME	Multipurpose Internet Mail Extensions
MQ	Message Queuing
MSN	Microsoft Network
NAICS	North American Industry Classification System
NAT	Network Address Translation
NDS	Novell Directory Services
NetBIOS	Network Basic Input Output System
OASIS	Organization for the Advancement of Structured Information Systems
ODBC	Open Database Connectivity
OEM	Other Equipment Manufacturer
OLAP	Online Analytical Processing
OO	Object Orientation
ORB	Object Request Broker
OSI	[ISO's] Open Systems Interconnection
PCDATA	Parsed Character Data
PDA	Personal Digital Assistant

PDF	Portable Data Format
PKI	Public-Key Infrastructure
PKIX	Public-Key Infrastructure Exchange
PO	Purchase Order
PU	Physical Unit
R&D	Research and Development
RA	Registration Authority
RAM	Random Access Memory
RAS	Reliability, Availability, and Serviceability or Remote Access Server/Services
RMI	Remote Method Invocation
ROI	Return on Investment
RPC	Remote Procedure Call
SAA	[IBM's] Systems Application Architecture
SAAJ	SOAP with Attachments API for Java
SAX	Simple API for XML
SCM	Supply Chain Management
SDK	Software Developer Kit or Software Development Kit
SGML	Standard Generalized Markup Language
SIC	Standard Industrial Classification
SMP	Symmetric Multiprocessing
SMTP	Simple Mail Transfer Protocol
SNA	[IBM's] Systems Network Architecture
SOAP	No longer an acronym as of SOAP 1.2—used to be Simple Object Access Protocol
SOHO	Small Office, Home Office
SQL	Structured Query Language
SSL	Secure Sockets Layer
SSO	Single Sign-on
STD	Sexually Transmitted Disease
SWOT	Strengths, Weaknesses, Opportunities, and Threats
TCP	Transmission Control Protocol

TLS	Transport Layer Security
tModel	Technical Model
tpaML	Trading Partner Agreement Markup Language
UBR	UDDI Business Registry or Universal Business Registry
UDDI	Universal Description, Discovery, and Integration
UN	United Nations
UNSPSC	United Nations Standard Products and Services Code System
URI	Uniform Resource Identifier or Universal Resource Identifier
URL	Universal Resource Locator
URN	Uniform Resource Names
UUID	Universally Unique Identifiers
VB	[Microsoft's] Visual BASIC
VM	Virtual Machine
VPN	Virtual Private Network
W3C	World Wide Web Consortium
WAS	[IBM's] WebSphere Application Server
WAS ND	[IBM's] WebSphere Application Server Network Deployment
WIN2003	[Microsoft's] Windows Server 2003
WinTel	Windows/Intel Platform
WML	Wireless Markup Language
WSDL	Web Services Description Language
WSDP	Web Services Developer Pack
WSFL	Web Services Flow Language
WS-I	Web Services Interoperability Organization
WSIA	Web Services for Interactive Applications
WSRP	Web Services for Remote Portals
WSTK	Web Services Toolkit
WSTP	[IBM's] WebSphere Transcoding Publisher
WSXL	Web Services Experience Language

XHTML	Extensible HTML
XKMS	XML Key Management Specification
XML	Extensible Markup Language
XSD	XML Schema Definition Language
XSL	Extensible Stylesheet Language
XSL-FO	XSL Formatting Objects
XSLT	XSL Transformations
XWSS	XML Web Services Security
Y2K	Year 2000

Glossary

3270 Once rampant family of IBM terminal offerings, where the term now refers to the data stream still widely used for mainframe application access.

5250 IBM terminal family for AS/400 systems, where the term now refers to the data stream still widely used for iSeries application access.

ActiveX Microsoft's strategic object-oriented technology, which applies to COM and Object Linking and Embedding (OLE) technologies.

Apache Doyen of the open-source movement that is particularly active and germane in the areas of XML, Java, and Web server technology.

Applet Small, mini-applications that run within a Web browser or an applet viewer and have strictly limited access to host resources, in particular any kinds of files.

Application Server Service-rich (e.g., load balancing) software platforms for executing contemporary applications written in languages such as Java and C++.

AS/400s Highly successful IBM mini-computer family introduced in 1988. Now referred to as the iSeries.

ASP Microsoft's server-side scripting technology for creating dynamic Web content.

Asynchronous Transfer Mode A once swaggering, Layer 2 data transfer mechanism, based on the very fast switching of fixed-length, 53-byte cells, which was considered the only way to realize the bandwidth required for supporting multimedia applications.

Authentication Process of uniquely identifying and validating a person, application, or Web service.

Autonomic Computing Self-managing, self-healing systems epitomized by IBM's Project eLiza technology.

AWT Java components for building user interfaces.

BEEP Nascent, connection-oriented, asynchronous protocol that permits simultaneous and independent exchanges of messages between peers.

BizTalk Server Microsoft server offering targeted at e-business and application integration.

BPEL4WS Defines how business processes interact with each other when it comes to Web services.

Business Process Management Software systems that enable companies to create, model, map, and manage their business processes.

Bytecode Intermediary, platform-independent pseudocode into which all Java programs are first compiled.

C# A Microsoft developed, object-oriented hybrid of C and C++, targeted for .NET initiatives and meant to compete with Java.

Cascading Stylesheets Simple but powerful mechanism for adding formatting styles to Web documents.

Certificate Authority A trusted authority that issues digital certificates.

CLR .NET's Windows-specific run-time environment—in essence the .NET JVM.

Clustering Combining multiple machines to increase processing power and resilience.

Collaboration Tools, such as e-mail, bulletin boards, and calendering, to facilitate fast interpersonal interactions and communications.

COM Microsoft's highly influential and widely used component architecture that was unveiled in 1993.

Container In the context of Java, the preferred terminology for a JVM as of Java 2.

CORBA Object Management Group's standard framework for distributed computing, formalized in 1989, which, similar to Web services, enables interoperability between objects, irrespective of the language they were written in or the platform on which they are running.

Corporate Portal A secure, Web-based, easy-to-use focal point of access to a diverse range of potentially personalized corporate information, services, applications, and expertise—to both internal and external users.

CRM   Everything to do with adroitly handling all interactions that an enterprise has with its customer base.

CSS   Stylesheet that tells Web browsers certain document formatting preferences, such as font type, font size, and margin settings.

Data Mining   Computerized system that utilizes complex artificial intelligence (AI)–inspired algorithms to sift through large amounts of data and highlight convoluted but highly relevant relationships and patterns buried within the data.

DCE   A set of open standards, which, among other things, popularized RPCs.

DCOM   Networked COM.

Digital Certificate   Electronic credential that vouches for a person's identity.

Digital Signature   The tamper-detection seal for digital certificates and other digital documents.

DIME   Lightweight binary message format for encapsulating multiple payloads in the context of SOAP.

Distinguished Name   Identifying information pertaining to a digital certificate holder.

DMZ   A subnetwork containing all key enterprise servers, including Web, application, and portal servers, protected from both the internal network and the Internet via firewalls.

DOM   One of two popular APIs for reading XML documents, which parses an XML document and creates an object representation of that document in the form of a tree. The other XML API is SAX.

DTD   The original XML mechanism for describing the structure of an XML document; this is based on a 20-year-old modeling concept pioneered by SGML.

DUNS   Nine-digit identification sequence that uniquely identifies a particular business.

EAI   Data interchange–based application integration within a company, involving both new and legacy systems, to gain IS synergy.

e-business   Doing business processes over the Web.

ebXML   Modular suite of specifications, sponsored by OASIS and the United Nations, to facilitate global e-business using XML.

e-commerce   A subset of e-business related to buying or selling products or services over the Web.

EJB   Server-side version of JavaBeans fortified with built-in access to various Java services (e.g., Java directory and naming).

Enterprise Portal   Ambiguous term, which could mean either a partners-only portal or a consolidated, partitioned corporate portal serving both internal and external users.

ERP   Rapidly becoming a generic term to describe all the mission-critical, business-related IT applications essential for running a contemporary corporation.

Extranet   Intranets interconnected over the Internet.

Firewall   Security technology to control and monitor access to and from the Internet (and other networks).

FTP   Preferred Internet protocol for exchanging files.

Green Pages   Technical information containing sections vis-à-vis the UDDI phone book analogy.

Host Integration   Technology that permits the proven business logic in existing host applications to be reused when creating new e-applications or Web services.

Host Publishing   Host application access Web-to-host solutions that work by converting host terminal data stream to HTML (or XML) via a server-side component.

HTML   Language used to describe the format of a Web page.

HTTP   The transport protocol most often used between Web servers and Web browsers.

HTTPR   A guaranteed packet delivery version of HTTP.

IDS   Electronic burglar alarm for IT systems.

IIS   Microsoft's ubiquitous Web server.

Intranet   Private, enterprise-specific internal network based on Internet technologies.

IPSec   Framework of open standards developed by the IETF to ensure the secure exchange of packets at the IP layer.

iSeries   New name for IBM's mid-range computers, née AS/400.

J2EE   Strategic, service-rich, server-side Java platform targeted at supporting distributed, enterprise class, *n*-tier modular applications.

J2SE   Subset of J2EE targeted at building and deploying client-side Java applications.

Java   Platform-independent, highly object oriented, third-generation programming language and software development methodology developed by Sun and introduced to the world in 1995 as a strategic technology for realizing dynamic, interactive Web applications, though it was conceived c. 1990.

Java 2   Umbrella term that refers to all Java initiatives that came after December 1988 when the Java 1.2 specification was released.

Java API   Extensive collection of predefined, ready-to-run software components and services for expediting and simplifying the development of Java programs.

Java Platform   A JVM (or container) along with the Java API.

JavaBeans   Java's powerful component architecture for creating and exploiting reusable, platform-independent software modules.

JavaScript   Simpler scripting version of Java, developed by Netscape, which only can run within Web browsers and is related to Java in the way that cheesecake is related to cheese.

JavaServer Faces   New Java technology for facilitating the building of user interfaces for server-side Java applications.

JavaServer Pages   Java technology to decouple the user interface aspects of a Web application from that of content generation.

JAXP   Java's extensible API for XML document processing that is based on the concept of using external plugged-in parsers.

JAXR   Java API for accessing and querying XML registries, in particular UDDI and ebXML registries.

JDBC   Database connectivity à la Java.

JIT   Just-in-Time Java compilers that speed up the performance of Java programs by recompiling byte code into a native machine code.

JNDI   Java's directory and naming services.

JScript   Microsoft's version of JavaScript.

JVM   A run-time, platform-specific environment for executing Java applications or applets.

Knowledge Management   Tools to help turn information into useful knowledge.

LDAP   TCP/IP-specific, directory access protocol that is modeled around X.500-*lite*.

Legacy Modernization   A new term for host integration, which refers to reusing the proven business logic embedded in mission-critical legacy applications when creating new applications.

Liberty Alliance   Single sign-on alternative to Microsoft's now discredited Passport backed by AOL, Sun, H-P, Novell, VeriSign, and others.

Media Access Control   Lower portion of the Layer 2 (i.e., Data Link Layer), specified via the IEEE 802.*x* standards.

Message Queuing   Asynchronous interapplication communications, particularly between applications running on different platforms, via the exchange of queued request-response messages.

NAICS   Usurped by SIC.

Namespaces   Mechanism used by XML to guarantee the unambiguity of elements specified in an XML document without sacrificing extensibility.

.NET   Microsoft's umbrella term (à la IBM's WebSphere), which encompasses all of its initiatives that pertain to XML, Web services, and post-Y2K e-business.

.NET Framework   Programming model within the .NET initiative for building, deploying, and running Web-based applications, smart client applications, and XML Web services.

OASIS   Not-for-profit, global consortium to promote e-business standards.

OSI   Now defunct ISO standard that was meant to be what TCP/IP ended up being in terms of seamlessly facilitating any-to-any networking on a global basis.

Partitioning   Virtual and dynamic system clustering on the same machine by dividing the machine's resources into multiple virtual machines.

Passport   Microsoft's now beleaguered single sign-on service for the Web.

PCDATA   Fancy way to say "a string of data" within an XML DTD.

PDF   Adobe Systems highly popular scheme for creating lavishly formatted documents that are platform independent.

PKI   Incisive framework for facilitating secure but at the same time easy-to-use public-key encryption and digital signatures.

Portal   A Web-based, easy-to-use focal point of access to a diverse range of content, services, resources, and applications.

Portlet   Content channel or an application window within an overall portal view.

Public-Key Cryptography   Data encryption scheme that uses a pair of associated keys, known as public and private keys, for encryption and decryption.

Public Portal   The likes of AOL, Yahoo!, Lycos, and Excite, where the primary business of the portal per se is that of running the portal for revenue and profit.

Python   Interpreted, open-source, object-oriented programming language supported on many platforms.

RPC   Mechanism that allows applications running on one system to dynamically invoke a procedure, replete with input parameters, running on a distant (and possibly different) platform and get back the required results in real time.

SAX   One of two popular APIs for reading XML documents—which works in event-driven mode, where it triggers a prespecified process each time it encounters an XML document construct it recognizes. SAX is best suited for interprogram interactions, as in the case of Web services, while the other XML API, DOM, is better suited for XML presentation-oriented applications.

Schema   The new strategic XML approach for precisely describing the structure of an XML document, where a schema per se is also an XML document.

SCM   Managing the entire business process—starting from sourcing supplies to build a product to handling faulty returns.

Service Provider   Provider of one or more Web services in this context.

Servlet   Essentially server-side applets.

SGML   The granddaddy of all electronic markup languages, including HTML and XML, which was developed by IBM in the early 1980s and became an ISO standard in 1986.

SIC   U.S. taxonomy for industry classification that has usurped NAICS.

Single Sign-On Obviates the need to individually sign on to separate applications or services once a user has been initially authenticated.

SMTP Most prevalent protocol used for Web-based e-mail operations.

SNA IBM's widely popular basis for mission-critical corporate networking from the late 1970s to the mid-1990s.

SOAP Totally XML-centric messaging scheme, the currently preferred means for Web service I/O, which consists of a lightweight communications protocol for exchanging structured information between applications, peer to peer, in a decentralized, distributed environment.

SSL Widely used client/server security scheme, developed by Netscape, which operates at the Transport Layer and provides authentication and data privacy.

Studio Today's favored marketing term to describe visual software development environments.

Swing Java components for building GUIs.

Tag Fundamental SGML construct used by both HTML and XML.

Thin Client In this context, computing solutions where client-side applications are executed on a server as opposed to the client, à la Microsoft's Windows 2000 Terminal Server.

TLS The latest version of SSL.

tModel Technical information about a [Web] service maintained in a UDDI Registry.

Tomcat Apache's highly acclaimed, open-source Java servlet server.

Trojan Horse Something that masquerades as another in order to intercept transmissions meant for others.

Two-Factor Authentication Scheme whereby users have to identify themselves using two unique factors: one that they know (e.g., PIN) and the other being something they physically possess (e.g., a magnetic stripe card).

UAN Siebel's XML-centric, standards-based, vendor-independent application integration scheme.

UDDI Standard for Web-based, electronic directories that contain detailed information about businesses, the services they provide (including Web services), and the means for utilizing these services.

UDDI Keys Unique identifier assigned to each entity defined in a UDDI Registry.

UDDI Node   A software implementation that supports one or more of the APIs specified in the UDDI standard.

UDDI Operators   The companies—IBM, Microsoft, SAP, and NTT Communications—that at present, working collaboratively, host and maintain the UBR.

UDDI Registry   Actual implementation of a UDDI service made up of at least one UDDI node.

Universal Business Registry   Global public UDDI registry service, on the Web, that is open to all.

UNSPSC   U.N.-sponsored standard for product and service classification.

URI   Short strings that uniquely identify resources on the Web.

URL   Global addresses, based on URIs, used to identify Web pages and Web sites.

UUID   128-bit-long keys, generated using an amalgamation of hardware addresses, timestamps, and random seeds, which are used to uniquely identify resources over time and space.

Virtual Private Network   Using Internet bandwidth, securely, via tunneling and encryption technology, to emulate a private packet switching network.

Visual BASIC   Microsoft's highly graphical, drag-and-drop version of BASIC, which, following its introduction in 1990, has become the accepted baseline for visual software development tools.

Visual C++   Microsoft C++ for Windows.

Visual J#(/J++)   A Windows-specific variant of Java developed by Microsoft that is not platform independent.

Web Services   Web-oriented software component methodology that deals with modular, self-contained, self-describing, reusable software components whose public interfaces are described using XML. They are an enabling technology for providing applications with software functionality in a standardized form from within an enterprise or from third-party service providers.

Web Services Gateway   Application-level firewall for application-to-Web service interactions that go outside the corporate firewall.

WebEx   A form of Web-based videoconferencing.

Web Logic   BEA's brand name for its family of Web-oriented products.

WebSphere   IBM's umbrella brand name for most of its offerings pertaining to the Web, e-business, Java, and Web services.

Web-to-Host   Technology to integrate pre-Web legacy applications with the Web.

WS-Coordination   Extensible protocols for coordinating the actions of distributed applications, especially in the context of completing a specific business process.

WSDL   XML derivative that defines the high-level functionality of a Web service, in terms of its external I/O interface, and describes how that Web service can be accessed over the Web.

WSFL   Now superseded by BPEL4WS.

WSIA   A specification for adding GUIs to Web services that is now being amalgamated into WSRP.

WS-Inspection   Complements UDDI and WSDL and allows Web-services requester to drill down further into the services offered by a provider.

WS-Policy   Framework to describe and communicate the policies of Web services, including service requirements, preferences, and capabilities.

WSRP   IBM's proposal for Web services with their own built-in GUIs.

WS-Security   Enhancement to SOAP to provide message integrity, confidentiality, and authentication.

WS-Transaction   Works with WS-Coordination to monitor the success or failure of short- or long-term transactions.

WS-Trust   Builds on top of WS-Security to cater for security token exchange and multidomain credential management.

WSXL   Web services–centric component model for interactive Web applications that is designed to achieve two main goals: enable businesses to deliver interactive Web applications through multiple distribution channels and enable new services or applications to be created by leveraging other interactive applications across the Web.

X.500   An ISO standard for global directory structures.

X.509   Seminal standard for digital certificates.

Xerces   Apache's family of validating XML parsers.

XHTML   Rather than being a formatting scheme for XML, this is instead an XML-compliant version of HTML that adheres to the stringent document structuring rules of XML (e.g., all tags have to be closed).

XKMS   XML-oriented scheme to integrate PKI with the Internet.

XML   A platform and programming language–independent scheme for sharing data among applications and corporations in an unambiguous, consistent, and extensible manner through the use of mutually understood vocabularies.

XML Document   Fundamental framework used by XML to describe any and all data.

XML Elements   Basic building blocks of an XML document.

XML Parser   Software tool that verifies that an XML document is well formed (i.e., has no missing tags). A validating parser goes further by validating the content of a well-formed XML document against an appropriate DTD or schema.

XSL   Allows formatting to be added to an XML document using stylesheets.

XSL-FO   XML's rather sophisticated equivalent of HTML, when it comes to document formatting.

XSLT   The scripting language component of XSL.

z/OS   IBM's flagship operating system for its latest mainframes.

Bibliography

Much of the research and reference pertaining to this book was done dynamically on the Web. I only made reference to a very few books. These were as follows:

Bremner, Lynn M. et al. *Intranet Bible*. Las Vegas, NV: Jamsa Press, 1997.

Cauldwell, Patrick et al. *Professional XML Web Services*. Birmingham, UK: Wrox Press, 2001.

Gurugé, Anura. *Corporate Portals Empowered with XML and Web Services*. Woburn, MA: Digital Press, 2003.

Gurugé, Anura. *Integrating TCP/IP i•nets with IBM Data Centers*. Reading, MA: Addison-Wesley, 1999.

Gurugé, Anura. *Reengineering IBM Networks*. Hoboken, NJ: John Wiley & Sons, 1996.

Marchal, Benoît. *XML by Example*. Indianapolis, IN: Que, 2002.

Morrison, Michael. *Teach Yourself XML in 24 Hours*. Indianapolis, IN: Sams Publishing, 2002.

Oliver, Dick. *Teach Yourself HTML in 24 Hours*. Indianapolis, IN: Sams Publishing, 1998.

Index

About the Author

Anura Gurugé is an independent technical consultant who specializes in all aspects of contemporary networking, corporate portals, and Web services, particularly if they involve IBM host systems. He has first-hand, in-depth experience in Web-to-host, SNA, Frame Relay, Token Ring switching, and ATM. He was actively involved with the Token Ring switching pioneer, Nashoba Networks, which was acquired by Cisco Systems in 1996, and the ATM broadband access company, Sonoma Systems, which was acquired by Nortel in 2000.

He was the founder and chairman of the SNA-Capable i•net Forum in 1997. He also ran a boat-based, take-out delivery service in New Hampshire called "Waiters on Water." In his spare time he has been known to sell restaurant point-of-sales (POS) systems and Wi-Fi solutions. He also teaches graduate and postgraduate computer technology and marketing at Southern New Hampshire University (SNHU)—Laconia/Gilford and Portsmouth campuses.

He is the author of *Corporate Portals Empowered with XML and Web Services* (2002), *Integrating TCP/IP i•nets with IBM Data Centers* (1999), *Reengineering IBM Networks* (1996), and the best-selling *SNA: Theory and Practice* (1984). He coedited *Communications Systems Management Handbook* and *Web-to-Host Connectivity* (Auerbach Pub.). He also publishes a highly acclaimed 16-page, monthly electronic newsletter called "i-BigBlue Professionals' Monthly," which deals with most issues related to IBM systems. In addition, he has published over 320 articles. In a career spanning 29 years, he has held senior technical and marketing roles at IBM, ITT, Northern Telecom, Wang, and BBN.

He can be contacted at (603) 455-0901 or anu@wownh.com. His Web sites are www.inet-guru.com and www.wownh.com.